A Practical Approach to Cognitive Behaviour Therapy for Adolescents

Manju Mehta · Rajesh Sagar
Editors

A Practical Approach to Cognitive Behaviour Therapy for Adolescents

Springer

Editors
Manju Mehta
Department of Psychiatry
All India Institute of Medical Sciences
New Delhi
India

Rajesh Sagar
Department of Psychiatry
All India Institute of Medical Sciences
New Delhi
India

ISBN 978-81-322-2240-8 ISBN 978-81-322-2241-5 (eBook)
DOI 10.1007/978-81-322-2241-5

Library of Congress Control Number: 2014957632

Springer New Delhi Heidelberg New York Dordrecht London

Printed on acid-free paper

Springer (India) Pvt. Ltd. is part of Springer Science+Business Media (www.springer.com)

Preface

Adolescence (11–19 years age) has been recognized as a period of turmoil. This is a transitional stage characterized by rapid biological, psychological and interpersonal changes. The adolescent has dreams but many times fails in methods to achieve them. In the present scenario, many adolescents have to face high competition, unrealistic expectations and multiple distractions. It is not surprising that different types of psychological problems are manifested during adolescence.

Although, there is evidence that only 3–12 % of the adolescent population need help for various mental disorders, 25 % need help for adjustment problems and almost 40 % need help in developing life-skills and competencies to learn to deal with their problems effectively. Psychosocial support through Cognitive Behavioural Therapy (CBT) helps to bring changes in patterns of thinking, feeling and behaviour in an individual. CBT is a collaborative approach that teaches adolescents and their parents new ways of thinking (cognitive) and acting (behavioural) which are more balanced, less negative and lead to improvements in psychological well-being.

CBT empowers adolescents to solve problems and cope with their own difficulties while supporting parents with strategies to help their children achieve success. CBT also helps to improve psychosocial competence and builds resilience. Psychological empowerment is an adolescent's cognitive state characterized by a sense of perceived control, competence and goal internalisation. This is a proactive approach to life, which helps in adaptation, capacity building, provides a sense of well-being and prevents development of mental disorders.

There are different approaches to deliver CBT, namely individual CBT; group CBT; TF—Trauma Focused CBT; and self-help approach which includes Computerized CBT, Internet-based CBT and manual-based CBT; and Tele-CBT. Computer-assisted/Internet-based therapies have great potential to make psychological assessment and treatment more cost-effective than other approaches. These forms of therapies are feasible and efficacious and can reduce the stigma of visiting mental health professionals.

This book comprises 19 chapters and is divided into three parts. The first part provides an overview of problems faced by adolescents and the psychological techniques that can be used to help them deal with mental health problems. Chapter 1 describes the prevalence and magnitude of mental health conditions among adolescents in India. Chapter 2 provides an introduction to Cognitive Behavior Therapy, its basic principles and applications in various mental health disorders. Chapter 3 enumerates the significance of community-based interventions for Indian adolescents.

The second and third part of the book (Building Skills and Interventions) has been developed out of intense research carried out on clinical populations. Each of the chapters describes modules in detail, including assessment of the adolescent and practical steps to be followed to bring change in the behaviour. Modules on building skills can be used in the school set-up by school counsellors and other mental health professionals working with adolescents. Chapter 4 imparts study skills that may help adolescents cope with academic difficulties. Different strategies are given to develop effective studying styles and to make studying more rewarding. Chapter 5 deals with relationship issues often precipitating emotional problems in adolescents. The chapter describes skills that may aid in interpersonal problem solving. Chapter 6, Anger Management, addresses the prevalent problem of anger and aggression in adolescents and imparts techniques for management of the same. Chapter 7 deals with Sleep Disorders in adolescents and elaborates on techniques for sleep management as well as sleep hygiene. Stress is a common problem among adolescents and is widely seen as a precipitating factor for many mental health issues, therefore, Chap. 8 focuses on imparting skills for effective stress management. Chapter 9 deals with management of pain-related issues in various disorders such as psychosomatic pain, fibromyalgia, etc.

The next few chapters (Interventions) focus on mental health disorders. The interventions described can be practiced, after training in clinical skills by professionally trained clinical psychologists. The practice of CBT requires extensive supervised training. It is imperative that only trained professionals practise CBT with utmost efficiency. Chapter 10, the management of Anxiety disorders, lays the foundation for CBT techniques. As anxiety is an underlying condition in many psychiatric and psychophysiological disorders, the techniques described have a wider application. Chapter 11 on Depression in adolescents, is very relevant to current mental health needs. Depression is manifested in adolescents in a different way compared to adults. Currently this disorder is becoming very common due to psychosocial stressors, which need specialized intervention. Obsessive Compulsive Disorder covered under Chap. 12 also provides self-help methods. Somatoform Disorder in adolescents are often seen in Indian and Asian cultures, but there is a scarcity of standardized psychological intervention and Chap. 13 aims at bridging this gap. Chapter 14 elaborates on a transdiagnostic approach to the management of headaches in adolescents, employing more recent modules to the practice of CBT in management of comorbid conditions. Chapter 15 focuses on management of Attention Deficit Hyperactivity Disorder in adolescents. ADHD is no longer limited to childhood, the adolescent period aggravates some other problems, which are being addressed in this chapter. Chapters 16–18 are based on more recent lifestyle-based issues faced by adolescents, namely Substance Abuse,

Internet Addiction and Obesity. These chapters enumerate intervention modules to address these concerns.

The final Chap. 19, Effectiveness of Cognitive Behaviour Therapy in Adolescents, focuses on the efficacy studies and applicability of cognitive behaviour therapy in various mental disorders.

All the modules are presented as practical steps in session format and guides the practitioner through the various techniques. This book aims at disseminating CBT techniques which are culturally adapted and are likely to empower adolescents with skills to make their life more meaningful, happier and worthy.

Manju Mehta
Rajesh Sagar

Acknowledgments

We express our sincere thanks to all the contributors for consolidating research work into a book. We are thankful to all the members of the doctoral committee from Psychiatry and Biostatistics Department of All India Institute of Medical Sciences, New Delhi, for giving critical feedback during the development of treatment modules. We wish to acknowledge help provided by Prof. Girishwar Mishra, Vice Chancellor, Wardha University; Ex Prof. of Psychology, Delhi University and Chairman of ICSSR, New Delhi for peer review of the chapters.

Our heartfelt thanks to patients of Psychiatry OPD, All India Institute of Medical Sciences, New Delhi, on whom the modules were administered and refined.

We extend our thanks to Dr. Paulomi Sudhir for her unconditional support and valuable suggestions at every step of development of this book.

Our special thanks to Ms. Sneh Kapoor, Ms. Paakhi Srivastava and Ms. Pragya Sharma for help in organizing and editing the material.

Thank you all

Manju Mehta
Rajesh Sagar

Contents

Part III Interventions

Contributors

Atul Ambekar National Drug Dependence Treatment Centre and Department of Psychiatry, All India Institute of Medical Sciences, New Delhi, India

A.C. Ammini All India Institute of Medical Sciences, New Delhi, India

Anubha Dhal Global Health Strategies Emerging Economies Pvt. Ltd., New Delhi, India

Anju Dhawan National Drug Dependence Treatment Center, All India Institute of Medical Sciences, Ghaziabad, India

Deepika Gupta Department of Psychiatry, Ram Manohar Lohia Hospital, New Delhi, India

Tanu Gupta Department of Psychiatry, All India Institute of Medical Sciences, New Delhi, India

Swati Kedia Gupta NIMHANS, Bangalore, India

Vandana Jain Department of Paediatrics, All India Institute of Medical Sciences, New Delhi, India

Angela Ann Joseph Department of Psychiatry, All India Institute of Medical Sciences, New Delhi, India

Suparna Kailash Connecticut, USA

Sneh Kapoor Department of Psychiatry, All India Institute of Medical Sciences, New Delhi, India

Garima Srivastava Malhotra Department of Psychiatry, Ram Manohar Lohia Hospital, New Delhi, India

M. Manjula Department of Clinical Psychology, NIMHANS, Bangalore, India

Manju Mehta Department of Psychiatry, All India Institute of Medical Sciences, New Delhi, India

Monica Mongia Lady Shriram College, University of Delhi, New Delhi, India

Usha Naik Osmania Medical College, Hyderabad, India

Vidhi M. Pilania Department of Psychiatry, All India Institute of Medical Sciences, New Delhi, India

Rajesh Sagar Department of Psychiatry, All India Institute of Medical Sciences, New Delhi, India

Anamika Sahu Department of Psychiatry, All India Institute of Medical Sciences, New Delhi, India

Vandita Sharma Department of Psychiatry, All India Institute of Medical Sciences, New Delhi, India

Pragya Sharma Department of Psychiatry, All India Institute of Medical Sciences, New Delhi, India

Renu Sharma Department of Psychiatry, All India Institute of Medical Sciences, New Delhi, India

Manoj Kumar Sharma Department of Clinical Psychology, NIMHANS, Bangalore, India

Garima Shukla Department of Neurology, All India Institute of Medical Sciences, New Delhi, India

Paakhi Srivastava Department of Psychiatry, All India Institute of Medical Sciences, New Delhi, India

Paulomi Matam Sudhir Department of Clinical Psychology, NIMHANS, Bangalore, India

P. Thamil Selvan NIMHANS, Bangalore, India

Part I
Introduction

Chapter 1
Magnitude of Mental Health Problems in Adolescence

Usha Naik

1.1 Introduction

1.1.1 Adolescence—A Work in Progress

> WHO identifies adolescence as the period in human growth and development that occurs after childhood and before adulthood, from ages 10 to 19. It represents one of the most critical transitions in the life span and is characterized by a tremendous pace in growth and change. "The biological determinants of adolescence are fairly universal; however, the duration and defining characteristics of this period may vary across time, cultures, and socioeconomic situations" (WHO).

Adolescence is also defined "as a critical period, characterized by neurobiological and physical maturation leading to enhanced psychological awareness and higher level social, cognitive and emotional responses". Adolescence is viewed as *neurobiological works in progress* faced by emotional academic and personal challenges (Pataki 2009).

Adolescence is a time of great promise, enthusiasm and limitless possibilities. It is a time of emerging talents in several fields. It represents a metamorphosis from child to adult, from dependency to independence and a movement away from the family to the peer group and to the larger world without. Adolescents question their place here on earth and their relevance to the universe, justice, morality, inequality, their changing bodies, their need to do well in academics, sports and in social relationships. Within families, an attempt by the adolescent to move towards independence is met with confrontation from the adult world. A similar situation exists at school. Questioning, demanding explanations and a need to conform to

U. Naik (✉)
Osmania Medical College, Hyderabad, India
e-mail: naikusha@gmail.com

M. Mehta and R. Sagar (eds.), *A Practical Approach to Cognitive Behaviour Therapy for Adolescents*, DOI 10.1007/978-81-322-2241-5_1

peer-group norms lead to conflict. Physiological changes, curiosity, interest in the opposite sex, and behavioural and emotional individuation is a given. Parenting styles also evolve from engaging in conflict or withdrawal to a focus on problem solving, changing from vertical to more horizontal or less authoritarian, in later adolescence (Van Doorn et al. 2011). For the majority of children, adolescence is mastered appropriately, but about 20 % of young people have challenges they cannot overcome adequately. It is these young people who need support services.

1.1.2 Risk Factors

Felitti first studied the impact of adverse childhood events (ACEs) in the ACE study and found considerable differences between individuals who had no adverse events as compared to those who had 4 or more events. Four major types of child maltreatment namely physical abuse, sexual abuse, psychological abuse and neglect have been categorized (Leeb et al. 2007). Behavioural problems, depression, PTSD, substance abuse, violence, criminality and chronic diseases like cardiac and respiratory conditions were considerably increased with ACEs. For example, there was a 4- to 12-fold increase in health risks for alcoholism, drug abuse, depression and suicide attempts in individuals with 4 or more ACEs. Poverty, with all its attendant disadvantages, can be a further compounding factor (Fang et al. 2012; Felliti et al. 1998; Hamburger et al. 2008).

1.1.3 Risk Taking

The increase in mortality and morbidity in adolescence relates to inadequate control of behaviour and emotions. Unintentional injuries were reported to be a leading cause of death and disability in adolescents, and road traffic injuries, drowning and burns were the most common types. Injury rates among adolescents are highest in developing countries.

The leading causes of death in 15–29-year-olds are RTA or road traffic accidents. The particulars of these avoidable deaths are speeding, drunken driving and failure to wear seatbelts and helmets. In 2011, 1,42,485 individuals were killed in road traffic accidents and 5,11,394 were injured. Of these, 30.3 % were between 15 and 24 years. The police records for these accidents state that it was the driver's fault in 77.5 % of the cases. Inexperience, aggression and a casual approach along with risk taking and alcohol consumption were important factors (Ruikar 2013).

An interesting neurobiological explanation is based on the differential maturation of different circuits in the teenage brain. Brain areas, like the ventral striatum concerned with motivation and reward seeking, are myelinated and mature before the prefrontal cortex which performs the executive functions of restraint and self-control. There is an early increased reactivity to motivational stimuli, whereas executive or cognitive control lags behind and is established later. This disparate rate of myelination can explain the impulsivity of adolescence (Casey et al. 2008).

1.1.4 Peer-Group Influence

While families and school stay as constants, it is a moving towards the peer group that is the most important change in this period. Friends and schoolmates largely determine smooth sailing or otherwise, for the impressionable adolescent. Several studies have shown that birds of a feather do flock together.

1.2 Demographic Data

Beyond a certain number, demographic data becomes impossible to conceptualize. The current world population in 2014 is about 7.2 billion and about one in every five people in the world is an adolescent. Eighty-five per cent of these young people live in developing countries. As the population of India moves towards the 1.25 billion mark, our estimated number of adolescents is 243,492 million (www.world-population.com, UNICEF 2011). If one were to extrapolate the prevalence figures to a reasonable and approximate 20 %, in India alone, the numbers would be 48 million or about 5 crore adolescents in need of therapeutic mental health services. This enormous figure does not account for that multitude of children who do not fulfill diagnostic criteria but are in distress and would benefit from problem solving and assertiveness training, and interpersonal and life skills counseling.

1.3 Magnitude of Mental Health Problems and Disorders

The prevalence of mental health problems is not always easy to ascertain. Several factors determine the recognition of a problem by parents and teachers. Externalizing problems are reported to a greater extent by Asian teachers. They even rate the same behaviour as more severe, given the same case data. This would reflect a cultural expectation of what is appropriate child behaviour (Sharan 2013). Conversely, internalizing behaviours are noted more readily by Western teachers who find child withdrawal to be more worrisome. Epidemiological studies are innately difficult to conduct. Several issues arise in adolescence which do not necessarily amount to cases by ICD or DSM criteria. The screening and assessment tools used, the language and cultural context, the stages of screening and final level of case confirmation, whether conducted by professionals or trained community level workers, may all affect the level of impairment needed to define *caseness,* thus leading to widely different prevalence rates (Sharan and Sagar 2008; Srinath et al. 2010). Moreover, the definition of adolescence as the period from 10 to 19, currently accepted by the WHO has not been the norm in earlier reports. National records for young people are documented as for the 15–24 group. To extract precise information regarding the 10–19 bracket is not always possible.

At least 20 % of young people will experience some form of mental illness, such as depression, mood disturbances, tobacco and substance abuse, suicidal behaviours and eating disorders (UNICEF). The relevance of identifying and treating mental health disorders of adolescence is further enhanced through recent studies that confirm that half of all lifetime cases of mental illness are now recognized to begin by age 15 and three-quarters by age 24. Even in developed countries, the median number of years from the time a child first experiences psychiatric disturbance and receives treatment is 9 years and 2 years for psychotic illnesses (Kessler et al. 2005).

A. *Important Studies*

In an early epidemiological study of child and adolescent psychiatric disorders, conducted at Bangalore and Lucknow, the prevalence rate of psychiatric disorders was found to be 14.3 % among males and 12.6 % among females in the Bangalore centre and 13.6 and 10.6 % for male and female children, respectively, in Lucknow. The commonest disorders were enuresis, pica, stuttering, specific developmental disorders, phobic anxiety disorders and oppositional defiant disorder (ICMR Bulletin 2001). In a review of epidemiological studies from 51 Asian countries, the prevalence of child and adolescent mental health problems and disorders were in the range of 10–20 % (Srinath et al. 2010). In one meta-analysis, the prevalence rate of child and adolescent psychiatric disorders in the community was found to be 6.46 % and for school based studies, the figure was 23.33 % (Malhotra and Pradhan 2013).

A review by Achenbach, prevalence studies from the USA and India, and one incidence study will be briefly covered here. They refer both to general psychopathology and the prevalence of single conditions. A reference will be made to one US study and one Indian study highlighting comorbidity in adolescence. The age ranges of some studies overlap with adolescence but include younger children as well.

(i) *Review by Achenbach in 2012*

A recent review by Achenbach in 2012 evaluated several prevalence reports and studies including two Indian studies. The review looked at general population studies with sample sizes greater than 300, where standardized diagnostic interviews were used along with dimensional rating instruments to assess childhood psychopathology. Prevalence rates based on diagnostic interviews differed considerably probably because of methodological variation. A few of the studies from the original table have been included in Table 1.1, divided into Development and Well-Being Assessment (DAWBA) and Diagnostic Interview Schedule for Children (DISC) studies. These prevalence figures represent a wide spectrum of disorders including, anxiety, depression, phobias and in some cases epilepsy as well. The two Indian studies found different rates of prevalence (Table 1.1). The Bangalore study has prevalence figures similar to those from the USA. Prevalence in the Goa study is much lower than in other studies. The disparities in rates may not reflect a true difference in prevalence but methodological differences. The review supported the use of rating instruments for diverse background population-based studies, if appropriate normative data were available.

Table 1.1 Epidemiology of child and adolescent psychopathology

Location	Author	Ages	Prevalence (%)
Development and well-being assessment (DAWBA) studies			
Goa	Pillai et al. (2008)	12–16	1.8
Israel	Farbstein et al. (2010)	14–17	11.7
Italy	Frigerio et al. (2009)	10–14	8.2
Diagnostic interview schedule for children (DISC) studies			
Bangalore	Srinath et al. (2005)	4–16	12.5
USA National	Merikangas et al. (2010)	8–15	13.1

Achenbach 2012

(ii) *The National Comorbidity Survey–Adolescent Supplement (NCS-A)*

Using the World Health Organization Composite International Diagnostic Interview (CIDI), the US National Comorbidity Survey–Adolescent Supplement (NCS-A) surveyed 10,123 adolescents aged 13 to 18 years. This study was launched as an initiative to address the lack of national statistics on mental health in children. The methodology was of a dual frame with a household subsample and a school subsample. The CIDI was modified for use with adolescents, and information from both the parent and adolescent was combined for major depression and behaviour problems. DSM-IV criteria were used (Merikangas et al. 2010).

The overall lifetime prevalence of disorders with severe impairment or distress was 22 %. The details are given in Table 1.2. Anxiety disorders were the most commonly reported with 8 % having severe impairment. It is important to note the early age of onset of anxiety disorders, followed by behaviour, mood and substance abuse disorders. The early age of onset of disorders highlights the need for early intervention (Table 1.2) (Merikangas et al. 2010).

(iii) *Community-based study of Epidemiology of Child and Adolescent Psychopathology* (Srinath et al. 2005)

In this important study undertaken in Bangalore, a sample size of 1,578 children was selected including 438 urban children, 481 slum children and 659 rural children. The prevalence rate in the 4–16-year-old children was 12.0 %. Enuresis, specific phobias, hyperkinetic disorders, stuttering and oppositional defiant disorder were the most frequent diagnoses. When impairment associated with the disorder was assessed, significant disability was found in 5.3 % of the 4–16-year-olds. Middle-class urban families were more likely to report psychiatric morbidity but

Table 1.2 Lifetime NCS-A 2010 (Merikangas et al. 2010)

Disorder	Cases (%)	Severe impairment or distress (%)	Median age of onset of disorder (years)
Anxiety disorders	31.9	8.3	6
Mood disorders	14.3	11.2	13
Behaviour disorders	19.1	9.6	11

Table 1.3 Community-based study of epidemiology of child and adolescent psychopathology (Srinath et al. 2005)

Disorders	Percentage	Disorders	Percentage
Specific isolated phobias	2.9	OCD	0.1
Social phobia	0.3	Depressive episode	0.1
GAD	0.3	Hyperkinetic disorders + hyperkinetic conduct disorder	1.7
SAD	0.2	ODD	0.9
Agoraphobia	0.1	Conduct disorder	0.2
Panic disorder	0.1	Behaviour disorder NOS	0.2
Social anxiety disorder	0.1	Speech and language disorders	2.0

also recorded the maximum drop in rates, when impairment criteria were included. The urban slum areas had the lowest total prevalence rates possibly due to greater toleration of deviance and low awareness of problems (Table 1.3).

(iv) *Non-traditional lifestyles and prevalence of mental disorders in adolescents in Goa, India* (Pillai et al. 2008)

In the Goa study, 2,048 adolescents aged 12–16 years were evaluated for psychiatric disorders. The most common diagnoses were anxiety disorders (1.0 %), depressive disorder (0.5 %), behavioural disorder (0.4 %) and attention-deficit hyperactivity disorder (0.2 %). Where both sets of informants were interviewed, a higher rate of diagnosis was made. Of the 20 individuals diagnosed with anxiety disorders, 10 individuals had a depressive disorder, 9 individuals had behavioural disorders and 4 had ADHD. In this study, the authors stated that the prevalence could be low for three possible reasons: methodological factors, the scope of the study and the prevalence of protective factors (Table 1.4).

(v) *Psychopathology of school-going children in the age group of 10–15 years* (Bansal and Barman 2011)

In a cross-sectional study, the Childhood Psychopathology Measurement Schedule (CPMS) was used to screen 982 students in the age group of 10–15 years from four randomly selected schools. The screening was followed by detailed evaluation in which children were diagnosed by ICD-10 criteria. One hundred and ninety-nine (20.2 %) students had psychiatric morbidity. Specific phobias were the largest group amounting to nearly 20 % followed by sleep disorders. Tension headache was reported in 11.5 %. Hyperkinetic disorder was found in 6 %, conduct disorder in 1 %, and depressive episodes in 2 % of children (Bansal and Barman 2011).

(vi) *Depression in School-based Adolescents* (Nair et al. 2004)

In a sample of 1,014 school- and college-based adolescents aged 13–19 years, the Beck's depression Inventory was used to find the prevalence and pattern of depression. School dropouts had the most severe and extreme forms of depression. There was 3 % depression in school-going adolescents and none in college-going

Table 1.4 Non-traditional lifestyles and prevalence of mental disorders in adolescents in Goa, India (Pillai et al. 2008)

		No. of cases	Diagnostic break up
Anxiety disorders	1.0 %	20	Social phobia 4
			Panic disorder 4
			OCD 4
			GAD 2
			AD NOS 6
Depressive disorders	0.5 %	10	MDD 5
			DD NOS 5
Behavioural disorders	0.4 %	9	Conduct disorder 3
			ODD 1
			Disruptive behaviour disorder NOS 5
ADHD	0.2 %	4	Combined type 3
			Predominantly inattentive type 1

adolescents. Prevalence of severe and extreme depression among adolescents using BDI was 9.5 and 1.7 %, respectively, among school dropout girls, 2.6 and 0.2 %, respectively, among school-going girls, 1.4 and 0.2 %, respectively, among school-going boys and nil among college-going girls (Nair et al. 2004) (Table 1.5).

The BDI has been found to be a sound measure for use in a primary care setting in India (Basker et al. 2007).

(vii) *Anxiety disorders in Rural Adolescents* (Nair et al. 2013)

In a rural sample of 500 rural adolescents, the prevalence for all anxiety disorders was 8.6 % when the international cut-off of 31 was used for SCARED and 25.8 % when the Indian cut-off of 21 was used and 14.4 % when DSM-IV-TR criteria were used. The respective figures for boys and girls were boys = 2 %; girls = 6.6 % (cut-off 31); boys = 6.6 %; girls = 19.2 % (cut-off 21) and boys = 4.8 %; girls = 9.6 % (DSM IVTR) (Table 1.6).

(viii) *Comorbidity needs also to be considered*

In the NCS-A study, of the affected adolescents, 61 % met criteria for a single disorder. Twenty-five per cent of adolescents affected by one disorder also met

Table 1.5 Incidence of childhood psychiatric disorders in India (Malhotra et al. 2009)

Diagnosis			
Depressive episodes	3	Pathological stealing	1
Mixed anxiety and depressive disorder	3	Specific developmental disorder of scholastic skills	2
OCD, mixed thoughts and acts	1	ADHD	2
Adjustment disorder brief depressive reaction	3	Conduct disorder	1
Histrionic personality disorder	1	Emotional disorder with onset specific to childhood	2
Childhood disorder of social functioning	1	$n = 20$	

Table 1.6 Anxiety disorders in rural adolescents (Nair et al. 2013) and depression in school-based adolescents (Nair et al. 2004)

Anxiety Rural adolescents = 500	13–19	SCARED cut-off 31	8.6 %
		SCARED cut-off 21	25.8 %
		DSM-IV-TR criteria	14.4 %
Depression	13–19	School dropouts Severe depression	11.2 %
		School-going	3 %
		College-going	nil

criteria for a second disorder, 11.0 % were affected by three classes of disorders, and 3 % were affected by four classes of disorder (Merikangas et al. 2010).

In the Trivandrum sample, depressive disorders were concurrently present in 23.7 % of adolescents with AD. Conversely, 20 % of adolescents with panic disorder, 12.1 % with generalized anxiety disorder, 5.3 % with separation anxiety disorder and 12 % with social anxiety disorder also had depressive disorders (Nair et al. 2004).

(ix) *Incidence studies*

In the only Indian incidence study on childhood psychopathology, in a 6-year follow-up study in Chandigarh, children who scored below the cut-off for psychiatric disorder ($N = 727$) on both the screening instruments used were recontacted 6 years later. Assessments were done by qualified psychiatrists and by well-structured and standardized scales, using ICD 10 criteria. Assessment scales included lifetime versions of symptoms. The follow-up strategy was intensive door-to-door survey. One hundred and eighty-six children and their families were available for re-evaluation. Twenty children out of 186 followed up were identified to have psychiatric disorder. This gives the incidence rate of 18/1000/year. Ten (50 %) children fell into the category of neurotic, stress-related and affective disorders, and 2 (10 %) children had personality and behaviour disorders. These conditions are basically adult disorders which had onset during childhood. Only 8 (40 %) children presented with disorders that have onset specific to childhood (Table 1.5). The methodology excluded children with severe psychopathology as it was a school-based study. Brief disorders of adjustment might have been missed as the group was assessed after a period of six years.

B. *Individual Disorders*

(i) *ADHD*

In the NCS-A study, the prevalence of ADHD was 8.7 %, with three times as many males being affected by this condition as females. The prevalence of severe ADHD was 4.2 %, or approximately half of all cases in the sample. Srinath et al. reported a point prevalence estimate for hyperkinetic disorder to be 1.6 %. Pillai et al. reported a rate of only 0.2 % in adolescents aged 12–16 years. In a recent study, in 770 children aged between 6 and 11, the prevalence of ADHD was found to be 11.32 % (Venkata and Panicker 2013).

(ii) *Conduct Disorders*

ODD was present in 12.6 % of the sample (6.5 % for severe cases) and 6.8 % met criteria for CD (2.2 % for severe cases). Although the rates of ADHD and ODD remained relatively stable by age group, rates of CD increased to a peak of 9.6 % among the oldest adolescents (Merikangas et al. 2010). The median 12-month prevalence rate of disruptive behaviour disorders (i.e., conduct disorder or oppositional defiant disorder) is 6 % (range 5–14 %) in studies conducted in developed countries. Srinath reported the prevalence for conduct and oppositional defiant disorder to be 1.3 % whilst Pillai, reported a rate of 0.4 % for disruptive behaviour disorders (Srinath et al. 2005; Pillai et al. 2008).

In a random sample of 240 school students, conduct disorder was found in 4.58 %, the ratio of boys to girls being 4.5:1. Childhood onset was found in 73 % and adolescent onset in 27 % (Sarkhel et al. 2006).

(iii) *Somatoform Diorders, Pain and Headache*

In community samples, estimating prevalence rates of somatic symptoms, somatoform disorders and pain disorders including headache can be fraught with dangers. Epidemiological studies cannot rule out the prevalence of organic disorders. Early studies of abdominal pain from developing countries have cited high rates of infestations and other *organic* underlying conditions (Balani et al. 2000). Clinic-based figures tend to give a better idea of the number of referrals that fit the diagnosis which has features of prominent somatic symptoms associated with distress or impairment (Fiertag et al. 2012).

In a Norwegian cross-sectional study of 230 boys and 189 girls in grades 1–10, perceived loneliness showed strong and positive associations with sadness, anxiety and headache, with consistently stronger associations for girls than boys. Necessary help from teachers was associated with lower prevalence of stomach ache in girls (Løhre et al. 2010).

In an older German study, with lifetime prevalence of DSM-IV somatoform symptoms, syndromes and disorders in a representative sample of 3,021 adolescents and young adults aged 14–24, an overall prevalence rate of 12.6 % was found. Somatoform disorders were relatively rare with a lifetime rate of 2.7 %, but a considerably higher proportion of respondents met criteria for other disorders like undifferentiated somatoform/dissociative syndrome USDS lifetime prevalence 9.1 % (Lieb 2000).

In a report of hospital-based prevalence, children and adolescents attending the behavioural Paediatrics Unit made up 2.71 % of the annual attendance. Somatoform disorders accounted for 12.12 % of psychiatric referral (Jayaprakash 2012).

In another clinic-based survey, the prevalence of somatoform disorders was 0.59 % (103 among 17,500) and 0.78 % (21 among 2,678) among outdoor and indoor paediatric patients, respectively. The mean age of the study group was 13.2 ± 2.8 years. Among the 124 children (40 boys and 84 girls) meeting ICD criteria, conversion disorder was the commonest (57.3 %), followed by undifferentiated somatoform disorder (25.2 %). Fainting attacks and ataxia were common in conversion disorder. Pain in abdomen and headache were more frequent in other somatoform disorders.

Stressors were identified in 73.4 %, and acute precipitating stressors were present in 14.4 % children (Bisht et al. 2008). In another school-based study, tension headache was reported in 11.5 % of adolescents (Bansal and Barman 2011).

(iv) *Obesity*

In a study carried out by the National Institute of Nutrition in Hyderabad, in 2003, adolescents aged 12–17, overall prevalence of overweight was 6.1 % among boys and 8.2 % among girls; 1.6 and 1.0 % were obese, respectively. The prevalence was significantly higher among adolescents who watched television ≥3 h/day or belonged to a high socio-economic background, whereas it was significantly lower among those participating regularly in outdoor games ≥6 h/week. In another urban study, 4,700 school students in the age group of 13–18 years were studied. Overweight was 17.8 % for boys and 15.8 % for girls. It increased with age and was higher in adolescents with less physical activity and in the higher socio-economic group (Ramachandran et al. 2002). In another cross-sectional study carried out on 2008 school children aged 9–15 years, the overall prevalence of obesity and overweight was 11.1 and 14.2 %, respectively (Chhatwal et al. 2004). In a study conducted to see the change in prevalence of adolescent obesity over two time points with a 3-year gap, age, gender and Asian Indian-specific cut-offs of body mass index (BMI) were used to define overweight and obesity. Three thousand four hundred and ninety-three school children were studied in the year 2006 and 4,908 in year 2009. The prevalence of obesity increased significantly from 9.8 % in 2006 to 11.7 % in 2009. These rising figures would emphasize the need for intervention both for the medical and the psychological difficulties caused by obesity (Gupta et al. 2011).

(v) *Stress*

In a recent review article focusing on determinants of psychological stress and suicidal behaviour in Indian adolescents, it was highlighted that in 2011, 2,381 children committed suicide because of failure in examinations. The prevalence of stress among Indian adolescents varies from 13 to 45 % (Verma et al. 2002; Kumar and Talwar 2004). For example, it was found that students in the "board classes", i.e., 10th and 12th as compared to the classes 9th and 11th, had significantly higher stress levels (Bhasin 2010).

(vi) *Scholastic skills*

In an adolescent sample in Chandigarh, details of academic performance of all the students was taken, subjectively from class teachers and objectively from the marks obtained in the last academic session. In phase I, 2402 students of classes VII–XII were assessed. In phase II, 108 students were randomly selected for evaluation for assessing sensitivity and specificity. A total of 124 students from phase I and all students in phase II were assessed in detail. Thirty-eight students were found to be having specific developmental disorder of scholastic skills in phase I, which gave a prevalence of 1.58 % (Arun and Chavan 2009). In Bangalore, in a primary school study of children aged 8–11, the prevalence of specific learning disabilities was 15.17 % in sampled children, whereas 12.5, 11.2 and 10.5 % had dysgraphia, dyslexia and dyscalculia, respectively (Mogasale et al. 2012). 9.4 % of children in the Bangalore epidemiological study had scholastic problems (Srinath et al. 2005). In evaluating scholastic problems, in a study sample that consisted of 1,892 adolescents, 597 boys and 1,295 girls of Class IX–XII belonging to five schools, the predictor variables for poor scholastic performance were as follows: not studying daily lessons, poor concentration in studies, lower education status of father and unhappy family (Nair et al. 2003). In another Bangalore-based study, 615 students from corporation and private schools were studied. 39.76 % (489) were high achievers, and 13.5 % (166) were low achievers. In the low achievers, 12.03 % were from the corporation schools and 1.46 % from private schools. The predictor variables for poor scholastic performance were adolescent having refractory error, not having help for study at home, not doing homework regularly, not solving question bank papers and reading only before examinations (Shashidhar et al. 2009). These studies concluded that it is possible to identify determinants of scholastic performance and plan appropriate intervention.

(vii) *Sleep Habits*

Worldwide, there is concern about the sleep habits of adolescents and the implications for long-term possibilities of substance abuse. In a recent review, sleep timing was noted to delay with increasing age, restricting night sleep, on school nights. Asian adolescents' bedtimes were later than peers from North America and Europe, resulting in less total sleep time and a tendency for higher rates of daytime sleepiness (Gradisar et al. 2011). In a school-based survey in an urban setting, 1,920 adolescents aged 12–18 completed a questionnaire related to sleep habits. Sleep debt of approximately one hour per day was seen in all adolescents and progressed with higher grades (Gupta et al. 2008). Sleep disorders were found in 25.5 % which included sleep terrors, nightmares, sleepwalking and other sleep disorders like bruxism (Bansal and Barman 2011).

(viii) *Obsessive Compulsive Disorder*

Geller reviewed reports from a number of epidemiological studies, most using school surveys and noted a prevalence rate of paediatric OCD varying between 2 and 4 % with a mean age of onset between 7.5 and 12.5 years (Geller 2006). In a comparative study of children (3–9 years) and adolescents (10–18) with OCD, older youth demonstrated a stronger intensity of obsessive and compulsive symptoms and more comorbid depression whereas younger children had less resistance and control over compulsions and more comorbid ADHD. A different emphasis on symptoms while screening the two groups may have advantages (Selles et al. 2014). In Indian prevalence studies, where adolescents are included, figures are lower-0.1 % (Srinath et al. 2005) and 0.2 % (Pillai et al. 2008). The only incidence figure is 0.09 % over a 6-year period (Malhotra et al. 2009).

(ix) *Substance Abuse*

In the *Youth in India—Situation & Needs Study by IIPS & the Population Council* 2010, the reported usage of tobacco, alcohol and various drugs is provided (see Table 1.7) (IIPS 2010). When these data are extrapolated to the adolescent population, the figures for select type of drug abuse becomes over 160 million for tobacco, 62 million for alcohol, 8 million for cannabis and 2 million for opiates (Tables 1.7 and 1.8) (Adolescence UNICEF 2013).

Table 1.7 Number of users of select drug type (approximate in millions based on 1991 census male population)

Ever use	Males	Females
Tobacco and products (%)	30.4	2
Alcohol (%)	17.5	0.7
Drugs: Ganja, Charas, Brown Sugar, Cocaine, Bhang, Others (%)	0.5	??

Adolescence UNICEF (2013)

Table 1.8 Youth in India—situation and needs study by IIPS and the Population Council 2010, users in millions

Drug type	Ever use	Current use
Tobacco	168.99	162.86
Alcohol	75.59	62.46
Cannabis	11.96	8.75
Opiates	2.92	2.04
Sedatives/hypnotics	0.58	0.29

Adolescence UNICEF (2013)

In a study from Wardha of 15–19-year-old rural adolescents, 68.3 % of rural males and 12.4 % of rural females were found to have consumed tobacco products in the previous 30 days (Dongre et al. 2008). In another community-based, cross-sectional study that was carried out among 260 randomly selected adolescents in an urban slum area, with the objective of studying the prevalence and determinants of substance use among adolescents aged 10–19 years, the overall prevalence of substance use was 32.7 %. About 31 % initiated substance use at 13–15 years of age, and the reason was peer pressure in 52.9 % (Kokiwar and Jogdand 2011). In certain more hazardous situations like urban slums, in 10–19-year-olds, substance use is as high as 32–50 % (Pagare et al. 2004; Kokiwar and Jogdand 2011). In an observation home in Mumbai, the rate of drug abuse by adolescents below 18 was 44.2 % (Naik et al. 2011). Parental alcohol use has been linked to early initiation and higher prevalence of alcohol use in male adolescents (Chopra et al. 2008).

A study was commissioned by the WHO, "Bollywood": Victim or Ally? A WHO study on the portrayal of tobacco in Indian Cinema, to know the frequency of smoking in films because of the power this media form wields in shaping adolescent behaviour. "Tobacco companies have found an ally in Indian cinema. For transnational tobacco companies, India's film industry offers a huge opportunity to reach out to millions of film-crazy youngsters. This is particularly significant because increasingly tobacco brands are finding it impossible to advertise their products". The fact that some superstars smoke off-screen has helped establish "a strong triangular relationship between their public image, their personal lives and tobacco". Increasingly smoking is depicted as cool, or a sign of rebelliousness and assertiveness. The message sent out is of a trendy lifestyle option (WHO).

(x) *Internet Addiction*

In 1998, Young proposed a new diagnosis which has found its way into DSM 5 as Internet gaming disorder which is also called Internet gaming addiction. With a prevalence of about 8.4 % for males and 4.5 % of females aged 15–19 years, it most closely resembles gambling disorder (Young 1998). Defining features include preoccupation with Internet games, tolerance and withdrawal symptoms, with functional impairment in academic, job or relationship areas (DSM-5). India is a country with 72/100 population mobile phones and 10/100 Internet users (UNICEF 2011), and this condition is likely to surface increasingly. One recent study of 552 students from English-medium schools in Ahmedabad used Young's Internet Addiction Test reported 11.8 % of students to have Internet addiction (Yadav et al. 2013).

1.4 Areas of Concern

1.4.1 Adolescents Are not Created Equal

It must be remembered that adolescence means different things to different young people. In a special issue devoted to adolescents in India, UNICEF collated these pertinent facts in a desk review. Twenty-seven per cent of women aged 20–49 were married before 15 years of age, and more than half were married before 18 years of age (Kumar et al. 2013). The mean number of years of completed education was 5.12 years well below the average for developing countries, which is 7.09. Twenty-two per cent of girls aged 15–19 had no education at all as compared to 7 % of boys. The reasons for not attending school were "education not considered necessary, had to support household income, had to attend domestic chores and school too far" (Bandyopadhyay and Subramanian 2008). Thirty-three per cent of girls aged 11–18 were undernourished (UNICEF Adolescents in India 2013). About 12 % of children aged 5–14 worked in their own household or for someone else. Over 35 % of all reported AIDS cases in India occur among young people in the age group of 15–24 years, yet only 35 % males and 19 % of female adolescents had a comprehensive knowledge of AIDS.

1.4.2 Violence Against Young People

In 2007, the Ministry of Women and Child Development surveyed 12,477 children, across 13 states to learn of their experience of abuse. About 69 % of all Indian children are the victims of physical, mental or emotional abuse. One in 12 children reported suffering from sexual violence. Physical abuse was reported in 50 % of children. It was the highest in Assam and Mizoram at 84 %, followed closely by Delhi at 83 %. The perpetrators of violence were family members 89 % of the time. "It is a staggering fact: half of all Indians have encountered abuse before they became adults". In hazardous situations like Juvenile Homes, boys at New Delhi's Child Observation Home, 76.7 % reported physical abuse (Pagare et al. 2004). It was distressing to note that violence in the home in the form of wife beating was considered justified by 57 % of males and as many as 53 % of adolescent females (UNICEF 2011). Violence against children can leave permanent emotional scars and cause post-traumatic stress disorders which may go unrecognized. The National Crime Bureau for 2010 reports 26,694 crimes against children. Of these, kidnapping and abduction accounted for 40 %, rape for 20.5 %, murder 5.3 %, abandonment 2.5 % and other crimes 31.5 % (National Crime Records 2011). In 2013, there were 24,923 cases of rape in India, according to the government's official statistics. That is about two per 100,000 Indians. About 585 cases of rape were reported in Delhi in 2012. About 58 % of men arrested for rape in India in 2010 were aged 18–30.

1.4.3 Suicide—Indian Figures

About 170,000 deaths by suicide are reported every year. Of all suicides, 40 % in men and 56 % in women occur in the ages 15–29; 13 % of all deaths in this age group were due to suicide (NCRB 2011; Kumar and Talwar 2014). A 15-year-old Indian has a 1.3 % risk of dying of suicide before 80. In adolescents, it is the second cause of death after road accidents. The rate is estimated at 25.5 per lakh population with a much higher rate in the southern states, for example 66.3 per lakh in Kerala compared to 6.3 in Bihar (Patel et al. 2012).

1.4.4 Non-suicidal Self-injury

Non-suicidal self-injury (NSSI) and deliberate self-harm (DSH) are related behaviours. A recent review of 52 studies suggested the prevalence of both conditions appear similar across countries at 18 % for NSSI and 16.1 % of DSH. The DSM 5 term of non-suicidal self-injury could be used for comparing data (Lewis et al. 2012; Muehlenkamp et al. 2012).

1.5 Bridging the Gap

There is an acute shortage of qualified personnel. For example, India's first child psychiatrists would have qualified in August 2014, from NIMHANS. The USA has 8,300 practicing child and adolescent psychiatrists (AACAP 2013). It is concerned about an undersupply of child and adolescent psychiatrists with a maldistribution causing shortage in rural and low SES areas!

Even in developed countries, the mental health needs of adolescents are unmet (Patel et al. 2007).

To quote Myron Belfer, former Head of Child Psychiatry at WHO,

> While epidemiological data appears relatively uniform globally, the same is not true for policy and resources for care. The gaps in resources for child mental health can be

> categorized as follows: economic, manpower, training, services and policy.- lack of program development in low income countries; lack of any policy in low income countries and absent specific comprehensive policy in both low and high income countries; lack of data gathering capacity including that for country-level epidemiology and services outcomes; failure to provide social services in low income countries; lack of a continuum of care; and universal barriers to access (Belfer 2008).

Several government schemes exist to address the needs of adolescents. Adolescent-friendly centres set up through paediatric initiatives are serving to decentralize sources of help and be user-friendly. "To increase help seeking behaviour of adolescents, apart from health and life skill education, medical screening with a focus on reproductive health by trained physicians, parental involvement, supported by adolescent friendly centres, for counseling, referral and follow up are essential" (Joshi et al. 2006). One community-based programme has been successful at the district level through careful strategy planning, sensitization, training of personnel to handle medical and psychosocial problems of adolescents and most importantly, monitoring of the effort (Nair et al. 2012). These tested methods could be emulated and taken to scale.

The propagation of highly efficacious methods of treatment like cognitive behaviour treatment by well trained psychologists would serve the needs of the adolescent population and greatly mitigate suffering of adolescents and their families.

References

Achenbach, T. M., Rescorla, L. A., & Ivanova, M. Y. (2012). International epidemiology of child and adolescent psychopathology I: Diagnoses, dimensions, and conceptual issues. *Journal of the American Academy of Child & Adolescent Psychiatry, 51*(12), 1261–1272.

Arun, P., & Chavan, B. S. (2009). Stress and suicidal ideas in adolescent students in Chandigarh. *Indian Journal of Medical Sciences, 63*(7), 281–289.

AACAP. (2013). https://www.aacap.org/App_Themes/AACAP/docs/Advocacy/policy_resources/cap_workforce_crisis_2013

Balani, B., Patwari, A. K., Bajaj, P., Diwan, N., & Anand, V. K. (2000). Recurrent abdominal pain-A reappraisal. *Indian Pediatrics, 37*(8), 876–881.

Bansal, P. D., & Barman, R. (2011). Psychopathology of school going children in the age group of 10–15 years. *International Journal of Applied and Basic Medical Research, 1*(1), 43.

Bandyopadhyay, M., & Subrahmanian, R. (2008). Gender equity in education: A review of trends and factors. http://sro.sussex.ac.uk/1866/ Official URL: http://www.create-rpc.org/pdf_documents/PTA_18.pdf

Basker, M., Moses, P. D., Russell, S., Swamidhas, P., & Russell, S. (2007). The psychometric properties of beck depression inventory for adolescent depression in a primary care paediatric setting in India. Child and adolescent psychiatry and mental health. *Child and Adolescent Psychiatry and Mental Health, 1*, 8.

Belfer, M. L. (2008). Child and adolescent mental disorders: The magnitude of the problem across the globe. *Journal of Child Psychology and Psychiatry, 49*(3), 226–236.

Bhasin, S. K., Sharma, R., & Saini, N. K. (2010). Depression, anxiety and stress among adolescent students belonging to affluent families: A school-based study. *The Indian Journal of Pediatrics, 77*(2), 161–165.

Bisht, J., Sankhyan, N., Kaushal, R. K., Sharma, R. C., & Grover, N. (2008). Clinical profile of pediatric somatoform disorders. *Indian Pediatrics, 45*(2), 111–115.

Casey, B. J., Jones, R. M., & Hare, T. A. (2008). The adolescent brain. *Annals of the New York Academy of Sciences, 1124*(1), 111–126.

Chhatwal, J., Verma, M., & Riar, S. K. (2004). Obesity among pre-adolescent and adolescents of a developing country (India). *Asia Pacific Journal of Clinical Nutrition, 13*(3), 231–235.

Chopra, A., Dhawan, A., Sethi, H., & Mohan, D. (2008). Association between parental and offspring's alcohol use–population data from India. *Journal of Indian Association for Child & Adolescent Mental Health, 4*(2), 38–43.

Dongre, A. R., Deshmukh, P. R., Murali, N., & Garg, B. S. (2008). Tobacco consumption among adolescents in rural Wardha: Where and how tobacco control should focus its attention? *Indian Journal of Cancer, 45*(3) 100–106.

DSM-5. (2013). *Diagnostic and statistical manual of mental disorders* (5th ed., pp. 795–798). Washington, DC: American Psychiatric Publication.

Fang, X., Brown, D. S., Florence, C. S., & Mercy, J. A. (2012). The economic burden of child maltreatment in the United States and implications for prevention. *Child Abuse and Neglect, 36*(2), 156–165.

Farbstein, I., Mansbach-Kleinfeld, I., Levinson, D., Goodman, R., Levav, I., Vograft, I., & Apter, A. (2010). Prevalence and correlates of mental disorders in Israeli adolescents: results from a national mental health survey. *Journal of child psychology and psychiatry, 51*(5), 630–639.

Felitti, M. D., Vincent, J., Anda, M. D., Robert, F., Nordenberg, M. D., Williamson, M. S., et al. (1998). Relationship of childhood abuse and household dysfunction to many of the leading causes of death in adults: The adverse childhood experiences (ACE) study. *American Journal of Preventive Medicine, 14*(4), 245–258.

Frigerio, A., Rucci, P., Goodman, R., Ammaniti, M., Carlet, O., Cavolina, P., & Molteni, M. (2009). Prevalence and correlates of mental disorders among adolescents in Italy: the PrISMA study. *European child & adolescent psychiatry, 18*(4), 217–226.

Fiertag, O., Taylor, S., Tareen, A., & Garralda, E. (2012). Somatoform disorders. In J. M. Rey (Ed.), *IACAPAP e-textbook of child and adolescent mental health*. Geneva: International Association for Child and Adolescent Psychiatry and Allied Professions.

Geller, D. A. (2006). Obsessive-compulsive and spectrum disorders in children and adolescents. *Psychiatric Clinics of North America, 29*, 353–370.

Gradisar, M., Gardner, G., & Dohnt, H. (2011). Recent worldwide sleep patterns and problems during adolescence: A review and meta-analysis of age, region, and sleep. *Sleep Medicine, 12*(2), 110–118.

Gupta, D. K., Shah, P., Misra, A., Bharadwaj, S., Gulati, S., Gupta, N., et al. (2011). Secular trends in prevalence of overweight and obesity from 2006 to 2009 in urban Asian Indian adolescents aged 14–17 years. *PLoS One, 6*(2), e17221.

Gupta, R., Bhatia, M. S., Chhabra, V., Sharma, S., Dahiya, D., Semalti, K., et al. (2008). Sleep patterns of urban school-going adolescents. *Indian Pediatrics, 45*(3), 183–189.

Hamburger, M. E., Leeb, R. T., & Swahn, M. H. (2008). Childhood maltreatment and early alcohol use among high-risk adolescents. *Journal of Studies on Alcohol and Drugs, 69*(2), 291.

Shashidhar, S., Rao, C., & Hegde, R. (2009). Factors affecting scholastic performances of adolescents. *The Indian Journal of Pediatrics, 76*(5), 495–499.

ICMR Bulletin. (2001). Epidemiological study of child and adolescent psychiatric disorders in urban and rural areas. *ICMR Bulletin, 31*, 54–55.

International Institute for Population Studies (IIPS) and Population Council. (2010). *Youth in India: Situation and needs 2006–2007*. Mumbai: IIPS.

Jayaprakash, R. (2012). Clinical profile of children and adolescents attending the behavioural paediatrics unit OPD in a tertiary care set up. *Journal of Indian Association for Child & Adolescent Mental Health, 8*(3), 51–66.

Kumar, C., Rai, R. K., Singh, P. K., & Singh, L. (2013). Socioeconomic disparities in maternity care among indian adolescents, 1990–2006. *PLoS ONE, 8*(7), e69094.

Joshi, B. N., Chauhan, S. L., Donde, U. M., Tryambake, V. H., Gaikwad, N. S., & Bhadoria, V. (2006). Reproductive health problems and help seeking behavior among adolescents in urban India. *The Indian Journal of Pediatrics, 73*(6), 509–513.

Kessler, R. C., Berglund, P., Demler, O., Jin, R., Merikangas, K. R., & Walters, E. E. (2005). Lifetime prevalence and age-of-onset distributions of DSM-IV disorders in the National Comorbidity Survey Replication. *Archives of General Psychiatry, 62*(6), 593–602.

Kokiwar, P. R., & Jogdand, G. S. (2011). Prevalence of substance use among male adolescents in an urban slum area of Karimnagar district, Andhra Pradesh. *Indian Journal of Public Health, 55*(1), 42.

Kumar, V., & Talwar, R. (2014). Determinants of psychological stress and suicidal behavior in Indian adolescents: A literature review. *Journal of Indian Association for Child and Adolescent Mental Health, 10*(1), 47–68.

Leeb, R. T., Paulozzi, L., Melanson, C., Simon, T., & Arias I. (2007). *Child maltreatment surveillance: Uniform definitions for public health and recommended data elements* (version 1.0). Atlanta, GA: Centers for Disease Control and Prevention, National Center for Injury Prevention and Control.

Lewis, S. P., Heath, N. L., Michal, N. J., & Duggan, J. M. (2012). Non-suicidal self-injury, youth, and the internet: What mental health professionals need to know. *Child and Adolescent Psychiatry and Mental Health, 6*(1), 1–9.

Lieb, R., Pfister, H., Mastaler, M., & Wittchen, H. U. (2000). Somatoform syndromes and disordersin a representative population sample of adolescents and young adults: prevalence, comorbidity and impairments. *Acta Psychiatrica Scandinavica, 101*(3), 194–208.

Løhre, A., Lydersen, S., & Vatten, L. J. (2010). Factors associated with internalizing or somatic symptoms in a cross-sectional study of school children in grades 1–10. *Child and Adolescent Psychiatry and Mental Health, 4*(1), 33.

Malhotra, S., Kohli, A., Kapoor, M., & Pradhan, B. (2009). Incidence of childhood psychiatric disorders in India. *Indian journal of Psychiatry, 51*(2), 101.

Malhotra, S., & Pradhan, K. B. (2013). Childhood psychiatric disorders in North-India: Prevalence, incidence and implications#. *Adolescent Psychiatry, 3*(1), 87–89.

Mogasale, V. V., Patil, V. D., Patil, N. M., & Mogasale, V. (2012). Prevalence of specific learning disabilities among primary school children in a South Indian city. *The Indian Journal of Pediatrics, 79*(3), 342–347.

Muehlenkamp, J. J., Claes, L., Havertape, L., & Plener, P. L. (2012). International prevalence of adolescent non-suicidal self-injury and deliberate self-harm. *Child and Adolescent Psychiatry and Mental Health, 6*(10), 1–9.

Merikangas, K. R., He, J. P., Burstein, M., Swanson, S. A., Avenevoli, S., Cui, L., et al. (2010). Lifetime prevalence of mental disorders in US adolescents: results from the National Comorbidity Survey Replication–Adolescent Supplement (NCS-A). *Journal of the American Academy of Child & Adolescent Psychiatry, 49*(10), 980–989.

Naik, P. R., Gokhe, S. S. B., Shinde, R. R., & Nirgude, A. S. (2011). Street children of Mumbai: Demographic profile and substance abuse. *Biomedical Research, 22*(4), (0970-938X).

Nair, M. C., Paul, M. K., & Padmamohan, J. (2003). Scholastic performance of adolescents. *The Indian Journal of Pediatrics, 70*(8), 629–631.

Nair, M. K. C., Paul, M. K., & John, R. (2004). Prevalence of depression among adolescents. *The Indian Journal of Pediatrics, 71*(6), 523–524.

Nair, M. K. C., Chacko, D. S., Indira, M. S., Siju, K. E., George, B., & Russell, P. S. (2012). A primary care approach for adolescent care and counseling services. *The Indian Journal of Pediatrics, 79*(1), 79–83.

Nair, M. K., Russell, P. S., Krishnan, R., Russell, S., Subramaniam, V. S., Nazeema, S., et al. (2013). ADad 4: The symptomatology and clinical presentation of anxiety disorders among adolescents in a rural community population in India. *Indian Journal of Pediatrics, 80*(Suppl 2), 149–154.

NCRB. (2011). http://ncrb.nic.in/CD-CII2011/Statistics2011.pdf

Pagare, D., Meena, G. S., Singh, M. M., Saha, R., Gwadz, M. V., Clatts, M. C., et al. (2004). Risk factors of substance use among street children from Delhi. *Indian Pediatrics, 41*(3), 221–225.

Pataki, C. (2009). Adolescent development. In B. J. Sadock, V. A. Sadock, & P. Ruiz (Eds.), *Kaplan and Sadoc's comprehensive textbook of psychiatry* (Vol. 2, pp. 3356–3365). Philadelphia: Lippincott Williams & Wilkins.

Patel, V., Flisher, A. J., Hetrick, S., & McGorry, P. (2007). Mental health of young people: a global public-health challenge. *The Lancet, 369*(9569), 1302–1313.

Patel, V., Ramasundarahettige, C., Vijayakumar, L., Thakur, J. S., Gajalakshmi, V., Gururaj, G., & Jha, P. (2012). Suicide mortality in India: a nationally representative survey. *The lancet, 379*(9834), 2343–2351.

Pillai, A., Patel, V., Cardozo, P., Goodman, R., Weiss, H. A., & Andrew, G. (2008). Non-traditional lifestyles and prevalence of mental disorders in adolescents in Goa, India. *The British Journal of Psychiatry, 192*(1), 45–51.

Ramachandran, A., Snehalatha, C., Vinitha, R., Thayyil, M., Sathish Kumar, C. K., Sheeba, L., et al. (2002). Prevalence of overweight in urban Indian adolescent school children. *Diabetes research and clinical practice, 57*(3), 185–190.

Ruikar, M. (2013). National statistics of road traffic accidents in India. *Journal of Orthopedics, Traumatology and Rehabilitation, 6*(1), 1.

Sarkhel, S., Sinha, V. K., Arora, M., & DeSarkar, P. (2006). Prevalence of conduct disorder in school children of Kanke. *Indian Journal of Psychiatry, 48*(3), 159.

Selles, R. R., Storch, E. A., & Lewin, A. B. (2014). Variations in symptom prevalence and clinical correlates in younger versus older youth with obsessive–compulsive disorder. *Child Psychiatry & Human Development, 45*(6), 666–674.

Sharan, P., & Sagar, R. (2008). The need for national data on epidemiology of child and adolescent mental disorders. *Journal of Indian Association of Child Adolescent Mental Health, 4*(2), 22–27.

Sharan, P. (2013). *Classification, culture and child psychiatry*. Presidential Address, 25th September IACAMH.

Srinath, S., Girimaji, S. C., Gururaj, G., Seshadri, S., Subbakrishna, D. K., Bhola, P., & Kumar, N. (2005). Epidemiological study of child & adolescent psychiatric disorders in urban & rural areas of Bangalore, India. *Indian Journal of Medical Research, 122*(1), 67.

Srinath, S., Kandasamy, P., & Golhar, T. S. (2010). Epidemiology of child and adolescent mental health disorders in Asia. *Current Opinion in Psychiatry, 23*(4), 330–336.

UNICEF Adolescents in India. (2013). *A desk review of existing evidence and behaviours, programmes and policies*. New Delhi: UNICEF.

UNICEF State of the World's Children 2011.

Van Doorn, M. D., Branje, S. J., & Meeus, W. H. (2011). Developmental changes in conflict resolution styles in parent–adolescent relationships: A four-wave longitudinal study. *Journal of Youth and Adolescence, 40*(1), 97–107.

Venkata, J. A., & Panicker, A. S. (2013). Prevalence of attention deficit hyperactivity disorder in primary school children. *Indian Journal of Psychiatry, 55*(4), 338.

Verma, S., Sharma, D., & Larson, R. W. (2002). School stress in India: Effects on time and daily emotions. *International Journal of Behavioral Development, 26*(6), 500–508.

WHO. http://www.who.int/maternal_child_adolescent/topics/adolescence/dev/en/

WHO. http://www.who.int/tobacco/wntd/2003/en/bollywood-exesum

Yadav, P., Banwari, G., Parmar, C., & Maniar, R. (2013). Internet addiction and its correlates among high school students: A preliminary study from Ahmedabad, India. *Asian Journal of Psychiatry, 6*(6), 500–505.

Young, K. S. (1998). Internet addiction: The emergence of a new clinical disorder. *CyberPsychology & Behavior, 1*(3), 237–244.

Chapter 2
Cognitive Behaviour Therapy with Adolescents

Paulomi Matam Sudhir

2.1 Introduction

The period of adolescence is undoubtedly one of the most challenging periods in one's life. As a transition period, the adolescent faces many challenges. Negotiating these academic, interpersonal and intrapersonal challenges is crucial for adjustment. Many adolescents face emotional disorders that make it necessary for them to seek and receive psychological interventions, and most emotional disorders have their onset and peak during this period.

Helping adolescents deal effectively with these tasks is therefore important. This has been addressed through training in life skills and coping skills (assertiveness, problem-solving skills). While effective life skills and coping skills are important in order to negotiate situations and may at times be preparatory in nature, many psychological interventions are designed to address psychological problems that have already been identified.

2.2 A Brief Overview of Psychological Treatments for Adolescents

There is increasing recognition that psychological interventions are important in the management of psychological problems in adolescents. There is a need to adopt evidence-based therapies in practice in order to make interventions more scientific and effective. Evidence-based interventions are practices that are based on

P.M. Sudhir (✉)
Department of Clinical Psychology, NIMHANS, Bangalore, India
e-mail: paulomi.sudhir@gmail.com

M. Mehta and R. Sagar (eds.), *A Practical Approach to Cognitive Behaviour Therapy for Adolescents*, DOI 10.1007/978-81-322-2241-5_2

empirical research and carried out on populations with similar diagnoses or problems. These interventions have been demonstrated to be superior to no treatment or alternative interventions for people with specific diagnoses. They are specifically matched to target problems/needs. In the absence of this fit, the effectiveness of therapy is reduced. They may sometimes be harmful or worsen problems, if they are used for persons who do not have the criterion disorder or belong to the targeted group. Clinicians must be able to accurately and reliably identify problems and make diagnoses for evidence-based interventions to have greater utility.

Psychological interventions in children and adolescents are of three types, **therapeutic**, **preventive** or **focused on enhancing specific skills** (Kendall 2006).

Researchers have identified several different types of psychological interventions that are considered either well established or probably efficacious. These include behaviour modification, multisystemic therapy, functional family therapy, graduated exposure, modelling, exposure and response prevention (ERP), cognitive behaviour therapy (CBT) for a variety of problems and parent management training (Ollendick and King 2004). More recently, in addition to CBT, dialectic behaviour therapy and interpersonal therapy have also been reported to show promising outcome. These psychological interventions target anxiety, mood disorders such as bipolar disorder, depression, eating disorders, disruptive and oppositional behaviours, self-harming or self-injurious behaviours, anger and aggressive behaviours, major psychiatric disorders such as schizophrenia and also substance use disorders (Ollendick and King 2004; Report of the Children's Evidence Based Practices Expert Panel 2005).

Psychological interventions for adolescents face special challenges often due to the nature of problems. Many problems seen in later years and managed in therapy are those that may be present even earlier, without being problematic (e.g. aggression, shyness). Another challenge lies in the fact that adolescents are often referred by significant others such as teachers, parents and health professionals, and this makes participation and decision-making in therapy different from that of adults. This also leads to an often-asked question of whose problem is it? Adolescents face multiple influences by way of family and peer, and these influences are likely to impact the nature of problems and manifestations.

2.3 Cognitive Behaviour Therapy as an Effective Treatment in Adolescents

CBT is a time-oriented and problem-focused psychological therapy. Cognitive behaviour therapies are a group of therapies that include both cognitive and behavioural interventions. Dobson (1988) identified nearly 22 varieties of therapies that come under the categories of cognitive and cognitive behavioural therapies. Broadly, three major groups of CBT have been recognized. These include therapies aimed at **cognitive restructuring** such as the approaches by Beck et al. (1979), Ellis (1958), the **coping skills training** (CST) that includes interventions such as stress inoculation training and self-instruction training (Meichenbaum and Goodman 1971) and finally **problem-solving skills training** (PSST) (D'Zurilla 1986). CBTs include a variety of cognitive and behavioural techniques that target symptom reduction and changes through identification and modification of dysfunctional thoughts and skill building. While it appears that CBT is a unitary therapeutic approach, CBT actually is diverse in its components. CBT is developed within the context of learning theories and gradually moved on to incorporating the mediational role of cognitions in the maintenance of emotional disorders, while behaviour therapy focuses more on non-mediational models, that is, the direct relationship between stimulus and response.

All CBTs share some common features that include a comprehensive cognitive and behavioural assessment of thoughts, emotions and behaviours using a functional analysis, a therapeutic model for psychopathology based on cognitive theory, recognition of thought patterns and subsequently strategies to modify them, using behavioural and cognitive strategies.

The core ingredients with which the cognitive therapist works are negative automatic thoughts, information processing errors (distortions) and schema. Cognitive or thinking errors can be either inferential or attributional in nature. For example, personalization, magnification and minimization (attributional errors), selective abstraction and jumping to conclusions (inferential errors).

CBT is becoming the treatment of choice for adolescents with various psychological issues with reviews providing evidence for this form of psychological intervention. This is due to the fact that CBT is flexible and includes a variety of both behavioural and cognitive strategies that the therapist can choose to adopt while continually monitoring the progress of the client. CBT also allows the therapist to choose from a combination of therapeutic strategies that can bring about reduction in symptoms and prevent relapse.

2.4 CBT for Adolescents and Adults Same or Different?

Cognitive behavioural theory as applied to adults works on the assumption that appraisals of events or situations are crucial for the regulation of affect or emotions and behaviour. These appraisals are in turn shaped by various processes, including early learning experience. Thus, therapy focuses on various levels of cognition such as negative automatic thoughts, dysfunctional assumptions, cognitive errors and schema or cognitive structures.

2.5 The Need to Adopt a Developmental Perspective in CBT

The approach to understanding emotional disorders in CBT has been developed for adult clients. A core aspect of CBT is the need for the client to become aware of thought processes, to be able to detect, identify, document and then develop alternative perspectives. Therefore, for a long time, there was hesitation in the use of CBT in younger clients, particularly children and adolescents.

In an attempt to understand the applicability of CBT to younger clients, researchers have referred to theories of cognitive development (Inhelder et al. 1958; Vygostsky 1988). These theories are influential and are considered to be the basis of understanding cognitive development. Their description of the role of language and the linkages between cognition and action has significant relevance to CBT. However, while Piaget's works suggest that CBT in young children has limited applicability, this is not always true in all young children or adolescents, as many are able to engage in the process of CBT.

Two major theoretical approaches relevant to children and adolescents are the **social attribution and social information processing models** (Dodge 1993; Garber and Flynn 2001). Research on social cognitions addresses issues related to the processing, encoding and interpretation of social information and cues that are relevant for the development of appraisals (Why did the other child do this to me?). They are also essential for the development of problem-solving skills and conflict resolution skills and have been used in studies on adolescents with anger problems.

Thus, it was believed that as cognitive techniques in particular rely heavily on the level of cognitive development or tasks that could be carried out, CBT was not considered suitable for younger clients. However, more recent research has suggested that there is not much clarity on this assumption, that younger children would be able to participate in behaviour-oriented therapies only and that cognitive techniques could be introduced only after adolescence. Researchers now conclude that developmental processes that are necessary for a therapy such as CBT may occur over years, without a definite cut-off. On the other hand, some studies also hold the view that by adolescence, there is a clear emergence of formal operations. Therefore, there is a need for the clinician to consider the developmental stage of the child (O'Connor and Creswell 2005).

The second major theoretical influence is from **the attachment theory** (Ainsworth et al. 1978; Bowlby 1982), which explains the process of how a child's experiences with early relationships shape his/her representations of later relationships and help in building 'internal working models' (Bowlby 1982).

Despite the emphasis on cognitive mediation, CBT is flexible with a scope to include behavioural and cognitive strategies. These different techniques target different problems.

2.6 Assessment and Case Formulation in CBT—Cognitive Theory Versus Case Formulation

The three main assumptions in CBT are that thoughts precede changes in emotions and behaviours, thoughts can be monitored and assessed, and changes in thinking can lead to changes in emotions and behaviours.

2.7 Assessment

Assessment of symptom severity, beliefs and assumptions and other cognitive phenomena such as negative automatic thoughts, hopelessness, suicidal ideation and self-concept is an important step in carrying out the therapy. Assessment can be carried out using self-report measures, rating scales as well as self-monitoring or diaries and functional analysis. Many of the measures, in particular the rating scales are suitable for use in the Indian setting. Silverman and Ollendick (2005), provide a comprehensive list of interview-based as well as self-report measures that can be used in adolescents.

2.8 Case Conceptualization

Case conceptualization or case formulation in CBT considers the contributions of early experiences in the subsequent development of schema. The model takes into consideration the appraisals or thought processes at various levels, from core schema to dysfunctional assumptions and negative automatic thought. Cognitive theory must be separated from case formulation. Case formulation is specific to each individual and is thought to link theory with actual therapeutic planning. The unique aspect of a cognitive case formulation is that it remains open to new information and validation throughout therapy. Case formulations vary depending on the complexity of issues, age or developmental level of the client. In CBT, the case formulation is a shared understanding between therapist and client. Therefore, the client contributes to the development of the model and must be in agreement with the overall formulation. Starting with a simple formulation that identifies maintaining cognitions and behaviours and then gradually elaborating on this is one approach suggested for use when working with adolescents.

Several approaches to case formulation in children and adolescents have been suggested. In particular, Williams et al. (1997) suggest the use of what they call a 'mind map' to assist case formulation. In building a case formulation in children and adolescent, the clinician must remember that cognitions are still in the process of developing and are likely to be continually influenced by various factors including parents and peers. The case formulation needs to consider this as well along with family and peers as protective factors. Modelling as an influence on learning is also significant.

Some of the significant early learning experiences in adolescents are based on family environment, parenting styles and exposure to parental or significant other models. These early experiences interact with the temperament of the adolescent along with other vulnerabilities and lead to the formation of core beliefs.

Therefore, as with adult patients, the case formulation (Fig. 2.1) consists of identifying early experiences that contribute to the formation of core schema or beliefs (I must always be perfect, nobody loves me, the world is a dangerous place, I must be careful), critical incidents that trigger or activate the core schema

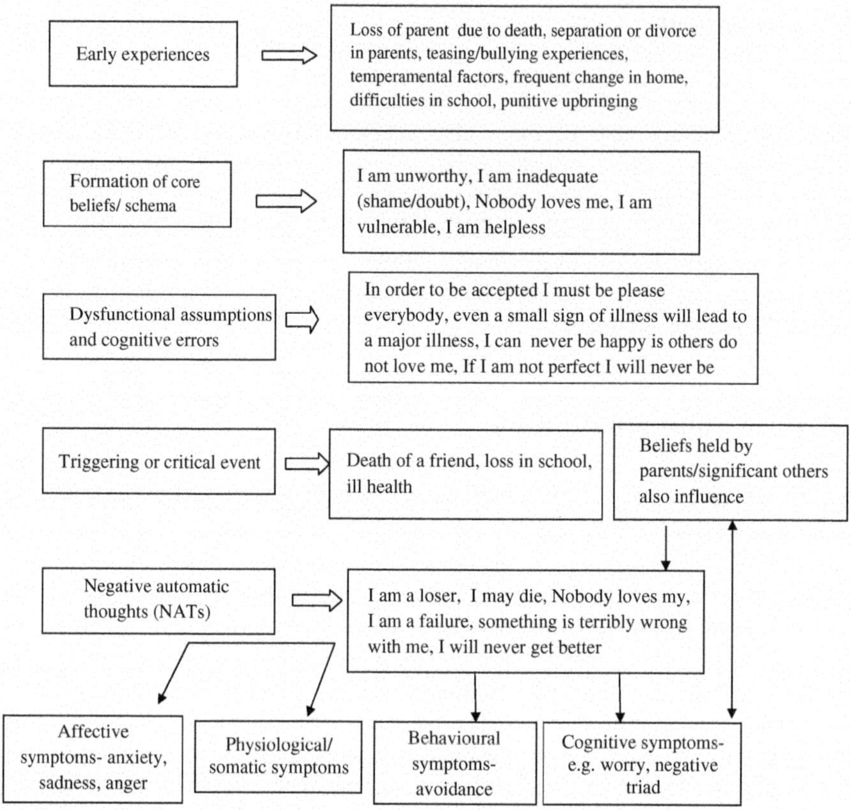

Fig. 2.1 The cognitive behavioural framework for emotional disorders

leading to dysfunctional assumptions (only if I am perfect can I be successful) and subsequently identifying the symptoms in terms of **behavioural** (restlessness, being fidgety, withdrawn), **affective** (sadness/anxiety), **motivational** (lethargy, loss of interest), **physiological** (sweating, palpitations) and **cognitive** (negative automatic thoughts, decreased concentration). This developmental model then guides the therapist to formulate the plan of therapy in collaboration with the client. Case formulation in CBT for adolescents should also consider the changing nature of environment and ongoing events that continue to impact beliefs and assumptions.

Various strategies can be adopted to develop a case formulation in CBT. A detailed interview that guides the adolescent through various possible experiences and factors is the most reliable method. Often, as the adolescent cannot provide much of the early development information, significant others are also to be interviewed. Understanding the family structure, systemic factors as well as specific disabilities the adolescent presents with is important in arriving at a comprehensive formulation (Bailey 2001).

A cognitive behavioural interview uses a process of guided discovery and Socratic questions through which assumptions and cognitions are elicited.

Additionally asking the adolescent to elaborate on specific events and examples also helps in arriving at hypothesis about how cognitions develop over a period of time. Several other methods to elicit beliefs and assumptions have been recommended and these can also be used in working with adolescents. They include the use of imagery to recall thoughts, exposure to specific situations and then asking for thoughts that may have occurred and role-plays to recreate situations that can elicit dysfunctional thoughts.

The precipitating factor is often considered to be the **critical incident** which activates or triggers dormant beliefs and leads to activation of dysfunctional assumptions. Identifying the critical incident or incidents (such as failure in exam, loss of a parent, separation, break-up in relationship, teasing experience) provides the information as to what led the adolescent to begin experiencing difficulties and till what point was he/she functioning adequately.

The cognitive behavioural formulation or case conceptualization can be either **longitudinal** in nature, which is tracing the development of core beliefs based on early experiences and other vulnerabilities, or **cross-sectional**, which attempts to explain a typical cycle of trigger, interpretation and consequence. The longitudinal model is helpful in providing the therapist a broad understanding of contributory and maintaining factors from a developmental perspective and in identifying core beliefs how they develop as a result of an interaction of various factors.

On the other hand, a cross-sectional model attempts to provide the therapist and client an understanding of the here-and-now factors such as triggers and cognitive processes (thinking errors), behavioural and emotional changes as result of these thought processes. Several cross-sectional models are available to specific emotional disorders, such as panic, social phobia, obsessive-compulsive disorders (OCD) and GAD.

Despite the emphasis on early experiences, CBT is considered to adopt a **here-and-now** approach in the management of problems. This is reflected in the nature of strategies used in therapy. Common aims across CBTs include symptom reduction, modification of dysfunctional thinking and relapse prevention.

2.9 Therapeutic Relationship in CBT for Adolescents

The nature of relationship in CBT is one of **collaborative empiricism**. The term refers to the scientific or experimental nature of the approach to solving problems in therapy. Thus, in therapy, the therapist does not assume that he/she already knows better than the adolescent. Prescribing solutions or deciding for the adolescent is avoided. They work jointly on the discovery of dysfunctional patterns in thinking, setting goals and deciding on activities. Collaboration is to be followed at all points in therapy. This includes the start of therapy at which point goals are set. Thus, therapy is a joint effort between the adolescent and the therapist and the family as well.

When working with adolescents, it is important to involve parents at various points in the intervention and to keep the adolescent informed. This is particularly relevant in anxiety management, wherein parents are either cotherapists, facilitators or are part of the intervention due to their role in maintaining anxiety.

2.10 Homework in CBT

CBT involves the acquisition of skills for new patterns of thinking and coping. An important way of achieving this is through practice. Homework compliance has been found to be a major predictor of treatment outcome. Factors such as poor understanding of the therapy, anxiety, cognitive distortions and inadequate motivation/opportunities affect compliance. The therapist must be aware of these factors and work on them to ensure that compliance is maintained. CBT in adolescents involves the use of activities, worksheets and various other methods of communicating formulation, educating and increasing participation.

2.11 Ethical Practice in CBT for Adolescents

Several ethical concerns arise in the treatment of children and adolescents. These are governed by the basic ideas of do no harm, doing what is in the best interest of the child or adolescent and protecting the privacy of the child or adolescent. Respecting the child and family without any bias and promotion and supporting the highest level of development and autonomy in the child are some of the other important rules (Schetky 1995). The therapist additionally faces pressures to control the child and force compliance at the cost of the individuality of the client.

Several other concerns arise in working with adolescents. It is important to protect the privacy of the adolescent client and keep him/her informed about frequency of parent involvement. The exceptions to the rules of privacy and confidentiality are also to be made clear to the adolescent.

Ascherman and Rubin (2008) provide an excellent discussion about current ethical concerns in the practice of child and adolescent psychotherapy.

2.12 Cognitive Behavioural Strategies

The threefold aim of CBT is (a) symptom reduction, (b) belief modification or identification and modification of unhelpful thinking and (c) preventing relapse. Thus, CBT shares certain common strategies that help achieve these goals. Depression and anxiety in adolescents are two major mental health concerns.

A brief overview of some of the frequently used therapeutic strategies are described here.

Several cognitive and behavioural strategies have been found to be effective in adolescents. The choice of strategies is based on the case conceptualization and the functional analysis of problems. Rationale for each of the strategies must be established clearly, as also the monitoring of progress once they are implemented. Continuous monitoring by the therapist and adolescent also allows for the detection of changes and responses and allows the therapist to alter or change treatment strategies.

In the following section, a few frequently used strategies are briefly described. They are further described in the later sections of this chapter, in the context of conditions for which they have been found to be effective.

Arousal reduction methods: Anxiety or arousal reduction is an important therapeutic goal as it leads to symptom reduction. Several different types of strategies can be used to help the adolescent client reduce arousal or anxiety. They include deep muscle relaxation, biofeedback procedures (EMG and galvanic skin response), deep breathing and Eastern methods such as Shavasana and mindfulness-based stress reduction programmes. These methods have also been found to be helpful in anger management and help the adolescent in coping with anxiety and anger by teaching them self-regulation. Arousal reduction methods are most effective when practised regularly.

Applied relaxation (AR) (Öst 1987): The need for more portable and briefer methods of producing the relaxation response in anxiety management led to the development of the AR. It was first described by Chang-Liang and Denney (1976) and later developed by Öst (1987). AR is described as a coping skill, which has several steps. They include recording and identifying early signs of anxiety or worry that act as cues for anxiety and training in deep muscle relaxation or tension release relaxation (sessions 2 and 3), followed by release-only relaxation (session 4) and cue-controlled relaxation (session 5) in which the word cue or calm is paired with exhalation, differential relaxation and rapid relaxation (session 8). Sessions 10–11 are focused on application of these skills to actual situation, based on the cues recorded by the client. Finally, the client and therapist review the overall programme and its maintenance. AR has been found to be particularly effective in panic disorder, generalized anxiety disorder and social phobia.

Exposure and Response Prevention (ERP) is a treatment of choice in the management of OCD. It is based on the theoretical principle of habituation and extinction. ERP involves drawing a hierarchy of situations or triggers that provoke anxiety/fear/disgust, by collaboratively working with the adolescent. The situations/triggers are rated for their subjective units of distress (SUD). The adolescent may also be asked to state what would happen if he/she did not perform the neutralizing behaviour or compulsion so as to understand underlying beliefs. Systematic exposure to these cues is started with items that elicit moderate amounts of anxiety and the adolescent is asked not to engage in compulsions either overt or covert, till there is a significant reduction in anxiety (usually at least 50 %). This allows for habituation of the experience of anxiety, and with repeated practice, there is an extinction of the response of anxiety, even in the presence of these triggers. During the practice of ERP, the therapist must ensure that the adolescent has understood the rationale for response prevention, as well as the need to be able to tolerate distress that arises during exposure. Sufficient education regarding the symptoms, role of neutralizing behaviours in maintaining distress and beliefs is to be carried out before beginning ERP. This not only ensures adequate compliance but is also likely to be helpful in reducing attrition.

Adequate time for exposure is crucial factor in the practice of ERP. Insufficient or brief exposure can result in the enhancement of anxiety or inadequate learning. The therapist is also alert to use of cognitive compulsions in place of overt ones, avoidance or other subtle forms of neutralizing behaviours and this can be seen when clients report sudden decreases in anxiety.

Graded exposure is a behavioural strategy based on the learning principle of habituation and extinction. It is the treatment of choice in the management of specific phobia, panic disorder, social phobia and other anxiety disorders. Graded exposure addresses avoidance and fear, by systematic exposure to fear-evoking stimuli. The therapist and client prepare a hierarchy that includes fear-evoking situations or triggers and the level of anxiety or fear (subjective unit of distress). Based on this list of situations, the client is gradually exposed to cues, allowing for habituation to occur and subsequently extinction of fear.

Social skills training (SST) is a skills-based programme developed on the principles of social learning. SST assumes that social skills can be learned and acquired with training. Skill deficits in adolescents account for several emotional and behavioural problems such as anxiety, anger, poor interpersonal relationships and overall adjustment leading to stress. SST focuses on building verbal and non-verbal skills that are essential in initiating and maintaining interpersonal skills. Assessment plays a very important role in setting goals for SST. It includes both self-report and observation and behavioural data. Role-play and modelling are some of the important methods by which SST is imparted. Steps in SST include establishing a rationale for skill acquisition, discussing steps involved, modelling skill in role-play, reviewing role-play, engaging the client in a role-play of the same situation, providing positive and corrective feedback and finally assigning homework that will help consolidate gains. Repeated practice and practice across different situations are essential in making SST effective.

Assertiveness skills are an important component of SST and use role-play and modelling to teach skills in effective expression of positive and negative emotions. Assertiveness skills training involves training in refusal, requesting skills, accepting positive or commendatory feedback. In adolescents, assertiveness is particularly important for resisting peer pressure for risky behaviours such as sexual behaviours or substances.

PSST (D'Zurilla 1986): The absence of adequate problem-solving skills often results in the build-up of stressful states and subsequently anxiety and depression. Problem-solving skills are particularly helpful in adolescents who experience various sources of stress such as academic, peer-related and family. Steps in PSST are (a) orientation or set to formulate problems as potentially solvable. This includes the recognition of a problem and the ability to resist taking an action impulsively.

(b) Problem definition in which the central element is specificity as one must be precise, and specific (e.g. I have difficulty in getting to know people socially) (c) generate alternate courses of action: by using brainstorming and other such procedures) decision-making (e.g. refusing to go out with a friend where pressure to drink is high) (d) verification requires that the client be able to anticipate, rehearse and implement a decision. Here, social skills are required or even detailed anticipation of events in the person's life followed by a debriefing after these schedules are implemented. Thus, PSST is a cognitive behavioural programme.

In addition to these broad strategies, cognitive restructuring and many other behavioural strategies such as stimulus control (for study skills, weight management), behavioural activation (in depression) and self-instructional training may be incorporated into programmes that target specific problems.

2.13 Depression in Adolescents

Depression in youth and adolescents is a major concern for mental professionals, and nearly 1.5–8 % young adults (from late adolescence) suffer from depressive disorder (Rushton and Schectman 2002; Waslick et al. 2003). CBT is considered to be one of the most efficacious treatments for depression (Waslick et al. 2003), with a significant amount of evidence supporting it (TADS 2003; Kaufman et al. 2005).

Cognitive models of depression in older children and adolescents recognize that by around ages 8–11 years, most children can both identify and report several cognitions that are seen in adults (Harrington 2005). This is also the time when children are able to perceive self psychologically as well as understand the meaning of events such as death, separation or loss. The nature of presenting complaints appears to be a significant positive indicator for CBT in adolescents. Thus, adolescents who present with a primary problem of mood or depression appear to be more suited for CBT. In addition, the recognition and acknowledgement of the problem by the adolescent and family serve as positive indicators for the choice of CBT. When the family acknowledges the presence of depression and the need for psychological intervention, they will also assist and support the adolescent in therapy.

Contraindications include the developmental stage of the adolescent, severity of depressive symptoms and the social context. With respect to the developmental stage, many techniques used in CBT require knowledge about thought processes or cognition (metacognition). Therefore, if the adolescent is not able to do this, carrying out homework and other tasks will be difficult. The social context is an important factor in response. Many adolescents are caught in social contexts that are difficult to alter, and therefore, despite psychological treatments, problems may ensue. There is a little research on the role of comorbid disorders in impacting outcome of CBT in adolescents.

2.14 Anxiety Disorders in Adolescents

Anxiety disorders and other internalizing disorders form a major part of the psychiatric disorders seen in children and adolescents. Although many fears and anxieties may be transient, changing as the child grows up, others continue, developing into debilitating problems. OCD, social anxiety, specific phobia, school refusal and panic attacks are common anxiety disorders seen in adolescence.

Social phobia is known to have onset in childhood or adolescence; however, very often social anxiety goes unrecognized. This has resulted in far more research on adult samples than in adolescents. The presentation of social phobia is also likely to be different in adolescents, with greater externalizing and antisocial problems, excessive self-focused attention and avoidance (Kashdan and Herbert 2001).

Cognitive behavioural management of anxiety disorders assumes a multicomponent etiologic, involving biological, psychological/cognitive and behavioural components. The treatment that follows this understanding of anxiety disorders employs a group of techniques that try to break the vicious cycle of physiological responses, fear and safety behaviours. It is important to note that anxiety disorders also have comorbid depression, which may impact treatment outcomes.

2.15 Cognitive Behavioural Strategies in the Management of Anxiety and Depression

CBT for depression and anxiety shares many common strategies. An overview of these main strategies is provided below with reference to depression and anxiety.

Education and engagement is an important stage in CBT. Depending upon the severity of depressive or anxiety symptoms and existence of comorbid disorders, the process of engagement can vary in terms of time and difficulty. The process of engagement can be challenging, particularly with difficult adolescents.

CBT for anxiety disorders in adolescents includes an **educational component** in which the therapist provides information about the role of biological processes in the maintenance of anxiety and skills training which would help the adolescent **identify the early signs of anxiety** through self-monitoring.

Behavioural activation through activity scheduling aims at increasing activity levels as well as enhancing mastery and pleasure, thereby improving mood. This is particularly important in depression wherein low motivation and activity could be a presenting complaint as well as in anxiety disorders in the form of avoidance. This is achieved through pleasant events as well as tasks that are graded in terms of difficulties. In anxiety disorders, activity schedules can also incorporate tasks that have been previously avoided and provoke anxiety.

Self-monitoring (thought diary) is used to identify these patterns of dysfunctional thinking, and through this activity, the adolescent is helped to gain an understanding of the vicious cycle between thoughts, emotions and behaviours. Exposure, role-plays and other behavioural methods are also helpful in eliciting dysfunctional cognitions.

Cognitive restructuring is a key component of CBT and aims at identifying and modifying typical patterns of dysfunctional thinking that maintain depressed affect and reduce social behaviours. The process of restructuring dysfunctional patterns of thinking involves both **verbal and behavioural strategies**. Verbal reattribution techniques include using a cost–benefit analysis, developing a pie chart to understand the various factors that lead to a predicted outcome (error of personalization) and identifying the use of double standards to challenge excessive self-criticality, all of which are aimed at taking a more rational perspective. Behavioural reattribution techniques include behavioural experiments, role-plays, exposure sessions and poll surveys. These strategies complement the verbal strategies and also aim at cognitive change.

Learning relaxation skills help manage arousal symptoms. Several types of relaxation skills have been found to be helpful including deep muscle or progressive muscle relaxation, deep breathing, guided or positive imagery and biofeedback. Behavioural strategies are also helpful in the reduction of anxiety and are based on the learning principles such as habituation and extinction and social learning. These include, in session exposure, role-play and modelling, imagery-based methods and graduated exposures (or step ladders). For specific anxiety, symptoms such as worry and worry management techniques can also be recommended. These include worry postponement, worry exposure and prevention of worry behaviours such as checking and reducing reassurance by seeking help from the parents. Cognitive components of the anxiety management programme include identification of negative cognitions that are frequently encountered in anxiety disorders or anxious self-talk. The use of **coping self-statements** has been recommended to deal with anticipatory anxiety. This is carried out through the use of self-statements and cognitive restructuring that can address misinterpretation of anxiety symptoms and catastrophization.

PSST is a core component in the depression treatment protocol for adolescents (Kazdin 2002). It has also been found useful in the management of anxiety disorders. In both conditions, it can effectively prevent relapse. In depression, PSST is based on the assumption that deficits in interpersonal problem-solving skills contribute to and maintain depressive symptoms. It includes skills for interpersonal or social problem-solving, such as dealing with peers, conflicting relationships within the family and dealing with everyday problems that can potentially generate stress in adolescents. Social problem-solving allows the adolescent to anticipate and deal with situations as well as learn to respond to social cues (others' anger, sadness) and also helps in negotiating interpersonal problems that are common in this period. The steps in PSST are similar to those in adults, beginning with identifying a problem that is to be solved, generating as many potential solutions as possible, without at this point judging quality of solutions, choosing the best options while keeping backup solutions, implementing based on skills and resources and finally reviewing outcomes.

CST is helpful in the management of both anxiety and depression. The behavioural model of depression emphasizes skill deficits as an important aspect in the maintenance of depressive symptoms (Lewinsohn and Clarke 1999). Skill deficits are seen in the interpersonal and social problem-solving domains. These skills are important to earn and sustain positive and supportive relationships as well as in regulating difficult emotions. There are different approaches to CST. They share a few common features such as the identification and modification of schema related to depression or anxiety, correction of cognitive errors, skills training to improve social interactions that include conversational skills, social problem-solving (conflict resolution skills) and other skills and competencies relevant to enhancing self-esteem (e.g. setting performance goals and reaching them), relaxation training to reduce the physiological arousal that could interfere with experience of pleasure and structured experience in selecting and engaging in mood-enhancing activities to increase rates of positive reinforcement.

CBT and CST share similar components, as both modify faulty and depressogenic and anxiety-producing cognitions and involve in session exposures and modelling.

2.16 Treatment Modules and Research on CBT in Adolescents with Depression

Although depression is a major mental health concern in adolescents, there have been relatively fewer research studies on psychological interventions, in particular CBT for adolescent depression as compared to problems such as anxiety and aggression (Para 2008). Reviews by Kazdin and Weisz (1998) and by Kaslow and Thompson (1998) suggest that CBT for adolescents with depression is one of the relatively few childhood or adolescent treatments that met the criteria for at least probable efficacy as an empirically supported treatment. They point out that components of successful CBT for depression in young people include methods to increase participation in pleasant, mood-enhancing activities, to increase and improve social interactions, to improve conflict resolution and social problem-solving skills to reduce physiological tension or excessive affective arousal and to identify and modify depressive thoughts and attributions.

Brent and Poling (1997) and Lewinsohn et al. (1985, 1990) also suggest the inclusion of mood monitoring, goal setting, presentation of a clear treatment rationale and socialization of the adolescent and parents to the treatment model based on this rationale.

Treatment for Adolescents with Depression Study (March 2004; TADS 2003) is a pioneering attempt to treat depression in adolescents, based on key components of CBT for depression described by Beck et al. (1979). It combines CBT for adolescents with parental involvement.

Adolescent coping with depression (CWD-A) is another group cognitive behavioural programme that has been used with adolescents between 14 and 18 years of age in the community settings (Lewinsohn et al. 1984). It is conducted for a mixed gender group over 16 years of age, 2-h sessions (Lewinsohn et al. 1985). The components are based on the coping with depression programme for adults. It is based on the social learning theory and includes skills training and pleasant activities through self-monitoring, self-reinforcement and goal setting.

Reviews of CBT for adolescents suggest mixed results for the effectiveness of CBT (Compton et al. 2004; James et al. 2013). There is an absence of long-term follow-up to establish durability. Few studies have conducted controlled trials, and the relative contribution of different components in CBT to outcome is also not clear. There is limited evidence that CBT is more effective than active controls or TAU or medication at follow-up (James et al. 2013). Therefore, there is a need for controlled research with active treatment controls and longer follow-up to further establish the efficacy of CBT for adolescent depression.

2.17 Programmes Based on Cognitive Behavioural Framework for Other Anxiety Disorders

The Coping Cat programme is a programme that was developed for the management of anxiety disorders in children and adolescents (Kendall 2006). It is a frequently recommended and used treatment programme for the management of anxiety in children and adolescents. The Coping Cat programme involves roughly those with 14–18 years of age, 60 min sessions, delivered over a 12–16-week period. The entire programme is designed to teach the child/adolescent skills and provide opportunities to practise the skills acquired, through exposure. The main aspects of the programme in addition to recognition of anxiety reactions include identifying cognitions in anxiety-provoking situations and making a plan to cope (such as self-talk, exposure, review, evaluation of action and reinforcing one self). Skills taught in the programme include identifying signs of anxious arousal that serve as cues or for the child to employ the skills in anxiety management they have acquired. The **Cool Kids programme** is based on the Coping Cat programme. It follows a group format, involving the family. The main goals of this programme are helping the adolescent learn anxiety management skills, graded exposure or 'step ladders', cognitive restructuring and parent management. Optional modules include SST, assertiveness and handling teasing/bullying.

The Coping Cat programme has also been used in a recent Indian study that demonstrated its effectiveness in early adolescents in a community school setting (Selvi 2013). This study demonstrated the efficacy of the Coping Cat programme in a school setting in reducing anxiety.

Reviews on CBT for childhood and adolescent anxiety disorders indicate that while they are effective psychological interventions, more studies on their comparative efficacy with alternate treatment are required (Cartwright-Hatton et al. 2004).

2.18 CBT for Specific Anxiety Disorders

CBT for specific anxiety disorders has also been formulated. OCD is one such anxiety disorder. About 0.5–1 % of children and adolescents receive a diagnosis of OCD (March et al. 1997). Like older patients, CBT has shown to be effective in dealing with OCD in adolescents. While it is the most recommended treatment for OCD, clinicians document the difficulties in implementing CBT for this disorder, due to poor compliance, attrition, difficulties in belief modification and family accommodation that maintains the symptoms.

A typical CBT protocol for OCD includes a detailed phase of education and socialization to the CB model, **exposure and response prevention** (**EXP/RP**), along with **cognitive restructuring** for handling beliefs related to performance of compulsions, **reducing family accommodation** and proxy compulsions (March and Mulle 1998; Mehta 1990) and behavioural interventions such as **modelling and shaping** which help develop appropriate coping behaviours and in enhancing compliance with EX/RP. However, the effectiveness of EX/RP is enhanced with the inclusion of cognitive interventions (Soechting and March 2002). The family also plays an important role in providing positive reinforcements when the adolescent completes tasks successfully and for other positive behaviours.

Most treatment protocols based on CB framework accomplish these goals over a 12-week period with about 14–16 sessions and are dependent on severity of problems and compliance (March and Mulle 1998).

2.19 Cognitive Behavioural Management for Problems Related to Anger and Aggression

Anger, aggression and difficulties in regulating similar negative emotions directed at external events or people are a major problem that clinicians encounter when working with adolescents. Anger and aggression may be seen as part of a larger psychological problem, such as conduct disorder, as anxiety disorder or as an independent problem maintained by contingencies in the environment. They impact the interpersonal relations of the adolescent negatively.

Kazdin (2002) describes a five-step self-instruction approach as part of comprehensive programme to help adolescents build competencies in dealing with anger and aggression. This includes the steps that have been described in the previous section in this chapter. The problem-solving approach used with adolescents with conduct disorder is also referred to as the **cognitive problem-solving skills** (Kazdin 1997) as it involves a variety of cognitive and behavioural processes such as being able to identify the problem accurately, think of it from various points of view before generating a variety of solutions. It also attempts to teach the adolescent skills in delaying impulsive decision-making and use of coping self-talk or self-instructions that can act as effective ways to reduce impulsive acts by allowing the adolescent to reflect before responding.

SST is based on the social learning theory proposed by Bandura (1977). Social skills are an integral and an important component of many emotional and behavioural disorders. The development of social skills is said to occur through vicarious learning. However, many children fail to acquire the desired social skills to successfully manage challenging situations in life. The failure to acquire social skills can be attributed to a variety of factors, including biological factors that hinder learning, inadequate role models/ opportunities and symptoms such as anxiety or depression that interfere with the effective use of social skills.

SST includes a variety of skills designed to address skills in managing difficult or challenging social situations. They include behavioural and social skills, training in social perception, which involves accurate interpretation of social cues from others, self-instruction/self-regulation training which is the use of self talk, self-reinforcement in response to appropriate social behaviours, social problem-solving, which is similar to PSST, but is applied in an interpersonal context. SST also includes the reduction of inappropriate, inhibiting or competing social behaviours that interfere with appropriate social interactions. This is achieved through the practice of strategies such as contingency contracting, parent management training or even cognitive restructuring where cognitive distortions may interfere or inhibit social interactions (Spence 2003). SST is an essential component in the treatment of emotional disorders.

Assertiveness training is an important component of SST. Deficits in assertiveness have been identified as being an important factor in substance use disorders, high-risk sexual behaviours, aggression and internalizing disorders such as anxiety and depression. Training in assertiveness involves identifying specific areas in which the adolescent has difficulties, such as refusal skills, requesting skills, accepting compliments or expressing positive and negative emotions effectively. Assertiveness training is most effectively delivered through role-plays, role reversals and feedback.

2.20 Parental Involvement

While many of cognitive behavioural programmes are carried out with the adolescent, additional parental involvement becomes important for many of the behavioural problems. Research evidence suggests that parent involvement is likely to improve treatment outcome in anxious children and adolescents (Albano and Kendall 2002; Barrett et al. 1996). The therapist can involve the parents as cotherapists, as collaborators or as consultants who provide important assistance to the therapy. Thus, parents can function as '**cognitive behavioural coaches**'. The frequency at which parents may be called can vary depending upon the tasks required. Parents are often involved in planning exposure activities, in desisting reassurance giving or in carrying out proxy compulsions. Parents are also instructed to provide positive reinforcements during the course of treatment.

The active involvement of parents in the child or adolescent's treatment plan will vary depending upon a number of factors including degree of impairment, comorbidity, age and developmental level of the child (i.e. degree of independent functioning). Parent involvement may be impeded by marital discord, parental psychopathology or other psychosocial stresses such as economic or environmental problems. Thus, the clinician will assess each individual situation and 'dose' the parental involvement accordingly.

For problems such as attention-deficit/hyperactivity disorder, conduct disorders and other externalizing disorders, interventions involve both the adolescent and the parent. A variety of behavioural strategies such as contingency management have been found to be effective. Conflict resolution skills and handling negative self-talk affect regulation skills such as learning to relax or use social problem-solving skills that are used in the management of problems related to anger (Novaco 1979).

Parent management training (PMT) refers to procedures in which parents are trained to alter their child's behaviour in the home (Kazdin 2005). The parents meet with a therapist and acquire skills in specific procedures that aim to alter interactions with their child, to promote pro-social behaviour and to decrease undesirable behaviour. PMT is based on the assumption that problem behaviours are maintained by coercive and maladaptive parent–child interactions in the home setting. Multiple aspects of this interaction that foster the behavioural problems including harsh punishment along with use of ineffective commands by parents in addition to a failure by parents to positively reinforce the child when he/she shows appropriate behaviour are said to be major reinforcing factors (Patterson 1982).

Recent advances in this field include the application of **mindfulness-based interventions** for adolescents in the management of anxiety (Urvashi 2013), conduct disorder, aggressive behaviours (Singh et al. 2007) and attention-deficit/hyperactivity disorder (Zylowska et al. 2007). Mindfulness-based interventions, considered to be the third wave in behaviour therapy, are considered to be a promising approach in the management of psychological problems in adolescents (Burke 2009).

2.21 Varied Forms of CBT Delivery

Since the development of CBT in the last few decades, varied forms of CBT delivery have been reported. Face-to-face delivery of CBT has been the most common mode of CBT practice. However, in the recent years, as the need to reach out to more adolescents and to make CBT more easily available to clients, CBT has been delivered through Internet (Internet CBT or Web-based), telephone (Tele-CBT) and computer- assisted CBT. More recently, CBT is also made available as a telephone application. Evidence for the clinical effectiveness of Internet-based CBT has been recently reported with respect to depression (Ruwaard et al. 2009). One such programme that has been studied is the MoodGYM, which is a free Web-based CBT programme developed to prevent and treat mild-to-moderate depression and has been studied in adolescent population (Groves et al. 2003). These forms of delivering CBT have been most often used in non-clinical settings or in clients with mild levels of symptoms. They have the distinct advantage of being accessible to more people and also overcome the difficulties associated with lack of time and availability of therapist, as well as cost.

2.22 Conclusions

CBT is a problem-focused, time-oriented and evidence-based psychological intervention. It has been adapted to suit both children and adolescents as well. The therapist stance in CBT is one of collaborative empiricism, and this approach ensures that the adolescent feels that he/she is an active collaborator in therapy. The main focus in CBT for adolescents is the identification and modification of depressogenic or anxious thinking patterns and teaching skills in problem-solving, anxiety management and similar skills that will help the adolescent in dealing with challenging situations. Problem-solving skills and coping skills are effective for a variety of emotional and behavioural problems in adolescents. In addition to core cognitive components such as cognitive restructuring, CBT also includes behavioural techniques such as relaxation training, exposure, role-play and activity scheduling. Parental involvement has been recommended in many formats of CBT for adolescents; however, care needs to be taken to inform the adolescent, and parental involvement must be defined clearly.

Recent reviews support the effectiveness of CBT in adolescents; however, there is a need for long-term studies, with active treatment controls to further substantiate these conclusions. Future research must also focus on understanding how different mechanisms operate in CBT to bring about outcome. Studies must also focus on mediators and moderators of change in therapy (Kazdin and Weisz 1998; Kazdin and Nock 2003). This can be made possible through dismantling studies. Psychological interventions based on the cognitive behavioural framework are effective in treating a wide variety of psychological problems seen in adolescents.

References

Ainsworth, M. D. S., Blehar, M. C., Waters, E., & Wall, S. (1978). *Patterns of attachment: A psychological study of the strange situation*. Hillsdale, NJ: Erlbaum.

Albano, A. M., & Kendall, P. C. (2002). Cognitive behavioural therapy for children and adolescents with anxiety disorders: Clinical research advances. *International Review of Psychiatry, 14*, 129–134.

Angold, A., Prendergast, M., Cox, A., Rutter, M., Harrington, R., Simonoff, E., & Rutter, M. (1995). The child and adolescent psychiatric assessment (CAPA). *Psychological Medicine, 25*, 739–754.

Ascherman, L. E., & Rubin, S. (2008). Current ethical issues in child and adolescent psychotherapy. *Child Adolescent Psychiatric Clinics of North America, 17*, 21–35.

Bandura, A. (1977). Self-efficacy: Toward a unifying theory of behavioral change. *Psychological Review, 84*, 191–215.

Bailey, V. (2001). Cognitive behaviour therapies for children and adolescents. *Advances in Psychiatric Treatment, 7*, 224–233.

Barrett, P. M., Dadds, M. R., & Rapee, R. M. (1996). Family treatment of childhood anxiety: A controlled trial. *Journal of Consulting and Clinical Psychology, 64*(2), 333.

Beck, A. T., Rush, A. J., Shaw, B. F., & Emery, G. (1979). *Cognitive therapy of depression*. New York: Guilford.

Bowlby, J. (1982). *Attachment and loss*. Volume 1. Attachment (2nd edn.). New York: Basic Books.

Brent, D., & Poling, K. (1997). *Cognitive therapy treatment manual for depressed and suicidal youth*. Pittsburgh, PA: University of Pittsburgh.

Burke, C. A. (2009). Mindfulness-based approaches with children and adolescents: a preliminary review of current research in an emergent field. *Journal of Child and Family Studies*. doi:10.1007/s10826-009-9282-x.

Cartwright-Hatton, S., Roberts, C., Chitsabesan, P., Fothergill, C., & Harrington, R. (2004). Systematic review of the efficacy of cognitive behaviour therapies for childhood and adolescent disorders. *The British Journal of Clinical Psychology, 43*, 421–436.

Chang-Liang, R., & Denney, D. R. (1976). Applied relaxation as training in self-control. *Journal of Counseling Psychology, 23*(3), 183–189.

Compton, S. N., March, J. S., Brent, D., Albano, A. M., Weersing, R. V., & Curry, J. (2004). Cognitive-behavioral psychotherapy for anxiety and depressive disorders in children and adolescents: an evidence-based medicine review. *Journal of the American Academy of Child and Adolescent Psychiatry, 43*(8), 30–959.

Dobson, K. (Ed.). (1988). *Handbook of cognitive-behavioral therapies*. New York: Guilford Press.

Dodge, K. A. (1993). Social-cognitive mechanisms in the development of conduct disorder and depression. *Annual Review of Psychology, 44*, 559–584.

D'Zurilla, T. J. (1986). *Problem-solving therapy: A social competence approach to clinical intervention*. New York: Springer.

Ellis, A. (1958). Rational psychotherapy. *The Journal of General Psychology, 59*(1), 35–49.

Garber, J., & Flynn, C. A. (2001). Predictors of depressive cognitions in young adolescents. *Cognitive Therapy and Research, 25*, 353–376.

Groves, C., Griffiths, K., & Christensen, H. (2003). *Working out MoodGYM: A user's guide*. Canberra, Australia: Centre for Mental Health Research.

Harrington, R. (2005). Depressive disorders. In P. Graham (Ed.), *Cognitive behaviour therapy for children and families* (2nd ed., pp. 263–280). Cambridge, United Kingdom: Cambridge University Press.

Inhelder, B., Piaget, J., Parsons, A. T., & Milgram, S. T. (1958). *The growth of logical thinking: From childhood to adolescence.*

James, A. C., James, G., Cowdrey, F. A., Soler A., Choke, A. (2013). Cognitive behavioural therapy for anxiety disorders in children and adolescents. *Cochrane Database of systematic reviews*, 6. Art. no. CD004690. doi:10.1002/14651858.CD004690.pub3.

Kashdan, T. B., & Herbert, J. D. (2001). Social Anxiety disorder in childhood and adolescence: Current status and future directions. *Clinical Child and Family Psychology Review, 4*, 1.

Kaslow, N., & Thompson, M. (1998). Applying the criteria for empirically supported treatments to studies of psychosocial interventions for child and adolescent depression. *Journal of Clinical Child Psychology, 27*, 146–155.

Kaufman, N. K., Rohde, P., Seeley, J. R., Clarke, G. N., & Stice, E. (2005). Potential mediators of cognitive-behavioral therapy for adolescents with comorbid major depression and conduct disorder. *Journal of Consulting and Clinical Psychology, 73*(1), 38–46.

Kazdin, A. E. (2002). Psychosocial treatments for conduct disorder in children and adolescent. In P. E. Nathan & J. M. Gorman (Eds.), *Guides to treatments that work* (2nd ed.). New York: Oxford University Press.

Kazdin, E. A. (1997). Practitioner review: Psychosocial treatments for conduct disorder in children. *Journal of Child Psychology and Psychiatry, 38*(2), 161–178.

Kazdin, A., & Weisz, J. (1998). Identifying and developing empirically supported child and adolescent treatments. *Journal of Consulting and Clinical Psychology, 66*, 19–36.

Kazdin, A. E., & Nock, M. K. (2003). Delineating mechanisms of change in child and adolescent therapy: Methodological issues and research recommendations. *Journal of Child Psychology and Psychiatry, 44*(8), 1116–1129.

Kazdin, A. E. (Ed). (2005). *Parent management training: Treatment for oppositional, aggressive, and antisocial behavior in children and adolescents.* New York: Oxford University Press.
Kendall, P. C., Hedtke, K. (2006). *Cognitive-behavioral therapy for anxious children: Therapist manual.* 3. Ardmore, PA: Workbook Publishing.
Lewinsohn, P. M., & Clarke, G. N. (1999). Psychosocial treatments for adolescent depression. *Clinical Psychology Review, 19*(3), 329–342.
Lewinsohn, P. M., Antonuccio, D. O., Steinmetz-Brekenridge, J., & Teri, L. (1984). *The coping with depression course.* Eugene, OR: Castalia Press.
Lewinsohn, P. M., Hoberman, H., Teri, L., & Hautzinger, M. (1985). An integrative theory of depression. In S. Reiss, & R. R. Bootzin (Eds.), *Theoretical issues in behavior therapy* (pp. 331 – 359). San Diego, CA: Academic Press.
Lewinsohn, P., Clarke, G., Hops, H., & Andrews, J. (1990). Cognitive-behavioral group treatment of depression in adolescents. *Behavior Therapy, 21*, 385–401.
March, J., Frances, A., Kahn, D., & Carpenter, D. (1997). Expert consensus guidelines: Treatment of obsessive compulsive disorder. *Journal of Clinical Psychiatry, 58*(Suppl 4), 1–72.
March, J. S., & Mulle, K. (1998). *OCD in children and adolescents: A cognitive-behavioural treatment manual.* New York: Guilford Press.
March, J. (2004). The treatment for adolescents with depression study (TADS) short term effects and safety outcomes. *Journal of American Medical Association, 292*, 807–820.
Mehta, M. (1990). A comparative study of family-based and patient-based behavioural management in obsessive-compulsive disorder. *The British Journal of Psychiatry, 157*, 133–135. doi:10.1192/bjp.157.1.133.
Meichenbaum, D. H., & Goodman, J. (1971). Training impulsive children to talk to themselves: A means of developing self-control. *Journal of Abnormal Psychology, 77*(2), 115–126.
Novaco, R. W. (1979). *Therapist manual for stress inoculation training. Therapeutic interventions for anger problems.* Irvine: University of California.
O'Connor, T., & Creswell, C. (2005). Cognitive behavioural therapy in developmental perspective. In P. Graham (Ed.), *Cognitive behaviour therapy for children and families* (2nd ed., pp. 25–47). Cambridge, United Kingdom: Cambridge University Press.
Ollendick, T., & King, N. J. (2004). Empirically supported treatments for children and adolescents: Advances toward evidence-based practice. In P. M. Barrett & T. H. Ollendick (Eds.), *Handbook of interventions that work with children and adolescents: Prevention and treatment* (pp. 3–25). London: Wiley.
Öst, G. (1987). Applied relaxation: Description of a coping technique and review of controlled studies. *Behaviour Research and Therapy, 25*(5), 397–409.
Para, E. A. (2008). CBT for the treatment of depression in young adults: A review and analysis of the empirical literature, *Graduate Journal of Counselling Psychology, 1*(1), Article 14.
Patterson, G. R. (1982). *The coercive family process.* Eugene, OR: Castalia Publishing Company.
Report of the Children's Evidence Based Practices Expert Panel. (2005). Submitted to DSHS-children's administration, mental health division.
Rushton, J. L., Forcier, M., & Schectman, R. M. (2002). Epidemiology of depressive symptoms in the national longitudinal study of adolescent health. *Journal of American Child Adolescent Psychiatry, 41*(2), 199–205.
Ruwaard, J., Schrieken, B., Schrijver, M., Broeksteeg, J., Dekker, J., Vermeulen, H., & Lange, A. (2009). Standardized web-based cognitive behavioural therapy of mild to moderate depression: A randomized controlled trial with a long-term follow-up. *Cognitive Behaviour Therapy, 38*(4), 206–221. doi:10.1080/16506070802408086.
Schetky, D. H. (1995). Preface. Child adolescent psychiatric clinics of North America, *4*(4), XIII–XXIV.
Selvi, M. (2013). Effectiveness of cognitive behaviour therapy for children with anxiety disorders in school setting. Unpublished PhD thesis. Bangalore: NIMHANS (Deemed University).
Singh, N. N., Lancioni, G. E., Singh Joy, S. D., Winton, A. S. W., Sabaawi, M., Wahler, R. G., et al. (2007). Adolescents with conduct disorder can be mindful of their aggressive behavior. *Journal of Emotional and Behavioral Disorders, 15*, 56–63.

Silverman, W. K., & Ollendick, T. H. (2005). Evidence-based assessment of anxiety and its disorders in children and adolescents. *Journal of Clinical Child and Adolescent Psychology, 34*(3), 380–411.

Soechting, I., & March, J. (2002). Cognitive aspects of obsessive compulsive disorder in children. In. R. Frost & G. Steketee (Eds.), *Cognitive approaches to obsessions and compulsions: Theory, assessment, and treatment* (pp. 299–314). Amsterdam: Pergamon/Elsevier Science Inc.

Spence, S. H. (2003). Social skills training with children and young people: Theory, evidence and practice. *Child and Adolescent Mental Health, 8*(2), 84–96.

Treatment for Adolescents with Depression Study Team (TADS). (2003). Treatment for adolescents with depression study (TADS): Rationale, design, and methods. *Journal of the American Academy of Child and Adolescent Psychiatry, 42*, 531–542.

Urvashi Anand. (2013). Effectiveness of a mindfulness-based stress reduction (MBSR) program in reducing stress in adolescents. Unpublished PhD thesis. Bangalore: NIMHANS (Deemed University).

Vygostsky, L. S. (1988). *The genesis of higher mental functions*. In J. V. Wertsch (Ed.), *The concept of activity in soviet psychology* (pp. 144–188). New York: M. E. Sharpe Inc. (Reprinted in *Cognitive development in adolescence*), pp. 61–80, by K. Richardson & S. Sheldon, Eds., 1990, Hove: Lawrence Erlbaum Association.

Waslick, B., Schoenholz, D., & Pizarro, R. (2003). Diagnosis and treatment of chronic depression in children and adolescents. *Journal of Psychiatric Practice, 9*(5), 354–366.

Williams, C. J., Williams, S., & Appleton, K. (1997). Mind maps- an aid to effective formulation. *Behavioural and Cognitive Psychotherapy, 25*, 61–71.

Zylowska, L., Ackerman, D. L., Yang, M. H., Futrell, J. L., Horton, N. L., Hale, S. T., et al. (2007). Mindfulness meditation training with adults and adolescents with ADHD. *Journal of Attention Disorders, 11*, 737–746.

Chapter 3
Community-Based Mental Health Interventions in Adolescents

M. Manjula

3.1 Need for Community-Based Interventions

Unaddressed mental health problems in adolescents are found to have serious implications. About 24–39 % of them are known to experience such consequences as discontinuation of the education, risky sexual behaviors, substance abuse, unemployment and involving in antisocial activities; poor interpersonal relationships, and lack of skills to cope with problems (Kjelsberg and Dahl 1999). Though most of the mental health problems of the adults have their onset in the adolescence and often are not identified as psychological in nature, help is not sought till it becomes entrenched and disabled in nature. There are strong perceived and actual barriers in seeking help, and the percentages of those who seek help are as less as 10–15 % (McGorry and Purcell 2009; Rickwood et al. 2007). These figures are largely based on young adult population; thus, the adolescents seeking help may even be lesser. If the problems have their onset in young age, interventions should follow suit, before they become ingrained, because shorter duration and reduced severity of symptoms are associated with better outcomes (Kessler et al. 2005). The mental health interventions offered are largely child or adult focused, neither the setting nor the types of interventions are appropriate for the adolescents' needs. Since most often the problems are sub-syndromal in nature, the early intervention and preventive/promotive interventions can go a long way in early recovery and prevention.

The community-based interventions are carried out on the premise that the psychological problems experienced by the adolescents are determined by the interaction of individual, environmental, family, and parental factors. Thus, community-based

M. Manjula (✉)
Department of Clinical Psychology, NIMHANS, Bangalore 560029, India
e-mail: drmanjula71@gmail.com

M. Mehta and R. Sagar (eds.), *A Practical Approach to Cognitive Behaviour Therapy for Adolescents*, DOI 10.1007/978-81-322-2241-5_3

approaches focus on (a) promoting positive mental health by educating the community to recognize the early signs of mental illness, without stigmatizing or discriminating; (b) addressing the risk factors in the whole population (universal prevention, e.g., anti-stigma campaign); (c) targeting young people at risk for developing mental health problems; and (d) providing early intervention/prevention services for people with mild emerging mental health difficulties (Catalano et al. 2004).

When the interventions are carried out in the community (schools, community mental health clinics, hospitals, and residential treatment programs, and work places), it is easy to access without fear of stigma since the professionals reach to young people facilitating trusting relationships (Rickwood et al. 2007). Also, that the responsibility for intervention is shared (by individuals, families, parents, carers, teachers, policy makers, professional organizations etc.), makes the enforcement and maintenance of gains easy.

The current scenario is such that, even in the countries having programs for young people are at the best fragmented, not well integrated resulting in negative experiences and young people struggling to seek help (Vision for Change 2006). In India, mental health needs of the youth are largely unmet leading to poorer clinical outcomes and chronic mental health problems as they become adults (Murthy 2011; Farooq et al. 2009). Also, there is severe lack of community-based interventions designed specifically for adolescents. Given the current status of mental health systems, the requirement of the day is a community-based system comprising of integrated, youth-focused, evidence-based, prevention, and early intervention services which takes into account the setting, timing, kind, and the intensity of the intervention required when they need it the most (Patel et al. 2007).

3.2 Community-Based Interventions for Adolescents

The chapter attempts to give an overview of the community-based, early and preventive interventions carried out across the countries. This chapter is not all inclusive; however, an attempt is made to focus on large-scale studies and major interventions for mental health problems. There is substantial work in the area of juvenile delinquency/violence prevention and substance abuse; however, the paper does not cover the literature and programs on the same. Similarly, though promotive interventions lie on a continuum of preventive interventions with a universal focus, and largely aiming at enhancing resilience, for the lack of space, it is not covered.

The interventions based on cognitive-behavioral models, life skills, problem-solving and stress management techniques are known to decrease depressive and anxiety symptoms by more than 50 % and reduce the risk of anxiety and depression disorders by more than 2/3rds. They also lead to positive changes in psychological and behavioral adjustment, academic performance, and cognitive skills (Durlak et al. 2011). Improving mental health literacy is one of the most important strategies to facilitate early intervention; this is achieved through four categories of interventions: whole-of-community campaigns; community campaigns aimed at a youth audience; school-based interventions teaching help-seeking skills, mental health literacy, or resilience; and programs training individuals to intervene in a mental health crisis (Kelly et al. 2007).

Several interventions are identified as evidence based in the treatment of adolescent mental health problems. Therapies based on the behavioral, cognitive behavioral, models such as exposure therapy, modeling therapy, coping skills, communication skills, relaxation therapy, and anger coping therapy are used across disorders such as anxiety, autism, ADHD, schizophrenia, depression, bipolar disorder, and conduct/oppositional defiant disorder. Some of the well-established evidence-based practices are cognitive behavior therapies (CBT), trauma-focused CBT (TF-CBT), adolescent community reinforcement approach (A-CRA), aggression replacement training (ART), dialectical behavior therapy (DBT), seven challenges, for substance abuse; multisystemic therapy (MST)—a brief but intensive, clinician-provided, home-based treatment; preparing adolescents for adulthood (PAYA) and motivation interviewing (MI). Other evidence-based therapies are parent management training, family education and support, interpersonal therapy, multisystemic therapy, functional family therapy, brief strategic family therapy and mentoring (NAMI 2007). Both clinic- and community-based approaches use the same modules; however, the community-based programs are largely group based.

Apart from the diagnosable mental health problems, often parents of adolescents also are equally in need of knowing how to deal with the undesirable behavior of an adolescent. The behaviors included fighting with siblings, talking back to adults, moodiness, and school difficulties (Ralph et al. 2003). Similarly, adolescents enlist causes of stress as difficulties in academics, problems in interpersonal relationships with parents, friends, peers, heterosexual relationships, low self-esteem, and fears about sexuality-related issues (Das and Manjula 2009).[1]

3.3 Interventions Carried Out in Community Health Clinics

Keeping in mind the prevalence of the psychiatric problems in the adolescents and feasibility of carrying out intervention in the primary care services and to facilitate referral to secondary care services, a briefer intervention (1–5 sessions) called SCREEN was developed. It included assessments as well as interventions specific to the problems. The brief intervention was sufficient for about 37 % ($n = 2{,}071$) of them resulting in improved psychosocial functioning implying the need for replicating the briefer intervention strategies at the primary care services (Laukkanen et al. 2010).

Preliminary attempts to examine efficacy of lifestyle interventions using a socio-ecological framework for such disorders as obesity and eating disorders is underway (Wilfley et al. 2010). In a community- and clinic-based RCT carried out in USA, Weisz et al. (2009) used CBT for youth aged 8–15 years ($n = 57$), who were

[1] Unpublished dissertation work from NIMHANS, Bangalore.

selected based on the initial complaints of any internalizing symptoms by parents and then were evaluated for depressive spectrum disorders. CBT was found to be cost-effective, briefer, resulted in reduced usage of medication, and more parent engagement. In a similar attempt, RCT was carried out in community clinic setup to examine the feasibility of CBT in youth (8–15, $n = 48$) diagnosed with anxiety disorders. Though there was significant improvement in anxiety symptoms, there was no difference between CBT and usual clinical care (Southam-Gerow et al. 2010).

3.4 Early Intervention, Prevention, and Promotion Interventions Carried Out in the Community

3.4.1 Early Interventions

The early intervention modules typically include identifying early signs of distress, provide help on a first aid basis, prevent self-harm, ameliorate the course of mental illness, facilitate recovery, guide young people toward the right support, and reduce stigma (Clark et al. 2002). There is definitive evidence for early interventions in youth leading to reduction in prevalence and progression of illness (McGorry et al. 2007). A very good example of deployment and validation of early interventions are carried out under the leadership of McGorry and colleagues in Australia. Community-based youth mental health centers operated by Headspace, Orygen Youth Health, the National Youth Mental Health Foundation, (more than 60 such centers) operating across the country serve a large number of youth. They help young people with emerging serious mental health and substance disorders, and also conduct training programs to share knowledge and enhance service system functioning. Realizing the need for the early intervention and prevention and to facilitate help-seeking among adolescents, Australian Red Cross has formulated various culturally appropriate, youth centered, peer education support programs.

Work of McGorry has been modeled after in many countries such as 'headstrong' program in Ireland originated by Prof. Hewitt B. Clark, which carries out such activities as research and support (education and training, communication, service evaluation, and fund raising). The uniqueness of the headstrong program has been youth engagement, enablement, and leadership across all areas of work such as local and national youth advisory panels (YAPS) and youth lead mental health promotion (Think Big). Recently, there has been considerable efforts in replicating the Australian model, in countries such as Canada, England, Scotland, and Wales targeting people who work with, live with or care for adolescents (11–18) (Kitchener and Jorm 2006). In US, the prominent evidence-based program for adolescents and young adults is the Transition to Independence Process (TIP) model developed by the National Network on Youth Transition (NNYT).

One of the most important community-integrated collaborative early intervention approach including the researchers, community/local therapists, community organizations, and family members has been carried out with respect to youth experiencing ongoing traumas (domestic, community and school violence; verbal, physical, sexual abuse, bullying). Series of projects were carried out such as the Children Recover after Family Trauma (CRAFT) Project; Women's Center and Shelter of Greater Pittsburgh (WCS) (Cohen et al. 2011; Murray et al. 2010) at U.S. and Zambia using the trauma-focussed–cognitive behavior therapy (TF-CBT). TF-CBT includes components to enhance youth resiliency-based coping skills (enhancing safety), actively includes parents or caregivers in treatment, developing trauma narratives and addressing youths' maladaptive cognitions about ongoing traumas and helping youth differentiate between real danger and generalized trauma reminders. The studies indicated significant improvement in the youth and the parents.

3.4.2 Preventive Interventions

The mental health promotion and prevention interventions typically are built upon strengthening the existing skills, the components of such programs are: Mental health literacy, Coping skills to cope with daily stressors, Self care and community connectedness, Improving access to social support, Strengthening community action for better understanding of illness to reducing stigma and discrimination and help-seeking. Examples of such programs are Beyondblue, Mindmatters, and Mental health first aid (Davis et al. 2000).

Lot of work has gone in terms of the suicide prevention intervention in youth, and there are various preventive models that are established as effective. In a systematic review study, Gould et al. (2003) examined the school-based suicide prevention programs (conducted over 10 years). The identified promising interventions included—school-based skills training for students, screening at-risk youths, media education and education of primary care physicians, and lethal means restriction. The psychological therapies that are effective included dialectical behavior therapy and cognitive behavior therapy. Direct education and awareness through pamphlet ('Toughin' it out'), to School Gatekeeper training model or signs of suicide (SOS) prevention programs have resulted in greater awareness, openness to discuss about suicide, more help-seeking, lower attempts and more adaptive attitudes about depression and suicide (Bridge et al. 2007; Kataoka et al. 2007; Aseltine et al. 2007). In contrary, the efficacy of national youth suicide prevention strategy (NYSPS) implemented in Australia from 1995–1998 and a subsequent period (1999–2002), did not show significant differences in decline in rates of suicides in areas which targeted the prevention and areas which were not targeted. Including the parents along with the adolescents in suicide prevention intervention is found to have significant impact in reducing the risk factors, enhancing the protective factors and greater sustainability of improvements (15 months) (Hooven et al. 2012). A suicide prevention program enhancing the sources of strength among the peer leaders (453) trained for conducting school-wide awareness program (18 schools and 2,675 students) was found to be beneficial both for the students and the peer leaders (Wyman et al. 2010).

The preventive protocols for depression have typically addressed the youth at risk for depression because of family history of mood disorder or current sub-syndromal mood symptoms. Studies involving youth at risk also use the term 'high symptom' studies; they recruit the participants by screening large numbers of unselected youth from class rooms and primary care screening. These studies exclude current diagnosable major depression. The interventions are based on a coping model, though have the elements of CBT protocols, they differ in terms of dose, emphasis on cognitive versus behavioral techniques and format; with most programs using group formats. The components include psycho-education, pleasant activity scheduling, social skills training, problem-solving training, and cognitive restructuring. Some of the manuals used for preventive intervention are Coping With Depression for Adolescents (CWD-A; Clark et al. 1990) which was used by more than 50% of the studies on high symptom groups, brief CBT and Pittsburg cognitive program have shown to be effective (Weersing and Brent 2006). In a review of the preventive interventions conducted for adolescents in high risk environments in US, Opler et al. (2010) concluded that 'primary preventive intervention has the potential to be effective for some mental health disorders such as anxiety disorders, eating disorders, substance abuse, disruptive behavior disorders, and suicide, whereas for attention-deficit/hyperactivity disorder (ADHD) and early onset schizophrenia, the results are not uniform and encouraging.'

Neil and Christensen (2009) did a systematic review of about 20 individual school-based early intervention and prevention programs for anxiety. Results indicated that most of the universal, selective, and indicated prevention programs were effective in reducing the symptoms of anxiety in adolescents and most of them used CBT. Similarly, a systematic review was conducted of 42 RCTs related to 28 individual school-based programs addressing depression. It was found that CBT (8–12 sessions) targeting students exhibiting elevated levels of depression were most effective (Calear and Christensen 2010). In one of the largest meta-analytical study of 213 school-based, universal, social and emotional learning programs ($N = 270{,}034$), it was found that participants of the program showed significant improvement in social and emotional skills, attitudes, behavior, and academic performance (Durlak et al. 2011).

Recently, since about 20 years an approach known as *wraparound* has been extensively explored in planning and coordinating community-based care for children and adolescents with severe emotional and behavioral disorders. It encompasses wide array of services and supports serving the youth and the families in their home communities. It encourages the full participation of families and youth consumers in planning, evaluating, and delivering services and supports. Few quasi-experimental and RCTs conducted show positive outcomes in areas such as improved community adjustment, behavior, decreased functional impairment, fewer social problems, fewer placements, lower rates of delinquency, and fewer days of absence from school (Burchard et al. 2002). The components include addressing behavioral and emotional difficulties during transition, planning their own future, social problem-solving, prevention planning related to high-risk behaviors and situations, and accessing developmentally appropriate services and supports (Clark et al. 2002). American Psychological Association (2004) has brought out a model of preventive interventions for LGBQ youth, wherein it talks about the addressing the issue by the school counselors, nurses, psychologists, and social workers, in the school and college setup and providing interventions for any psychological problems.

3.5 Indian Scenario

In Indian also, preventive interventions are developed and implemented, while most of them are unpublished and local programs, very few are published. Two important preventive programs that are manualized and implemented successfully are worth a mention here. The 'Students Counseling for College Teachers' (Chandrashekhar 2002) was developed to identify, provide intervention, and prevent mental disorders among college students. College teachers were trained in a group workshop format, in mental health issues of college students (substance abuse, academic problems, aggression, etc.), and basic counseling skills. A total of 1,091 teachers were trained in 44 batches starting from 1975 till 2010. The 'life skills education program' (Bharath and Kumar 2010) is a cascade model of comprehensive health promotion for secondary school students delivered by trained teachers. The effect of the program was evaluated at the end of 1year in 605 adolescents and 100 trained teachers selected randomly. Results showed that the adolescents in the program had significantly better self-esteem, perceived adequate coping, better overall adjustment with respect to teachers, and school, and prosocial behavior. Similarly, 'expressions' was developed in VIMHANS, Delhi (Nagpal 2011), a school-based program, to understand and identify mental health problems and dissemination of life skills education among adolescents. It follows a cascade strategy which includes training the counselors/teachers followed by training the 'peer trainers', who in turn train students. A program addressing parents called Society for the Care of Adolescents (SCAN) aims to assist parents to improve the physical and mental health of their adolescents through seminars educating on mental health problems, parenting skills, sexuality education and communication skills (WHO 2007).

While there can be many unpublished preventive interventions, a few are mentioned here. The 'coping skills training—power to empower' (Chugh et al. 2010) designed at AIIMS, Delhi for adolescents (13–16 years) to build competencies to deal with their daily stressors and decrease emotional distress. It is a group intervention and includes components such as anxiety management, managing emotions, and rational thinking, problem-solving, anger management, and social skills training. 'Stress management in Pre University Students' (Manjula 2011)[2] was developed in NIMHANS, Bangalore, to help students (16–18 years) understand the causes of stress and to deal effectively with stress, in the following areas:

[2] Unpublished project work from NIMHANS, Bangalore.

academic, interpersonal relationships, and self (body image, confidence, and self-esteem). The program used a workshop format and preliminary efficacy has been established. The intervention group showed improvement in coping skills compared to the control group. Another study incorporated a classroom-based universal prevention approach to enhance the resilience of students pursuing professional course (Engineering, $n = 80$) called 'Resilience-based Intervention for College Students' (Herbert and Manjula 2013).[3] The intervention was a 6-session program with components such as stress and coping, resilience, responsibility, perceiving stress as challenge, and creating meaningful connections. Following intervention, the participants showed significant improvement in resilience, problem-solving and negative emotion. In an indicated intervention with adolescents (13–18 years) having sub-syndromal depression, 'School-based Group Coping Skills Program' was carried out (Meghna and Manjula 2014).[4] The intervention was delivered in groups of 4–8 adolescents each of same gender ($n = 65$ in intervention and $n = 55$ in control group). The components addressed negative cognitions, academic stress, and interpersonal relationships. The components are chosen based on the exploratory study as well as the existing modules of therapy. The results showed significant improvement in depressive symptoms, negative cognitions, academic stress, social problem-solving, and coping skills which was maintained at 3-months follow-up.

3.6 Conclusions

There is substantial evidence for usefulness and efficacy of early intervention and preventive, psychosocial interventions; however, its effectiveness and cost-effectiveness is not adequately tested in comparison to clinic-based interventions (Graeff-Martins et al. 2008—review of 34 programs). Each country comes up with different modules and dissemination procedure. Though there are identified evidence-based interventions in adolescents, there is no body of evidence to confirm the way the services should be organized to deliver the same. There is lack of early screening methods/tools to assist in determining who is 'at risk' and there is significant overlap with respect to the age groups included in the studies often making it difficult to dismantle 'what' works for 'whom'. There is a lack of clear consensus about what approaches work best in what circumstances and how long or how many sessions are sufficient (e.g. community-focused compared with classroom-based, skills training compared with social support). Though early intervention/prevention programs for mental health are given enough importance in other countries (Australia, Ireland, UK, America, Canada), there are no coordinated efforts in India. There is lack of clarity with regard to models of care at individual, community, professional, and policy levels. There are significant lacunae in the longer follow-ups of the interventions. There are very few attempts at establishing

---

[3] See footnote 2.

[4] See footnote 2.

the fidelity of some of the programs, and largely, it is insufficient. Similarly, replication of the programs has just begun and there is some evidence for few of the interventions; however, many of the programs are still not considered as evidence based. Also, much needs to be done in the direction of coordination with school operations, implementation, and evaluation, comprehensive models covering all (social, health, academic) aspects, and the educational policies.

At the best, it can be said that importance of the mental health in the economic productivity is recently been realized worldwide; however, the strides made in the direction of prevention remains still just as aspiration, while there is some work in early intervention (McGorry 2013). Thus, there is still a lot more to be done in the area of community-based interventions in youth population. Since this is the only way to reach out to larger population, it is necessary that this area has to be given utmost importance.

References

American Psychological Association. (2004). *Model of preventive interventions for LGBQ youth*, Washington DC.

Aseltine, R. H., James, A., Schilling, E. A., & Glanovsky, J. (2007). Evaluating the SOS suicide prevention program: A replication and extension. *BMC Public Health, 7*, 161.

Bharath, S., & Kumar, K. K. (2010). Empowering adolescents with life skills education in schools—school mental health program: Does it work? *Indian Journal of Psychiatry, 52*, 344–349.

Bridge, S., Hanssens, L., & Santhanam, R. (2007). Dealing with suicidal thoughts in schools: Information and education directed at secondary schools. *Australasian Psychiatry, 15*, 58–62.

Burchard, J. D., Bruns, E. J., & Burchard, S. N. (2002). The wraparound approach. In B. J. Burns & K. Hoagwood (Eds.), *Community treatment for youth: Evidence based interventions for severe emotional and behavioral disorders* (pp. 69–90). New York: Oxford University Press.

Calear, A. L., & Christensen, H. (2010). Systematic review of school-based prevention and early intervention programs for depression. *Journal of Adolescence, 33*(3), 429–438.

Catalano, R. F., Berglund, M. L., Ryan, J. A. M., Lonczak, H. S., & Hawkins, J. D. (2004). Positive youth development in the United States: research findings on evaluations of positive youth development programs. *The Annals of the American Academy of Political and Social Science, 591*, 98–124.

Chandrashekhar, C. R. (2002). *Manual on students' counselling for college teachers*. Bangalore: Department of Collegiate Education, Government of Karnataka, and National Institute of Mental Health and Neurosciences, Bangalore.

Clark, G. N., Lewinsohn, P. M., & Hops, H. (1990). *Adolescent coping with depression course*. Eugene, OR: Castalia Publishing.

Clark, H. B., Belkin, M. T., Obradovich, L. D., Casey, R. E., Gagnon, R., Caproni, P., et al. (2002). Transition from school to community: Navigating rough waters. In K. L. Lane, F. M. Gresham, & T. E. O'Shaughnessy (Eds.), *Interventions for children with or at risk for emotional and behavioral disorders* (pp. 299–316) Boston: Allyn & Bacon.

Cohen, J. A., Mannarino, A. P., & Iyengar, S. (2011). Community treatment for PTSD in children exposed to intimate partner violence: A randomized controlled trial. *Archives of Pediatrics and Adolescent Medicine, 165*, 16–21.

Davis, C., Martin, G., Kosky, R., & O'Hanlon, A. (2000). *Early intervention in the mental health of young people: A literature review*. Australia: The Australian Early Intervention Network for Mental Health in Young People.

Durlak, J. A., Weissberg, R. P., Dymnicki, A. B., Taylor, R. D., & Schellinger, K. B. (2011). The impact of enhancing students' social and emotional learning: A meta-analysis of school-based universal interventions. *Child Development, 82*(1), 405–432.

Farooq, S., Large, M., et al. (2009). The relationship between the duration of untreated psychosis and outcome in low-and-middle income countries: A systematic review and meta analysis. *Schizophrenia Research, 109*(1–3), 15–23.
Gould, M. S., Greenberg, T., Velting, D. M., & Shaffer, D. (2003). Youth suicide risk and preventive interventions: A review of the past 10 years. *Journal of the American Academy of Child and Adolescent Psychiatry, 42*(4), 386–405.
Graeff-Martins, A. S., Flament, M. F., Fayyad, J., Tyano, S., Jensen, P., & Rohde, L. A. (2008). Diffusion of efficacious interventions for children and adolescents with mental health problems. *Journal of Child Psychology and Psychiatry, 49*(3), 335–352.
Hooven, C., Walsh, E., Pike, K. C., & Herting, J. R. (2012). Promoting CARE: Including parents in youth suicide prevention. *Family & Community Health, 35*(3), 225–235.
Kataoka, S. H., Stein, B. D., Nadeem, E., & Wong, M. (2007). Who gets care? Mental health service use following a school-based suicide prevention program. *Journal of the American Academy of Child & Adolescent Psychiatry, 46*, 1341–1348.
Kelly, C. M., Jorm, A. F., & Wright, A. (2007). Improving mental health literacy as a strategy to facilitate early intervention for mental disorders. *Medical Journal of Australia, 187*(7), 26–30.
Kessler, R. C., Berglund, P., Demler, O., Jin, R., Merikangas, K. R., & Walters, E. E. (2005). Lifetime prevalence and age-of-onset distributions of DSM-IV disorders in the national comorbidity survey replication. *Archives of General Psychiatry, 62*, 593–602.
Kitchener, B. A., & Jorm, A. F. (2006). Mental health first aid training: Review of evaluation studies. *Australian and New Zealand Journal of Psychiatry, 40*(1), 6–8.
Kjelsberg, E., & Dahl, A. A. (1999). A long-term follow-up study of adolescent psychiatric in-patients. Part II. Predictors of delinquency. *Acta Psychiatrica Scandinavica, 99*, 237–242.
Laukkanen, E., Hintikka, J. J., Kylma, J., Kekkonen, V., et al. (2010). A brief intervention is sufficient for many adolescents seeking help from low threshold adolescent psychiatric services. *BMC Health Services Research, 10*, 261.
McGorry, P. D. (2013). Prevention, innovation and implementation science in mental health: The next wave of reform. *The British Journal of Psychiatry, 202*(s54), s3–s4.
McGorry, P. D., Nelson, B., Amminger, G. P., et al. (2007). Clinical staging: a heuristic model for psychiatry and youth mental health. *Medical Journal of Australia, 187*(7), S40–S42.
McGorry, P. D., & Purcell, R. (2009). Youth mental health reform and early intervention: Encouraging early signs. Youth mental health reform and early intervention: Encouraging early signs. *Early Intervention in Psychiatry, 3*, 161–162.
Murray, L. K., Skavenski, S., Familiar, I., Bass, J., Bolton, P., & Jere, E. (2010). *Catholic relief services, SUCCESS return to life*. Zambia TF-CBT Pilot Project Report to USAID.
Murthy, R. S. (2011). Mental health initiatives in India. *The National Medical Journal of India, 24*(2), 98–107.
Nagpal, J. (2011). Expressions 2009: Delhi experience. Symposia/Workshops. *Indian Journal of Psychiatry, 53*, 10–26.
National Alliance on Mental Illness. (2007). *Choosing the right treatment: What families need to know about evidence-based practices*. Arlington, VA: National Alliance on Mental Illness.
Neil, A. L., & Christensen, H. (2009). Efficacy and effectiveness of school-based prevention and early intervention programs for anxiety. *Clinical Psychology Review, 29*(3), 208–215.
Opler, M., Sodhi, D., Zaveri, D., & Madhusoodanan, S. (2010). Primary psychiatric prevention in children and adolescents. *Annals of Clinical Psychiatry, 22*(4), 220–234.
Patel, V., Flisher, A. J., Hetrick, S., & McGorry, P. D. (2007). Mental health of young people: A global public-health challenge. *Lancet, 369*, 1302–1313.
Ralph, A., Toumbourou, J. W., Grigg, M., Mulcahy, R., Carr-Gregg, M., & Sanders, M. R. (2003). Early intervention to help parents manage behavioural and emotional problems in early adolescents: What parents want. *Advances in Mental Health, 2*(3), 156–168.
Rickwood, D. J., Deane, F. P., & Wilson, C. J. (2007). When and how do young people seek professional help for mental health problems? *Medical Journal of Australia, 187*, 35–39.

Southam-Gerow, M. A., Weisz, J. R., Chu, B. C., McLeod, B. D., Gordis, E. B., & Connor-Smith, J. K. (2010). Does cognitive behavioral therapy for youth anxiety outperform usual care in community clinics? An initial effectiveness test. *Journal of the American Academy of Child and Adolescent Psychiatry, 49*, 1043–1052.

Vision for Change. (2006). *Report of the Expert Group on Mental Health Policy*. Dublin: Department of Health and Children, Stationery Office.

Weersing, R. V., & Brent, D. A. (2006). Cognitive behavioral therapy for depression in youth. *Child and Adolescent Psychiatric Clinics of North America, 15*, 939–957.

Weisz, J. R., Southam-Gerow, M. A., Gordis, E. B., Connor-smith, J. K., Chu, B. C., Langer, D. A., et al. (2009). Cognitive-behavioral therapy versus usual clinical care for youth depression: An initial test of transportability to community clinics and clinicians. *Journal of Consulting and Clinical Psychology, 77*(3), 383–396.

Wilfley, D. E., Van Buren, D. J., Theim, K. R., et al. (2010). The use of biosimulation in the design of a novel multilevel weight loss maintenance program for overweight children. *Obesity, 18*(1), 91–98.

World Health Organization (WHO). (2007). *Helping parents in developing countries improve adolescents' health*. Geneva: WHO Press.

Wyman, P. A., Brown, C. H., LoMurray, M., Schmeelk-Cone, K., Petrova, M., Yu, Q., et al. (2010). An outcome evaluation of the sources of strength suicide prevention program delivered by adolescent peer leaders in high schools. *American Journal of Public Health, 100*(9), 1653–1661.

Part II
Building Skills

Chapter 4
Study Skills

Garima Srivastava Malhotra and Manju Mehta

4.1 Introduction

Study skills are fundamental to academic competence. Effective study skills are associated with positive outcomes across multiple academic content areas and for diverse learners. Academic competence is associated with the knowledge and application of effective study skills. Capable students at all grade levels may experience difficulty in school, not because they lack ability, but because they lack good study skills. Although some students develop study skills independently, even normally achieving students may go through school without having acquired effective approaches for studying (Nicaise and Gettinger 1995). Implementing study skills instruction relies on an understanding of the theoretical foundation for teaching and using study skills, as well as knowledge of current research on the effectiveness of study strategies.

The purpose of this chapter is to articulate a theoretical perspective on the contribution of study skills to academic competence, and to identify evidence-based strategies that are effective in helping students study. Study skills are often viewed as academic enablers; they function as critical tools for learning. Study skills encompass a range of coordinated cognitive skills and processes that enhance the effectiveness and efficiency of students' learning (Devine 1987). According to Hoover and Patton (1995), study skills include the competencies associated with

G.S. Malhotra (✉)
Department of Psychiatry, Ram Manohar Lohia Hospital, New Delhi, India
e-mail: srivastavagarima9@gmail.com

M. Mehta
Department of Psychiatry, All India Institute of Medical Sciences, New Delhi, India
e-mail: drmanju.mehta@gmail.com

M. Mehta and R. Sagar (eds.), *A Practical Approach to Cognitive Behaviour Therapy for Adolescents*, DOI 10.1007/978-81-322-2241-5_4

acquiring, recording, organizing, synthesizing, remembering, and using information. These competencies contribute to success in both non-academic (e.g. employment) and academic settings. Studying, or the application of study skills, can be distinguished from other forms of school/university learning that occur under more proscribed conditions, such as teacher-led classroom instruction (Novak and Gowin 1984; Rohwer 1984). First, studying is skilful; it requires training and practice with specific techniques that help a learner to acquire, organize, retain, and use information. Although students are expected to apply study skills in completing homework or preparing for tests, teachers typically devote little time to providing explicit instruction in such skills (Zimmerman 1998). Second, studying is intentional. Effective studying requires not only the knowledge and application of skills, but volition as well. Studying differs from incidental learning; in that, it is purposeful and requires a deliberate and conscious effort on the part of the student. Third, studying is highly personal and individualized. Whereas classroom learning occurs within a social context through interaction and guidance from others (e.g. peers, teachers), studying is often an individual activity. Even when learning is fostered through a process of social communication, individual study behaviours still play a critical role in academic competence (Damon 1991; Kucan and Beck 1997). Finally, studying involves a self-regulatory dimension. According to Rohwer (1984), "studying is the principal means of self-education throughout life". Self-regulation (e.g. initiative, persistence, goal setting) is an important aspect of studying, not only during the initial development of study skills, but also during application of skills outside of formal learning contexts (Zimmerman et al. 1996).

A useful distinction has emerged in recent years to differentiate between a study tactic and study strategy (Lenz et al. 1996). A study tactic is a sequence of steps or a specific procedure, such as underlining or summarizing. A study tactic may be taught through explicit instruction wherein the skill is operationalized and presented as a sequence of observable, isolated behaviours. It is often assumed that good studying is synonymous with using study tactics correctly. The application and effectiveness of a tactic may be improved through the use of a study strategy. A strategy is an individual's comprehensive approach to a task; it includes how a person thinks and acts when planning and evaluating his or her study behaviour. A strategy consists of guidelines and rules related to selecting the best tactics and making decisions about their use. The goal of study strategy instruction is to teach a strategy in a manner that is both effective (the strategy is learned) and efficient (it is learned to an optimal level with minimal effort).

Cognitive-based study skills. The goal of cognitive-based study strategies is to guide students to engage in appropriate thinking about information they are required to learn.

According to information-processing theory, the greater knowledge students have about content, the more likely they are to think about, understand and remember it (Schunk 2000). Thus, studying is enhanced when new material is meaningful to learners and integrated with their existing knowledge. In addition, information that is stored as a network of connected facts and concepts, called schemata, is more easily learned and retained. It follows that good studying requires students to (a) activate and assemble background knowledge prior to studying a topic; (b) connect new ideas, information or concepts to what they already know; and (c) develop new schemata, when necessary, to integrate content to be learned (Bos and Anders 1990). Cognitive-based study skills are designed to achieve these goals.

Cognitive organizers also referred to as cognitive and semantic maps are effective tools to assist students in activating prior knowledge about a topic, organizing information during learning, and using schemata to establish connections among key concepts (e.g. Baumann and Bergeron 1993; Scanlon et al. 1991). Cognitive maps allow students to arrange the component ideas and details from text visually so that implicit relationships among ideas and details are made explicit.

Evidence-based approaches to enhance study skills

There is a lacuna of evidence-based CBT studies of effectiveness and efficacy of study skills and learning techniques especially in the last ten years; however, mostly before that period, both laboratory- and classroom-based research have provided evidence supporting the effectiveness of study skills to promote academic competence among students. Through study skills instruction, students become more efficient, thoughtful, and independent learners (Scheid 1993) and perform better in school. Research has shown that even students who develop study skills on their own can learn to study more effectively and efficiently through explicit instruction (Wood et al. 1995). Overall, study skills instruction has been shown to improve academic performance, strategic knowledge, and affective responses among students with learning problems across multiple academic domains (Harvey and Goudvis 2000). Research indicates that students, indeed, require explicit instruction in study skills; individuals assigned randomly to control conditions tend not to acquire or use study strategies on their own without training (Schunk and Zimmerman 1994).

A number of different theoretical perspectives support the benefit of equipping students with study skills to enhance their learning and academic competence. The most comprehensive approach to study skills stems from an information-processing model (Adams and Hamm 1994; Gettinger and Nicaise 1997; Harvey and Goudvis 2000; Schunk 2000). In brief, an information-processing model assumes that information to be learned is manipulated by the student to enhance acquisition and retention. The level of processing, or manipulation, is affected by the type of study strategy the learner uses. The more elaborate the strategy, the deeper the level of processing.

Within an information-processing framework, the development of study skills is conceptualized as strengthening cognitive processes across many information-processing systems (Schunk 2000). An information-processing perspective provides the theoretical framework for two broad areas of investigation related to study skills: (a) research evaluating the effects of four clusters of study skills on academic outcomes and (b) research identifying critical components of effective study skills instruction, irrespective of the specific skill taught. Key studies in both areas are reviewed next.

4.2 Importance of Developing Good Study Skills

There are four factors that support an effective study routine:

- showing independence in learning;
- being able to organize yourself;
- being actively engaged in your learning; and
- adopting a "deep approach" to learning.

An effective independent study routine means:

- being self-motivated and taking control of your learning
- setting, and then maintaining, your own goals and standards
- identifying your strengths and learning preferences.

4.3 Reviewing Your Learning Style (Scales Included in Annexure)

As an independent learner, it is advisable to think carefully about your learning style and how best you can use your learning strengths to support your academic studies.

This section will help you:

- To think about the different ways you perceive and understand information;
- Consider your most appropriate learning environment;
- To identify how you process information most effectively;
- To identify different strategies and skills that will benefit you as a learner;
- To understand multi-sensory techniques.
  - Barsch Learning Style Inventory
  - Approaches and Study Skills Inventory for Students (ASSIST; short form; Tait et al. 1998)

Learning Styles Questionnaire
Tick the response which best suits you.

1. Do you usually remember more from a lecture when:
   a) You do not take notes, but listen very carefully
   b) You sit near the front of the room and watch the lecturer
   c) You take notes
2. Do you usually solve a problem by:
   a) Talking to yourself or a friend
   b) Using an organized, systematic approach like lists, etc.
   c) Walking, pacing or some other physical activity

3. Do you remember phone numbers (when you cannot write them down) by:
   a) Repeating the numbers orally
   b) Seeing or visualizing the numbers in your mind
   c) Writing the numbers with your finger on the table or wall
4. Do you find it easier to learn something new by:
   a) Listening to someone explain how to do it
   b) Watching a demonstration of how to do it
   c) Trying it yourself
5. When you try to remember something do you:
   a) Try to see it happen in your mind
   b) Hear in your mind what was said or the noises that occurred
   c) Feel the way "it" reacted with your emotions
6. If you do not know how to spell a word, do you:
   a) Sound it out
   b) Try to see it work in your mind
   c) Write the word in several ways and choose the one that looks right
7. Do you enjoy reading most when you can read:
   a) Dialogue between characters
   b) Descriptive passages that allow you to create mental pictures
   c) Stories with lots of action in the beginning (because you find it difficult to concentrate early on)
8. Do you remember people you have met by their:
   a) Names
   b) Faces
   c) Mannerisms, movements, etc.
9. Are you distracted mainly by:
   a) Noises
   b) People
   c) Environment (temperature, comfort of furniture, etc.)
10. Do you have problems sitting still to read? If so, do you:
    a) Talk with a friend
    b) Watch TV or look out of the window
    c) Fidget in your chair, or cannot lie still in bed

Count the total number which fall into the following categories

a) .... Auditory (by hearing)
b) .... Visual (by seeing)
c) .... Kinaesthetic (by touching, doing or moving)

ASSIST—Approaches and study skills inventory for students (short version)

Table 4.1 Different types of motivation

Type of motivation	What is it?	Examples
Intrinsic motivation	Motivation from within	• I enjoy learning new things
		• I will be better equipped to obtain a degree
Extrinsic motivation	Motivation from external sources	• My parents will be disappointed if I do not succeed
		• I will get a pay rise if I finish my degree
Positive motivation	A positive attitude towards the task	• I have the ability to get a degree and I know I can do the work
		• My future income will be much greater when I graduate
Negative motivation	A negative attitude towards the task	• My parents will cut off my allowance if I do not study
		• My friends will think I am stupid if I fail
		• My family will be disappointed if I drop out

4.4 The Role of Motivation in Developing Effective Study Skills

"Motivation refers to processes which activate, sustain and direct behaviour towards achieving a particular goal" (Table 4.1).

Remaining motivated—some ideas to help

- Affirm that you can do it!
- Recognize the achievements you have attained already.
- Devise a list of all the reasons you originally decided to study. Ensure they are positive, and display them in your home and workplace.
- Identify your long-term, short-term and mini-goals. Write them down together with your objectives, and display these in your home and workplace. If you are struggling with motivation, place more emphasis on mini-goals, as these tend to be easier to achieve and will help lead to the completion of larger goals.
- Construct a realistic study plan and follow it.
- Consider your time management and decide if you need to develop a more realistic plan.
- Ensure that your study environment is comfortable and conducive to effective study.
- Seek support and encouragement—this may be in the form of family, friends or professionals.

4.5 Study Strategies for Different Learning Styles (Cottrell 2008)

4.5.1 Auditory

If you are an auditory learner, it means you will learn best by hearing information. Consider making use of sound in the following ways:

- Talk or read aloud to yourself as you learn information;
- Talk through and/or review information with friends;
- Record information on to tape or disc to enable you to listen back over information;
- Ask a friend to read text or lecture notes aloud to you;
- Have light, instrumental music playing in the background whilst you read or write;
- Work in a silent room.

4.5.2 Visual

Visual learners often learn best from seeing information presented in diagrams, charts or pictures. Try using some of the following visual techniques:

- Plan work using spider diagrams, lists or tables, pictograms and mind maps;
- Write down all information;
- Use coloured pens to highlight important information when reading and to link similar ideas and arguments as you identify them (But only if you are using your own text);
- Use coloured paper for different modules or subjects;
- Use large wall charts or planners to organize your work;
- Try to visualize information and ideas in your mind;
- Vary the environment or position in which you work as this may create a link between your visual setting with a particular subject area.

4.5.3 Kinaesthetic

A kinaesthetic learner will learn best by touching, doing or moving. Try to think physically by:

- Discussing ideas with friends;
- Putting different arguments and ideas on separate pieces of paper when planning essays, allows you to physically organize your answer;
- Going over information in your mind whilst walking, jogging or swimming;
- Using colour or draw pictures and diagrams alongside written notes;
- Moving around your environment during independent study time.

4.5.4 Multi-sensory

It does not matter how you learn as long as you use the methods which suit you. However, a combination of the use of all the senses is the best way to learn.
It appears that on average you will remember:

- 20 % of what you read;
- 30 % of what you hear;
- 40 % of what you see;
- 50 % of what you say;
- 60 % of what you do.

But you will remember 90 % of what you say, hear, see and do.

Multi-sensory learning can help anyone to enhance the experience of learning and improve recall of important information. Information is received by the brain through the sensory channels. These channels are as follows:

- Visual (seeing information)
- Auditory (hearing information)
- Kinaesthetic (touching, moving or doing)
- Olfactory (smelling and making associations related to smell)
- Taste (what we experience from the mouth and tongue)

Consider how strongly a smell, taste or hearing a piece of music can remind you of a previous situation or event. This is because all your sensory channels have worked simultaneously to link into your emotions to create that experience.

Multi-sensory learning involves activating as many of the senses as possible at the same time to aid understanding and recall.

The learning style questionnaire is attached in the Appendix.

4.6 Classroom Applications of Study Skills Research

Over the past two decades, much has been learned about the process of effective studying. Research has demonstrated that success in all academic content areas is often associated with good study skills. Whereas some students develop effective ways to study on their own, the majority of students will not become proficient at studying without systematic instruction and repeated practice. In response to research on the importance of study strategies, comprehensive models have been developed and evaluated for implementing strategy training, including the SIM by Deshler and Shumaker (1988) and Pressley's Good Information Processing Approach (Pressley et al. 1995). Such models have played a vital role in helping to promote the translation of research on study skills into effective classroom practice. A critical role for school psychologists is to maximize the success of efforts to enhance study skills through an understanding of the nature of study skills and knowledge of evidence-based approaches that facilitate the acquisition of effective study skills. Despite the potential benefits of study skills, instructional challenges exist that may limit the widespread application of study skills training. For strategy instruction to be implemented in classroom contexts, adaptations for group situations may be necessary (Palincsar and Brown 1988; Pressley et al. 1995).

Strategy instruction that requires lengthy one-to-one interaction between the teacher and student is not feasible in most classrooms. Scanlon et al. (1994) found that many teachers were not willing to sacrifice coverage of curriculum content in order to teach study skills to students who need them. One way to address this concern is for teachers to merge their teaching of specific content with the teaching of study strategies that aid students in learning the content. That is, teachers can teach and prompt the application of specific study strategies that are effective for their particular course content. In a study by Scanlon et al. (1996), for example, teachers were taught to incorporate intensive and explicit study strategy instruction within the context of their social studies teaching. In this study, teachers exhibited relatively low levels of implementation of strategy teaching (less than half of the targeted teaching behaviours), raising questions about the extent to which teachers are able to successfully merge instruction with strategy training.

Additional key principles derived from research on improving study skills are important to keep in mind when designing study skills training. First, students must recognize the need for varied approaches to studying. Not all strategies are appropriate for all study tasks. For example, the most effective strategy for studying spelling words is likely to be different from an effective approach for studying for a history test. Furthermore, any single study tactic will likely require some modification and personalization on the part of students themselves. In developing an awareness of different strategies, students should be encouraged to explain the appropriateness of a particular study strategy for different tasks.

Second, the key to effective study strategy training is to help students guide their own thinking, organizing and study behaviours. The most effective study strategy instruction helps children to develop strategies that work for them. Unlike the focus of commercially available study skills curricula, students should be actively involved in developing their own, personalized study strategies, instead of being taught a scripted set of steps. Including students in developing their own strategies enhances maintenance and generalization to other study situations. Future research is needed to identify instructional conditions that are most conducive to the successful integration of study strategy instruction with classroom learning. For example, given the relationship between study skills and other academic enablers, effective strategy training should include some means of motivating students to engage in study strategy usage, to reinforce engagement in studying and to increase parental encouragement and support of studying.

4.7 Study Schedule: How to Make One and Stick to It

Study/Revision Planner (Table 4.2)

Week beginning …………/………/……….

Table 4.2 Study/revision planner

Time	Monday	Tuesday	Wednesday	Thursday	Friday	Saturday	Sunday
8–9 a.m.							
9–10 a.m.							
10–11 a.m.							
11 a.m.–12 p.m.							
12–1 p.m.							
1–2 p.m.							
2–3 p.m.							
3–4 p.m.							
4–5 p.m.							
5–6 p.m.							
6–7 p.m.							
7–8 p.m.							
8–9 p.m.							
9–10 p.m.							
10–11 p.m.							

4.8 How to Study

4.8.1 Goal Setting

Many people have a dream of where they want to be or what they want to do in the future. Their dream provides a clear vision or goal that is ideal to them, and the motivation to achieve that goal. In order to obtain the "dream", it is important to set specific goals and work out realistic steps to achieve those goals.

The best way to set and achieve your goals is to write them down, so think about it. What do you want to achieve?

4.8.1.1 Long-term Goals

Long-term goals relating to your studies are outcomes you would like to achieve after you finish your course. These goals are generally set around three to five years into the future. For example, you may want to work as a counsellor in private practice, work as a school guidance counsellor, set up your own business in conflict resolution and mediation, work as a clinical psychologist, or be a more effective leader in management.

4.8.1.2 Short-term Goals

Short-term goals relating to your studies are outcomes you would like to achieve over the next year and up to the completion of your course. They tend to be stepping stones towards your long-term goals. For example, completing three units successfully over the next term of study, achieving a credit average in each of your subjects over the year or finishing your degree by the end of the following year are all short-term goals.

Mini-goals relating to your studies are outcomes you would like to achieve over the next day or week, or by the end of the term. They tend to be stepping stones towards your short-term goals. Breaking larger tasks into smaller ones will help to provide a sense of achievement. For example, spend two hours completing your weekly readings tonight, write a plan for your essay by the end of tomorrow and complete a first draft of your assessment by the end of the week. Mini-goals can also include goals that relate to extracurricular activities along with academic goals.

Checklist: Elements of a useful goal

- Specific – Does it describe what you want to do in great detail?
- Measurable – Does it describe your goals in ways that can be evaluated objectively?
- Challenging – Does it require energy and dedication to achieve?
- Realistic – Are you capable of achieving this goal? Is it possible?
- Timely– Does this goal clearly state when it will be finished?

In order to complete any goal, you must decide what needs to be done to attain this outcome. An objective is something you can do to achieve your goal. Like goals, objectives must be specific and will detail what will be done, how and when.

For example,

> My goal is to achieve a credit average in each unit this term.
> My objectives are to attend each class/log on each week, engage with the material of the subject, complete the assigned readings each week, review my notes several days after the class/frequently, and begin each assessment according to my timetable.

Your goal-setting plan may look something like what is depicted in Table 4.3.

Goal-setting plan

Goal	Objectives	Time frame	Done?
	1. What I need to do to achieve my goal? 2. Steps I need to take to achieve my goal		
1.			
2.			
3.			

Table 4.3 Goal-setting plan outline

Goal	Objectives	Time frame	Done?
1. Complete my developmental psychology Assignment for internal examination	• Ensure I understand the essay topic	• 2 h	√
	• Complete extensive research and ensure I fully understand the material	• 3–4.5 days	
	• Complete an essay plan	• 2–3 h	
	• Develop the first draft of the essay	• 2 days	
	• Ask a trusted friend/colleague to proofread my draft and suggest feedback	• 1 day	
	• Redraft	• 1 day	
	• Submit essay on time		

- The Smart Technique

The SMART technique helps in planning and organizing your study schedule to enhance one's performance:

S—Study only a **specific** topic/area to begin with, e.g. Section 3 "from the history lesson"
M—What you are studying should be **measurable** or your goal should be able to be quantified.
A—The goal that you set for yourself should be **achievable**; thus, it keeps you motivated to keep going
R—You should **reward** yourself when the goal is achieved in order to provide yourself some incentive and keep yourself motivated, e.g., deciding to watch your favourite TV show that you have recorded only after having completing your specific goal/task that you had set for yourself.
T—The goal that you set for yourself should be "**time bound**" so you have a deadline to follow.

The following can be an example to summarize the SMART technique: "I have to complete section 2.1 of history lesson "which is 2 pages long in 40 min which according to me is an achievable goal and once I complete this task I set for myself, I will reward myself with the chocolate I have really been wanting to eat".

- The SQ3R Method

Another useful tool for reading effectively is the SQ3R model, the details of which are presented in this Table 4.4.

Adapted from: Study Guides and Strategies. (nd). The SQ3R reading method. Retrieved from http://www.studygs.net.

Table 4.4 SQ3R model as an effective reading tool

Survey	Scan the section of text in order to get an overview. You are not trying to read in detail for understanding here, just to get an overall idea of the content of the text. This may involve reading subheadings, the abstract, the section, summarize the first and last paragraphs and/or review questions
Question	As you survey, ask questions yourself. You may do this by turning chapter or section headings into questions, or by asking yourself how this new information relates to previously learned information
Read	As you start to read, look for answers to the questions you first raised. Note any words that have been underlined, italicized or bold printed. Study any diagrams, charts, graphs, etc. Slow down your reading and if necessary re-read parts which are not clear. After a short section, stop and recite what you have understood
Recite	Summarize the text in your own words, and say your summary aloud
Review	Create flashcards with the new terms or ideas, develop questions about the content and then answer them, briefly re-survey the text (as you did in the survey section), create a glossary page with key terms, develop a mind map of new ideas, or use mnemonic devices to remember the material

4.9 Effective Time Management and Organization (Cottrell 1999)

Misuse of time is probably the most common form of sabotage that students use to undermine their attempts to study. However, planning your time makes you think about it strategically and, even if you have to alter your study plans, you will benefit from having previously defined your tasks and prioritizing your activities.

Why is it important to manage your time?

There are many good reasons to try to manage your time. Benefits of time management include the following:

- It is essential for success.
- It allows you to spread your workload over the course.
- It helps you to prioritize your workload.
- It helps you to work out how to use your time as efficiently as possible.
- It reduces the anxiety and stress that is common whilst meeting the demands of study.
- It decreases the likelihood of tasks being left to the last minute which often compromises your performance.
- It helps you to schedule time for fun (Table 4.5).

Study Checklist

Before the test or examination

☐ Study schedule complete
☐ Study space organized and equipment ready
☐ Books/notes, etc. organized
☐ Know what you need to study

Table 4.5 Common problems and solutions centring around time management

Common time problems	Possible solutions
Are you disorganized and frequently misplace things?	Organize your learning space. Take control of where you work, and you can then control how you work
	• Keep a clear desktop
	• Place pens, pencils, etc. in a desk tidy or jar
	• Organize your notes by using a separate ring binder for each subject
	• Use coloured dividers to separate lecture notes into date order
	• File handouts with the appropriate lecture notes
Put off doing coursework and assignments	Use a diary or wall planner to clearly mark assignment deadlines for every module
	• Start tasks sooner rather than later
	• Be realistic about how long things will take and set appropriate time slots for specific tasks, e.g., planning an essay will take longer than reading a short extract
	• Break tasks down into manageable parts and allow time to tackle some of it every week
Easily distracted	Negotiate study time with friends and flatmates so that they know when you are not to be disturbed
	• Be aware of the times of day you can learn and concentrate
	• Set clear start and finish times for each study session
	• Take regular short breaks
Over commitment and leaving things to the last minute	Try not to over commit your time
	• Plan social time into your week and mark clearly in a diary or wall planner
	• Prioritize tasks; do the most urgent tasks first

☐ Study Session 1 completed
☐ Completion of study sheets/flashcards, etc.
☐ Study Session 2 completed
☐ Study Session 3 completed
☐ Prepare materials for examination/test (stationery, etc.)

On the test/examination day

☐ Relax
☐ "Dump" information you are worried about forgetting by writing it on the test
☐ Read over examination before you begin to write
☐ Read/follow directions carefully

☐ Write test/examination questions that you know best
☐ Complete all other questions
☐ Review/re-read test and make any necessary corrections

Often we over or underestimate the amount of time any given task may take. It is a good idea to time yourself to see how long various tasks actually take. Keep a diary for a full week and note every hour how you have spent your time (blank "weekly time log" in the Appendix).

4.9.1 Prioritization (or "It is as Simple as ABC")

What is really important? What can possibly wait? What can be left until next day or the weekend?

It is not enough just to use your time efficiently; it is vital that you prioritize commitments in order to optimize your time and enhance your effectiveness.

The ABC approach

Categorise commitments according to the following groups:

Absolutely urgent (high importance)

Better do it soon (medium importance)

Can wait (low importance)

For example, your "To do" list might include the following tasks:

- watch latest episode of my favourite TV soap
- clean my room
- buy a gift for my parents anniversary
- ring my cousin to wish him on his birthday
- write my essay plan
- read pages 34–52 of the introduction to psychology textbook on my essay topic

They may then be categorized as follows in Table 4.6.

Table 4.6 Priority management charting

Absolutely urgent	Better do it soon	Can wait
• Read pages 34–52 of the introduction to psychology textbook on my essay topic	• By a gift for my parents anniversary	• Do the laundry
• Ring cousin to wish her a happy birthday		• Watch my favourite TV show (tape it now and watch at a low productivity time)
• Write my essay plan		

Weekly Time Log

Time	Monday	Tuesday	Wednesday	Thursday	Friday	Saturday	Sunday
8–9 a.m.							
9–10 a.m.							
10–11 a.m.							
11 a.m.–12 p.m.							
12–1 p.m.							
1–2 p.m.							
2–3 p.m.							
3–4 p.m.							
4–5 p.m.							
5–6 p.m.							
6–7 p.m.							
7–8 p.m.							
8–9 p.m.							
9–10 p.m.							
10–11 p.m.							

Daily Planner

Things to do today	Done
______________________	____________
______________________	____________
______________________	____________
______________________	____________

Term Planner

Week	Unit	Assessment details	Due date	Plan	Requirements
1					
2					
3					
4					
5					
6					
Break					
7					
8					
9					
10					
11					
12					

A good example of prioritization is doing your topic research prior to writing interview questions for a research report. This can save you time by enabling you to write the best possible questions through understanding past research and theory.

4.9.2 Constructing a Time Management Plan

A realistic time management plan will include the following:

- commitments: classes, work, family time, sports, gym, committees, etc. (including travel time)
- personal time: grooming/hygiene, relaxing, watching TV, listening to music, shopping, socializing, emailing, phone calls, etc.
- essential time: eating, sleeping
- housework: meal preparation, house cleaning, washing dishes, doing laundry, etc.

Daily planning

It is also a good idea to plan your daily tasks and one way to do this is to write a "To do" list. On your "To do" list, it is a good idea to prioritize your tasks according to the ABC approach as indicated by the letter in brackets after each task in the example below. This helps you to work out what should be done first. Breaking up large tasks into smaller ones makes achievement easier, as does being specific in your task details.

Things to do today...	Done
1. Deposit the collegefee (B)	____________
2. Complete readings for History project (A)	____________
3. Buy a birthday present for brother (B)	____________
4. Get membership to new collegelibrary (C)	____________
5. Finish Spanish assignment (A)	____________

Table 4.7 Various strategies to manage procastination

Do you?	Then you could...
Fear failure?	• Focus on goal setting
	• Reframe thoughts more positively
	• Simply begin, knowing you can redraft later
Have anxiety about the task?	• Break the task or goal into mini-goals
	• Seek assistance in ensuring you properly understand the task
Manage your time badly?	• Prioritize tasks
	• Create realistic daily, weekly and term plans
Have personal issues?	• Seek professional support
	• Seek support from family or friends
Have trouble concentrating?	• Ensure your study space is distraction-free and comfortable with good lighting
	• Study at a library where there are fewer distractions
	• Complete the more difficult tasks when you are most alert
	• Study when the house is most quiet, perhaps late at night or early in the morning, depending on when you are most effective
	• Ask family or friends to support you by not disturbing you during your study times

A blank "To do" list (daily planner) is attached in the Appendix.

- Procrastination: why do we put it off, find an excuse or allow ourselves to be distracted?

Generally, all the thinking we do about the difficulty in starting or continuing a task is worse than the task itself. Often getting started is the hardest part, and so the best way to counter procrastination tends to be to take the first step.

4.9.3 Strategies to Manage Procrastination

The first step is to identify why you may be procrastinating. This allows you to find solutions to meet your study goals (Table 4.7).

4.10 Specific Study Techniques

4.10.1 Memory and Learning Techniques

4.10.1.1 Active Learning

Learning is most effective when an active, rather than a passive, approach to study is adopted. Watching TV, for instance, is a passive process; it requires little or no action on our part. Whatever information we receive is probably soon forgotten. However, effective study requires the learner to take action. It means that the student becomes an active participant in the study process.

1. *Preview* Before you begin any detailed study, first preview course material, study guides and textbooks in order to gain the big picture.
2. *Browse* Quickly scan through relevant readings or textbook chapters to pick up on themes and main ideas. Use headings, captions, charts and graphics to guide you through unknown learning territory.
3. *Take notes* As you read, make notes in your own words. There is little value in copying the exact words of a text. Learning is not about reading a whole lot of material in the hope that something might sink in. It is about making sense of new ideas and concepts, of internalizing them and incorporating them into your existing knowledge. Use concept maps to provide a visual representation of ideas, concepts and themes and help define relationships between them.
4. *Walk and Talk* Walk around the study area, reciting facts out loud or explaining concepts as if an interested adult was in the room with you. You will have to clarify your understanding in order to "teach" someone else. Hearing the talk may help you recall details later for assignments and examinations.
5. *Highlighting* Use highlighters (sparingly) to emphasize significant points and ideas in a text. Experiment by using two colours; also try using underlining, * asterisks *, ← arrows □ and margin notes as further means of text summary.

6. *Ask yourself questions* As you read, engage with the author by questioning the text: *What is the author trying to say? How does this information fit in with what comes before, or after?* Asking *So what? Why?* and *What if?* can help you to explore the implications of what is being stated and to make sense of new material. Set yourself a small set of relevant questions before you read a text, then see whether you can find the answers as you read.
7. *Re-reading* A good practice is to re-read important material relating to the course and to review your own notes on a regular basis, either to confirm or to add details.
8. *Discussion* Learning does not happen in a vacuum. Be prepared to explore key concepts and specialized knowledge relating to the study discipline through discussions with other students, and with lecturers too. Form a study group or find a study buddy:

- Quiz each other
- Talk through ideas
- Make up questions.
- Brainstorm on a wall chart or the board in an empty tute room.
- Create concept maps.
- Take advantage of synergy. The combined energy of a pair or group is likely to be more than the sum of each individual's efforts.

4.10.1.2 Deep Approach to Learning

You are more likely to be effective in your study when you adopt a deep approach to learning. You will focus not so much on reproducing something for the next assignment task but on maximizing your understanding of the whole topic. Using this approach, you are more likely to initiate opportunities to learn rather than wait for directions from course material or a lecturer. Some deep learning strategies are as follows:

- making sense of new knowledge and developing understanding rather than simply learning sets of facts and information to be reproduced when required
- looking for what is significant like key concepts and principles, relationships between ideas, lines of reasoning
- employing higher order thinking skills through examining issues, clarifying problems, producing own ideas, and thinking critically
- asking questions about what you are learning, and discussing ideas with others relating new ideas to previous knowledge and experiences
- reflecting upon what is learned and reviewing the effectiveness of your learning strategies
- finding the link between conceptual knowledge and real-world applications
- accepting the challenge that learning involves you in actively constructing knowledge for yourself

4.10.1.3 Acronyms

An acronym is a word that is made by taking the first letter of the words you want to remember, and creating a new word. For example, HOMES is an acronym to remember the Great Lakes, Huron, Ontario, Michigan, Erie and Superior.

4.10.2 Acrostics

An acrostic is a sentence that is made by taking the first letter from each word or symbol you want to remember and inserting another word beginning with the same letter. For example, KING PHILIP CAME OVER FOR GREEN STAMPS is an acrostic for the classification of living things: Kingdom, Phylum, Class, Order, Family, Genus, Species.

4.10.3 Chunking

Short-term memory can generally hold about seven (give or take two) bits or "chunks" of information. However, the size of these chunks can vary. By grouping several pieces of information into a single chunk, it is possible to remember larger bits of information. Therefore, chunking information involves taking pieces of information and grouping them to create a single "chunk".

> For example:
>
> A phone number may be difficult to remember as single digits, however grouped into three separate groupings or chunks it becomes easier to recall.
>
> 1800809299 or 1800 809 299

In the same way, relevant course material can be grouped or chunked to assist with recalling information, for example, by using acronyms or mnemonics (Egan 2007).

Chunking involves the following:

- Breaking tasks into more manageable bite-sized pieces, and
- Seeing the completion of each piece as a success.

For example, in an essay, a student can succeed in many ways, including (a) fully understanding the question, (b) breaking the question into parts, (c) doing an initial search for information at the library or on the internet, (d) summarizing the information they read and (e) organizing the information under subheadings, and so on.

Not only does this strategy provide multiple success experiences, it is also a very effective way of building intrinsic motivation: the student is being rewarded with success throughout the essay and this sustains interest and persistence. Chunking can also be applied to non-academic activities such as dealing with personal issues or problems, working towards a personal goal, settling into a new job, or training for an upcoming sporting meet.

SOLER

S Face the client Squarely.
O Adopt an Open posture.
L Remember that it is possible at times to Lean towards the other.
E Maintain good Eye contact.
R Try to be relatively Relaxed or natural in these behaviours

4.10.4 Note Making

Effective note taking is a vital skill in writing an assignment task as efficiently and productively as possible. Developing a good method of note taking can help you to recognize the main ideas, think critically, analyse, question, remain focused, establish connections and draw conclusions about the text being read. Good note taking skills will also ensure that you are able to identify where various ideas have been found which makes proper referencing much easier. There are many ways to take effective notes. Some people find it good to use catalogue cards; others prefer to use sheets of A3 paper. It is a matter of working out what suits you best. Generally you need to make sure you include the following information:

- reference details—author, year of publication, title of book/article, journal title, place of publication, publisher, page numbers, Web address, date accessed, etc.
- paraphrased or summarized ideas of the text and possibly several direct quotes
- personal responses to the text and various ideas found within it

It is important that one choose a note taking method which suits ones learning style.

Consider whether you prefer linear methods or visual formats such as spider diagrams (Table 4.8).

Table 4.8 An example of linear note making

29.8.03	Note taking by Mr. Smith	Two-column method	Main idea place the main idea or heading in the left-hand column write the further details in the right-hand column
	Linear note taking		
	1. Use a number strategy		
	2. List key information		
	3. Do not try to write down every word		
	4. Use abbreviations		
	5. Use the margin to make a note of the date		________________
	6. Use the margin to list key words and references	Subject	____________

4.10.5 *Spider Diagrams*

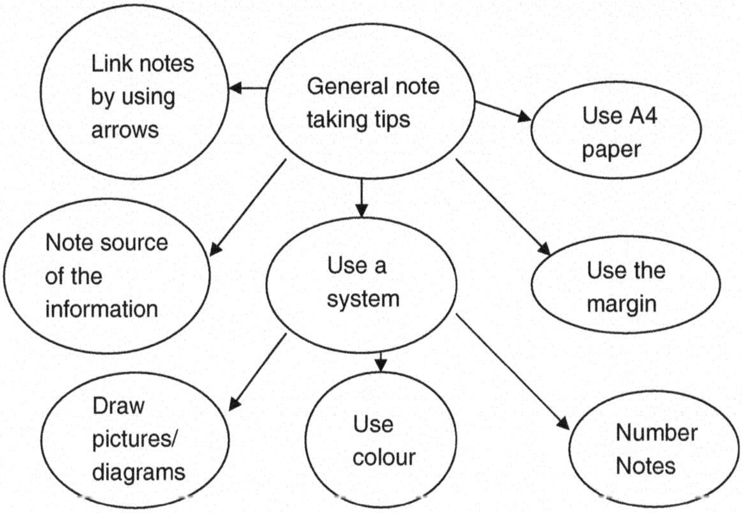

4.10.6 *Reading Skills*

Aim to develop ones reading skills to help assimilate information and understand ideas. Reading is simply a tool which helps one access the thoughts of others.

Academic reading requires you to:

- Identify arguments;
- Recognize whether they support or oppose the main premise;
- Identify the evidence;
- Identify conclusions and whether the evidence supports the conclusions;

Information Searching

Reading for study is time-consuming and tiring. Therefore, before you begin reading, ask yourself:

- What information do I need to find?
- Will this text provide the information I need?

To decide if a text book contains the information you need, use the clues provided in the following:

- Contents page;
- Preface;
- Index;
- Introduction;

Table 4.9 Some common reading problems with solutions

Problem	To alleviate the problem
Glare from white paper or text blurs, distorts or jumps about	Try using a coloured acetate or coloured plastic folder over the text to remove glare
Print size makes it difficult to concentrate or focus on reading	Use a photocopier to enlarge text, scan text onto a PC and enlarge
Difficulties understanding a particular section of text	Read the section aloud, ask a friend to read it aloud to you. Scan text into PC and use read back facility in Text Help Read & Write to listen to the words

- Chapter headings;
- Illustrations and diagrams;
- Section headings;
- Summaries;
- Reference section.

The SQ3R method that has been discussed earlier in the chapter is a good technique for improving reading comprehension.

Many learners, particularly those with dyslexia, may experience the following difficulties when reading. Some suggested solutions are given in Table 4.9.

- Writing Skills

Planning

Use the following checklist to help you keep track of your progress.

- Examine the question

This should include your first thoughts, asking yourself what you already know about this topic.

- Re-examine the question

Do you really understand all the terms used and have you highlighted the key verbs?

- Identify gaps

What else do you need to know or to find out before you are able to answer the question?

- Prioritize tasks

How long will it take you to get the information you need? Do you need to work with others or see your lecturer to clarify information at this stage? Act now to keep your attitude positive—do not let little snags become reasons for not working.

- Set realistic targets

You will not write a good essay quickly. It is also very unlikely that you will be able to write coherently without a plan. Remember, give yourself enough time to think and organize your thoughts before you start to write.

- Complete reading and note taking

Set yourself a deadline for completion of background reading and research. Make sure you take adequate notes and make a note of references for your bibliography or reference section.

- Devise your plan

4.11 Coping with Examination Anxiety

4.11.1 Before the Examination

Examinations can lead to a certain amount of anxiety and stress in students, but these can be minimized by good preparation and study time management before the examination.

4.11.1.1 Prepare Notes with the Examination in Mind

Reading your subject material weekly is essential. Revise after each lecture or class. Revising as you go helps you to identify areas or topics that you have not understood well and gives you the opportunity to seek help or do extra research. Leaving study until the end of the term usually means you are leaving it too late. Preparing your own summary notes is preferable to using ready-made notes, because you are actively engaging with the material. Preparing notes helps to develop a better understanding of the connections between areas of the subject. Understanding the whole subject and not just the isolated parts is very useful in doing well in examinations, because it helps you to see the reasons for and the connections between the concepts. Mind maps, diagrams and flow charts can be used to create associations. Summary tables are also good for organizing material.

4.11.1.2 Managing Your Time

Develop a weekly study timetable. Revision needs to be regular and continuous.

Studying for the examination at the end of the term should be the final step in the ongoing learning process, so plan your study during term to avoid last minute frenzy and cramming session.

4.11.1.3 Getting Started

- Draw up a realistic revision timetable—this should include some social time to allow you to relax;
- Organize your notes by module or topic—if you have followed advice in the Note Taking section, you will find getting started on revision easier;
- Decide what topics to revise;
- Use past examination papers to guide your revision;
- How many questions do you have to answer for each paper?
- Use past papers to practice writing answers to examination questions;
- Be positive about your learning;
- Ask tutors for help or to clarify information if necessary.

4.11.1.4 Practice

Practicing with past examination questions helps you to prepare for and predict the sort of questions that will be asked. Practice also helps to identify gaps in your understanding.

4.11.1.5 Studying with Others

Studying with others in pairs or groups helps understanding and memory, and it facilitates the sharing of ideas and perspectives.

4.11.1.6 Memory

Recall of information is essential for successful performance in examinations. Better recall can be achieved by time management of study periods and regular over learning.

- Try to keep concentrated study to no more than 40 min at one time;
- Take regular short breaks;
- Over learning is essential for recall of information:
  - After each break spend 10- to 15-min reviewing work covered in the previous study period
  - Review again after 24 h
- Be aware of when your concentration slips—it may be shorter than 40 min;
- Find a quiet place to work to avoid being distracted during revision periods;
- Make sure you drink plenty of water to keep your body hydrated and eat regularly.
- Use multi-sensory methods—write it, say it, see it, hear it;
- Use Survey, Question, Read, Recall, Review, when reading through text;

- Summarize key information onto one page using coloured paper;
- Use mind maps;
- Put key information into poster format and stick on your wall;
- Use coloured pens to highlight important facts, to link ideas or to separate arguments;
- Use technology—Text Help Read & Write programme allows you to hear and read information simultaneously;
- Record your revision notes or answers onto to tape or disc. Hearing the information may help you to remember it;
- Group revision—you may find it helpful to spend some time revising with friends.
- During the Examination

During the examination, it is important to concentrate, manage your time well and read the instructions carefully, and it is essential to answer the questions.

Examinations usually allow 10-min reading time before the examination proper starts. During reading time:

Before you turn over the examination paper, write down key dates, definitions, quotes names or other information you feel you may forget;

- Read the instructions on the question paper carefully. They will tell you if there is a Compulsory question and how many questions you must answer. Many students lose marks because they do not read the instructions carefully. It is very easy to think that this is an obvious point and that it would not happen to you, but stress and anxiety can lead even the best prepared student to skim over a sentence or a paragraph and lose the meaning. Read the instructions and then read them again. For example, if the instruction states "Answer three of the following five questions" then answer three, not all five.
- Scan through the paper and tick all questions you could answer. Read through all of the sections of the examination paper so that you know what is expected.
- Calculate the time needed to answer each question and the order you wish to attempt them;
- Read each of your selected questions carefully underlining key words or phrases. Also check how many parts there are to each question;
- Plan your answer to the first question and write it. Keep to the plan and avoid including information which is not relevant;
- Plan your answers for all the remaining questions to avoid panic towards the end of the examination.

Assign the time available to each of the questions according to the marks allocated to each question.

Example 1

You have a two-hour examination (120 min) with two essays worth 50 % each. Leave 10 min at the end for review so allocate 55 min per essay.

Example 2

You have a two-hour examination which has two sections—a short answer section with five short answers worth 10 % each (50 % total) and 50 multiple choice questions worth 50 %. Leaving 10 min at the end for review, this means that you would allocate 11 min (55 divided by 5) of the first 55 min for each short answer and a minute for each of the multiple choice questions.

Tips In examinations which have mixed types of assessments, many students find it better to write the essays first, but it is best to develop your own strategy.

In the case of essays and short answer questions, remember to answer the question. Irrelevant information does not attract marks so do not be tempted to include information that you have learnt only because you have learnt it.

If you have not finished a question in the time you have allocated, leave that question and move on to the next. Come back to it if you have time at the end.

Answer or attempt to answer all required questions or tasks. A mark, no matter how small, is better than no mark at all. Allow 10 min at the end to review your paper and finish off any incomplete answers. During the examination, do not be tempted to spend more time than you have allocated for any task. Come back to that task if there is time at the end.

- Psychological management of anxiety

Symptoms such as extreme fear, shortness of breath, racing heartbeat, insomnia, nausea, trembling and dizziness are not only associated symptoms of anxiety disorders but also common among students that experience anxiety in relation to studies or examination. Therefore, psychological management of anxiety symptoms is extremely important.

- Deep breathing

When we are tensed, we breathe shallowly and rapidly. When relaxed, we breathe more fully and more deeply, from the abdomen. By using deep abdominal breathing, we stimulate the relaxation response of our bodies, promoting calmness.

Additionally, attending to our breath helps us connect our minds to our bodies.

The following exercises can help you change your breathing pattern, especially if practiced regularly. Just 3 min of deep breathing practice will usually induce a state of relaxation. Practice for 3–5 min every day for at least two weeks. If possible, find a regular time each day to do this so that your breathing exercise becomes a habit. With practice, you can learn in a short period of time to "damp down" the physiological reactions underlying anxiety and panic. Once you feel you have gained some mastery, apply it when you feel stressed, anxious, or when you experience the onset of panic symptoms. By extending your practice of either breathing exercise to a month or longer, you will begin to retrain yourself to breathe from your abdomen. The more you can shift the centre of your breathing from your chest to your abdomen, the more consistently you will feel relaxed on an ongoing basis.

4.11.1.7 Abdominal Breathing Exercise

1. Note the level of tension you are feeling. Place one hand on your abdomen right beneath your rib cage.
2. Inhale slowly and deeply through your nose into the "bottom" of your lungs—in other words, send the air as low down as you can. If you are breathing from your abdomen, your hand should actually rise. Your chest should move only slightly whilst your abdomen expands. (In abdominal breathing, the diaphragm—the muscle that separates the lung cavity from the abdominal cavity—moves downward. In so doing it causes the muscles surrounding the abdominal cavity to push outward.)
3. When you have taken in a full breath, pause for a moment, then exhale slowly through your nose or mouth depending on your preference. Be sure to exhale fully. As you exhale, allow your whole body to just let go. (You might visualize your arms and legs going loose and limp like a rag doll.)
4. Do ten slow, full, abdominal breaths. Try to keep your breathing smooth and regular, without gulping in a big breath or letting your breath out all at once. It will help to slow down your breathing if you slowly count to four on the inhale (1–2–3–4) and then slowly count to four on the exhale. Remember to pause briefly at the end of each inhalation. Count from ten down to one, counting backwards one number with each exhalation. The process should go like this: Slow inhale…Pause…Slow exhale…Count "ten" Slow inhale…Pause…Slow exhale…Count "nine" Slow inhale…Pause…Slow exhale…Count "eight" and so on down to one. If you start to feel light-headed whilst practicing abdominal breathing, stop for 15–20 s and then start again.
5. Extend the exercise if you wish by doing two or three sets of abdominal breaths, remembering to count backwards from ten to one for each set. (Each exhalation counts as one number.) Five full minutes of abdominal breathing will have a pronounced effect in reducing anxiety or early symptoms of panic. Some people prefer to count from one to ten instead. Feel free to do this if it suits you.

4.11.1.8 Calming Breath Exercise

The calming breath exercise was adapted from the ancient discipline of yoga. It is a very efficient technique for achieving a deep state of relaxation quickly.

1. Breathing from your abdomen, inhale through your nose slowly to a count of five. (Count slowly "one…two…three…four…five" as you inhale.)
2. Pause and hold your breath to a count of five.
3. Exhale slowly, through your nose or mouth, to a count of five (or more if it takes you longer). Be sure to exhale fully.
4. When you have exhaled completely, take two breaths in you normal rhythm, then repeat steps 1 through 3 in the cycle above.
5. Keep up the exercise for a least three to five minutes. This should involve going through at least ten cycles of in-five, hold-five. As you continue the exercise,

you may notice that you can count higher, or count higher when you exhale than when you inhale. Allow these variations in you counting to occur if they do and just continue with the exercise for up to five minutes. Remember to take two normal breaths between each cycle. If you start to feel light-headed whilst practicing this exercise, stop for thirty seconds and then start again.

6. Throughout the exercise, keep you breathing smooth and regular, without gulping in breaths or breathing out suddenly.
7. Optional: Each time you exhale, you may wish to say "relax", "calm", and "let go", or any other relaxing word or phrase silently to yourself. Allow your whole body to let go as you do this. If you keep this up each time your practice, eventually just saying your relaxing word by itself will bring on a mild state of relaxation.

- Relaxation with Guided Imagery

Many people experience anxiety associated with examination taking. This guided imagery helps one relax and visualize the process of taking an examination successfully. Visualizing success can promote increased confidence. Relaxation can help you manage the anxiety so that you can do the best you can on the examination.

Begin by becoming very relaxed. Make yourself comfortable in a setting free of distractions for the next few minutes. Find a naturally relaxed sitting position and open posture, your hands resting in your lap or at your sides, your legs uncrosse, and your head balanced in a neutral position.

Start to relax your body. Take a deep breath in…hold it gently…and let it out…

Breathe in again…pause…and exhale fully… Keep breathing naturally. With each breath, you become more and more relaxed. If any anxious thoughts linger, leave them where they are for the moment. You can tend to them later.

Pick a spot in the room for your eyes to comfortably focus on. Hold the focus briefly and then let that focus go soft. You can let your eyes close anytime you like.

Notice some areas in your body where tension tends to linger: your shoulders, jaws, neck, back, chest, stomach and hands.

Focus first on your shoulders. See how your shoulders relax as your attention is focused on them. Feel the muscles as they loosen and your shoulders as they ease off. Allow your jaws to relax. Let your lower jaw drop slightly, allowing a space between your upper and lower teeth. Feel the muscles of your face become smooth, loose and relaxed. Turn your attention to your neck. See how you can let the tension go as you relax the muscles of your neck. Let the relaxation flow down the length of your spine, relaxing all the muscles along the way. Feel the relaxation in your neck and back.

As you become aware of the rhythm of your breathing, let the tension in your chest dissipate with each breath and feel your stomach muscles smooth themselves out and the calm settle in. Now focus on your hands. Open and close your hands a few times…wiggle your fingers… and then relax. Let your hands be limp and loose.

Scan your body now for any other areas that might be tense. For each area, imagine directing your breath to that area. Imagine breathing in relaxation… and breathing out tension. Breathing in a feeling of relaxation, and exhaling all the tension. Feel your muscles relax with each breath. Continue to scan your body, relaxing each area.

Now you are feeling calm and relaxed. Your whole body feels heavy, and you feel grounded and centred. Begin to visualize now the process of taking an examination.

Imagine yourself on the day of the examination. You are feeling a little excited to take the examination and share what you know; at the same time, you are feeling confident. You imagine walking calmly into the room where the examination is going to be. You say, "*When I get to my seat, just think about the situation, not my anxiety*".

You see yourself sitting in your chair. You notice your surroundings. You hear the other students shuffle in their seats. You smile to them. You feel the desk. You feel the pen in your hand. You see the test being handed out. You feel a hint of the old anxiety rising. You say, "*I can be anxious later, now is the time to take the exam*".

Now, the examination is in front of you. You are scanning over the entire examination calmly and confidently. You discover that you already know something about each answer. You feel relaxed, happy. You start to organize your time. You say, "*I will think rationally and not allow my anxiety to take over.... I've done well on exams before so there's no reason I can't today.... Breathe and relax.... I am ready to rise up to meet this challenge. It's time for me to show the professor what I know*".

Take in a deep breath and, slowly and calmly, let it all out. You feel your body relax and allow your mind to become calm. In this state of calm, you are able to concentrate and see things clearly. Now you begin writing quickly and deliberately. You effortlessly recall the information you studied. The ideas are flowing from your pen with ease. Some of the questions are easy and straightforward, and you answer them quickly. Some questions take more thinking. You expect this, and you are prepared. You find ways to show what you know.

You are now finished and you close the examination and calmly put away your writing tools. Finally, you are handing in the test with a big smile on your face. The proctor smiles back. Savour this feeling.

You imagine that you did ok on the examination. You feel proud of yourself for your accomplishment of working through the examination calmly and confidently. You say to yourself, "*It worked. I got through it without blanking out! I did feel stress but I managed it. Good for me!*" Imagine getting the examination results. Feeling confident and excited… and seeing the results: You get an excellent grade, exactly what you were hoping for. This feeling of success and accomplishment is so wonderful, you want to take another examination just to experience it all again. Now you have completed this visualization experience, you are feeling more mentally prepared for the process of taking an examination. You may even find that completing this guided imagery exercise helps you feel motivated, helps you feel calm, confident, and in control.

- Distraction
- Activity Scheduling

Table 4.10 Some examples on how to maintain diary entry for activity scheduling

	Pleasurable activity	Activity with a sense of achievement	Activities that keep you physically active	Social activities
Monday				
Tuesday				
Wednesday				
Thursday				
Friday				
Saturday				
Sunday				

It is helpful to have an everyday schedule that includes not just the study schedule but some pleasurable activities as well. Activity scheduling can include activities from the following groups:

- Pleasurable activities
- Activities which give you a sense of achievement
- Activities which make you physically active
- Social activities

It is important to do a balance of activities from each group. So, for example, each day try scheduling in an activity from a different group to the day before.

Of course, each activity might fit into more than one group—a coffee and cake with friends can be both pleasurable and sociable (Table 4.10).

4.12 Conclusion

Study skills are fundamental to academic competence. Good study skills minimize failure and enable students to take advantage of learning opportunities. To be effective learners, students must (a) have a wide array of study strategies at their disposal, and (b) know where, when, and how to use these strategies. Research has documented that effective study skills can be taught. The importance of study skills in terms of academic competence underscores the need for a strong emphasis on the development and maintenance of effective study skills across the curriculum and for all grade levels. Many students pass through our educational system without having achieved a level of academic competence necessary for success in and out of school. Although study skills are just one reason for educational failure, research on classroom implementation of strategy instruction and how to promote effective studying among all students should remain a high priority.

References

Adams, D., & Hamm, M. (1994). *New designs for teaching and learning: Promoting active learning in tomorrow's schools.* San Francisco: Jossey-Bass.

Baumann, J. F., & Bergeron, B. S. (1993). Story map instruction using children's literature: Effects on first graders' comprehension of central narrative elements. *Journal of Reading Behavior, 25*, 407–437.

Bos, C. S., & Anders, P. L. (1990). Effects of interactive vocabulary instruction on the vocabulary learning and reading comprehension of junior-high learning disabled students. *Learning Disability Quarterly, 13*, 31–42.

Centre for Research on Learning and Instruction, University of Edinburgh. (1997). *Scoring key for the approaches and study skills inventory for students.* Retrieved from Enhancing Teaching- Learning Environments in Undergraduate Courses Project Web site http://www.ed.ac.uk/etl/questionnaires/ASSIST.pdf.

Chong, J. (2007). *Time management.* Sydney, Australia: University of New South Wales.

Cottrell, S. (1999). *The study skills handbook.* Basingstoke: Palgrave Macmillan.

Cottrell, S. (2008). *The study skills handbook* (3rd ed.). New York, NY: Palgrave Macmillan.

Damon, W. (1991). Problems in direction in socially shared cognition. In L. B. Resnick, J. M. Levine, & S. D. Teasley (Eds.), *Perspectives on socially shared cognition* (pp. 384–397). Washington, DC: American Psychological Association.

Deshler, D. D., & Schumaker, J. B. (1988). An instructional model for teaching students how to learn. In J. L. Graden, J. E. Zins, & M. J. Curtis (Eds.), *Alternative educational delivery systems: Enhancing instructional options for students* (pp. 391–411). Washington, DC: National Association of School Psychologists.

Devine, T. G. (1987). *Teaching study skills: A guide for teachers.* Boston: Allyn and Bacon.

Egan, G. (2007). *The skilled helper: A problem management and opportunity development approach to helping* (8th ed.). Belmont, CA: Wadsworth.

Gettinger, M., & Nicaise, M. (1997). Study skills. In G. G. Bear, K. M. Minke, & A. Thomas (Eds.), *Children's needs II: Development, problems, and alternatives* (pp. 407–418). Bethesda, MD: National Association of School Psychologists.

Harvey, S., & Goudvis, A. (2000). *Strategies that work: Teaching comprehension to enhance understanding.* York, ME: Stenhouse.

Hoover, J. J., & Patton, P. R. (1995). *Teaching students with learning problems to use study skills: A teacher's guide.* Austin, TX: Pro-Ed.

Hoult, E. (2006). *Learning support: A guide for mature students.* London, England: Sage.

Kucan, L., & Beck, I. (1997). Thinking aloud and reading comprehension research: Inquiry, instruction, and social interaction. *Review of Educational Research, 67*, 271–299.

Lenz, B. K., Ellis, E. S., & Scanlon, D. (1996). *Teaching learning strategies to adolescents and adults with learning disabilities.* Austin, TX: Pro-Ed.

Nicaise, M., & Gettinger, M. (1995). Fostering reading comprehension in college students. *Reading Psychology, 16*, 283–337.

Novak, J. D., & Gowin, D. B. (1984). *Learning how to learn.* New York: Cambridge University Press.

Palincsar, A. S., & Brown, A. L. (1988). Teaching and practicing thinking skills to promote comprehension in the context of group problem solving. *Remedial and Special Education, 9*(1), 53–59.

Paris, S. G., & Winograd, P. (1990). Promoting metacognition and motivation of exceptional children. *Remedial and Special Education, 11*(6), 7–15.

Pressley, M., Woloshyn, V., & Associates. (1995). *Cognitive strategy instruction that really improves children's academic performance* (2nd ed.). Cambridge, MA: Brookline.

Rohwer, W. D. (1984). An invitation to an educational psychology of studying. *Educational Psychologist, 9*, 1–14.

Scanlon, D. J., Duran, G. Z., Reyes, E. I., & Gallego, M. A. (1991). Interactive semantic mapping: An interactive approach to enhancing LD students' content area comprehension. *Learning Disabilities Research & Practice, 7,* 142–146.

Scanlon, D. J ., Deshler, D. D., & Schumaker, J. B. (1994). Collaborative dialogues between teachers and researchers to create educational interventions: A case study. *Journal of Educational and Psychological Consultation, 5,* 69–76.

Scanlon, D. J., Deshler, D. D., & Schumaker, J. B. (1996). Can a strategy be taught and learned in secondary inclusive classrooms? *Learning Disabilities Research & Practice, 11,* 41–57.

Scheid, K. (1993). *Helping students become strategic learners: Guidelines for teaching*. Cambridge, MA: Brookline.

Schunk, D. H. (2000). *Learning theories: An educational perspective*. Upper Saddle River, NJ: Prentice-Hall.

Schunk, D. H., & Zimmerman, B. (Eds.). (1994). *Selfregulation of learning and performance: Issues and educational applications*. Hillsdale, NJ: Erlbaum.

Tait, H., Entwistle, N. J., & McCune, V. (1998). *ASSIST:* a reconceptualisation of the *Approaches to Studying Inventory*. In C. Rust (Ed.), *Improving students as learners*. Oxford: Oxford Brookes University, The Oxford Centre for Staff and Learning Development.

University of Queensland. (2009). *Time and study management*. Retrieved from http://www.uq.edu.au.

Wood, E., Woloshyn, V. E., & Willoughby, T. (Eds.). (1995). *Cognitive strategy instruction for middle and high school*. Cambridge, MA: Brookline.

Study Guides and Strategies (1997). The SQ3R reading method. Retrieved from http://www.studygs.net.

Zimmerman, B. J. (1998). Academic studying and the development of personal skill: A self-regulatory perspective. *Educational Psychologist, 33*, 73–86.

Zimmerman, B. J., Bonner, S., & Kovach, R. (1996). *Developing self-regulated learners: Beyond achievement to self-efficacy*. Washington, DC: American Psychological Association.

Chapter 5
Interpersonal Skills

Deepika Gupta, Manju Mehta and Rajesh Sagar

5.1 Introduction

Adolescent period is often described as a period of friction, fights and fireworks; correctly encapsulating the internal and external dilemmas that an adolescent as well as those around him/her go through. Beginning roughly from the age of 10 years till 18 years, teenagers, as they are also called, pass through all phases of development such as physical, emotional, personal and interpersonal. In addition to the normal changes that are expected and the consequent flux in the environment that is created, at times, individuals in this age group, like individuals in any other life stage, also experience distress and need psychological intervention. Most researchers have grouped adolescence into three developmental periods, entailing early adolescence (typically ages 10–13), middle adolescence (ages 14–17) and late adolescence (18 until the early twenties).

In the growth and development of any individual, the family and family's environment plays a central and nurturing role. A family which provides adequate physical, material, emotional and social resources to its members shapes a healthy and creative individual. However, the period of adolescence is the time when gates to multitude of other relationships also open up. Significant amongst these are

D. Gupta (✉)
Department of Psychiatry, Ram Manohar Lohia Hospital, New Delhi, India
e-mail: deepika101@gmail.com

M. Mehta · R. Sagar
Department of Psychiatry, All India Institute of Medical Sciences, New Delhi, India
e-mail: drmanju.mehta@gmail.com

R. Sagar
e-mail: rsagar29@gmail.com

M. Mehta and R. Sagar (eds.), *A Practical Approach to Cognitive Behaviour Therapy for Adolescents*, DOI 10.1007/978-81-322-2241-5_5

parents, siblings, friends/peers and romantic relationships. Also, since this is the period of self-discovery and establishment of one's own identity, relationship with one's own self is also a very significant milestone in this period.

Difficulties with forming and maintaining healthy interpersonal relationships in this age group stem from one or more of the following reasons: under-confidence or over-confidence in one's abilities; unrealistic appraisal of one's body; over sensitivity about one's family background; tendency for self-evaluation by constant comparison with peers; broadening of one's exposure to social situation by way of parties/outings; introduction to new habits like making friends with seniors at school; exposure to smoking/drinking; missing classes; defiance and rebellion; feeling constantly judged or misunderstood; unbalanced spending of time with self/parents and peers—less interest in talking to parents or sharing time/thoughts with family and increased identification with peers; and development of infatuations and development of one's own sexual identity and gender preferences.

5.2 Significant Relationships in the Life of Adolescents

5.2.1 Siblings

Siblings, both younger and older, form an important role in shaping the adolescent. Their relationships are characterized with conflicts as well as companionship and affection. From older siblings, the adolescent learns problem solving, morality and consequences for positive and negative actions. From younger siblings, the adolescent learns to manage power play, be a caring/teaching role model and nurturing/guiding behaviour. According to social learning theory, older siblings may serve as models for younger siblings when perceived as likable and nurturing. In contrast, sibling de-identification theory posits that adolescents respond to parents' differential treatment by defining themselves as different from each other, pursuing different domains of competence and interest to avoid comparison and rivalry.

5.2.2 Parents

It is a predominant notion that the period of adolescence is characterized by moodiness, lack of responsible adult-like behaviour, rejection of adult/societal values/norms as well as significant defiance and disobedience in relation with parents across cultures. The adolescent spends less time with parents owing to both the friction in the relationship as well as preoccupation in other developmental activities such as increased academic pressure, excelling at co-curricular activities and investing in establishing peer relations amongst others. Parents of offspring in early adolescence adopt a more authoritarian/authoritative parenting style, whereas parents of offspring in late adolescence adopt a more democratic and egalitarian parenting style.

Whether the conflict is furthering adolescent adjustment or disengages him/her from the family depends on:

(a) the frequency and intensity of conflict,
(b) whether the conflict is directed at a single parent or both,
(c) whether conflict is elevated during periods of personal crisis for the adolescent (exam stress, quarrel with peer, difficulty in intimate relation with partner, personal frustration and feeling of inadequacy),
(d) whether the conflict is in response to a structural change in the family (divorce, remarriage and death), and
(e) manner in which the conflict is resolved.

In situations where conflict is frequent and of high intensity, it is suggestive of ongoing family issues which escalate as the adolescent grows to differentiate himself/herself from the family. Conflict directed at a single parent is suggestive more of conflicting interpersonal relationship between the two individuals and less on the adolescents' rebellion against parenting in general. It is also important to understand that in the presence of such conflict what is the stance of the other parent and significant others. At times, manner of resolving conflict is at polar opposites—either defiance and rebellion or disengagement and devaluing. And thus, conflict resolution training becomes important.

Adolescents share a different personal relationship with mothers and fathers. The quality of the relationship is dependent on the perceived likeness of either parent for certain topics and dislikes for certain others. For instance, adolescents prefer to share about private matters such as dating and sexual/gender attitudes with mothers and impersonal issues such as school work and future plans with either parent. Steinberg and Silk (2002) attribute this difference to the perception that fathers provide informational and material support while mothers provide more emotional support.

5.2.3 Peers

The platform for interacting with and joining with peers is provided at school, tuitions, hobby classes, shared group work tasks and neighbourhood, amongst others. The peer group may form a similar or a different influence than parents, or they influence different areas of the adolescent's life. Adolescents look at peer group approval and acceptance for matters which may be short term (style, preferences, inclusion in social groups and conformity to norms) or habits (study patterns, picking up of new habits like smoking/lying) or (less often) long term (career choices and values).

Brown (2004) classified peer relations in three levels—dyadic friendships/romantic relations developed on functional significance and personal choice;

small groups of peers called cliques that come together based on a shared activity like hobby class; and crowds which come together based on a shared identity/stereotyped images. As adolescents mature, so does the quality of friendship deepen. The construct of jealousy outside the parental sphere starts emerging which if unaddressed may impact an individual's self-esteem and efficiency and enhance feelings of loneliness, social withdrawal, interpersonal aggression opening the way to negative habits such as substance use and decreased academic/vocational performance. They may develop internalizing/externalizing problems based on their coping with the situation.

5.2.4 Romantic Relationships

In continuation with the peer relations, a unique developmental aspect from the adolescent life stage is involvement in romantic relationships. Though viewed as fleeting and transitory across many cultures and societies, these relationships do foster greater self-esteem, help polish one's identity by exposing the adolescent to choices and alternatives, promote greater social inclusion and provide companionship in times of stress and happiness. Some of these relationships do stay stable across time as well and mature into adult relationships. However, the red flags appear when the individual is unable to balance the intimate relationships with other developmental tasks such as academic performance, vocational mastery, developing healthy peer relations and differentiating in a healthy manner from the family. 'Break-ups' can also have damaging consequences to the adolescent by threatening the stoppage of goals such as companionship and social inclusion. They can also have deeper psychological consequences such as loss of self-esteem, feelings of rejection and depression. An individual may also cope with such a scenario by jumping in and out of new relationships which they call 'flings'.

5.3 Case Vignette

Amita, 15 year old, girl, student of class 11, was referred to the psychologist by the general physician whom the family regularly visited. She belonged to an urban, middle-class, nuclear family. Mother, 43 year old, educated up to MA and presently working as an assistant in a bank and father, 46 year old, educated up to MSc and presently working in the administrative department of a multinational company. Amita has one younger brother, 13 year old, student of class 9. The parents were getting repeated complaints from the school regarding lack of concentration in class, missing classes with friends and not completing assignments on time. Coupled with this, the parents observed significant increase in the time Amita spent talking on the phone, going for social gatherings with friends and less with family members. Her parents also do not approve of the friend circle she belongs to citing them to have habits such as smoking and hailing from discordant families from upper socio-economic strata. They also felt that she was not devoting adequate time to her studies. Whenever corrected, Amita would flare up with the parents and lock herself in the room. There were regular fights at home regarding Amita's behaviour towards her parents, poor academic performance and her over involvement with own self and friends.

CBT sessions planned for Amita and the family would begin with assessment of the family dynamics (such as parenting styles, contingency management adopted for appropriate and inappropriate behaviour and relationship between siblings). This would be followed by setting joint goals between the therapist and the family. Success of therapy would be dependent upon not only fulfilling the parent's expectations from the adolescent but also exploring the adolescent's expectations from own self and from the family, improving communication between the two subsystems and improving role efficiency for both the daughter and parents so as to enhance healthy interpersonal relationships. CBT formulation would be explained to build motivation and compliance towards receiving desired results. Post completion of treatment goals, review of techniques and feedback is provided. Booster sessions as and when needed are also planned.

5.4 Cognitive Behaviour Therapy Sessions

CBT sessions begin with an intake session, followed by assessment. The rest of therapy sessions are divided as beginning phase, middle phase and ending phase. These are given below.

5.4.1 Intake Session

One of the salient aspects of the CBT approach in psychotherapy is the structure and time-limited fashion in which it operates. Number of sessions taken depends upon the problem at hand, client's motivation, therapists' skills and client–therapist relationship amongst other variables.

Intake session is the first session, usually brief, aimed at achieving the following:

(a) Collect factual information such as socio-demographic history, client profile, family history, treatment history and contact details
(b) Elicit presenting problems both from the adolescent and parents/significant others who accompany the client
(c) Explore reason for referral when referred from another professional/school
(d) Explain CBT formulation vis-à-vis importance of collaborative relationship, appointments, homework assignment and joint responsibility taking

(e) Explain trust and confidentiality agreements
(f) Clarify fee structure and institutional guidelines to be followed, if any.

It is suggested that in the first session, time is given individually with the adolescent in the absence of parents/significant others to enable the adolescent feel empowered, trusted and responsible as well as build trust with the therapist. This is then further followed by interviews with parents and others.

5.4.2 *Assessment*

Assessment of presenting complaints forms an important initial step to begin therapy. Appropriate evaluation has benefits as follows:

(a) Clarification of expectations and goals of treatment
(b) Identification of problem from perspective of adolescent
(c) Identification of problem from perspective of others such as parents and teachers
(d) Identification of contributing issues otherwise not reported
(e) Baseline understanding of functioning and setting of realistic targets
(f) Overall evaluation of adolescent vis-à-vis strengths, weaknesses and assets.

Assessment is done through interviews as well as incorporation of reports of referees, school records and objective assessment as and when needed.

How to assess?

1. Interview the adolescent and summarize to arrive at workable goals
2. Interview parents and understand their concerns
3. Take a joint session with parents and adolescent and arrive at goals for sessions
4. Identify need for objective assessment

S. no.	Area of assessment	Tool available
1	Self-esteem	Rosenberg self-esteem scale
2	Screening tool for behavioural and emotional problems in children and adolescents	Youth self report inventory
3	Family conflict	Family environment scale
4	Interpersonal dynamics between family members	Kinetic family drawing test
5	Elicit attitudes, beliefs and motivations about self and other aspects related to self	Sentence completion test

5. Incorporate findings from assessment to enrich treatment goals and use in therapy.

5.4.3 *Beginning Phase*

Therapy begins with goal setting to jointly arrive at problem areas which are workable. It is important to narrow the scope of goal setting so as not to aim to change personalities of parents/others and temperament of the adolescent completely but to find a healthy balance between the two. The role of the therapist to enable the adolescent develop skills to both build effective relationships, maintain them as well as effectively resolve conflicts as and when they arise which needs to be clarified at the outset.

Joint activities for teens and parents can be planned to enhance the bond between them and create opportunities for healthy interaction where the sole purpose of communication is not expression of what parents dislike in the adolescent and the adolescent's complaints about perceived bad parenting. It can be helpful for parents to get connected to what is the 'fad' of the moment, what excites the adolescent and what would he/she view as a reward. Parents can also know about the role model that the adolescent aspires for and bring out the good in him or her.

Parenting tips that are shared at this stage are as follows:

(a) Send clear signals to the adolescent that disrespectful behaviour will not be tolerated, without responding with anger to the agitated adolescent.
(b) Do not say 'No' for everything. Let some things which are not grossly wrong slide.
(c) Pick the right time to correct aberrant behaviour. When the teen is in a bad mood, that is not the best time to correct him/her about how badly he/she keeps their room.
(d) Pick one point at a time. Do not begin with one problem behaviour and pile it with all other problem behaviours also at one go.
(e) Talk about issues that need one-to-one attention where there is least distraction by, for example phone/other siblings/others who may happen to listen.
(f) Celebrate small efforts and successes by the adolescent even when the big break through is not coming in.
(g) Set aside quality time.

5.4.4 *Mi+ddle Phase*

The middle phase of therapy is focused on building social adaptive skills necessary for initiating and sustaining relationships, whether they may be with family, friends or romantic relationships. Being armed with realistic self-evaluation, healthy communication, conflict resolution and anger management can help the individual in different areas of relationship functioning.

5.4.4.1 Behaviour Change

The adolescent age group is often associated with mood swings and temperaments that are difficult to handle by those around them and are often a cause of disruptive relationships. In this step, adolescents are encouraged to reflect on their behaviour and see where there is a need for change.

Worksheet

(a) Make a list of things you do which are good
(b) Make a list of things you do which may cause trouble to others around you
(c) Make a list of behaviours that you would like to do more often
(d) Make a list of behaviours that you would like to do less
(e) I want my family to support me in changing my behaviour by doing …. and not doing ….
(f) Were there any things in the past 2 weeks that you thought you did without thinking and the consequences were not so nice?
(g) What can you do next time before acting impulsively?

Parents and significant others can help the teen in behaviour change by following simple steps as follows:

(a) Modelling: model the correct behaviour. It would not be very beneficial to scream at the adolescent in anger criticising the same action in him/her.
(b) Give cues: when you pick up that the adolescent is getting frustrated or unable to express himself/herself or needs assistance but is uncomfortable asking for it, give subtle cues such as 'look here' and 'you look frustrated' amongst others.
(c) Gradually withdraw adult support: encourage adolescents to think and act independently but also seek accountability and responsibility for actions. Be present to guide and offer advice in a manner and tone that the adolescent feels comfortable accepting.

5.4.4.2 Thought Monitoring and Modification

In this step, the role of the therapist is to psychoeducate the client about the T-F-A cycle which elucidates the relationship between thoughts, feelings and actions. By way of examples, it can be explained that the way we think influences the way we feel which in turn determines the course of action we take. The consequences of this action further fuel into the way we think and the cycle continues. In order to have desired results in terms of consequences, it is important to bring out a behaviour change which also stems from changing the way we think or perceive situations. The adolescent is explained about the negative automatic thoughts that tend to flood in as a situation presents itself. The salient characteristics of negative automatic thoughts are as follows: they are automatic, distorted, unhelpful, unreasonable and involuntary.

Cognitive biases are also included with examples of situations that the adolescent brings up where he/she felt misunderstood or a conflict opened up. Adolescents are encouraged to think about times when something they thought had an impact on something they did. For example, the client stopped talking to his friend because the latter refused to share his class notes with him. The client thought the reason was so as to get better marks than him, but in reality, his friend had incomplete notes which he did not want anyone else to know.

Worksheet

Think of one situation in the last two weeks where you had a disagreement with someone. Answer the following questions to elicit your negative automatic thoughts at work.

(a) What is the evidence for my negative automatic thinking?
(b) What alternative ways of looking at things are there?
(c) What effect does thinking this way have on me?
(d) Did I 'predict the future, over-generalize, think selectively, think in terms of black and white or jump to conclusions'?

5.4.4.3 Building Effective Communication Skills

Good communication means 'being able to tell others what you feel and think and being able to hear what others tell you about what they feel and think'. The adolescent is guided about effective communication to fulfil the following points:

(a) Make communication positive, clear and specific.
(b) Recognize that each individual sees things from a different point of view.
(c) Be open and honest about your feelings and accept others' feelings.
(d) Ask questions for clarification on an issue.
(e) Learn to listen.
(f) Use 'I-statements'.

Effective communication involves maintaining eye contact, using gestures such as affirmative nods, asking relevant questions, paraphrasing, not interrupting the speaker. The adolescent is encouraged to develop the habit of seeking help and not feeling rejected when the other does not 'magically' understand the need for help.

5.4.4.4 Use of 'I-Statements'

The three components of an I-statement are as follows:

(a) An 'I-statement' starts with letting people know whose feeling you are talking about: 'I feel …'
(b) An I-statement names clearly for people how you are feeling: 'I feel happy/sad/angry/frustrated/lonely or whatever…'
(c) An I-statement ends by explaining to people why you feel the way you do: 'I feel happy when my friends call around to see if I want to hang around with them'.

Assertiveness is an important aspect of communication training essential to adolescence to train them in not giving into peer pressure. Activity can be started by exploring the meaning of assertiveness and how it differs from submissiveness as well as aggressiveness. The adolescent can explore situations in the past one month in interacting with others where he/she felt that being more assertive could have been beneficial. Pros and cons of aggressive and assertive behaviour can be discussed by making posters. Role-play situations to play out dialogues with the adolescent being the one giving pressure as well as resisting pressure can be enacted within session. Helping the adolescent understand their emotions alongside each step would further be a self-reinforcing feature that would encourage him/her to use more assertiveness.

Worksheet

Which of the following steps would lead to better communication?

Which of the following steps would lead to better communication?		
1. Making eye contact	Yes	No
2. Listening without interruption	Yes	No
3. Stating needs clearly	Yes	No
4. Becoming easily frustrated	Yes	No
5. Speaking in a loud dominating voice	Yes	No
6. Allowing others to take advantage of you	Yes	No

5.4.4.5 Conflict Resolution

Conflicts are inevitable in any relationship. The problem arises when we fail to address the root of conflict or repair the damage that the conflict creates. The adolescent needs to be trained in effective conflict resolution as an important life skill to enhance quality of their relationships.

Steps for conflict management shared in session are as follows:

(a) Focus on the problem and not the person
(b) Talk to the person directly and not use other people to carry messages or interpret meanings
(c) Listen
(d) Use I-statements
(e) Do not jump to conclusions
(f) Take a timeout: when the conflict is elevated to a point of extreme anger and frustration, it is helpful to take a break and give a gap before resuming communication
(g) Apologize if you have done something wrong or hurt someone
(h) Work at resolution by arriving at a mid-point
(i) Come up with ideas so that the same situation does not repeat itself.

These steps can be followed using method of role-play discussing a hypothetical situation or a conflict situation in the last month with the client.

Worksheet

Brainstorm with the client what all he/she thinks does and does not work while resolving a conflict and note the points down.

What does not work?	What does work?
Yelling	Negotiation
Refusing to change or compromise	Mediation
Refusing to work out the conflict	Looking at both sides
Name calling	A win–win attitude
Hitting	Listening
Walking out	Timeout
Belittling	Relaxed attitude

5.4.4.6 Anger Management

The therapist and client can jointly brainstorm about what the consequences could be of handling a situation in anger versus handling the same situation in a calm manner. Discussing about anger and trigger for anger reactions is an important activity. The discussion can be shaped to bring out important themes as follows:

(a) We all try to manage anger—sometimes effectively (e.g., solve a problem) and sometimes ineffectively (e.g., walk away from a problem)
(b) We can be selective in when we want to express our anger (e.g., scream at a parent who corrects us for driving fast and apologize to a police man who catches us driving fast)
(c) Bringing down the 'hotness' in the angry moment can pave the way to resolution of anger provoking event
(d) What can lead to better resolution of a problem situation—dealing it in a calm way or angry way, even when one's stance is legitimate
(e) How can anger be expressed in a healthy, non-abusive and non-threatening way.

Steps for anger management are given in Chap. 6.

5.4.5 End Phase

Usually, all the above steps and skills are not needed and there is no set order in which to proceed. It is determined by the need of the client, the number of sessions for which the client is available and the pace of therapy. Each session when followed up by home work assignments where the adolescent practices in real life what has been discussed during the sessions brings good results.

During the ending phase of therapy, the initial goals are revisited and the progress achieved is highlighted. The adolescent's strengths are brought out and the changes achieved applauded. The adolescent's ability to bring out change in his/her environment and relationships by dealing more effectively with their own self and making needful changes is highlighted. The importance of this is to empower the adolescent to imbibe the training and believe in own self without feeling dependent on the therapist. Follow-up sessions are planned where the techniques are revised and clients' progress monitored. Any new challenges, if shape up, are dealt with subsequently.

5.5 Specific Issues in Adolescence

5.5.1 *Conflicting Relationship with Parents*

The above described pattern is followed beginning as follows:

(a) Define the problem behaviour as departure from otherwise normal interactional patterns between the parent and adolescent. The therapist must validate the client's feelings and then help define the problem in a specific and tangible manner. Next, it is important to remain focused in session to focus on solutions and not problems by directing towards understanding role of environment on one's own behaviour and thinking.

(b) Introduce behaviour charting to identify triggers to defiant/aggressive behaviour. The A-B-C chart used is as follows:

Date/ Time	Antecedent condition	Behaviour	Consequence
	What happened in the environment that triggered a negative response from me	Describe my own behaviour	What was the result of this/what happened after my reaction

(c) Use the chart to modify dysfunctional behaviour patterns and arrive at realistic evaluation of the interactional pattern.

5.5.2 *Romantic Relationships: Creating the Balance and Dealing with Break-Up*

Adolescent relationships can be a great source of social support but also lead to poor psychological/personal and social consequences if the adolescent is unable to manage their time effectively or not cope adequately with broken relationships.

5.5.2.1 Creating the Balance

The focus here is to enable the adolescent strike a balance between his/her different relationships and effectively manage study without being lopsided and consumed over their relationship. Towards this, the steps are as follows:

(a) Accept the relationship as meaningful to the adolescent in some way. If he/she doesn't have to spend effort in hiding it, they can be more relaxed and focus on all things holistically
(b) Encourage family to not compare them with their own teen years. Times are changing
(c) Create trust between parents and adolescents with a balance that both sides' thoughts and boundaries are respected
(d) Create red flags for the adolescent which includes what all would friends/girlfriend/boyfriend not influence in their life. These could be activities of personal growth such as tuition/study time/family time. The adolescent can identify number of hours they would put into their studies and co-curricular regardless of other interests. This can be compared with number of hours put in before entering a relationship or other adolescents who do and do not have a relationship
(e) Share the importance of spending quality and quantity time with friends other than romantic friendship only
(f) Create flags for the parents as what all activities would be allowed, for example phone time and leisure time
(g) Thought monitoring and modification for the adolescent so as to not having to make a choice between family and personal relationship
(h) Communication building for both adolescent and family to understand their thinking and reasons for the same
(i) Use of conflict resolution skills as and when disagreements come up.

5.5.2.2 Romantic Relationship and Sexuality

Engaging in dyadic intimate relationships provides the adolescent with the opportunity to explore one's own sexuality. Often, this is coupled with incomplete and incorrect information about one's own body; unrealistic expectations from self or partner; pressure to conform to group norms; and pressure to conform to partner's demands or even experimentation. It is beneficial for the adolescent if the therapist can create an environment for discussion about these pertinent topics. An important area worth outlining is the difference between physical and emotional love. The former entails attraction, the intense feeling of likeness, also understood as a bodily arousal or a hormonal rush in the physical presence or the thought of the romantic partner. The tendency of such a feeling is to emerge and leave with same quickness. Emotional or mental love on the other hand is the feeling of harmony between the thought process and ideology of two individuals who like and complement one another. The latter is based on deep friendship and mutual likeness with an inclination towards future commitment. It is important to enable the adolescent to be able to make a choice about one's own sexual involvement based on the understanding between the two. In addition, skills training as discussed earlier in the chapter including assertiveness to be able to consent or decline consent based on personal preferences, understanding one's personal ideology, comfort level with self and the relationship, autonomy of decision, decision not stemming from a fleeting impulse and being aware of one's family's value system amongst other reasons personal to the adolescent are important factors to be discussed in session. Empowerment of making a choice along with guided decision-making is helpful in helping the adolescent make the right decision at the right time with respect to his/her sexuality.

5.5.2.3 Dealing with Break-Ups

Often, school counsellors and psychologists are faced with young adolescents in a depressed state with lack of motivation, broken self-concept and feelings of gloominess about future with a declining academic and co-curricular performance. At times, the reason for this is a split in their relationships. It is important for the therapist to acknowledge this loss with same sensitivity and seriousness as they would have had the case been the loss of any other significant relationship.

(a) Allow expression: give space and time for the adolescent to share about the relationship, memories and hopes he/she had from it
(b) Explore the reasons for the break-up and what mental schemas are attached to it. Often, adolescents feel they were not good enough
(c) The therapist must help the teen to come to accept the reality of the loss and not continue based on empty hope
(d) Explore emotions such as anger, guilt and loneliness
(e) Explore quality of the relationship, functions fulfilled by it, roles and activities, avoided, if any by the adolescent due to relationship
(f) Engage adolescent in pleasurable activities not out of distraction but to enhance the life state and broaden opportunities to step out of their shell
(g) Help adolescent re-focus on making a new plan for their life
(h) Identify depressogenic and defeatist thought process and challenge it based on skills on realistic self-evaluation and problem solving mentioned earlier in the chapter
(i) Set small goals with the client and deliver timely reinforcements.

5.5.3 Beyond 'Normal' Defiance: Oppositional Defiance Disorder

Defiance and disobedience, or following a mind of their own, is a common trait in majority of adolescents. They may express their defiance by arguing, disobeying or talking back to their parents, teachers or other adults. When this behaviour lasts longer than six months and is excessive compared to what is usual for their age, it may mean that the teen has a type of behaviour disorder called oppositional defiant disorder (ODD). ODD is a condition with an ongoing pattern of uncooperative, defiant, hostile and annoying behaviour towards people in authority. This behaviour often disrupts their normal daily activities, including activities within the family and at school.

Symptoms of ODD may include:

- Throwing repeated temper tantrums
- Excessively arguing with adults
- Actively refusing to comply with requests and rules
- Deliberately trying to annoy or upset others, or being easily annoyed by others
- Blaming others for your mistakes
- Having frequent outbursts of anger and resentment
- Being spiteful and seeking revenge
- Swearing or using obscene language
- Saying mean and hateful things when upset.

In addition, many individuals with ODD are moody, easily frustrated and have a low self-esteem. They also sometimes may abuse drugs and alcohol. Parents can be helped in how to manage such behaviour. Some strategies are responding without anger, being clear and consistent, not taking adolescent's attacks personally, creating a balance between being the friend and the parent.

5.6 Tips to Build Healthy Relationships

In addition to the social skills needed to build effective relationships and cope with discordant ones, there are some generic tips that can be shared with the adolescents to increase their repertoire of skills. Some of these are as follows:

1. Build trust in yourself and others: be reliable, responsible and dependable
2. Always try and keep channels of communication open
3. Communicate emotions and disagreements
4. Follow through with promises made
5. Use respectful words, avoid verbal abuse/belittling words
6. Build effective boundaries by understanding your and the other's values. State them clearly
7. Spend time adequately with all different relationships such as friends, romantic friends, parents and siblings.

5.7 Barriers to Treatment

5.7.1 Practical Barriers to Care

These barriers are present because adolescents are dependent on adults and society for multiple reasons. Some of these are as follows:

(a) Transportation: An adolescent is unlikely to reach therapy outside school settings by their own self as they are usually not independently using public transport systems

(b) Scheduling: Matching appointment time that the adolescent can regularly take out between school, tuitions and co-curricular activities
(c) Social stigma: Often, the first point of contact for the adolescent is via the school counsellor. Some adolescents may be shy to seek this help or continue in the school setting for fear of reactions by teachers and peers. Seeking therapist outside school setting involves the parents battling social stigma and accepting professional help for their adolescent and family
(d) Caregiver limitations: Monetary and temporal limitations that prevent caregivers to bring adolescent to health care setting.

5.7.2 *Client Focused Barriers to Change*

These barriers are present as factors personal to the adolescent. Some of these are as follows:

(a) Lack of intention to change
(b) Lack of identification of the problem
(c) Recognition of the problem but unwillingness to do anything about it
(d) Understanding that an adult would be unable to understand their problem
(e) Personal temperament of shyness, hesitancy and introversion that may hamper the treatment seeking and engagement of adolescent with therapist
(f) Personal thoughts such as 'I can solve my problems myself', 'It is embarrassing to share my personal problems with others', 'If my parents/friends do not understand me, how can a stranger understand me?'

5.7.3 *Therapist Focused and Therapeutic Setting Based Barriers to Change*

(a) Distracting and impersonal therapeutic environment
(b) Inability to build confidentiality and respect
(c) Adopting a talk-down approach instead of a joint approach.

5.8 Summary

The period of adolescence is one of the most turbulent and challenging phases of development for both the individual and others in his/her social context. It is the phase of identity formation, self-exploration and beginning of establishment of first few stable relationships outside the family. Hence, it is associated with challenging both intrapersonally and interpersonally. Presence of negative and defeatist schema can hamper the growing adolescents' productivity in relationships, and the social context can itself become one of the most stressful areas of his/her life. Use of cognitive and behavioural modification techniques for social skills training and modification of cognitive errors and negative thinking have been found to enhance the quality of interpersonal relationships.

References

Abras, C. (2003). *Determining success in online education and health communities.* Unpublished PhD thesis, University of Maryland, Baltimore County, MD.

Brown, B. B. (2004). *Adolescents' relationships with peers* (2nd ed.). New York: Wiley.

Judith, G. S., Campione-Barr, N., & Metzger, A. (2006). Adolescent development in interpersonal and societal contexts. *Annual Review of Psychology, 57*, 84–255.

Kendall, P. C., Kane, M., Howard, B., & Siqueland, L. (1990). *Cognitive-behavioral treatment of anxious children: Treatment manual.* Philadelphia, United States: Department of Psychology, Temple University.

O'Reilly, G. (2004). *A CBT Workbook for children and adolescents.* Dublin: University College Dublin.

Schachter, F. F. (1985). Sibling de-identification in the clinic: Devil vs. angel. *Family Process, 24*, 415–427.

Steinberg, L., & Silk, J. (2002). Parenting Adolescents. In M. H. Bornstein (Ed.), *Handbook of Parenting, 1* (pp. 103–133). Mahwah, NJ: Erlbaum.

Updegraff, K. A., McHale, S. M., & Crouter, A. C. (2000). Adolescents' sex-typed friendship experiences: Does having a sister versus a brother matter? *Child Development, 71*, 10–1597.

Walker, L., & Taylor, J. H. (1991). Family interactions and the development of moral reasoning. *Child Development, 62*, 83–264.

Wright, K. (2000). Perceptions of on-line support providers: An Examination of perceived homophily, source credibility, communication and social support within on-line support groups. *Communication Quarterly, 48*, 44–59.

Chapter 6
Anger Management

Vidhi M. Pilania, Manju Mehta and Rajesh Sagar

6.1 Anger

Anger is one of the most talked about human emotion and has come to occupy an important role in our lives. Theorists also characterize anger as a negative arousal state that is maintained through its consequences. Spielberger et al. (1983, 1985) have offered a descriptive definition of anger as an emotional state that varies along a continuum ranging from irritation to rage or fury.

Anger is a natural response to those situations where we feel threatened, we believe harm will come to us, or we believe that another person has unnecessarily wronged us. Also, anger may result from frustration when our needs, desires, and goals are not being met. People often confuse anger with aggression. Aggression is *behavior* that is intended to cause harm to another person or damage property. This behavior can include verbal abuse, threats, or violent acts. Anger, on the other hand, is an *emotion* and does not necessarily lead to aggression. Therefore, a person can become angry without acting aggressively.

A term related to anger and aggression is hostility. Hostility refers to a complex set of attitudes and judgments that motivate aggressive behaviors. Whereas anger is an emotion and aggression is a behavior, hostility is an attitude that involves disliking others and evaluating them negatively.

V.M. Pilania · M. Mehta (✉) · R. Sagar
Department of Psychiatry, All India Institute of Medical Sciences, New Delhi 110029, India
e-mail: drmanju.mehta@gmail.com

V.M. Pilania
e-mail: vidhi1309psychologist@gmail.com

R. Sagar
e-mail: rsagar29@gmail.com

M. Mehta and R. Sagar (eds.), *A Practical Approach to Cognitive Behaviour Therapy for Adolescents*, DOI 10.1007/978-81-322-2241-5_6

6.2 Problems Caused Due to Unmanaged Anger

Anger becomes a problem when it is felt too intensely, is felt too frequently, or is expressed inappropriately. During prolonged and frequent episodes of anger, certain divisions of the nervous system become highly activated. Consequently, blood pressure and heart rate increase and stay elevated for long periods. This stress on the body may produce many different health problems, such as hypertension, heart disease, and diminished immune system efficiency. Thus, from a health standpoint, avoiding physical illness is a motivation for controlling anger. Inappropriate expression of anger, such as verbal abuse or intimidating or threatening behavior, often results in negative consequences. For example, it is likely that others will develop fear, resentment, and lack of trust toward those who subject them to anger outbursts, which may cause isolation from individuals, such as family members and friends.

6.3 Anger and Adolescents

Adolescents experience a number of social challenges and developmental challenges that require effective coping skills in order to function adaptively in society. They experience increased social stress caused by peer expectations, and they resist adult (i.e., parents and teachers) rules and authority. The stressors associated with these new challenges often appear to affect adolescent's emotions (e.g., frustration and anger). Consequently, adolescents who demonstrate poor self-control and limited positive coping strategies are more likely to be angry and to become perpetrators of crime and delinquent behavior (Peterson and Hamburg 1986).

6.4 Anger and Psychopathological Conditions

Researchers have identified many behavioral responses of increased anger in adolescence. Dodge and Coie (1987) have found an increase in rates of delinquent behaviors resulting from anger (i.e., indicative of conduct disorder and oppositional defiant disorder) during middle to late adolescence. Kazdin (1987) reported that among adolescents, 50 % admit to theft, 35 % admit to assault, 45 % admit to property vandalism and destruction, and 60 % admit to participating in other forms of antisocial behavior.

It is important to anticipate co-occurring negative outcomes and co-morbidity of risk factors. For example, aggressive children who are also socially rejected by their peers have twice the risk rate for middle school adjustment problems than do aggressive-only children (Coie et al. 1992). Because aggression is a broad risk factor, it has become an important focus for intervention. Anger is one critical factor associated with aggression and violent behavior in our children (Averill 1983).

6.5 Prevalence of Anger in Adolescents

The National Center for Education Statistics (2010) reported that approximately 1.9 million crimes occurred in elementary and secondary schools throughout the nation, meaning about 40 students per 1,000 were victims of some type. These statistics do not include bullying or cyber-bullying, which are also serious types of aggression. In 2009, 28 % of students ages 12–18 reported feeling bullied by one or more of their peers (Institute of Educational Sciences). In an Indian study, it was found that 23.9 % of female students as against 19.4 % of boys had problem with managing their own anger. 20.4 % of girls and 21.5 % of boys stated problem of disturbing thoughts. These findings suggest that the adolescents need to be made aware of the emotional ups and downs in their life and how they can effectively manage their anger.

6.6 Determinants of Anger Among Adolescents

Social factors, such as peer relationships and social skill deficits, are important in determining anger in adolescents. Negative peer interactions may increase anger levels in children. Preadolescents who demonstrate poor social skills and difficulty in making and keeping friends manifest more anger problems. Adolescents that witness conflict between parents may learn to respond to difficulties by using aggressive behavior (Sigfusdottir et al. 2004). Regarding family stressors, research has shown that anger may be influenced by factors such as physical abuse, neglect, or parental psychopathology that increase strain within the family unit. Preschool and adult studies conducted on anger have yielded mixed reviews; the majority of studies conducted on anger expression differences of school-aged and adolescent males and females have suggested that males experience and demonstrate more anger than females.

6.7 Case Vignette

Aditya, a 15-years-old boy visited the counselor with his mother. He belongs to an upper socioeconomic status. Aditya is facing problem in managing his anger both in school as well as at home. He has lost many of his good friends because of frequent expression of anger, he is facing academic difficulties, his grades are going down, and his mother also reported that these days he is having frequent arguments with his father. As per mother and Aditya, these behavioral problems are recently developed. He was a very popular student till he was 13 years old, he was captain of school football team, but now, he has also lost the captaincy. They further reported that Aditya was always an outstanding performer in studies, but in class Xth, he was not able to get marks as per the family and his own expectations.

His father is a senior IAS officer and has a lot of expectations from his only child. Aditya has a passion for football but he also wants to fulfill his parent's ambition of him becoming a good scholar. This conflict has made him so stressed that now he is having difficulties in managing his anger.

The management in such cases starts with initial assessment for anger. The assessment would help in understanding the nature and intensity of the anger problem. After assessment and behavioral analysis, actual anger management starts.

6.8 Measuring Anger

Anger is generally assessed in three ways: self-report, observed behavior, and psychophysiological recording. The use of self-report behavior rating scales is a common practice to assess the construct of anger as these measures provide an organized and scientific format to assess the frequency of individuals' behavior over time. The majority of rating scales that assess anger employ a self-report format that requires rating frequencies of behavior based on a Likert-type continuum response system (Table 6.1).

In addition to self-report measures, anger may also be recorded through direct and indirect observation techniques. Methods of observation may include behavioral analysis chart, anger diaries, and behavioral displays of anger. Finally, regarding psychophysiological recordings, these techniques involve the incorporation of biofeedback practices into measuring one's level of anger. Specifically, physiological responses that are related to respiratory and motoric functions are monitored and may include heart rate, irregular breathing, muscle stiffness, perspiring, and blood pressure.

6.9 Management of Anger

Anger management training typically involves providing information on the cognitive and behavioral components of anger, teaching cognitive and behavioral techniques to manage anger, and encouraging the application of newly learned skills in the real-world setting. Cognitive behavioral techniques attempt to intervene with cognitive, emotional, and physiological components of anger. Specifically, cognitive–behavioral interventions designed to address anger may include one or more of the following: self-awareness training, relaxation techniques, cognitive therapy, and conflict management skill training (Deffenbacher 1999). In a study, with objective of reviewing current approaches to assessment and management of anger and aggression in the youth, Blake and Hamrin (2007) found that cognitive–behavioral and skills-based approaches are the most widely studied and empirically validated treatments for anger and aggression in the youth.

Table 6.1 Measuring anger: some important self-report anger inventories

Self-report inventory	Developed by	Description
State-trait anger expression inventory-2 (STAXI-2)	Spielberger (1999)	57-item, self-report behavior inventory that measures the experience, expression, and control of anger of adolescents and adults, ages 16–63
Multidimensional anger inventory (MAI)	Siegel (1986)	Measures reports of anger frequency, duration and magnitude, range of anger arousing stimuli, mode of anger expression, and hostile outlook, of adults ages 40–63
Anger discomfort scale (ADS)	Sharkin and Gelso (1991)	15 items, that are designed to assess the construct of anger discomfort of individuals ages 18–38
Children's inventory of anger	Nelson et al. (1993)	Measures the intensity of anger of children ages 6–16. Specifically, this measure presents stick-figure drawings of facial expressions that correspond to a 4-point Likert-type scale
Multidimensional school anger inventory (MSAI)	Smith et al. (1998)	A self-report rating scale that assesses anger arousal, cynical hostility, and negative anger expression in students grades 6–12. It is composed of 36 items that involve responding to anger situations by referencing a 4-point Likert-type scale
Adolescent anger rating scale (AARS)	Burney (2001)	A 41-item, self-report, Likert-type rating scale designed to identify reactive anger, instrumental anger, anger control, and total anger of adolescents ages 11–19

6.10 CBT-Based Anger Management Training Module

This module emphasizes the interactive role of emotion, cognitions and behavior in the development and maintenance of mental health problems. This aims at enabling adolescents to acquire skills and techniques to deal with anger arousing stressors and help them to use these skills to understand and manage their anger. The techniques for anger management can be divided into two broad categories: quick anger control strategies and long-term anger control strategies. In this module, sessions 2 and 3 are about **quick anger control** training and sessions 4 and 5 talk about **long-term anger control** training.

6.11 Sessions

The module can be delivered across six sessions covering following broad areas as mentioned below:

- To develop understanding about anger.
- To learn to look for the triggers for anger.
- To learn relaxation skills.

Table 6.2 Sessions in anger management

Session no.	Aims of sessions
Session 1: psychoeducation	To make the client able to understand more about their own anger and how it affects and factors which can worsen it
Session 2: early warning signs and their quick control	To become able to recognize the early warning signs of anger and quick ways of controlling anger
Session 3: strategies to manage anger	To learn various strategies of managing anger, e.g., self talk and frustration tolerance
Session 4: communication skills	To develop more helpful and healthy ways of communication
Session 5: cognitive restructuring	To develop more helpful and healthy thoughts about situations that lead to anger
Session 6: review and challenge of maintaining the change	To cope with challenges to manage anger, setbacks, and how to increase the chances of success

- To learn and implement rational restructuring to identify and change irrational thoughts which are a cause of expressing anger.
- To learn positive social skills and assertiveness to communicate feelings and thoughts in a socially acceptable manner (Table 6.2).

6.11.1 Session 1: Psychoeducation: Understanding Anger

This session would focus on increasing understanding about anger. All of us experience anger. Anger is often a sign that indicates that something is not right. If we feel something wrong is happening, we may feel angry. Anger can lead to difficulties in handling interpersonal relationships, health related problems, declining work performance, and difficulties with law.

6.11.1.1 Anger Effects the Body

When people feel anger they may notice some of the following effects on their body:

- Muscular tension
- Faster breathing
- Dilation of pupil
- Sweating

6.11.1.2 Anger Effects Behavior

Angry behaviors are often the signs that are noticed. Some angry behaviors could be as follows:

- Hitting
- Screaming

- Throwing items
- Clenching fists
- Self-harm

6.11.1.3 Anger Effects Thought Process

It is actually not the situation itself that makes us feel angry, rather it is the way that a person appraises a situation that causes anger. For example,

- He is so jealous of my success.
- He always tries to make me feel like a fool.
- I hate this world.
- My teacher is biased.

6.11.1.4 Homework Assignment 1: Breaking up the Anger

Think about the times when you felt angry and give your responses to the following

How was your body effected	What types of thoughts come to your mind	How do you react when you get angry
.	.	.
.	.	.
.	.	.

6.11.1.5 Triggers for Anger

Anger is an emotional reaction to events or things which happen around us. Following are some of the main triggers which can cause anger (Fig. 6.1).

Now, let us see how a trigger can generate anger in a specific situation.

> Sarita, 17-years-old girl, had been on at her younger sister all day to arrange and clean her room and she kept saying she would do it in a minute or a bit later. Early in the evening, Sarita found her sister sitting in front of dressing table mirror just trying a new hairstyle. She saw her sister as deliberately provoking her saying "what are you going to do about it then?" (annoyance).
>
> She had felt stressed all day. When she saw her sister in front of the mirror, she completely lost her wits and she could feel her fists clench and her voice got louder. These changes happened in the space of a couple of minutes. She thought "my sister is completely useless, she has got no respect for me" She shouted and screamed at her sister for around 20 min. Later, her sister cleaned her room.

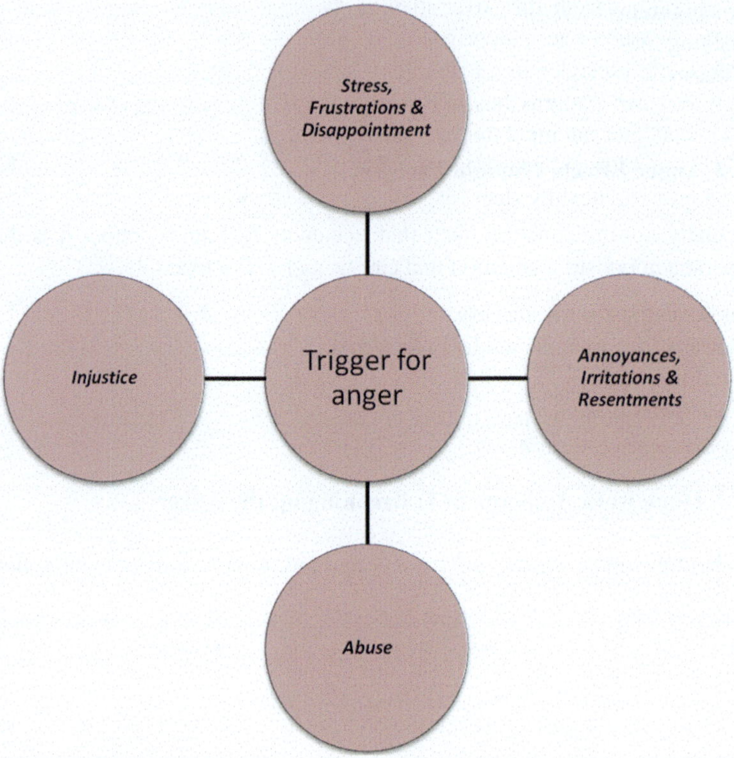

Fig. 6.1 Types of anger triggers

Here, the younger sister not doing her tasks is the trigger for Sarita's anger, and it was followed by the angry thought in Sarita's mind that her sister does not respect her she completely lost her temper, she clenched her fist and screamed louder and expressed her anger.

6.11.1.6 Homework Assignment 2: Getting to Know Your Anger Triggers

Think about what sort of things generate your anger and write them down.

- Particular place
- Certain people
- What really gets their anger going

6.11.2 *Session 2: Early Warning Signs and Quick Anger Control*

Recognizing when we get angry is the first important step in managing of our anger. This can be done easily by noticing the bodily sensations linked with anger.

6.11.2.1 Bodily Sensations

When we get angry, our body also reacts. These bodily sensations include feeling tension in muscles, sweating, and breathing faster. These sensations are a reaction to stressful condition and technically it is called "fight–flight response". A number of physical reactions occur when body goes into fight–flight, these include:

- Faster breathing
- Dilation of pupils
- Sweating

Anger Thermometer: Keeping a track of anger on an anger thermometer can be a useful way of measuring anger. Consider the following (Fig. 6.2).

When there is a change in our feelings, it goes up and down on the thermometer. It is not possible to jump from 0° to 100° without going through all the other temperatures. It is the same with anger, anger is also not an all or nothing emotion, and we move gradually upwards on the scale before we reach the top. Thus, when thinking about anger control, a person will need to do something before he gets "too hot" and go too far up the thermometer.

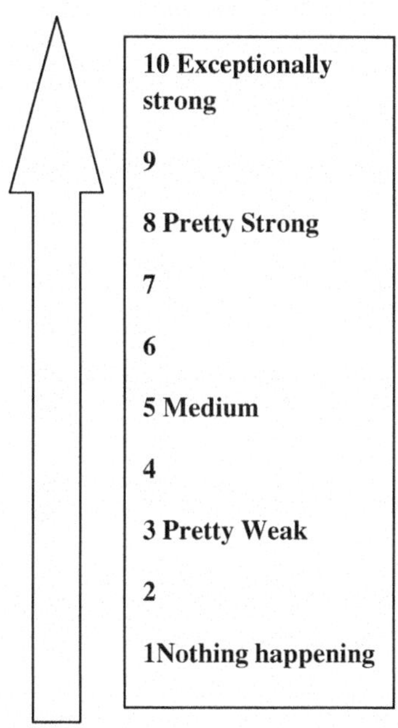

Fig. 6.2 Anger thermometer

6.11.3 Stop, Think, Go

The aim of this section is to learn and understand how one can act thoughtfully rather than reacting without thinking.

6.11.3.1 Time-Out

The principle behind this strategy is that all of us need time to think about what we are going to do to stop ourselves getting angry. Ways in which a person might buy himself some time include the following:

- Walk away
- Count to ten
- Distract
- Keep quiet/bite their tongue

6.11.3.2 Deep Breathing

Deep breathing is a quick way to calm the body. When we are stressed, our breathing becomes faster and shallower that results in increasing the effects of stress on our body. Calming down the breathing can help to control arousal levels of body quickly.

How to Practice Deep Breathing
See Annexure for detail.

6.11.4 Session 3: Strategies to Manage Anger

Anger is not always inevitable, and people can probably think of some instances which were anger arousing, but for some reason, they did not show their anger. There can be a number of reasons for not reacting angrily. One possible reason might be that they anticipated that the costs of getting angry would be too high. Another reason that people might not get angry could be that they use a strategy to manage their anger. For example,

Tanya
Tanya was really angry when she was standing in a queue to buy movie tickets. Someone had pushed her aside to get to the tickets and she was thinking "how rude, have they no manners". She realized she was beginning to boil and decided to walk away and count to 10.

6.11.4.1 Homework Assignment 1: Are There Things that You Already Do?

The strategies described in this session are research-based and are tried and tested and are very helpful in having a quick control on anger. Clients need to persevere, practise, and plan to get the best results from them. These ideas may be probably not new to the clients, and they are not the only way to stop or reduce their anger. They may already be doing other things that help. This session we will consider the following issues and strategies:

1. Positive self-talk
2. Frustration tolerance
3. Reducing venting
4. Controlling unhealthy rumination
5. Problem solving

Positive Self Talk

It is not necessary that all people get angry. Two people in the situation may not both get angry; the difference lies in how they think about the situation.

Example Your friends do not pass a smile to you when they see you in party. You think:

1. How rude, they must be deliberately ignoring me

or

2. I guess they did not see me; they seemed to be looking the other way.

The person who had the first thought is likely to get angry, while the person who had the second thought is more likely to stay calm. Thus, how we think can decide whether we get angry or not.

It may not be easy to identify the thoughts, but it can help to see them as "self talk". This is a normal thing to do, and it can be really helpful to think of "positive" thoughts. People can use "positive self talk" and it can help when they are facing a difficult situation in which they might express their anger, to get through the situation, or after the difficult situation, to review what they did. Here are some examples of calming "positive self talk".

- I should not take this too seriously.
- By getting angry, I will just be wasting my energy.
- Things could have been even worse.

6.11.4.2 Homework Assignment 2: My Calming "Positive Self Talk" Statements

Think of some calming "positive self talks" and write them down in the given space

…………………………………………………………………………………………

…………………………………………………………………………………………

…………………………………………………………………………………………

Frustration Tolerance

Frustration tolerance is the ability to continue staying in a balanced, healthy life despite facing repeated interferences. It refers to how strong we are to encounter life's stressors and challenges. Increasing tolerance for frustration is helpful to live with normal levels of annoyance. High frustration tolerance is helpful in developing more effective problem-solving skills. Example of high frustration tolerance statement:

- "This situation is difficult to bear but I can bear it"

What can be done to tolerate frustration?

- Knowing the causes for this frustration
- Knowing ourselves—unrealistic expectations and beliefs
- Accepting that we have a problem to solve
- Follow problem-solving routine
- Setting realistic and achievable goals for ourselves and others
- Communicating more effectively

Venting

Venting means letting out pent-up feelings of anger. When people vent out their anger, they often feel better immediately afterward, but not long after venting their anger, most people report having feelings of regret, guilt, shame, or sadness for the damage that they caused another person. Originally, venting was considered to be healthy and helpful for minimizing anger problems. However, recent researches have indicated that venting is not always healthy because it increases the possibilities of further anger in the future.

Reducing Venting

The following method would be helpful to express the anger in a healthy way:

1. Recognize the angry feelings
   - "I am angry because …"
2. Calm down (relaxation, self-talk, etc.)

3. Think:
   - Is it relevant or irrelevant?
   - If it is relevant, can it be controlled?
   - If it is relevant and can be controlled, are there procedures that are necessary to implement the actions?
   - If the incident is not relevant, dismiss it and move on to other more relevant and healthy issues.

Rumination

The word "ruminate" is taken from the Latin for chewing cud, in which cows grind up, swallow, then regurgitate, and re-chew their feed. People also mentally ruminate in the same way. Instead of bringing food back up and chewing it again, we bring thoughts into our mind (memories, imagined events), and chew them over and over again. Rumination is not good for mental health. Ruminating can lead to anxiety, depression, and anger. Rumination can also impair thinking, motivation, concentration, memory, and problem-solving skills. Anger rumination focuses on angry memories, thoughts of revenge, angry afterthoughts, and understanding of causes. In ruminative anger, cortisol and adrenalin levels increase as part of the fight-or-flight system. However, if the person does not run or fight, the cortisol and adrenalin stay in the body affecting the immune system, sleep, and emotional well-being.

Strategies for Managing Unhealthy Rumination

Whenever one starts to ruminate over something that makes him feel angry, he should recognize and accept to himself that he is ruminating, and then,

1. **Say to yourself** "stop ruminating"
2. **Calm yourself** by breathing, relaxation, or meditation.
3. **Question** yourself the purpose and advantages of ruminating:
   - Is it going to help me?
   - Would I ever advise someone to think in this way?
   - Am I looking at the incident from all dimensions?
   - Is it really a very important matter?
4. **Challenge** statements and questions:
   - Maybe I have misunderstood the situation
   - Am I sure about not overlooking some aspects?
   - How it is going to affect my health?

Problem-Solving Procedure

We may show anger when we are faced with various problems. The belief that the problems can be solved increases the chances of success. Using the problem solving skills, clients would learn to stop their anger becoming into something unmanageable.

Step by Step Problem Solving

1: What's bothering me ⟶ **2**: How does it make me feel ⟶ 3.Calm down

Now think

4 :Is this really need dealing with

↙ ↘

If Yes	**If No**
✓ This is just a problem to solve ✓ Blaming others does not solve it **Blaming is inflaming**	✓ It's not worth getting angry over. ✓ I deserve to keep myself calm! ✓ Remove yourself ☺ **Be Calm**

5: What do I want -Be specific. Be realistic

↓

6: What can I do ***Solution A, B, C***

↓

7: Consider the consequences of solutions A, B and C

↓

8: Take decision ⟶ 9: Execute ⟶ 10: Look how effective it is

6.11.5 Session 4: Communication Skill

The way we communicate with others can make a difference to the responses that we get from others. There are four main types of communication styles. All of us use all four of them at different times and in different situations as per the demand, but sometimes people get stuck in one style.

These communication styles are often defined as follows:

1. **Passive**—"Door mat" agreeing or saying nothing but boiling inside, people pleasing.
2. **Aggressive**—Forcing our opinion on others—making YOU statements, making the other person feel bad about holding a particular opinion and intimidating others with their opinion.

3. **Passive–Aggressive**—Being angry but never really being specific about what they are angry about. We may recognize this in the person who makes us feel bad about something with a smile on their face.
4. **Assertive**—Many people have never really learned or practiced how to be assertive. Often, it is confused with being aggressive, but it is very different. One way to understand assertive communication is that it is about expressing our own: *Feelings, Needs, Rights, and Opinions* and helping others to understand them. By being assertive:

    - We can listen and be open to new points of view
    - We will show that we care about the effect our communication has on others.
    - We are likely to reduce our own stress and frustration
    - Others are more likely to listen to us.

Being assertive is being able to outline the situation objectively, that is, to note the things we see, hear, or notice. We need to recognize our own feelings and let the other person know how their behavior has affected us without making the other person defensive. When describing feelings, it is helpful to use "I feel" language rather than saying "they make me feel". We must tell the other person what we want. Some ways in which we can make requests more effective are:

- Request should be specific.
- Request should be doable.
- One request should be made at a time.

6.11.6 Coping with Criticism

Receiving criticism is often difficult and it can make us feel angry. Instead of getting angry, one should find a way of dealing with it. It is important to stop any attack; we need to find out whether the criticism is justified or unjustified. Then, we should use anger management strategies.

If the criticism is justified:	*If the criticism is unjustified*:
	• Politely but firmly disagree
• Agree and admit to the mistakes	• Give an explanation, if needed
• Explain the reasons if you wish	• Ask what makes them think that
• Apologize if necessary	• Express how you felt—upset, etc.

6.11.7 Session 5: Cognitive Restructuring: Challenging Angry Thoughts and Beliefs

6.11.7.1 Our Thoughts Affect Our Anger

In order to understand anger, we need to pay attention to our thoughts. The reason for this is explained in the following sentence:

How we think directly affects how we feel

6.11.7.2 Homework Assignment 1: Do You Agree with This Statement? Why?

....

....

Anger is a feeling, our thoughts affect our anger, because

1. Our *appraisal* about things is directly related to our mood and feelings.
2. Change in one can change the other.
3. Learning how to pay attention to thoughts and beliefs can help in changing anger and its expression.

People have more of a choice about how they think and feel than they sometimes realize. This session will explain why this is so and how we can learn to stop automatic ways of thinking and behaving and help us pick alternative ways, in order to help us better manage our feelings of anger (Fig. 6.3).

6.11.7.3 Homework Assignment 2: Try to Recollect in Your Mind the Last Time You Remember Feeling Angry

I was thinking	I felt	I behaved
.	.	.

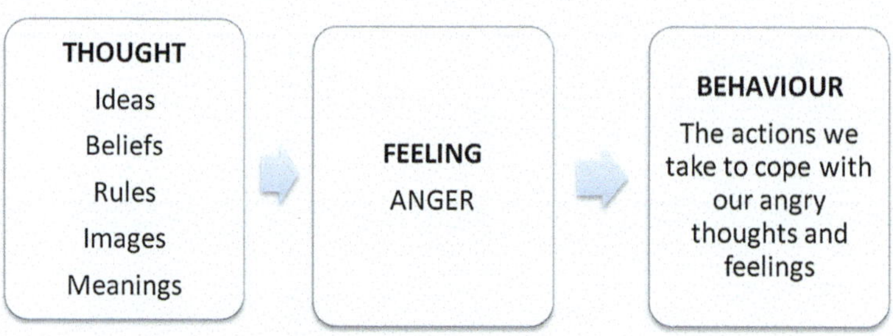

Fig. 6.3 Thoughts lead to angry behaviors

6.11.7.4 Behavioral Analysis: Learning Our ABCs for Anger

Anger is not caused by an event itself, rather it stems from how we *think* about those events. The same situation can deliver different meaning for different people at different times. To understand this, consider our ABCs:

Anger Trigger → **B**elief → **C**onsequence

Writing down the problem in ABC form can help to work in differentiating between the thoughts, feelings, and behaviors.

A is the anger trigger. These are the facts in the situation or event which make us feel angry. This could be a real event that has occurred in the outside world (such as someone verbally abusing) or an event that is inside the mind such as an image, sensation, or memory (remembering about a time when someone ridiculed us).

B is the beliefs. The beliefs include our thoughts and the meanings that we attach to the external and internal events (the triggers). It is important to note here that B comes in between A and C.

C is the consequences. Consequences can include the feelings (anger), physical sensations that accompany the angry feelings, and the behaviors (the actions we take to cope with the feelings). Anger may be only one of many feelings that we feel.

We cannot stop thoughts coming into our mind. However, developing a really clear ABC of the problem can make it much easier for us to realize how our thoughts at "B" lead to our emotional and behavioral responses at "C".

6.11.8 ABC Form—Example

Anger trigger	Belief	Consequence
Write down what triggered your feelings (it could be an outside event or something inside their mind)	Write down the thoughts and beliefs that went through your mind	Write down (a) your feelings and (b) what you did as a result (your actions and behaviors)
Someone jumping in front of me in the ticket counter queue	*That is not fair*	*Anger (feeling)*
		Irritation (feeling)
		Gave them an angry look (action)
Friend is not returning book when I asked twice	*He is taking my advantage*	*Anger (feeling)*
		Frustration (feeling)
		Shouted at him (action)

6.12 Some Common Themes in Angry Thoughts

When many different angry thoughts come to our minds, there are common themes when it comes to anger that one may be able to recognize in themselves. For example, we get angry in situations where we believe that

- We are being **threatened**
- An **injustice has been done**

- Something or someone has **prevented us from doing something we want to do**
- Someone has **attacked or criticized us** at a personal level
- Someone has **violated or broken a rule** which is important to us

In such situations, common thoughts that can make us angry include the following:

- People would take me for a ride
- This is dangerous
- This is unfair
- They are completely wrong
- They can not bully
- That is not correct way to do
- They can not do that with me

In all problematic situations, anger can be a very natural human response. Often we get angry not so much because of the event itself, but to our individual reaction for it. At times, we may even feel that our anger is completely justified. Difficulties can come when we start to respond automatically to our angry triggers, which means we are limiting our options.

6.12.1 Strategies for Changing Our Automatic Responses

Following are some strategies one can use in order to help in managing anger through controlling the automatic responses:

1. Increase self-awareness—get to know yourself better (using ABC forms)
2. Recognize most unhelpful thoughts
3. Challenge these thoughts
4. Discover more helpful strategies

6.13 Self-awareness

It is not the event that makes us angry, but how we appraise the event and what meaning we give to the event. For example, if something bad happens, and we take it personally, it is likely to trigger our anger. In order to understand our thoughts, we need to understand our feelings first. In order to do this, it is helpful to keep a simple diary of anger incidents including ABC form.

6.14 Recognize the Most Unhelpful Thoughts

Below, some of the common unhelpful patterns in anger are described (Table 6.3).

Table 6.3 Unhelpful thoughts behind anger

Type	Description	Example
All or nothing thinking	Categorizing things or event into clear-cut black and white with no shades of gray in between	*"It's all going totally against me"*
Jumping to conclusions	Guessing about results with out any facts to support for assumption	*"She hates me, so much for her friendship"*
Should' statements	Rigid forms of thinking that leads to feelings anger	*"I must never forget the way he insulted me"*
Blaming	Holding ourselves or others responsible for something that happened that was out of our control	*"I got angry because they messed up today"*
Labelling	Very quickly giving ourselves or others a negative label	*"He is irritating"*
Overgeneralization	Generalizing a single event as part of a regular and universal pattern	*"That's it, I'm always unlucky"*
Magnification	When an individual exaggerates the importance of the problem	*"How terrible, I've got no clothes to wear for the evening party, this is the end!"*
Emotional reasoning	When emotion is taken as an evidence for the truth	*"I feel angry, that proves that my friend must have treated me badly"*

6.15 Challenge the Unhelpful Thoughts

Our angry thoughts are often inaccurate and unrealistic because we mistakenly see the situation being thought of as threatening.

D here stands for Dispute. We need to challenge our unhelpful thinking by questioning and disputing our thoughts. We can do this by asking ourselves certain questions. When we lose our sense of looking to perspective in a holistic way, we often feel angry. Learning to see things differently can be helpful. All of us tend look at the world through our own pair of glasses. It can be helpful in preventing anger if we are able to see someone else's point of view. One easiest way of doing this is to ***put ourselves in the other person's shoes.*** Alternatively, we can try and keep things in perspective, by seeing the bigger and whole picture. The most handy strategy for managing anger is to ***keep a sense of humor***. It can help to be able to take a step back and see things in proportion. When trying to challenge our unhelpful thoughts, asking ourselves the following questions can be helpful.

Key questions we can ask ourselves:

- Is there another way to look at this particular event?
- What would someone else do if given the same situation?

- What is the worst thing that could happen?
- Am I right to think on these lines?
- How important it is here to give a reaction?

6.16 Helpful Strategies: Coping by Self Talk

Thinking affects our feelings through our self talk. Unhelpful thoughts can add fuel to the fire and play a large role in keeping anger going after the event has passed. However, using helpful self-statements (or "cooling thoughts") can be a good way to manage our anger and guide our behavior. Examples of these include the following:

- Calm down
- Breathe out anger
- Do not give others the satisfaction of seeing you angry
- Listen your favorite music

6.16.1 Session 6: Review and Challenge of Maintaining the Change

This session is dedicated in revising whatever learnt in previous sessions. Anger can be understood by thinking of its effects on body, thought processes and action. Anger is usually set off by obstacles, a sense of injustice, or feeling abused. At times, anger can be helpful, but often, anger can cause problems. In previous sessions, we looked at ways in which we might begin to manage the anger. We talked about problem solving and assertiveness. We also talked about anger triggers. There are also more general things that can make anger worse. These things can often be hidden and can be more difficult to notice than "immediate triggers". However, it can be difficult to control anger if we are not aware of what may be behind it.

The sort of things that might be behind the anger and need to be seriously addressed include the following:

- Poor sleep
- Relationships
- Stress, depression, anxiety, trauma, and bereavement
- Living con+ditions.

6.16.1.1 Barriers to Change

There are a number of obstacles to achieving the goals, and it is important to think how we might respond to them. Some common barriers are as follows:

1. **Non-acceptance and denial**—Denying anger as a problem is the first barrier. Many people do not even expect that their unmanaged anger is a problem with them; they approach to a counselor because people around them for example their parents, friends, and school teacher suggest them for this. Many respond that they do not have a problem and that it is someone else's fault or responsibility. These adolescents are in denial, and this attitude can be a barrier to the process of anger management. Also, since change will not occur without motivation and denial for need of change adversely impacts the level of motivation. Individuals change when there is motivation to change and when they have an understanding of who they are.

2. **Myths about anger**—Certain myths related to anger create an obstacle toward the direction of anger control and management. Some common myths are the following:

- **Anger is inherited**: The commonly existing myth about anger is that the way a person express anger is inherited and cannot be changed, and expression of anger is fixed and unalterable.
- **Anger symbolizes power**: This is common misconception that only powerful person can show anger and aggression through anger; one can get respect from people. Such attitude creates a barrier in anger management because adolescents consider that if they control their anger they will lose their powerful image among their peer group.

6.17 Conclusion

Anger is just like any other emotion. The aim of anger management program is not to make anger go away rather to help the person to express anger in a healthy way. Changes in one's thought process can help to control anger. For adolescents, anger management becomes very important as they need to develop coping skills like anger management to meet the challenges of their developmental phase. Anger management training typically involves providing information on the cognitive and behavioral components of anger, teaching cognitive, and behavioral techniques to manage anger and encouraging the application of newly learned skills in the real-world setting. Cognitive behavioral techniques attempt to intervene with cognitive, emotional, and physiological components of anger. Specifically, cognitive–behavioral interventions designed to address anger may include one or more of the following: self-awareness training, relaxation techniques, cognitive therapy, and conflict management skill training.

References

Averill, J. R. (1983). Studies on anger and aggression: Implications for theories of emotion. *American Psychologist, 38*(11), 1145–1159.

Blake, C. S., & Hamrin, V. (2007). Current approaches to the assessment and management of anger and aggression in youth: a review. *Journal of Child and Adolescent Psychiatric Nursing, 20*, 209–221.

Burney, D.M. (2001). Adolescent anger rating scale: professional manual. Psychological assessment resources. Lutz, Florida.

Coie, J. D., Lochman, J. E., Terry R, & Hyman, C. (1992). Predicting early adolescent disorder from childhood aggression and peer rejection. *Journal of Consulting and Clinical Psychology, 60*, 783–792 (American Psychological Association, Inc.).

Deffenbacher, J. L. (1999). Cognitive-behavior conceptualization and treatment of anger. *In Session: Psychotherapy in Practice, 55*(3), 295–309.

Dodge, K. A., & Coie, J. D. (1987). Social-information-processing factors in reactive and proactive aggression in children's peer groups. *Journal of Personality and Social Psychology, 53*, 1146–1158.

Kazdin, A. E. (1987). Treatment of antisocial behavior in children: Current status and future directions. *Source Psychological Bulletin, 102*, 187–203 (American Psychological association, US).

Nelson, W.M., Hart, K.J., & Finch, A.J. (1993). Anger in Children: A Cognitive behavioral view of assessment -therapy connection. *Journal of Rational-Emotive and Cognitive Behavior, 11*, 135–150.

Peterson, A. C., & Hamburg, B. A. (1986). Adolescent: A developmental approach to problem and psychopathology. *Behaviour Therapy, 17*, 480–499.

Sharkin, B.S. & Gelso, C.J. (1991). The Anger Discomfort Scale: Beginning reliability and validity data. *Measurement and evaluation in Counselling and Development, 24*,61–68.

Siegel, J.M. (1986). The Multidimensional Anger Inventory. *Journal of Personality and Social Psychology, 5*(1), 191–200.

Sigfusdottir, I., et al. (2004). The role of depressed mood and anger in the relationship between family conflict and delinquent behavior. *Journal of Youth and Adolescence, 33*(6), 509–522.

Smith, D.C., Furlong, M., Bates, M., & Laughlin, J. (1998). Development of multidimensional school anger inventory for males. *Psychology in Schools, 35*(1), 1–15.

Spielberger, C. D. (1983). State-trait anger expression inventory. Orlando, FL: Psychological Assessment Resources.

Spielberger, C. D. (1999). STAXI-2 State-Trait Anger ExpressionInventory-2: Professional manual. Lutz, FL: Psychological Assessment Resources.

Spielberger, C. D., Jacobs, G. A., Russell, S., & Crane, R. S. (1985). Assessment of anger: The State-trait anger scale. In J. N. Butcher & C. D. Spielberger (Eds.), *Advance in personality assessment* (Vol. 2, pp. 161–189). Hillsdale, NJ: Lawrence Erlbaum.

Chapter 7
Management of Sleep Problems

Angela Ann Joseph, Manju Mehta and Garima Shukla

I love sleep. My life has a tendency to fall apart when I am awake.

—Ernest Hemingway

7.1 Introduction

As Hemingway would agree, sleep is a precious gift during which there is a temporary escape from the adversities of the day. One can appreciate the value of sleep only when one is deprived of it. Sleep problems are predominant today with our hectic lifestyles in a technology-driven world. Insufficient sleep coupled with erratic sleep patterns has unfortunately become widespread among adolescents. This chapter attempts to elucidate some of the factors that influence adolescent sleep struggles and provides cognitive behavioural interventions to ameliorate them and promote healthy sleep.

A.A. Joseph (✉) · M. Mehta
Department of Psychiatry, All India Institute of Medical Sciences, New Delhi, India
e-mail: joseph.angela12@gmail.com

M. Mehta
e-mail: drmanju.mehta@gmail.com

G. Shukla
Department of Neurology, All India Institute of Medical Sciences, New Delhi, India
e-mail: garimashukla@hotmail.com

M. Mehta and R. Sagar (eds.), *A Practical Approach to Cognitive Behaviour Therapy for Adolescents*, DOI 10.1007/978-81-322-2241-5_7

7.1.1 What Is Sleep?

Like hunger and thirst, sleep is a basic drive of nature which provides nourishment and replenishes the brain (National Sleep Foundation 2000). An old Irish proverb states, "*A good laugh and a long sleep are the best cures in the doctor's book*". According to the behavioural definition of sleep, it is a reversible state that is characterized by reduced physical activity, stereotypical posture and reduced response to stimulation (Cauter 2012). Sleep may also be defined as a natural and periodic state of rest during which the consciousness of the world is suspended. It is an active process where body and mind are allowed to rest and become restored (Spriggs 2010).

7.1.2 Consequences of Sleep Deprivation

Studies conducted by Dr. William Dement a leading researcher on sleep deprivation have revealed that increased sleep debt is directly correlated with increased adverse effects, including daytime sleepiness, poor performance, lack of concentration and multiple health problems (Dement 1999). Other potentially harmful effects of chronic sleep deprivation are difficulty waking in the morning, irritability, lack of motivation and impulsivity (Spriggs 2010). A survey conducted by Dr. Xianchen Liu in China demonstrated the association between short sleep duration, nightmares and suicidal behaviour among adolescents (Liu 2004). Apart from the above-mentioned other neurobehavioral consequences of sleep deprivation include impairment in memory consolidation, diminished creative thinking and verbal fluency (Kotagal and Pianosi 2006).

Longitudinal studies by Agras et al. (2004), Reilly et al. (2005), Sugimori et al. (2004) have documented that shorter sleep predicts the later emergence of overweight (as cited in Beebe et al. 2007). Several hormones are secreted at night during sleep. When sleep patterns are disrupted, there is imbalance in hormonal secretion that accompanies the same. Poor sleep is related to increase in levels of cortisol which is known as a "stress hormone". Other hormones that are affected by poor sleep include Leptin and Grehlin. Leptin is a hormone that tells the brain to stop eating; it is responsible for generating feelings of satiety. In contrast, Grehlin provides hunger signals to the brain, making the person eat more. Sleep deprivation decreases the level of Leptin and increases the level of Grehlin such that it maximally pushes a person's appetite. This effect usually takes the form of binge eating at night when most often carbohydrate and sugar-rich foods are targeted.

Insulin is yet another hormone that is affected by poor sleep; it regulates glucose processing and fat storage. Inadequate sleep is linked to increase in insulin production after eating. Higher levels of insulin can also lead to weight gain which in turn is a risk factor for diabetes. Poor sleep also slows down glucose processing and studies have shown that getting less than 5 h of sleep at night is associated with the likelihood of developing diabetes later. Studies conducted by De La Eva et al. (2002) and Amin et al. (2005) have shown that similar to excessive weight, obstructive sleep apnoea and inadequate sleep share a causal relationship with insulin resistance and cardiovascular disease (as cited in Beebe et al. 2007).

People with hypertension who have insufficient sleep at night experience elevated blood pressure throughout the next day. Those affected with sleep apnoea experience multiple awakenings due to the closing of their airway during sleep. These multiple awakenings are also associated with increase in blood pressure. Over time, the cumulative effect of multiple awakenings leads to chronic elevation in blood pressure known as hypertension which is a major risk factor for cardiovascular disease (Harvard Medical School 2007).

When a person is suffering from an infection, the immune system produces antibodies to help fight infection. These antibodies also cause fatigue due to which most people prefer to sleep when they are sick. It is believed that the immune system evolved "sleep-inducing factors" because inactivity and sleep provides an added benefit. The benefit being that those who sleep better and sleep more are able to fight infection better than those who sleep less. It has also been noted in several animal and human research studies, the lack of sleep has been associated with lower white blood cell count (Harvard Medical School 2007).

7.2 Adolescent Sleep Struggles

In a 6-year longitudinal sleep laboratory study by Carskadon and colleagues (1980), total sleep time was held constant at 10 h in children within the age group of 10, 11 and 12 years during the initial 3-night assessment. The researchers hypothesized that by the time the participants enter their late teenage years, the young adolescents would sleep less and their total sleep time would decline to 7.5–8 h per night similar to what is observed in normal adults. Much to their surprise, they found that sleep quantity remained consistent at approximately 9.2 h across all pubertal stages. Contrary to popular belief that adolescents have a decreased need for sleep, sleep laboratory findings have brought to light the fact that adolescents need as much sleep as their younger counterparts. Despite this finding, research studies carried out by Allen (1992), Carskadon et al. (1982), and Williams et al. (1974) have shown that adolescents typically get much less sleep than pre-adolescents, the difference being 10 h during mid-childhood versus 7.5–8 h by age 16 (as cited in Wolfson and Carskadon 1998).

Most parents of adolescents wonder why it is so difficult for adolescents to fall asleep at night and why it is even harder to wake them up in the morning. Several factors play a strong part in keeping the adolescent awake for longer hours at night which is responsible for curbing their sleep time. As a child enters adolescence, parental involvement in bedtime routines decreases, but they are increasingly involved in waking them up since most often adolescents find it difficult wake up on their own. Late bedtime is the major culprit to be blamed for difficulty waking up in the morning. This finding is not surprising since the transition from childhood to adolescence is accompanied with a change in sleeping patterns.

The emergence of multiple social networking sites, smart phones and electronic gadgets with interactive media makes it difficult to retreat to bed because there is always one more post to "like" if not one more message to "tweet" and you can never really check your inbox enough times a day! Engaging in these stimulating but at the same time distracting activities during bedtime is highly incompatible with sleep. On the other hand, these digital devices emit blue radiation (light is a powerful zeitgeber) which dupes the brain into believing that it is not yet time to go to sleep and prevents sleep onset. However this alone is not responsible for late bedtimes, increased academic workload, social pressures and extra-curricular activities exert a heavy time crunch on adolescents. In their desperate attempt to try and fit everything in their daily schedule, sleep often takes a back seat. Apart from the above-mentioned factors, a circadian delay in the secretion of melatonin (sleep-inducing hormone whose levels peak just before sleep onset) is associated with the onset of puberty which makes it difficult for adolescents to fall asleep before 10:30 p.m. (Carskadon et al. 1998; Kotagal and Pianosi 2006).

As evident, a multitude of factors that include environmental, behavioural and biological factors are accountable for later bedtimes observed among adolescents. Given this delay in sleep onset and early wake up times as per existing school schedules, many adolescents are sleep deprived. This sleep deprivation keeps piling up during the week resulting in an accumulation of sleep debt. When the weekend arrives, both bedtime and wake up times are shifted even further, with adolescents sleeping later at night and waking up later in the morning. The average total sleep time over the weekend then exceeds that during the week. While waking up later can be attributed to the body's way of recovering from the sleep debt that was accumulated over the week, going to bed later on weekends could be due to attending social gatherings/parties and consumption of recreational drinks or caffeinated products that delay sleep onset.

It has been documented by Bearpark and Michie (1987), Petta et al. (1984) and Strauch and Meier (1986) that weekend total sleep times average 30–60 min more than school night sleep times in 10–14 years olds and this difference increased to over 2 h by 18 years of age (as cited in Wolfson and Carskadon 1998). Irregular week/weekend sleep schedules with a difference of over 90 min in total sleep time during the week as opposed to weekends has been associated with negative implications which include impaired academic performance, depressed mood and risk for substance abuse (Wolfson 2012). The predicament that follows after binge sleeping during the weekend is that on Sunday night adolescents find it difficult to fall asleep since they overslept on Sunday morning. This results in reinforcement of the circadian delay which leads to problems in initiating sleep. As wake up time is restricted by the time at which school commences, it is apparent that the teen has had inadequate sleep. Inadequate sleep is associated with excessive daytime sleepiness and has implications on the academic functioning and mood. It is associated with depressed mood, irritability, poor memory, attention and concentration (Colten and Altevogt 2006; Kotagal and Pianosi 2006). Carskadon and her colleagues (1980) demonstrated as part of the same longitudinal study that was mentioned previously, that even when nocturnal sleep amount did not decline as compared to their younger peers, adolescent's midday sleepiness increased significantly and remained at that level as measured on the multiple sleep latency

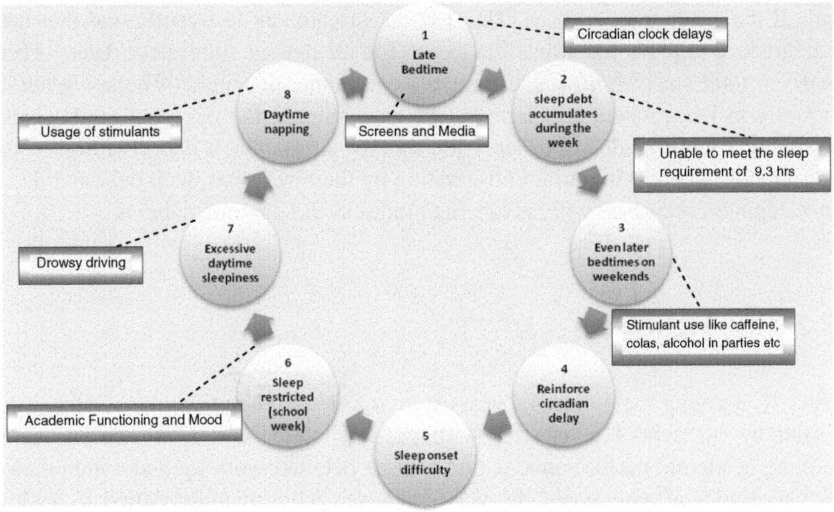

Fig. 7.1 The vicious cycle of adolescent sleep

test that measures excessive daytime sleepiness (EDS). Problems with daytime sleepiness can be potentially dangerous if the adolescent commutes long distances and experiences drowsiness while driving which can lead to impaired judgement thereby cumulating in unfortunate circumstances. When the drive to sleep becomes overbearing and relentless, most teens resort to afternoon napping if circumstances permit or try to counteract drowsiness by consuming caffeinated products and high energy drinks (such as Red Bull) during late afternoon and early evening hours. Caffeine is a stimulant and its effects are still present long after it has been consumed making it all the more difficult to fall asleep at night the consequence of which are late bedtimes and thus the vicious cycle repeats its course (Fig. 7.1).

7.2.1 Adolescent Sleep Research in India

Sleep patterns of 1920 urban school going adolescents were studied using a sleep habits questionnaire by Bhatia and colleagues (2008). The average age of the participants was 15.1 years and average total sleep time of 7.8 h per day which is much less than the optimal sleep requirement for adolescents. About 41.5 % of the participants went to bed by 11 p.m. and 42.6 % had to wake up by 5:00–6:00 a.m. which shows a similar trend of late bedtime and early rise times as their western peers. Although sleep efficiency was reported to be 92.6 %, only less than half the sample reported that they received refreshing sleep. Another finding that was consistent with the Western literature was that the total sleep time decreased with higher classes and sleep duration of the ninth graders was significantly higher from all the other three classes. This led the researchers to hypothesize that the tenth grade could be the transition point for change in total sleep time. This change in total sleep time was attributed to academic demands of higher grades, especially in India where adolescents face academic challenges from ninth grade onwards and tenth grade is probably the time of stress which is not witnessed in lower grades. Another important observation by them was that sleep debt and daytime sleepiness increased with advancing grades as did daytime napping.

7.2.2 Case Vignette

Master K, a young male aged 14 years studying in an urban school in Delhi, was referred by his school counsellor with primary complaints of inattention and declining academic performance. Upon routine detailed work up and comprehensive psychological assessment, he was diagnosed with attention deficit hyperactivity disorder predominantly inattentive subtype. His parents revealed that apart from difficulties in concentration their son also found it difficult to stay awake in class. This was reported by his teachers during the last PTA meeting that his parents attended. Moreover, his parents also reported that he went to sleep late and had difficulty waking up in the morning and almost always woke up with a negative mood. Sleep history and physical examination revealed no history of snoring, normal BMI, no history of RLS and no history of narcolepsy. Sleep log and actigraphy data revealed erratic sleep–wake patterns with a total time difference of more than 90 min of weekend versus weekdays sleep schedule. The average total sleep time was found to be 7 h for the two-week period during which sleep log and actigraphy data were recorded. Master K revealed that he often took a long time to feel alert in the morning, experienced fatigue and fell asleep in the school bus while travelling to the school. At times when his schedule permits he would also take a nap in the afternoon. Upon administration of adolescent sleep hygiene questionnaire, it was found that Master K had maladaptive sleep habits. These maladaptive habits included irregular/late bedtime, watching TV and instant messaging at bedtime, sleeping with his pet dog and a high intake of caffeinated drinks during the day. Paediatric sleepiness scale was also administered and the scores obtained were indicative of excessive daytime sleepiness. Master K's insufficient sleep was fuelled by his maladaptive sleep habits. Therefore, the cognitive rationale for treatment focussed on the need for sleep education and the role of faulty sleep habits in sustaining sleep difficulties. The treatment regimen consisted of sleep education, sleep hygiene and stimulus control. Initially, master K found it difficult to apply the sleep hygiene rules since he was involved with too many after school activities and found it difficult to manage school work, tuitions and after schools extra-curricular activities. Apart from that it was difficult for him to refrain from spending long hours texting/instant messaging at night as his close peer group would be online during those hours sending him messages. Moreover, he shared a bedroom with his brother who would also stay up late at night playing video games and surfing the net. Follow-up sessions were used to discuss these issues and the sleep hygiene rules were discussed with master K and his sibling. Time management was also discussed with master K and reorganization of extra-curricular activities with an attempt at taking on only so many activities that could neatly fit in his schedule without overburdening him was encouraged. Master K was also taught assertiveness skills such that he could effectively encounter peer pressure of not engaging in social media networking past bedtime. A sleep log was maintained throughout the whole treatment regimen to review his progress. Slowly but steadily there was a change in the average total sleep time which increased to about 9 h which is considered optimal for his age. Master K was also asked to write down the positive changes that he experienced during his daytime functioning as a result of adopting healthy sleep habits. Among the positive changes, he reported less trouble getting out of bed in the morning, feeling refreshed on waking up and not feeling drowsy during the day. He also reported being more alert in class and there were no teacher complaints of him dozing off in class.

7.3 Assessment

7.3.1 Clinical Interview and History Taking

The therapist builds a rapport with the adolescent by speaking to the adolescent separately before speaking with the parents. During this interview, the therapist makes an introduction and engages in conversation with the adolescent wherein discussions regarding current school/college schedules/personal schedules/choice of subjects/peer group/family relations/relationships with siblings/likes and dislikes/and current concerns are addressed.

Clinical interview and history can be taken with both adolescent and parents together at first and then the parent and adolescent can be interviewed separately if needed. This is done so that the adolescent may be given a chance to express his/her views regarding sensitive issues (some adolescents use nicotine, alcohol, etc., without the knowledge of their parents). It is important to take a thorough comprehensive history that encompasses psychosocial development, physical development, daytime functioning, bedtime routines and nocturnal behaviour (Ivanenko and Patwaria 2009; Kotagal and Pianosi 2006) (Fig. 7.2).

7.3.2 Scales and Questionnaires

Several scales and questionnaires exist which help clinicians to evaluate sleep disorders. As mentioned in the previous sections, insufficient sleep is of major concern among adolescents. Tools such as the adolescent sleep hygiene questionnaire, children's morningness eveningness preferences and Pediatric daytime

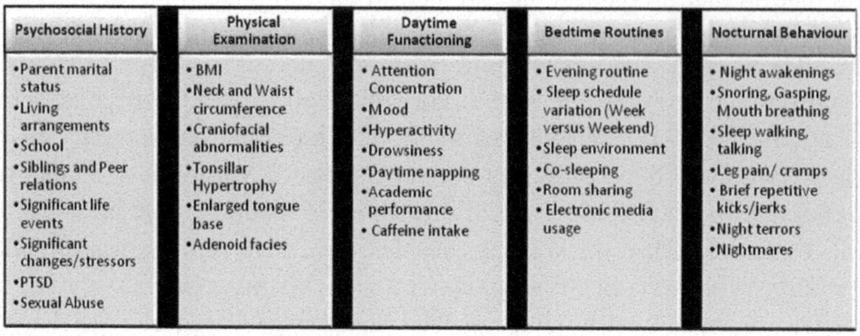

Fig. 7.2 Clinical interview and history taking

sleepiness scale help in identifying maladaptive sleep habits and possible circadian rhythm delay (which is indicated by endorsement of an evening type of orientation) that lead to insufficient sleep culminating in excessive daytime sleepiness. Automatic, irrational thoughts about sleep that interfere with the initiation or maintenance of sleep can be evaluated using the Dysfunctional Attitudes and Beliefs about Sleep Questionnaire and an extensive questionnaire for screening sleep disorders in teens is the Sleep Disorders Inventory for Students–Adolescent version (Table 7.1).

7.3.3 Sleep Log/Sleep Diary

A sleep log can provide insight into sleep habits, such as regularity/irregularity in daily bedtimes, variation/constancy in total sleep times, frequency of daytime

Table 7.1 Questionnaires and scales used commonly to assess adolescent sleep problems

Scale	Age range (years)	Domain assessed	No. of items
Paediatric daytime sleepiness scale	11–15	Excessive daytime sleepiness	8 items, self report
Adolescent sleep hygiene scale	12–18	Physiological, cognitive and emotional factors, sleep environment, daytime sleep, substances, bedtime routine, sleep stability, bed/bedroom sharing	28 items, self report
Children's morningness eveningness preferences	8–16	Morning orientation, evening orientation	10 items, self report
Dysfunctional beliefs and attitudes about sleep (DBAS-16)		Faulty beliefs and appraisals, unrealistic expectations, perceptual and attention bias	16 items, self report
Sleep disorders inventory for students-adolescent (SDIS-A)	11–18	Obstructive sleep apnoea, periodic limb movement disorder and delayed sleep phase syndrome RLS narcolepsy	30 items, self report

Table 7.2 Definitions of sleep log variables

Time in bed	The final part of the day the adolescent got in bed to sleep
Time out of bed	The time of day the adolescent got out of bed for the last time in the morning
Total time in bed	The total time in minutes the adolescent spent in bed during the night. This equals the time out of bed minus the time in bed
Time of sleep onset	The estimated time at night the adolescent fell asleep for the first time
Awake time	The estimated time of day the adolescent awoke for the last time in the morning
Total sleep time (TST)	The estimated amount of time the adolescent actually slept. It is the time taken from sleep onset to awake time minus WASO
Sleep efficiency (SE)	This is calculated by dividing the TST by total time in bed
Wake after sleep onset (WASO)	Sum of the duration of all night awakenings from sleep onset to awake time

Table 7.3 An example of a sleep log

Day/ Date	Daytime naps (frequency and duration)	Time in bed	Time out of bed	Total time in bed	Time of sleep onset	Wake after sleep onset	Awake time	Total sleep time	SE
1.									
2.									
3.									
4.									
5.									
6.									
7.									
8.									

napping and to clarify any misconceptions about sleep-related variables. Sleep logs are maintained for at least a week with entries made for each day (week and weekend). Given above is the list of variables that are entered in a sleep log (Tables 7.2, 7.3 and 7.4).

7.4 Sleep Management in Adolescents

7.4.1 Cognitive Behaviour Therapy—Treatment Rationale

Cognitive behaviour therapy for sleep difficulties is based on Spielman's 3P model. The 3 Ps stand for predisposing, precipitating and perpetuating factors that play a role in the development of sleep problems. Predisposing factors are those

Table 7.4 Sleep laboratory tests

Test	Description	Indication
Actigraphy	Movement tracking device which looks like a wrist watch. It works on the principle that movement indicates wakefulness. Used for tracking sleep–wake patterns	Circadian rhythm disturbances such as delayed sleep phase syndrome or insomnia
MSLT	It consists of 4–5 planned naps in a sleep conducive environment. Measures the likelihood of falling asleep and if there is a direct transition from Wake to REM stage	Daytime sleepiness or narcolepsy
Nocturnal polysomnography	Measures multiple neurophysiologic variables and examines sleep architecture	Obstructive sleep apnoea, periodic limb movement disorder

that contribute to the likelihood or the tendency of developing a problem. This could either be a genetic inclination, such as having a parent with a sleep problem or just being biologically prone to certain conditions such as being a sensitive or a light sleeper. Predisposing factors are not entirely accountable for causing a problem; they just contribute towards the chance of it being likely to surface. It is usually the interaction of multiple factors that are responsible for causing a problem. Precipitating factors are those that hasten the development of a problem or provide the impetus for it to become evident. Precipitating factors can include any stressful event, such parental divorce/separation, exam stress, change in residence, stressful relationships which can cause severe anxiety making it hard to fall asleep at night. Perpetuating factors are those that are liable for maintaining a problem such poor sleep habits which plays a critical role as a sustaining element in many chronic sleep disorders. Therefore, the current treatment protocol provided in the following sections will be primarily aimed at changing adolescent sleep habits that perpetuate sleep deprivation which is commonly observed among adolescents.

Before starting therapy, it is recommended that presenting the rationale for treatment to the adolescent will benefit not only in promoting acceptance but will also aid in fostering adherence to the treatment protocol.

7.4.2 Collecting Pre-treatment Data

Collecting baseline data is essential prior to starting treatment, since it is needed to determine time in bed which is exclusively tailored for each adolescent. This is done by monitoring sleep log and/or Actiwatch data for about 2 weeks before beginning therapy. Apart from the sleep log, it is recommended that the 5 scales mentioned in table be administered scored and analysed, since its findings can highlight areas of concern that can be targeted for change and can help the therapist in the choice of technique employed to correct the problem. While the first

2 scales cater to identifying different facets of insufficient sleep, the third scale is useful for determining a circadian phase delay associated with delayed sleep phase syndrome (a late evening orientation is thought to be correlated with delayed phase). Faulty sleep cognitions that interfere in the process of initiating or maintaining sleep can be evaluated using the Dysfunctional Beliefs and Attitudes Scale. Lastly and most importantly, the Sleep Disorders Inventory for Students–Adolescent version is useful to screen for sleep disorders which need medical attention from a sleep specialist such as obstructive sleep apnoea, restless legs syndrome, periodic limb movement disorder, and narcolepsy.

Session by Session Outline

I. Session 1: Introductory Session (45–60 min)
   A. Presentation of Treatment Rationale
   B. Sleep Education

II. Session 2: Sleep Hygiene (25 min)
   A. Presentation of Learning Aid: Mnemonic
      a. Sleep hygiene rules

III. Session 3: Stimulus Control (30 min)

IV. Session 4: Follow-up (30–45 min)
   A. Encourage and Reinforce Adherence
   B. Troubleshooting

7.4.3 Session I: Sleep Education: "Miles to Go Before I Sleep"

Once the adolescent is comfortable, the therapist introduces the purpose of the appointment and briefly describes the treatment rationale. The following statement can used to do the same.

> *"After carefully examining your assessment records and based on our clinical analysis, I think that it would empower you to become familiar with some background on sleep and some ideas intended to help you change your sleep habits. It has been known that when a sleep problem manifests for very long, usually sleep habits have a substantial role in maintaining the problem. This treatment is designed to enlighten you on your sleep needs and help you change your sleep habits so that you may enjoy better quality of sleep."*

The adolescent and the parents are then introduced to the basics of sleep, which includes educating the family about sleep, the need for sleep, characteristics of human sleep, consequences of sleep deprivation, regulation of sleep, sleep stages and effects of ageing on sleep. The following statement can be used to generate interest in the adolescent for sleep education.

> The treatment that will be provided to you will require you to evaluate your sleep habits so that you may be able to change those that are incompatible with sleep. However before you do so it is essential that you become acquainted with your sleep needs and what processes regulate the amount and quality of your sleep. The information that will be provided to you will help you understand your body's sleep cycle and prepare you for the treatment procedures that are to follow in subsequent sessions.

Parts of the documentary "Who needs sleep?" can be shown to demonstrate the effects of sleep deprivation. It was made by the Oscar winning cinematographer Haskell Wexler about his dear friend and colleague. The documentary is set in the movie industry and is based on the life of a cameraman. After putting in long hours of work, he was driving home from a film shoot when he met with an accident and lost his life due to sleep deprivation. Diagrams that explain the sleep–wake process can be handed out in a pamphlet with information regarding the regulatory mechanisms as well. These can be provided as learning aids. The essence of providing sleep education to adolescents is that it helps the adolescent to challenge dysfunctional beliefs about sleep and substitute them with realistic sleep expectations. It will also help in comprehension of the treatment procedures introduced in subsequent sessions. Apart from that, providing even a rudimentary understanding of the processes involved in sleep to adolescents may increase the chance of better adherence to treatment. Before terminating the session, any queries or concerns from the adolescents should be addressed and the next session should be fixed within a week.

7.4.4 Session II: Sleep Hygiene: "Sleep Smart for Sweet Dreams"

After completing the assessment and gathering enough information about family sleep habits and home sleep environment, an appropriate intervention strategy needs to be decided upon. Insufficient sleep as previously discussed is the most rampant problem plaguing adolescents. Most often adolescents suffer from insufficient sleep due to inadequate sleep hygiene. In the current session, the goal is to inculcate good sleep habits by sleep hygiene education. Using the mnemonic "Good night and sweet dreams" as quick recall method, the chief components of sleep hygiene can be taught effectively. Please refer to the diagrammatic representation of the same. As a learning aid a set of 5 small flip cards can be given to the adolescent, with one word of the mnemonic on one side and the sleep hygiene rule associated with it on the flip side. The cards should be ordered according to the diagram below:

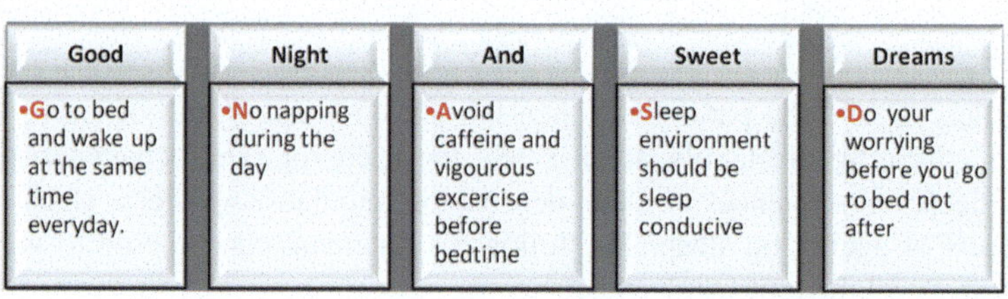

After handing out the cards to the adolescent, the therapist provides a brief rationale for each sleep hygiene rule corresponding to the first letter of each word in the mnemonic. The text that follows can be used to provide the explanation for each rule.

> You have been given a set of flip cards, with a word on one side and a sleep hygiene rule printed on the other side. Each of these rules are linked to the first letter of the word in the sentence '**G**ood **N**ight **A**nd **S**weet **D**reams'. Remembering this sentence will help you recall the rules once you become familiar with them. Shall we begin?
>
> Take a look at the first card, it reads the word '**G**ood' on one side, now flip it over to read the rule which says '**G**o to bed and wake up the same time everyday'. Following the rule will help establish a consistent sleep-wake pattern. As discussed in the sleep education session changes to sleep/wake patterns disrupt your sleep and are associated with negative circumstances. If you adhere to regular bed/wake up times then you will begin to notice that you tend feel drowsy at the same time each evening thereby making it easier for you to fall asleep each night.
>
> Moving on to the next card, it reads the word '**N**ight' one side, now flip it over to read the rule which says '**N**o napping during the day'. While sleeping during the day will help you satisfy your drive to sleep at that particular moment, it is not recommended to do so, because napping during the day will weaken your drive to sleep making it difficult for you to fall asleep at night.
>
> Take a look at the third card, it reads the word '**A**nd' on one side, now flip it over to read the rule which says '**A**void caffeine and vigorous exercise before bedtime' Caffeine and exercise are both stimulants as they both stimulate the brain to stay awake and alert. The effects of caffeine consumption stay long after it has been consumed. It is recommended that caffeine intake and exercise should be avoided 3 hours prior to bedtime.
>
> Let us now move on to the fourth card which reads '**S**weet' now flip it over to read the rule which says "**S**leep environment should be sleep conducive". The sleep environment plays a major role in determining the ease with which sleep is initiated and maintained. Keeping noise levels low, temperature cool/warm depending on the weather and light levels dim is beneficial in creating a sleep conducive environment.
>
> Take a look at the last card which reads, '**D**reams' now flip it over to read the rule which says "**D**o your worrying before you go to bed not after". Lying in bed and worrying about sleep is counterproductive and should be avoided. Keeping a small dairy on bedside table may be beneficial as it can be used for writing or planning daily activities before going to bed, rather than worrying about it while in bed already. Engaging in this practise will limit distress provoking, distracting thoughts while lying in bed.

The therapist can then ask the adolescent to review the rules by self assessment using the side of the flip card with the mnemonic word written to recall the rule printed on the other side, in case of any doubt, the adolescent can flip over and cross-check. Breaking a habit is tough and it will need a lot of encouragement from the therapist. It is a step by step process and many times adolescents feel that they are slipping back into the same routine. One day at a time approach needs to be employed. It helps to get the family members involved and if possible encourage family bedtime routines where there is a winding down period about 30 min before bedtime. Any questions or queries from the adolescent regarding the material presented should be addressed before terminating the session. The next session should be scheduled for a week later.

7.4.5 *Session III: Stimulus Control: "iPhone + iPad + iPod = i Can't Sleep"*

Stimulus control is a therapeutic strategy aimed at rupturing the association between the bed and not being able to sleep caused by the repeated pairing of unsuccessful attempts at sleeping in a sleep environment that in not sleep conducive. Stimulus control seeks to reassociate the sleep environment with falling asleep. It accomplishes this by eliminating sleep incompatible activities on the bed and in the bedroom. The following text can be used for enunciating the rationale and instructions to the adolescent.

> Today's session will focus on how behaviour influences the association between probability of falling asleep and the sleep environment. As you may remember during the last session recommendations were given on how to make the sleep environment conducive for sleeping by controlling external factors like light, temperature and noise levels. In the current session activities that are non-conducive to sleep and best abandoned at bedtime will be discussed. Any activity that is otherwise done during the day, which requires a person to be awake, is considered to be stimulating, these activities are considered sleep incompatible. The sleep environment i.e. bedroom needs to be re-associated with sleep so all stimulating activities like texting, surfing the web, talking over cell phones, watching movies, listening to music, chatting, doing homework, and emailing should be avoided and preferably all electronic gadgets should be kept away from the bedroom. The bedroom needs to be a quiet repose and the bed should only be used for sleeping. Using these gadgets at bedtime not only makes you associate the bed with staying awake but also fools the brain into believing that it's not yet time to sleep. As you might recall from the sleep education session light is a powerful zeitgeber and the bluish light emitted from laptops/tablet/phone screens promotes wakefulness rather than sleep onset. It is best to have these gadgets outside the bedroom and not engage with them past bedtime.
>
> If you find yourself lying in bed for more than 20 minutes but are unable to fall asleep within that time period it is recommended that you leave the bedroom and go to another room. This is done because the longer you stay in bed waiting to fall asleep, the stronger the association becomes between the bed and arousal. Try to relax or engage in something that does not require your brain to be on high alert like listening to light music till you feel sleepy again. Return to your bed only when sleepy. Following these recommendations will allow you to re-associate your bed and bedroom with sleep.

Any questions or queries from the adolescent regarding the material presented should be addressed before terminating the session. The next session should be scheduled for a week later.

7.4.6 *Session VI: Follow-up: "May You Sleep Happily Ever After"*

Follow-up sessions can be used for: (1) encouraging and reinforcing adherence with treatment procedures; and (2) troubleshooting adolescent's difficulties as therapy progresses.

Reinforcing Adherence: The therapist can assess adolescent's adherence to treatment recommendations by reviewing sleep logs/actigraphy data, reports by caregivers or by self reports. Another way to study adherence will be to review sleep education and sleep hygiene rules and ask the adolescent about the changes that he/she has made in view of them. Positive feedback for progress made should be given in a genuine way. Encouragement should be given even if the adolescent has not succeeded in efforts but has put in genuine effort. This ensures feeling of empathy, trust and genuine regard between therapist and the adolescent.

Trouble-shooting adolescent's problems: Most of the problems faced by adolescents are related to difficulty with sleep/wake schedules, daytime napping, using caffeine as a means of keeping awake, following sleep hygiene and stimulus control procedures. It is important to carefully review sleep logs/actigraphy records to identity non-adherence with sleep–wake schedules and involve family members and siblings as part of the sleep hygiene and sleep education sessions. Most often it is seen that even when the adolescent tries to change sleep habits, the family routines are such that the TV is on past bedtime. In such situations, it becomes quite distracting for the adolescent to follow treatment recommendations especially if the adolescent does not have a separate bedroom and sleeps in a common space where noise can travel. If the adolescent shares a bedroom with a sibling then the siblings sleep habits (such as studying at night keeping lamp on, listening to music, and talking on the phone) may affect the adolescent. Therefore, it is important to involve the family members so that they understand how valuable family support and collaboration is for the therapeutic process to prove beneficial for the adolescent. Another problem is that adolescents sometimes find it difficult to refrain from using Internet at night since most of their peers are online and a lot of social interaction on the net occurs during that time. Motivation enhancement and assertiveness training may help such adolescents. Other adolescents may prefer to study long hours into the night and nap during the day, for such adolescents including time management skills in their regimen may prove to be useful.

7.5 Barriers to Treatment

Annoyance boredom and discomfort have most often been associated with barriers to stimulus control. Vincent et al. (2008) have identified certain recommendations for therapists to enhance adherence that include the following (a) discuss anticipated discomfort/annoyance/boredom associated with stimulus control/in detail prior to implementation and engage patients in proactive problem solving (c) discourage patients from questioning the causes for their insomnia in the middle of the night when attempting to motivate themselves to get out of bed if unable to sleep (d) model and encourage positive self-statements (e) providing access to support groups or a website for patients to have interactive web discussions to increase their sense of support for engaging in these techniques.

7.6 Conclusions and Future Directions

It is not rare for adolescents to suffer from insufficient sleep which can have severe repercussions on their academic, physical/health, cognitive, emotional and social functioning. Insufficient sleep is caused by biological factors such as a circadian delay in sleep onset during adolescence, as well as a plethora of environmental and behavioural factors such as poor sleep hygiene (engaging in stimulating activities such as phone and Internet usage past bedtime), increased academic load in higher classes, intake of food that are stimulants (e.g., caffeine, colas, alcohol, and nicotine), increase in social extracurricular activities, decrease in parental control on setting bedtimes and early school start times. Biological, behavioural and environmental factors interplay with each other and contribute to the vicious cycle of insufficient sleep among adolescents. As a means to overcome this rampant problem, healthy sleep habits and sleep education should be included in school health education programs and it should be mandatory for students, teachers and management to attend. Public policies that encourage a shift to later school start times may prove to be beneficial so that students can get adequate hours of sleep and are not forced to skip breakfast in the morning as bid to reaching school on time. Apart from that food products which contain stimulants, such as coffee and colas, should have a statutory health warning on their labels due to their multiple detrimental effects. As far as possible, their sale within student canteens in schools should be restricted. Public health programs that spread awareness about sleep education should be encouraged. Last but not the least, as citizens who know about the deadly consequences of sleep deprivation can cause behind the wheel (avoid operating heavy machinery/ driving when drowsy or sleep deprived), we should fulfil our social responsibility by adhering to healthy sleep practises so that we neither cause harm to ourselves nor to those around us.

References

Agras, W. S., Hammer, L. D., McNicolas, F., & Kraemer, H. C. (2004). Risk factors for childhood overweight: A prospective study from birth to 9.5 years. *Journal of Pediatrics, 145*, 20–25.

Allen, R. (1992). Social factors associated with the amount of school week sleep lag for seniors in an early starting suburban high school. *Sleep Research, 21*, 114.

Amin, R. S., Kimball, T. R., Kalra, M., Jeffries, J. L., Carroll, J. L., Bean, J. A., et al. (2005). Left ventricular function in children with sleep disordered breathing. *American Journal of Cardiology, 95*, 801–804.

Bearpark, H. M., & Michie, P.T. (1987). Prevalence of sleep/wake disturbances in Sydney adolescents. *Sleep Research, 16*, 304.

Beebe, D. W., Lewin, D., Zeller, M., McCabe, M., Macleod, K., et al. (2007). Sleep in overweight adolescents: Shorter sleep, poorer sleep, sleepiness and sleep disordered breathing. *Journal of Pediatric Psychology, 32*(2), 67–69.

Borbely, A. A., & Achermann, P. (1999). Sleep homeostasis and models of sleep regulation. *Journal of Biological Rhythms, 14*, 557–558.

Cauter, E. V. (2012, December 12). *Sleep Disturbances Obesity and Type 2 Diabetes: Interacting Epidemics*. The Fifth Annual Obesity Symposium. UCSF Centre for Obesity Assessment, Study and Treatment. Health and Medicine. Show ID: 24581 [Video Lecture Series]. San Francisco, CA: University of California Television. Retrieved January 6, 2014, from http://www.uctv.tv/.

Carskadon, M., & Roth, T. (2000). *Adolescent sleep needs and patterns: Research report and resource guide*. Washington, DC, USA: National Sleep Foundation.

Carskadon, M. A. (1990). Patterns of sleep and sleepiness in adolescents. *Pediatrician*, 5–12.

Carskadon, M. A., Wolfson, A. R., Acebo, C., Tzischinsky, O., & Seifer, R. (1998). Adolescent sleep patterns, circadian timing, and sleepiness at a transition to early school days. *Sleep, 21*, 726–731.

Carskadon, M. A. (1982). The second decade. In *Sleeping and waking disorders. Indications and techniques* (pp. 1–16). Addison-Wesley.

Carskadon, M. A., Acebo, C., & Jenni, O. G. (2004). Regulation of adolescent sleep: Implications for behavior. *Annals of the New York Academy of Sciences, 1021*, 276–291.

Chervin, R. A. (2002). Association between symptoms of inattention, hyperactivity, restless legs and periodic limb movements. *Sleep, 25*, 213–218.

Colten, H. R., & Altevogt, B. M. (2006). Extent and health consequences of chronic sleep loss and sleep disorders. In H. R. Colten & B. M. Altevogt (Eds.), *Sleep disorders and Sleep Deprivation: An unmet Public Health Problem*. Washington DC: The National Academies Press.

De la Eva, R., Baur, L., Donaghue, K., & Waters, K. (2002). Metabolic correlates with obstructive sleep apnea in obese subjects. *Journal of Pediatrics, 140*, 654–659.

Dement, W. C., & Vaughan, C. (1999). *The promise of sleep*. New York: Dell.

Ebben, R. M., & Speilman, R. A. (2009). Non-pharmacological treatments for insomnia. *Journal of Behavioural Medicine, 32*, 244–254.

Harvard Medical School, Division of Sleep Medicine (2007, December). *Healthy sleep: Sleep and disease risk*. Retrieved January 6, 2014 from the WGBH Education foundation Web site: http://healthysleep.med.harvard.edu/healthy/matters/consequences/sleep-and-disease-risk.

Ivanenko, A., & Patwaria, P. P. (2009). Recognition and management of pediatric sleep disorders. *Primary Psychiatry, 16*, 42–50.

Kotagal, S., & Pianosi, P. (2006). Sleep disorders in children and adolescents. *BMJ, 332*, 826–832.

Liu, X. (2004). Sleep and adolescent suicidal behaviour. *Sleep, 27*(7), 1351–1358.

National Sleep Foundation. (2000). *Adolescent sleep needs and patterns*. Washington DC: National Sleep Foundation.

Owens, J., Maxim, R., McGuinn, M., Nobile, C., Msall, M., & Alario, A. (1999). Television viewing habits and sleep disturbance in school children. *Pediatrics, 104*(3), 1–8.

Petta, D., Carskadon, M.A., & Dement, W.C. (1984). Sleep habits in children aged 7-13 years. *Sleep research, 13*, 86.

Reilly, J. J., Armstrong, J., Dorosty, A. R., Emmett, P. M., Ness, A., Rogers, I., et al. (2005). Early life risk factors for obesity in childhood: Cohort study. *BMJ, 330*, 1357.

Spriggs, W. H. (2010). *Essentials of Polysomnography: A training guide and reference for sleep technicians*. Ontario: Jones and Bartlett.

Strauch, I., & Meier, B. (1986). Sleep need in adolescents: A longitudinal approach. *Sleep, 11*, 378-386.

Sugimori, H., Yoshida, K., Izuno, T., Miyakawa, M., Suka, M., Sekine, M., et al. (2004). Analysis of factors that influence body mass index from ages 3 to 6 years: A study based on Toyama cohort study. *Pediatrics International, 46*, 302–310.

Vincent, N., Lewycky, S., & Finnegan, H. (2008). Barriers to engagement in sleep restriction and stimulus control in chronic insomnia. *Journal of Consulting and Clinical Psychology, 76*(5), 820–828.

Wexler, H. (Director). (2006). *Who needs sleep* [Motion Picture].

Williams, R., Karacan, I., & Hursch, C. (1974). *EEG of human sleep*. New York: Wiley & Sons.

Wolfson, A. R. (2002). Bridging the gap between research and practise: What will adolescent's sleep-wake patterns look like in the 21st century? In M. A. Carskadon (Ed.), Adolescent Sleep patterns. Biological, Social and psychological influences. Cambridge: Cambridge University Press.

Wolfson, A. R., & Carskadon, M. A. (1998). Sleep schedules and daytime functioning in adolescents. *Child Development, 69*(4), 875–887.

Wolfson, A. (2012). *Adolescent Sleep*. USA: American Psychological Association/Clark University Workshop.

Chapter 8
Stress Management

Manju Mehta and Vandita Sharma

8.1 What is Stress

Stress is a part of everyday life for adolescents. Although they are young and energetic, their lives are also full of changes and challenges. When adolescents come for help, they are often dealing with experiences that leave them feeling physically and emotionally overwhelmed. Since adolescence is a stage involving major physical and psychological changes, during this stage, their minds and bodies become even more susceptible to major stressors. In simple words, stress can be defined as a state wherein the external demands outweigh one's internal resources to deal with it.

Stress can broadly be classified into two categories—*Eustress and Distress.*

A certain level of stress is beneficial. We need some stress to stimulate us. This is called *Eustress* (or positive stress). Eustress helps individuals to perform better and achieve their goals and is perceived within the coping abilities of the person. For example, participating in a marathon may require running regularly and yet one may thoroughly enjoy it. Becoming the head boy or head girl at school may be perceived as an overwhelming achievement even though it means more responsibility and work.

However, there are times when stress is associated feelings of anxiety, fear, tension and uncertainty. This is called *distress* (or negative stress). It leads to

M. Mehta (✉) · V. Sharma
Department of Psychiatry, All India Institute of Medical Sciences, New Delhi 110029, India
e-mail: drmanju.mehta@gmail.com

V. Sharma
e-mail: vandita0512@gmail.com

M. Mehta and R. Sagar (eds.), *A Practical Approach to Cognitive Behaviour Therapy for Adolescents*, DOI 10.1007/978-81-322-2241-5_8

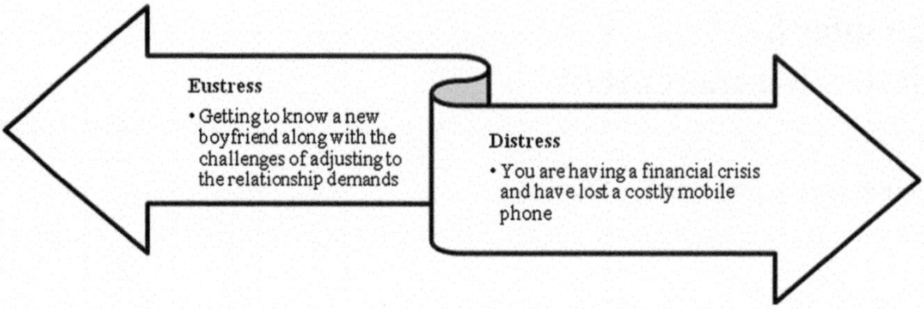

Fig. 8.1 Eustress and distress

poor health and well-being, hampers the individual's performance, and can lead to many physical and psychological problems. It usually arises when one has to adapt to too many negative demands. For example, when a close family member is sick, deadlines at work, deciding for career choices and transition from school to college (Fig. 8.1).

8.2 Prevalence of Distress Among Indian Adolescents

Stress is a condition of major public health concern, because of its high rate of prevalence and the high degree of dysfunction and suffering associated with it. Studies on stress in India are mostly based on the objective measures of stress and various causes of stress. Prevalence studies of stress in India have mostly been carried out in conjunction with prevalence of anxiety and depression. Daily hassles, academic pressure and career-related demands are the major causes of stress among Indian adolescents. According to Mehta (2000), majority of Indian adolescents experience mild to moderate levels of stress. Daily hassles are a significant cause of their stress. For many adolescents, examinations are a significant cause of emotional trauma and anxiety. Being labelled as "average" or "below average" may be extremely distressing and can lead to low self-esteem and poor academic concept. Even high achievers have high fears of failure and experience stress.

Figure 8.2 presents the prevalence rates of stress in adolescents in India.

Findings from other studies suggest that students in Government schools experience higher levels of stress than those in private schools. Students engage in higher use of avoidance coping (Augustine et al. 2011). Depression, anxiety and stress are higher among students in "board classes" (Bhasin et al. 2010). Findings from these studies reveal that managing stress among adolescents in India is the need of the hour.

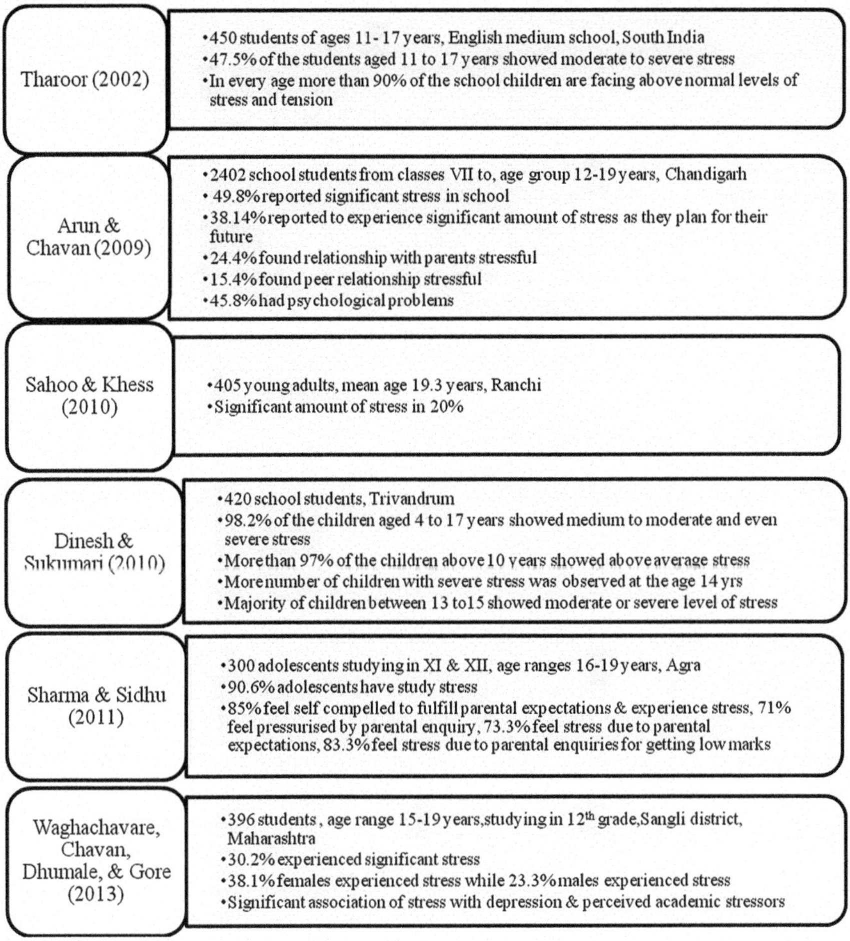

Fig. 8.2 Prevalence of stress among Indian adolescents

8.3 Causes of Stress in Adolescents

Certain stressful situations are more likely to occur during particular developmental periods. Adolescent stress is an important, yet often overlooked, health issue. During this period, adolescents undergo a time of rapid body growth. It is also during this phase that they have to make crucial academic and professional decisions. Adolescence is also a period associated with identity development. The main causes of stress arising during adolescence have been highlighted in Table 8.1.

Table 8.1 Causes of stress in adolescents

Common sources of stress in adolescence	
Academic stress	Pressure to perform well in school examinations, competitive college entrance examinations, apprehensions about not getting selected in a college of choice, examination anxiety, amount of time spent in school and tutorial classes
Conflicts with parents	Parental aspirations and pressures related to career choices, incompatibility between adolescent's demands for higher independence and parents continued thinking about them as children, higher reliance on peers, family beliefs about friendship and dating, arguments over substance use and automobile driving
Peer-related demands	Peer group expectations, social status, change in relationships with friends, dating and break of relationships, stress arising from close friendships and romantic relationships, peer victimization, Lack of assertiveness, bullying, pressure to experiment with drugs and alcohol
Body image issues	Poor body image, perception of being obese, pressure to have a particular body size or shape (Girls focussing on body weight, boys focussing on having muscular or athletic physique), concern related to physical appearance (having acne or other skin-related problems as a sign of being ugly), pressure to wear certain types of clothes, follow certain types of fashion trends
Mood disruptions related to adolescence	Rapid mood fluctuations naturally occurring during this stage, feeling easily self-conscious, embarrassed, awkward, lonely or ignored, poorer emotional understanding, difficulty managing negative emotions, poor confidence over ability to manage emotions, poor self-control, poor control over impulses

8.4 How Does Body React to Stress

According to Selye (1978), the state of stress can be recognized only by its physiological manifestations. He defined stress as "an adaptive or defensive reaction to an event or stimulus" and labelled it as the *General Adaptation Syndrome* (G.A.S.), which occurs in three stages: the *alarm reaction* (A.R.), the *alarm resistance* (A.R.) and the *stage of exhaustion* (S.E.).

The *alarm reaction* is a physiological response made by the body for alerting the defensive forces within the individual. In this stage, blood is diverted towards the skeletal muscles in order to prepare them for action in response to a stressor.

If the stress exposure remains, the stage of *resistance* follows. In this stage, the body begins to restore balance, recover depleted body sources, and start renewal and repair. If the stressor still persists, the body starts adapting itself with continued effort in resistance. During this phase, the body continues to remain in a state of arousal. If an individual accepts that the stressor is a necessary part of life, it may persist indefinitely. In such a condition, the person becomes highly vulnerable to a wide range of stress-related problems and diseases.

With long-term stress exposure, the individual enters the third stage, the stage of *exhaustion.* During this stage, the risk of emotional and physical problems increases and the individual starts experiencing symptoms such as loss of morale and feelings of loss of control and may finally collapse.

8.5 Signs of Stress Among Adolescents

The impact of maladaptive responses to stress can manifest in five main domains—physical, psychological, emotional, behavioural and social. The most common signs of stress seen in adolescents are highlighted in Fig. 8.3.

Adolescents may also experience certain types of thoughts that can precipitate, lead to, maintain or heighten the experience of stress. These thoughts generally represent certain dysfunctional styles in thinking and cognitive distortions. A list of cognitive distortions is provided in the Appendix.

Common examples of the thoughts experienced by adolescents during stress are included in Fig. 8.4.

While these thoughts can lead to experience of stress, they can also be seen as by-products of stress. The experience of these thoughts can prolong the effects of stress among adolescents. Cognitive behaviour therapy (explained in detail in subsequent sections) can serve as a promising treatment modality in dealing with these cognitions.

Physical	Psychological	Emotional	Behavioural	Social
•Body aches (headaches/stomach aches/back pain/jaw pains/chest pain/pain in neck & shoulders) •Feeling dizzy •Stiffness in neck •Mouth ulcers •Weight loss/ weight gain •Weakness •Nausea/vomiting/indigestion •Excessive sleeping/Inability to sleep •Overeating/Loss of appetite •Skin problems •Constant fatigue •Palpitations/Muscle tension/Restlessness •Disruption in menstrual cycle •Compromised immunity •Skin problems (Acne, hives disease, rosecea, eczema, trichotelomania)	•Difficulty Concentrating •Decreased memory •Indecisiveness •Mind going blank or mind racing •Confusion •Loss of sense of humour •Decreased libido •Inattentiveness •Bad dreams	•Anxiety •Anger •Irritability •Impatience •Short temper •Frustration •Worry •Fear •Tension •Nervousness	•Increased smoking, drinking, & drug use •Yelling •Swearing •Aggression •Changes in eating habits (increase or decrease) •Changes in sleeping habits (increase or decrease) •Nervousness (nail biting, fidgeting, pacing etc.) •Not caring about physical appearance •Walking or talking faster •Irritation with delays	•Fewer friends •Stay home more •Angry at others •Withdrawing from supportive relationships •Increased arguments •Isolation from social activities •Conflict with friends or classmates or family members •Overreactions •Frequent absenteeism

Fig. 8.3 Common signs of stress among adolescents

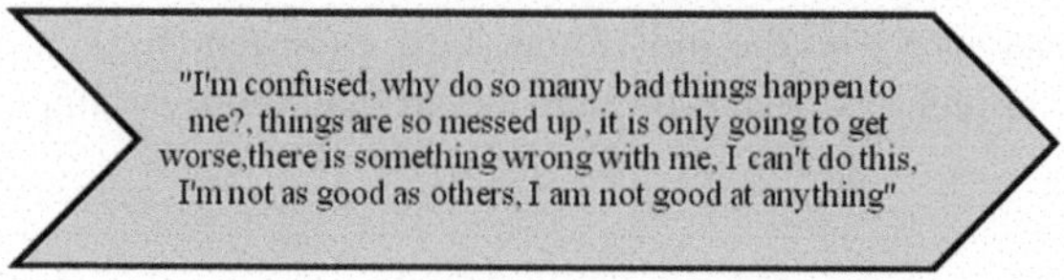

Fig. 8.4 Examples of common stress-related cognitions

8.6 Implications of Untreated Stress

Stress can have numerous detrimental effects on adolescents. Stress generally elevates the production of cortisol, a stress hormone, which not only impairs memory but also general health. Between 50 and 80 % of all diseases, at least in part, have stress-related origins (Humphrey 2004). There is a strong correlation between an increase in stressful events and a decrease in health and psychological functioning (Newcomb et al. 1981). In the longer term, stress can have a very cumulative and wide-ranged effects on health (Table 8.2).

8.7 Coping with Stress and Building Resilience

Effectively managing stress mainly involves taking charge over one's thoughts and feelings and finding a way to deal with the problems. Adolescents can learn to become more resilient by changing how they think about their problems and life situations. Resilience can be defined as the ability to cope well with challenging

Table 8.2 Effects of chronic stress

Effects of chronic stress	
Physical	**Psychiatric**
Increased blood pressure	Depression
Compromised immunity	Anxiety
Frequent cold and flu	Dissociation
Hormonal imbalance	Psychogenic vomiting
Indigestion/lack of appetite/ulcers	Forgetfulness
Irritable bowel syndrome	Somatisation
Crohn's disease	Panic attacks
Frequent exacerbation of asthma	Generalized anxiety
Acne	disorders
Eczema	Alcohol dependence
Hives	Nicotine dependence
Rosacea	Drug abuse
Psoriasis	
Vitiligo (de-pigmented white spots on skin)	

situations and a context of positive adaptation in light of adversity. Resilient individuals generally use more effective coping strategies, have a realistic understanding of situations and have better tolerance and control over their feelings.

Thus, building resilience essentially involves learning to develop good coping skills. Two main types of coping styles have been widely reviewed—problem-focussed coping (approach oriented) and emotion-focussed coping (avoidance oriented).

Problem-focused coping (approach-oriented coping) aims at changing the source of the stress. For example, if a student is stressed about an upcoming exam, the problem-focused approach for the student would be to devote more time for studying. The student may also ask friends and teachers for help. Emotion-focussed coping (avoidance oriented) aims towards reducing or managing the emotional distress related to a situation. Examples include denial, avoidance, and procrastinating. Studies suggest that females generally use more emotion-focused coping strategies while males tend to use more problem-focussed strategies. Adolescents often use less effective coping strategies such as wishful thinking, self-blame, complaining, making excuses, not communicating, bullying, becoming withdrawn, smoking or drinking. While these coping strategies may temporarily reduce stress, they are counterproductive and may worsen the stress and cause more damage in the long term. Adolescents can learn healthier ways to manage stress by learning more effective and problem-focussed coping strategies. These may include developing problem-solving skills, developing positive thinking, developing more flexible styles of thinking, maintaining an optimistic outlook, learning better time management, developing a balance between work and leisure, engaging in regular physical exercise, practising relaxation exercises, spending time with friends, sharing problems with a friend or family member, expressing feelings instead of bottling them up, developing more effective communication skills, maintaining healthy eating and sleeping habits, maintaining a stress diary, indulging in a hobby, reading a novel or comics, watching a funny movie or videos, listening to music, doing something creative such as drawing or painting and playing with pets. These coping strategies are more problem focussed and help in building resilience to stress.

8.8 Need for Management of Stress Among Adolescents

Stress is related to a wide range of health-related problems among adolescents. Chronic stress can cause hormonal imbalance and has emerged as a key risk factor in development of many physical and psychiatric illnesses and lifestyle-related diseases as seen in the previous section. Academic stress among adolescents is emerging as a leading problem which requires immediate concern. "Today stress levels among children and adolescents have been going up dangerously due to the pressure of their academic or cultural activities. Not all children can cope with such high levels of expectations and parents do not seem to realize or accept that their children are under severe pressure" says Elizabeth Vadakkekkara, a child psychologist and director of Thrani; a counselling centre in Kerala focussing on crisis intervention and suicide prevention (The Hindu 2003). Many adolescents believe that nothing can be done to avoid stress. Poor coping strategies used by adolescents can have significant short- and long-term consequences on their physical and emotional health. Stress management has thus become a need of the hour for adolescents in India. Teaching several coping strategies such as seeking social support, cognitive restructuring, positive self-talk, problem solving, relaxation, physical activity, sleep and diet regulation, cognitive restructuring and self-talk can serve to be successful in combating stress among adolescents and promising a healthy lifestyle.

8.9 Case Vignette

The case illustration provided in Fig. 8.5 highlights the case of a 19-year-old female with significant body image issues and cognitive distortions experiencing significant amount of stress and developing a stress-related condition (Irritable Bowel syndrome).

CASE VIGNETTE- I

S is a 19 years old college going teenager. While she is pursuing graduation through correspondence, she aims to become a renowned singer. She is receiving formal training in classical music and dreams of becoming a well known Bollywood playback singer and winning the next Indian Idol. S has a general predisposition to experience stressful thoughts more frequently and easily. Due to low stress tolerance, she has already developed Irritable Bowel syndrome at a tender age and has been enrolled in treatment since 2 years now. She believes that in order to become a successful singer, her physical appearance is quintessential and she must have to be looking glamorous all the time. She believes that a slight moderation in her looks will lead to her rejection in the competition and if her face and body do not look beautiful, she will not be allowed to appear on screen. Recently, she has developed a skin allergy on her face presenting in the form of a small red spot. While she visits her dermatologist, she overhears his conversation with another patient who presented with a similar complaint and was diagnosed with hives disease. During her consultation, the doctor tells her that she has a simple seasonal allergy which should go away after few days of medication. However, S is not convinced about this and confirms with the doctor on whether she too has developed hives. The doctor smiles and says that she does not have any severe skin condition and that she should not be worried. On her way back home, S feels extremely angry. She is convinced that her doctor was smiling at her because he found her stupid and later he must have been making fun of her. She thought that her doctor must be thinking that she is a "psycho". When she reached home, she started surfing the internet for various skin conditions and read in great details about eczema, hives, and rosacea. After gaining this information she started experiencing extreme amount of stress and worry over her condition. She started getting distressing thoughts like "What if my problem is not just an allergy", "What if the doctor has misdiagnosed", "What if I have developed rosacea", "These medicines may cause reactions and slowly my entire face will turn red", "I will look so ugly", "Nobody will select me in the competition", "What if the allergy starts growing and spreads though out my body and then the internal organs". In the evening, while she sat for her singing practise, she experienced slight itching and burning in her throat. She started thinking that the allergy must have spread to her tonsils and glands and slowly her voice will start cracking and become hoarse. If this happens she will never be able to become a singer. She stops eating her food and starts spending sleepless nights in mulling over her condition. Gradually, she stops interacting with her parents and reacts very angrily whenever talked to. She also stops going for her singing classes. She keeps laying in bed thinking that because of her allergy, she has started to look ugly and soon the allergy will develop into some serious skin disease, and her voice will also go away. In a few days she also started experiencing burning sensations in her stomach and anus and her condition of Irritable Bowel Syndrome (IBS) worsened. Now S was convinced that because of her IBS and skin allergy she will never be able to become a singer and that there was no use living any further. She refuses to visit the doctor because she is convinced that the other day, he made fun of her and that all doctors are like him and will make fun of her.

Fig. 8.5 Case illustration

8.10 Assessment of Stress

Assessment of stress involves identification of signs of stress, the causes (stressor), and the present demands and resources of the individual. This can be carried out using detailed interviews, providing the adolescents with self-assessment records, and through structured questionnaires and inventories.

8.10.1 Interview-Based Assessment

The experience of stress, level of stress, signs and symptoms, and nature of coping can be assessed using open-ended questions. Various questions that can be asked to assess for presence of stress and its related symptoms are provided in Table 8.3.

8.10.2 Self-monitoring

Adolescents can also be provided with daily logs to monitor stress. They may be asked to maintain a regular record of situations in which they feel stressed and the thoughts, feelings, and sensations they experience in order to monitor for signs of stress. Thus, in the case vignette given in Fig. 8.5, S can be asked to keep the record provided in Table 8.4.

Stress journals can be provided for monitoring the stressors and the usual coping responses. In the same example in the case vignette, S could be asked to maintain the journal as provided in Table 8.5.

Self-monitoring sheets to assess the level of stress among adolescents can also be provided. Adolescents can be asked to maintain a record that indicates their daily level of stress. Ratings may be done as provided in Table 8.6.

Table 8.3 Interview-based assessment of stress

List of questions used for eliciting stress
How do you know when you are feeling stressed?
What are the first things you notice when you experience stress?
What are your early warning signs of stress?
Where do you feel stress in your body?
What do you notice about your body, thoughts and feelings when things are difficult?
How do you behave when you are feeling stressed out?
Do you often feel weepy or irritable?
Do you feel things are getting on top of you?
How do you react to stress?
How do you currently cope with stress?
How do you usually handle stress? List your usual coping habits.
How effective are the coping behaviours you have used in the past? Do they reduce or eliminate the stress?

Table 8.4 Daily logs for recording stressful situations and responses to stress

Situation	Automatic thoughts	Emotions	Physical sensations
Saw the red spot on face deepen in colour	This is not a simple allergy. The doctor has misdiagnosed me. This is a sign for some serious skin disease. There is something terribly wrong with my looks. How will I go out? How will I face my friends? They will make fun of me	Anxious, tensed	Palpitations, heaviness in head

Table 8.5 Stress journal

Time	Stressor	Feelings	How you coped	Effect of coping • Effective • Partly effective • Not at all effective
Wednesday 2:30 pm	Missed my music class	Irritation, anger	Locked my room from inside and kept laying in bed thinking about how terrible my day was because I couldn't go for the music class	Not at all effective, felt worse about the whole thing

8.10.3 Questionnaires and Inventories

Several self-report measures for assessment of stress among adolescents are also available. These are given in Table 8.7.

8.11 Stress Management Interventions

Before introducing the techniques, let us consider another example of an adolescent experiencing high level of stress (Fig. 8.6).

Various techniques can be used by adolescents to manage stress. One can deal with stress by directly avoiding the stressors wherever possible. However, when the experience of stress seems unavoidable, individuals can learn ways to alter their responses to stressors. Another way of managing stress may include adapting oneself to stressors. Finally, one can also learn to accept stressors and bring about lifestyle-related changes in order to handle it well (Fig. 8.7).

Table 8.6 Daily stress monitoring log

1	2	3	4	5	6	7
Not at all Stressed	Very Mildly	Mildly Stressed	Moderately Stressed	Fairly Stressed	Highly Stressed	Extremely Stressed

	Sunday	Monday	Tuesday	Wednesday	Thursday	Friday	Saturday
Time 1 (10 am)	Rating 2						
Time 2 (12.30 pm)	5						
Time 3 (6.48 pm)	7						
Time 4 (10.32 pm)	4						
Day overall	5						

These stress management techniques can be taught in individual as well as group settings. When practised in group settings, the intervention serves to be cost and time effective modality. These techniques can be taught according to the needs of the individual/group.

8.11.1 Avoid Stressors

Direct avoidance of stressors can be done when possible. Many a times, adolescents know exactly when and in what situations they are bound to feel stressed. For example, an adolescent may be aware that going for a drive with friends in the evening may leave him with very little time to prepare for his test the next day. This individual can be asked to avoid going for the outing or attending calls from those friends for that evening.

8.11.1.1 Assertiveness Training

Often, the communication styles used by individuals can also lead to experience of stress. Effective communication skills in the form of assertive communication can

Table 8.7 List of tools for assessment of stress

Name of the tool	Description
Acute stress checklist for children (ASC-Kids), Kassam-Adams (2006)	ASC-Kids is a 29-item self-report measure used to assess acute stress reactions within the first month after exposure to a potentially traumatic event. The questionnaire can be administered within the age group of 8–17 years
Adolescent coping orientation for problem experiences (A-COPE); Patterson and Mc Cubbin (1987)	The A-COPE is a 54-item scale designed to explore the coping behaviours among adolescents that are associated with normal stress. The scale identifies 12 different coping patterns: ventilating feelings, seeking diversions, developing self-reliance and optimism, developing social support, solving family problems, avoiding problems, seeking spiritual support, investing in close friends, seeking professional support, engaging in demanding activity, being humorous and relaxing
Stressful life events scale (LES) (Aggarwal et al. 2007)	LES has been developed exclusively for Indian adolescents and is a culturally adapted version of social readjustment rating scale. It is a 40-item scale where the adolescents are asked to report only the events which had occurred in their lives in the past one year. The scores are interpreted as composite weighted scores and second-order groupings of controllable, uncontrollable and distressful events
Adolescent stress questionnaire (ASQ) (Byrne et al. 2007)	The ASQ is an inventory made up of items originally designed to measure common stressors that adolescents may experience in their daily life. The scale was developed with the intention to ensure that the list of stressors was based on adolescents' individual experience and broadly salient to the contemporary issues facing young people at that time
Child and adolescent needs and strengths—trauma comprehensive version, Kisiel and Lyons et al. (2011)	The measure is used to assess information on traumatic experiences and whether adjustment to trauma affects functioning. It is a comprehensive tool that can be assessed within age groups of 0–18 years
Dimensions of stressful events rating scale (DOSE), Fletcher (1996)	The DOSE is a 50-item clinician administered scale used to assess the specific characteristics of high-magnitude stressful events among age group of 6–18 years
Stress appraisal measure (SAM); Peacock and Wong (1990)	The SAM is a 28-item questionnaire that examines 6 dimensions of primary and secondary appraisal of stress. Three components measure primary appraisal: threat, challenge and centrality. Three components measure secondary appraisals relating to stress controllability: controllable-by-self, controllable-by-others and uncontrollable-by-anyone. The questionnaire also measures overall perceived stress, which is referred to as stressfulness
Responses to stress in adolescence questionnaire; Connor-Smith (2000)	The RSQ consists of 57 items assessing a range of volitional coping and involuntary responses to stress characteristic of adolescence. Separate versions were developed for adolescents' self-reports and parents' reports of their adolescents' responses. Items are rated on a scale from 1 to 4 that indicates the degree to which or frequency with which each response is enacted by the adolescent (from not at all to a lot)
Academic expectations stress inventory (AESI); Ang and Huan (2006)	The AESI is a 9-item inventory that measures expectations (from self, parents or teachers) as a source of academic stress in middle and high school adolescents. Responses are rated on a Likert-type scale ranging from 1 (never true) to 5 (always true). High scores indicate greater level of perceived academic stress from these expectations

(continued)

Table 8.7 (continued)

Name of the tool	Description
Youth outcome questionnaire-self-report (YOQ-SR), Wells et al. (2005)	The YOQ-SR is an adolescent self-report measure with 64 items that assess a wide range of troublesome situations, behaviours and moods that are common among adolescents. The measure has 6 scales: intrapersonal distress, somatic, interpersonal relationships, critical items, social problems, and behavioural dysfunction along with a total problem scale. It can be used for assessment in age groups of 12–18 years

CASE VIGNETTE II

R is a 16 year old boy from Nashik, Maharashtra who has shifted to Delhi with his family recently. He has been a high achiever throughout schooling and has been an all rounder. His teachers used to admire him and would give examples of his achievements to other school children in order to motivate them. He has finished his Class 10th exam in Nashik and secured a roaring 96.7% marks. However, his schooling has been done through a Hindi medium school where the spoken language has been mostly Marathi or else, Hindi. Because of his impressive scores he has got admission in one of the top notch schools in Delhi where he has enrolled in the medical stream in Class 11th. His first few days in Delhi have been full of excitement where R has felt delighted at being in the new city and exploring the new culture. However, within the first month at school, R has already started facing a lot of problems. Since he is now enrolled in an English medium school, language is becoming a major barrier in hampering his performance. He is not being able to make new friends since his interests differ. While most of his classmates are "party freaks", R doesn't end up gelling in. He has never been to night clubs. The new "lingos" and slangs used by his classmates (fuccha, thulle, jugaad, omg, rofl, bajaaod, bro, ciggie, cut surd, dude, sarky, vella, zapped) seem to be a foreign language to R. While in Nashik, the school houses were simply named by the colour-red house/blue house; in R's new school, houses have English names (Rangers for green house, Barrow for red house). Within the first few days at school, on being asked by his teacher as to which house he has been allotted, R mispronounces the name and feels embarrassed as everyone laughs at him. During the first few classes, R dares to ask doubts from teachers, however, after being scolded by one teacher for "asking a stupid question", R has stopped clearing his doubts for the fear of being humiliated. He misses his old days where every teacher would admire him. His classmates also end up assigning him many class related activities and then make fun of him. R is unable to refuse to perform these tasks. He has also joined a premier coaching institute for preparing for his pre-medical entrance exams. The classes happen daily for 3 hours leaving him with little time for anything else. He has also enrolled himself in English speaking classes that happen thrice in a week. R is also supposed to give regular tests at school at least once in a week for internal assessment. Many a times, he also has weekend assessments at his coaching centre along with a weekly test in school. The syllabus being covered school is totally different from that being covered at the institute. R feels as if a mechanical machine being made to work all the time-school to English classes to coaching centre and then coming back to finish homework and prepare for tests and assessments. He feels as if time flies through. He has started feeling irritated all the time and ends up arguing with parents without any significant reason. He also feels as if he is yearning for sleep but has no time to do so. R's scores have declined significantly. From being an A grader perpetually through school, he is now getting "C"s and "D"s. His appetite has decreased, he feels sleepy all the time but finds no time to sleep. The frustration from not being able to achieve, from being the clown of the class, from not being able to refuse his classmates when he is made to do petty jobs, and from lack of sleep are leaving R under a lot of stress. He has now started procrastinating working on his assignments and preparing for his tests and ending up in a panic state on the day before the test or the assignment submission.

Fig. 8.6 Case illustration II

help in decreasing the demands and increasing the personal resources. The main aim of assertive communication is to honestly communicate one's thoughts, feelings and needs in a respectful manner. The most important elements involved in assertiveness training have been discussed in detail in the Appendix.

A crucial part of assertiveness training involves learning to say "no". In the case cited above, R can be taught skills for assertive communication in order to deal with the problems he is facing with his classmates wherein he can learn to assertively refuse to carry out the petty jobs he is assigned that utilize his time and also make him feel more overloaded.

Avoid stressors	Alter the stressor	Adapt to the stressor	Accept the stressor
•Directly avoiding sources of stress wherever possible •Assetiveness training •Conflict management •Time management	•Jacobson's progressive muscle relaxation technique •Diaphraghmic breathing •Mindfulness meditation •Guided imagery •Visualisation •Expressing thoughts & feelings	•Distraction •Worry/rumination postponement •Cognitive restructuring •Practising positive thinking •Using positive affirmations •Problem solving	•Accepting that everything cannot be controlled •Looking at stressors as opportunities for growth •Lifestyle modification

Fig. 8.7 4 A's for dealing with stress

> **Simple:** "Thank you for the invitation, but I have already made some other plans for that day"

>**Alternative:** " I have too much work, I won't be able to help you, but let me help you find someone else who can help you with this'

> **Gracious:**"I really appreciate your asking me, but i have already committed for that time to someone else"

> **Someone else involved in the decision:** "I have promised my mother that I will not go to the party without asking her permission"

Fig. 8.8 Examples of saying "no" using assertive communication

The following are some examples of various ways to say "no" (Fig. 8.8): Instructions for assertiveness training have been provided in the Appendix (II-i)

8.11.1.2 Conflict Management

Conflicts can become a major source of stress among adolescents. By building conflict resolution skills, adolescents are able to resolve conflicts in a better manner, which in turn can eliminate stress. Conflicts involve differences between two or more persons about things such as values, ideas, perceptions and opinions. Adolescents may experience a significant majority of stress arising from conflicts with peers and parents, as well as psychological conflicts (between two ideas/thoughts/beliefs/decisions). Resolving these differences can best be achieved using the conflict resolution process. Figure 8.9 highlights the points that are important in managing conflicts that involve persons.

- Consider that the individual is separate from the problem
- Use only objective criteria for resolving the conflicts
- Think of as many options that involve mutual gain
- During resolution try to maintain your focus on the common interests and not the individual positions

Fig. 8.9 Essential points to be considered during conflict resolution with people

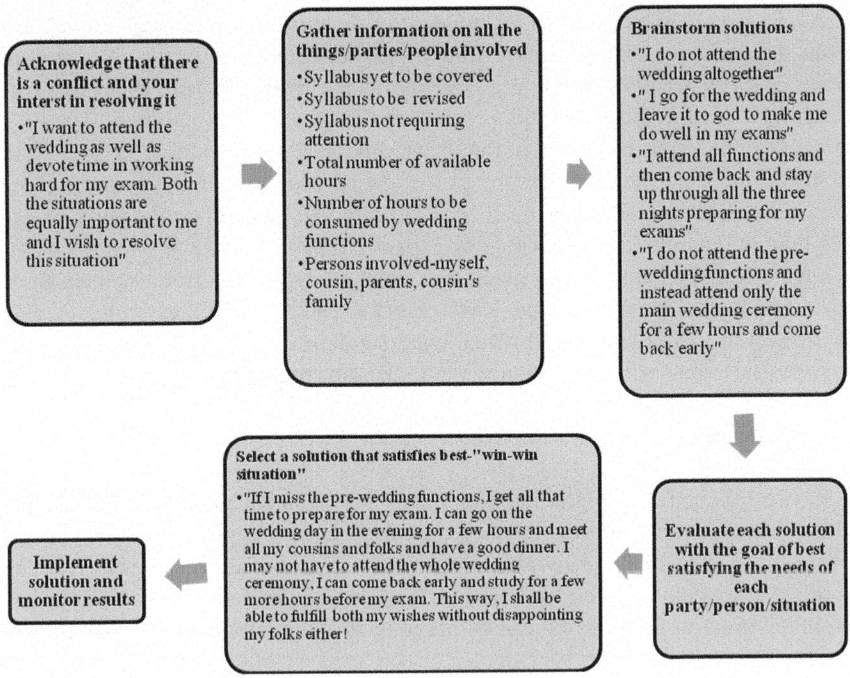

Fig. 8.10 Steps for conflict resolution

Let us understand this in detail using the following example:

In Case vignette II, R is facing a situation where he wants to go for a wedding of one of his closest cousins. R was excited about the wedding and wanted to attend all the functions. However, he had his mid-term examination in the same week as the wedding. He wants to attend all the events related to the wedding and spend maximum time there, however, he is as motivated to study hard and score as much as he used to in his old school in Nashik. This is termed as an "approach–approach" conflict. R can now be asked to follow the steps given in Fig. 8.10 to resolve this.

This can also be practised using case vignettes, and modelling and behavioural rehearsal.

8.11.1.3 Time Management

Under high levels of stress, the motivation to perform things decreases. Under these circumstances, one may find that they are giving up on hobbies and other activities that they previously enjoyed. This can lead to feeling even worse and it becomes a vicious cycle.

Procrastination and poor time management skills can be a major source of stress. Managing time can help adolescents plan their activities in advance, and it helps in incorporating pleasurable activities in daily routine in addition to usual daily tasks in order to combat stress.

Adolescents can be asked to maintain a to-do list in which they can make a list of all the activities that they have to-do, such as doing homework assignments, finishing a project and attending a coaching class. This will help them to know the amount of time they have that is free for other pleasurable activities. They can be asked to pace out time so that they have time to finish important tasks as well as spare time for relaxation. The free time can be used in meeting friends, going for a movie/outing, indulging in hobbies, exercising, etc. Time management can also help in planning and regulating bed times so that there is a regular sleep pattern which in turn helps in improving mood and energy levels. Adolescents can be asked to plan out daily activities, leave extra time in between appointments, plan their travel in such a way that it saves time, maintain a priority list, delegate some activities to others wherever possible and take advantage of wasted time such as reading while travelling in a metro.

Essential points to be considered have been provided in the chapter on study skills (Chap. 4).

In Case vignette II, R can be taught time management skills in order to deal with the stress evolving from attending coaching classes, English speaking classes, managing time for his homework assignments and preparing for his tests. He can be asked to maintain a to-do list for each day. On the days and weeks where he has too many tasks to perform, he can be asked to differentiate among them between urgent and important tasks. He can then choose urgent tasks to finish first followed by the important tasks and keep reviewing the list on a regular basis.

8.11.2 Alter the Stressor

If the stressful situation cannot be avoided, one can figure out ways to try and alter it. This requires figuring out what can be done to change things so that the problem does not present itself in future.

8.11.2.1 Progressive Muscle Relaxation Technique

Progressive muscle relaxation is a very effective technique for reducing stress and improving the overall mood. Instructions and guidelines for practicing the progressive muscle relaxation technique have been provided in the Appendix.

8.11.2.2 Diaphraghmic Breathing

Diaphraghmic breathing is a relaxation technique that releases tension from the body and mind, thereby reducing the experience of anxiety resulting from stress and improving overall physical and mental wellness. Detailed and structured instructions for practising the technique have been provided in the Appendix (II-a).

8.11.2.3 Mindfulness Meditation

Mindfulness is the quality of being completely engaged in the present moment, without trying to think about the experience. Mindfulness meditation switches the focus on what is happening right now, rather than worrying about the future or thinking about the past. Mindfulness meditation finds its roots in early Buddhist meditations. The first mindfulness-based stress reduction programme (MBSR) was developed by Kabat-Zinn (1990). This programme has been widely researched and modified for use in different populations and is proving to me a promising mode of treatment in dealing with a wide variety of problems. A modification of this programme for adolescents to deal with stress has been done by Biegel and colleagues in 2009 (MBSR-T; Biegel et al. 2009). Mindfulness exercises take effort to maintain concentration and to bring it back to the present moment when mind wanders off. But with regular practice, mindfulness strengthens the areas of the brain associated with joy and relaxation. Mindfulness provides a very effective treatment to the common causes of daily stress such as distraction, agitation, time pressure and interpersonal conflicts. Another variant of mindfulness meditation is called the *body scan technique*. Instructions for mindfulness meditation and body scan meditation are provided in the Appendix (II-c).

8.11.2.4 Guided Imagery

Guided imagery is a convenient and simple relaxation technique that can help in quickly and easily managing stress and reducing tension. This technique can help to ease tension and stress. Practice of guided imagery involves imagining a scene in which one feels at peace, and free from all tension and anxiety. Detailed instructions of a guided imagery practice exercise are provided in the Appendix (II-b).

8.11.2.5 Visualization

Visualization is a stress reducing technique where we can use our imagination to visualize situations that make us feel good. These feelings bring on the relaxation response. The first step in visualization is to close the eyes. The next step is to allow the mind to wander to a place that makes one feel good. This could be any relaxing environment. The key is to mentally take oneself to a positive place. Visualization can be used to foresee positive outcomes to situations. For example, you are preparing to give a presentation and you feel stressed. Take a deep breath and visualize that you are standing in front of your class giving an exemplary presentation. Everything has turned out to be great. This type of visualization is like a mental rehearsal. Again, the thoughts must be positive and everything must turn out well.

Visualization can be used along with positive self-affirmations to bring about a relaxing effect and help combat stress.

8.11.2.6 Expressing Thoughts and Feelings

The simple act of expressing what one may be going through can be very cathartic. Talking to a friend or a family member, sharing your feelings, confiding in a close one can help ventilate bottled up emotions that lead to significant amount of stress. When one feels that their problems cannot be directly shared with someone else, one can use other techniques that facilitate ventilation such as talking to a pillow or writing in a diary. Writing one's feelings helps in gradually easing the feelings of emotional trauma or stress. Writing or talking about emotional experiences has been found to be associated with significant health-related benefits. Adolescents can be asked to write for at least four days in a week for a minimum of 20 min per day. In their writings, they should be asked to acknowledge their emotions more openly and allow themselves to feel all the emotions associated with the event in question. Expressive writing exercise is a useful behavioural technique that can be used to facilitate ventilation of pent up emotions and in dealing with stress. Instructions for expressive writing are given in Fig. 8.11.

8.11.3 Adapt to the Stressor

If an individual cannot change the stressor, he/she can adapt to stressful situations and thus regain their sense of control by changing their expectations and attitude related to the situation.

I would like for you to write about your deepest thoughts and feelings about the stressful life experiences in your life. In your writing, i would like you to really let go and explore your very deepest thoughts and emotions. You can tie the sources of these emotions to your childhood, your relationships with others, including your parents, lovers, friends and relatives. You may also link these to your past, present or future or to who you have been, who you would like to be, or who you are now. You may write about the general issues and experiences on all days of your writing or on different topics each day. All your writing will be completely confidential. Do not worry about spelling, sentences or grammar. Only focus on acknowledging and expression of all the emotions that you feel. Express openly and honestly. You may feel a little low at the end of this exercise. It this happens, do not worry. It is a very temporary feeling and will go away in a few minutes. Writing about your feelings will help you vent your emotions and feel lighter and better.

Adapted from: Pennebaker, 1985

Fig. 8.11 Instructions for expressive writing exercise

8.11.3.1 Distraction

If excessive worry or rumination is causing stress for adolescents, then distraction may be appropriate technique to be used in response to stress. Distraction involves using behaviours that involve engaging in any kind of pleasurable activities to distract oneself from the stressful event. These may include listening to music, reading an interesting novel, watching television, exercising or indulging in any hobby. Distraction is a form of a passive coping strategy. The individual copes with the situation without directly confronting it or trying to solve the problem. By using distraction techniques, we stop thinking about what is bothering us for a while and instead think about something else. In the first case vignette, S could be taught distraction techniques to deal with stressful thoughts about her red patch. She could be told that in order to cope with her distressing thoughts, while she has stopped doing her daily chores and going for any outing and stays sitting in her bed thinking further about her looks and what could happen, this is only worsening her state further. She could be asked to use various distraction techniques such as humming a song loudly or start watching funny videos on Internet whenever these thoughts occur in her mind. A detailed list of distraction techniques has been provided in the Appendix (II-e).

8.11.3.2 Worry/Rumination Postponement

The worry/rumination postponement experiment is a strategy that helps strengthen control over excessive and persistent thinking. This technique is effective in challenging the beliefs about uncontrollability over negative thinking. For instance, if an adolescent feels stressed and has been experiencing a lot of negative and anxiety producing thoughts and believes that he has no control over these thoughts and he just loses his ability to disengage from the web of thoughts, he may be given the instructions given in Fig. 8.12 to practise the exercise.

"When you notice that you are worried, say to yourself, "stop, this is only a thought, I am not going to engage in it right now, I'll leave it here and worry about it later". Next, allocate a particulat time in the day, when you will allow yourself 15 minutes to worry. When that time comes you can engage in your worry for as much as you want. However, you do not have to necessarily use this time period in worrying about what was bothering you during the day. If you still decide for using this period, please make a note for why you decided to use it."

Adapted from: Wells (2009)

Fig. 8.12 Instructions for worry postponement exercise

S could be asked to allot 15 min in the evening, from 6 to 6.15 pm, to mull over her thoughts about her skin allergy. She could be asked that at any point during the day if these distressing thoughts occur to her mind, she can gently instruct herself to postpone the time of thinking to the allotted slot. She should also be told clearly that she is supposed to use this worry time only if she feels the need and not otherwise.

8.11.3.3 Cognitive Restructuring

Unhelpful thinking styles in the form of faulty and dysfunctional beliefs can lead to maintenance and worsening of stress and lead to further complications. Cognitive restructuring is a form of cognitive therapy that can help adolescents identify, challenge and alter stress-inducing thought patterns and beliefs. The main aim of cognitive restructuring was to help individuals to replace stress-inducing thought patterns with more accurate and flexible styles of thinking. During periods of heightened stress, the brain is designed to focus attention on potential threats and problems and exclude paying attention to the other important sources of information. In this process, several errors in thinking may occur. These errors lead to increase in the feelings of anxiety, worry and helplessness, which in turn can lead to avoidance instead of problem solving. Learning how to recognize when these thinking errors occur and how to correct them can help alleviate distress and facilitate more productive coping efforts.

- *Role of thought appraisals in experience of stress*:

We generally attribute the causes of stress in our lives to outside sources such as heavy traffic, difficulty in our relations with a classmate in school and demanding workload. But each of these can be stressful to one person and not stressful to another person. The difference here lies in perception. According to Lazarus and Folkman (1984), an individual's perception of an event results directly from their cognitive appraisal of that event. Two cognitive processes are important in the perception of stress: appraisal and coping. According to Lazarus and Folkman (1984), cognitive appraisal is the evaluative process used by a person to determine why and to what extent a particular experience or series of person-environment experiences result in stress. They found that increased levels of dysfunctional stress occur when individuals perceive that they do not have the necessary interpersonal and/or physical resources to be able to successfully negotiate or cope with the demands or pressures coming from the environment.

In general, the way we view a situation or event contributes more to the generation of a stress response than the situation itself. The manner in which we think can have a large affect on the chance that we will experience stress. This is because our style of thinking affects the way we process information, which in turn affects the way we perceive a situation or event. Certain ways of thinking can distort perceptions and make it more likely for individuals to see that they lack resources. These may include negative thinking, discounting the positive and maximizing the negative, overgeneralising, pessimism, over-analysing, self-criticism, rigid (black and white) thinking, exaggerating and catastrophizing, etc. These thoughts generally represent certain dysfunctional styles in thinking and cognitive distortions. A list of cognitive distortions is provided in the Appendix (II-h).

Here, we highlight the use of cognitive restructuring through case example highlighted in the Case Vignette I.

When S experiences stressful thoughts, she is experiencing many distortions in her thinking. For example, she is thinking of a common allergy as a form of some major dermatological disease. She is thinking that this will spread throughout her body and will affect her internal organs and her voice. Here, she is engaging in "catastrophizing". She has been thinking that what if the doctor has misdiagnosed her condition, what if this is a major disease, what if the allergy spreads and what if she loses her voice. Here, S is engaging in the "what if statements". She also believes that she must be good looking in order to be a successful singer and she should be having a beautiful face and body else she will be rejected. Here she is having the cognitive distortion of "Should and must statements". She has decided that she will compete only in the upcoming Indian Idol and no other platform and if she does not get selected, she will never try becoming a singer. Here, she is engaging in "All or none thinking".

The first step involves becoming aware of unhelpful irrational thoughts. This can be done by asking oneself, "What just went through my mind",

Some common examples of unhelpful and irrational thoughts are provided in Fig. 8.13.

The next step involves challenging unhelpful thoughts. For example in Case Vignette II (Table 8.8):

Situation: *R was unable to finish a particular homework assignment before the due date of submission due to ill health*

Now he can challenge his unhelpful thoughts by asking the questions given in Fig. 8.14.

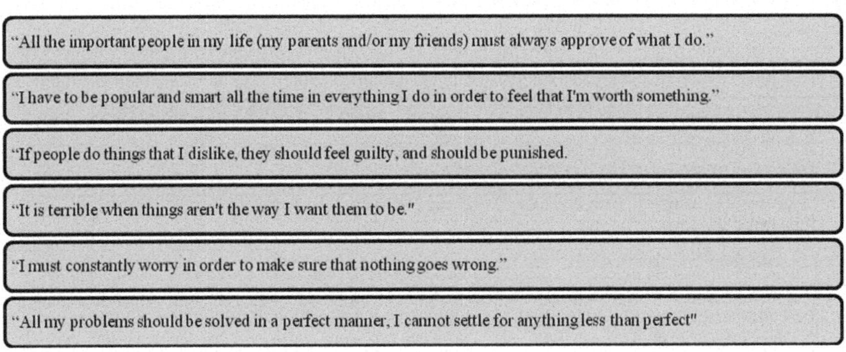

Fig. 8.13 Irrational thoughts

Table 8.8 Identifying cognitive errors

Unhelpful thought	Category
I am such a failure	Labelling
My teacher is going to send me to the principal and I will be expelled from school	Catastrophizing
What if she gives me a zero in my final internal assessment because I did not finish this homework	What if statements

The following exercise can also be used to dispute irrational thoughts. In this situation, an adolescent's friends made a plan to go for a movie but everybody then refused last minute. He can practise the following exercise provided in the illustration in Fig. 8.15.

Citing another example from Case vignette I, S has reacted angrily towards her sister on being asked to come along with her for shopping. She can be asked to do the exercise given in Fig. 8.16.

Adolescents can be asked to apply these techniques to challenge their unhelpful thoughts that result in experience of stress. These techniques can be used to test if the thoughts are realistic and balanced.

8.11.3.4 Practising Positive Thinking

An optimistic state of mind can have positive effects on health as well as well-being. Keeping a positive attitude overall and looking for the positive things in

Is there an evidence that contradicts this thought?

- I have finished all the rest of the assignments and submitted them on time
- I usually act responsibly and sincerely in school

Can you identify any patterns of unhelpful thinking described earlier?

- I'm catastrophising. Based on my failure to finish one assignment, I'm jumping to the worst possible conclusion
- I'm labelling myself based on one task

What would you say to a friend who had this thought in a similar situation?

- I would say-you can tell your teacher about your health and get an extension for the submission date, stop stressing

What are the costs and benefits of thinking in this way?

- Costs: It is really getting me down and I can't concentrate on anything else. I'm feeling so stressed out
- Benefits: i can't think of any

Is there a proactive solution to this unhelpful thinking?

- Maybe i could wait till tomorrow and talk to my teacher first; inform her about my illness and wait till then, without over-thinking

Is there another way to look at this situation?

- Maybe that I should tell myself that this is just one such event where i haven't been able to do my work properly, I should better not make any conclusive statements about myself based on a single event, I may be overthinking about what will happen, maybe my teacher understands and empathises with me over my illness and give me more time, or maybe she doesn't turn up to school tomorrow and i get another day and finish my work!

Fig. 8.14 Questions used for challenging dysfunctional thoughts

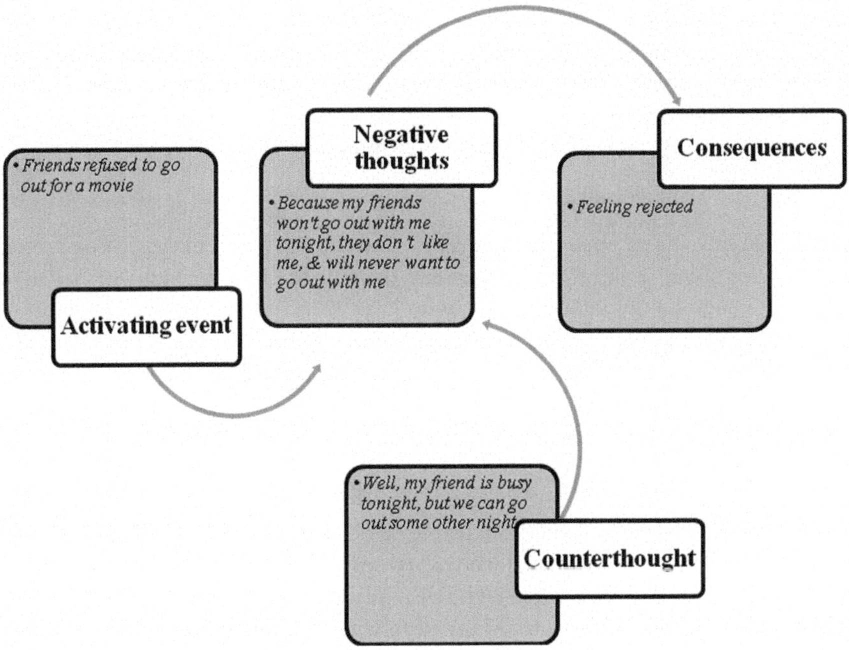

Fig. 8.15 Cognitive restructuring I

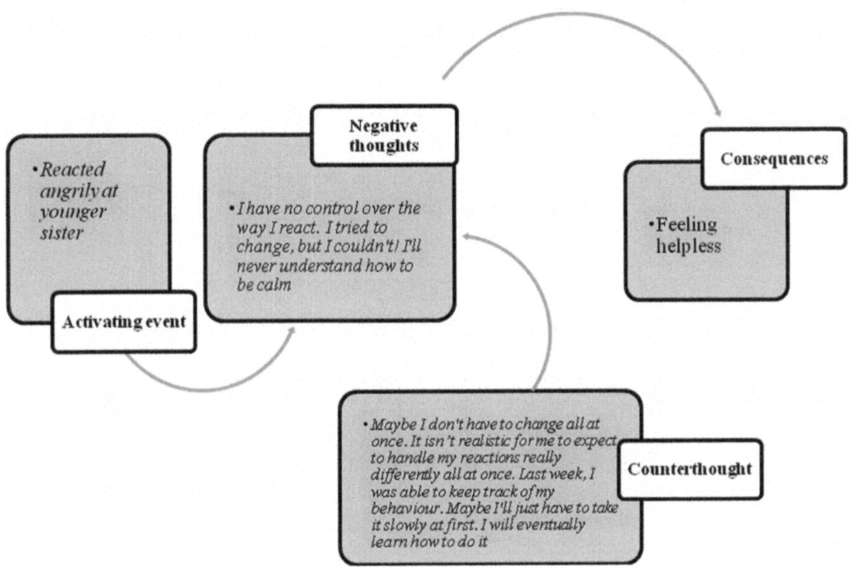

Fig. 8.16 Cognitive restructuring II

people and situations is an excellent stress strategy to reduce stress. Positive thinkers mostly tend to expect the best. When bad things happen to them, they consider this occurring to be unusual. Pessimists, on the other hand, expect bad things to happen to them.

Some important steps involved in positive thinking include:

- Ending any negative self-talk

Before you talk, think about what you are going to say to yourself. If you notice that you are taking a negative perspective, then stop. Look for signs of negative thinking, which mainly include words with negative connotations such as no, not, never, can't, shouldn't, couldn't, don't, and won't. When you find yourself thinking on these lines, make an effort to stop yourself in middle and find a positive way of saying the same thing.

The following techniques can be used to replace negative thinking:

- Thinking in a positive way

Speaking from a negative perspective always seems easier. Positive thinking involves employing extra efforts. One way to speak positively is to talk about what you would like, rather than what you don't. You can speak about what you want, rather than what you don't want. Many problems that create stress can be looked upon as opportunities. For instance, students may complain about an assignment, paper or test, but each of these can be seen as an opportunity to learn, practice and improve skills.

- Practicing positive language everyday

There are many opportunities throughout the day for practicing positive thinking. These may include what you think about a classmate or about general thoughts about life, etc. These opportunities can be used to practise positive language and use positive self-talk.

Examples of using positive language are included in Fig. 8.17.

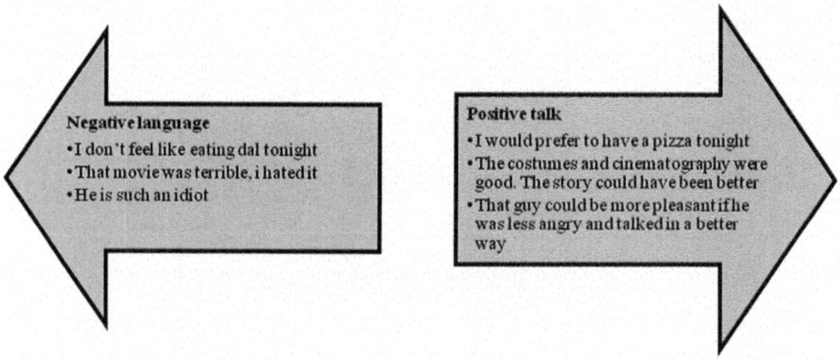

Fig. 8.17 Replacing negative with positive language

8.11.3.5 Using Positive Affirmations

Many adolescents experience negative thoughts very frequently. Negative thinking is self-fulfilling in nature. As a result of this, adolescents may easily tend to believe that they are not good enough. A useful strategy for dealing with this situation involves consciously doing just the opposite—using positive affirmations. Affirmations are positive, specific statements that help to overcome self-depreciating, and negative thoughts. They are usually short, positive statements that target a specific behaviour, belief or area that one may be struggling with. Positive affirmations can be used to help adolescents raise their confidence, control negative feelings such as frustration, impatience and anger and improve self-esteem. Some examples of positive self-affirmations are given in Fig. 8.18.

Affirmations should always be formed in the present tense, as if they are already happening. For instance, "I am well-prepared and well-rehearsed, and I can give a great presentation" can be used before starting a presentation.

The power of affirmations lies in their repetition. Thus, it is advised to recite the affirmations several times a day. One should also repeat them particularly when engaging in negative thinking.

8.11.3.6 Problem Solving

Deficits in problem-solving skills can be a major source of stress among adolescents. Adolescents with poor problem-solving ability may feel overwhelmed and this can make them feel extremely distressed. Problem solving involves a structured way of working through a problem. Training in problem-solving skills can be done using modelling and behaviour rehearsal as well as using case vignettes. The therapist can act as a model and demonstrate the steps involved in solving a hypothetical problem while the adolescent can be encouraged to learn and rehearse these skills. Adolescents can also be provided with case vignettes presenting a particular situation that demands a solution to a problem. A description of steps involved in problem solving has been provided in the Appendix (II-g).

To explain this further, let us consider the description provided in Case vignette II; R may be facing a lot of stress due to his lack of ability to solve problems.

Positive self talk

- I think I can do good work.
- I have very good friends.
- I have good control over my thoughts and feelings.
- I can find a solution for my problems.
- I have the capacity to successfully live through my adversities.
- I can take care of myself even when things are bad.

Fig. 8.18 Positive self-affirmative statements

Thus, on a particular day, when after many days of procrastination, R realizes that he has to submit an important assignment the next day and also has a test at his coaching institute on the day that follows; he may panic over how to solve this problem at the last minute. He can carry out the steps as highlighted in Fig. 8.19.

8.11.4 Accept the Stressor

Sometimes, stress may arise from unavoidable situations. In these situations, the best way to cope with stress is to accept things as they are. Accepting the situation

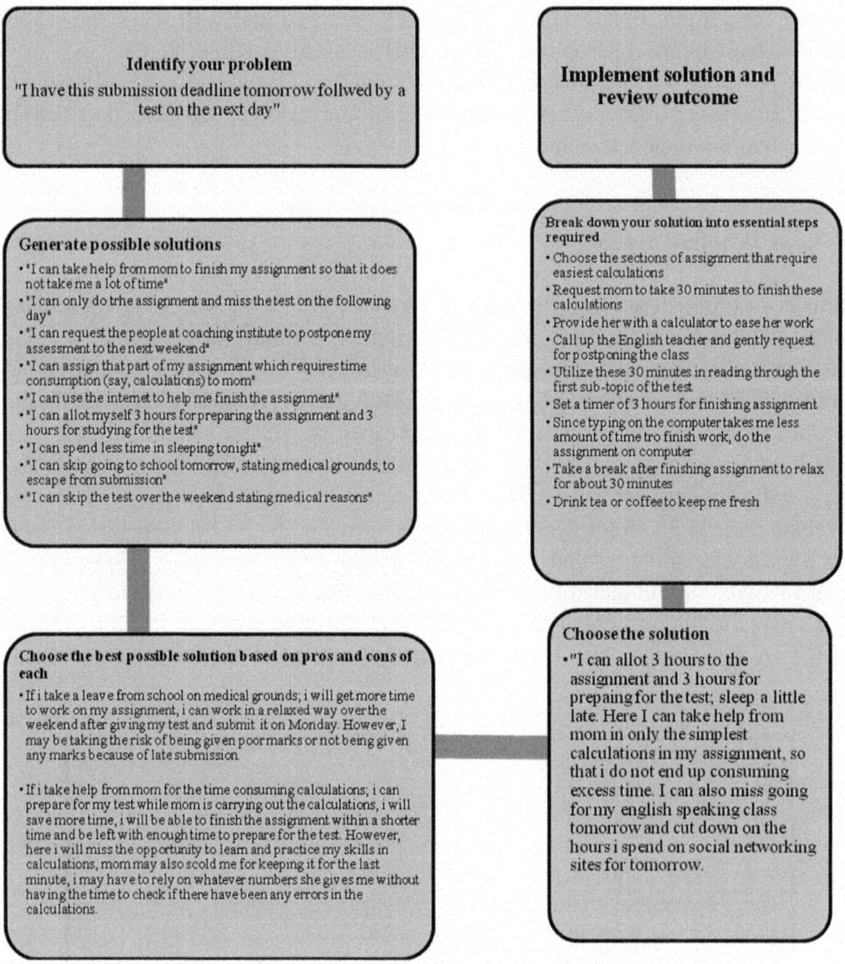

Fig. 8.19 Steps involved in problem solving citing case example

as it is may initially seem difficult, but eventually, one may learn to positively adapt oneself according to the demands of the situation, once it has been accepted. For instance, it is important to learn that we cannot control other people's thoughts and behaviours, so rather than stressing over them, we can learn to control our reactions towards such individuals. When stressors seem to be unavoidable, we can learn to look at them in an optimistic manner, changing our outlook to look upon these situations as learning opportunities for our overall growth. Other ways for accepting stressors include bringing changes in our lifestyle so that we are better able to cope with these situations.

8.11.4.1 Lifestyle Modification

A healthy lifestyle is essential for stress reduction. Adolescents can improve their general health by going for regular exercise, eating a healthy diet which is rich in a variety of whole grains, vegetables and fruits, and avoid taking excessive alcohol, caffeine and tobacco. Regular physical exercise can also serve as an effective distraction technique and may directly neutralize the harmful effects of stress on blood pressure and the heart. Nicotine, alcohol, caffeine and drugs are used by many adolescents to get away from stress. Consuming too much of these components has a powerful opposite effect. These substances only temporarily mask the problem but they do not eliminating it. Overuse of these substances can be harmful for health. Poor eating habits can also cause significant amount of stress. Not eating or eating less can make one feel tired and mentally exhausted and in turn makes the individual more vulnerable to daily stressors. Lack of sleep also makes one get agitated at small things. Sometimes excessive stress can cause stress-induced insomnia. Getting enough sleep, maintaining time for sleep and going to bed a little earlier can protect the mind against stress tremendously. Keeping pets can also reduce stress levels. Caring for a pet helps in reducing cortisol levels and blood pressure. Aside from making these changes, one can also include regular leisure time activities in daily routine. These lifestyle changes can be included in adolescent's behavioural plans.

8.12 Barriers to Treatment

Stress can mean different things to different people. It affects the way an individual deals with his/her life events and can have a serious impact upon health and well-being. However, since it is mostly viewed as a part of living, individuals may not realize the importance of seeking treatment for the condition. Many a times, most individuals do not acknowledge stress as a potential problem. Quite often, when stress is looked upon as inevitable, adolescents may start viewing themselves as passive, helpless victims of such states and allow stress to take complete control over their lives without taking necessary measures to combat it.

One may tend to ignore the impact that prolonged stress can have upon overall health and eventually develop many physical and psychological diseases related to stress. Another barrier to management of stress is its severity and co-morbidities. Stress is quoted often associated with depression and anxiety. Co-morbid psychopathologies related to severe stress levels can lead to dropout from therapy if they are not addressed on time. Extremely high levels of stress can also interfere significantly with skill building for managing stress. Other barriers to treatment may include rigidity in thinking styles, personality-related problems, poor motivation for change, resistance to change, procrastination and poor motivation to implement newly learnt plans for managing stress. Lastly, a common barrier to the treatment of most psychological conditions including stress stems from the fact that due to a heightened tendency for being easily self-conscious commonly associated with this stage of life, many adolescents may view seeking treatment as a sign of weakness and may hold generally oppositional attitudes towards help seeking.

8.13 Summary and Conclusion

Adolescents may experience stress everyday and can benefit from learning stress management skills. While some types of stressors may be perceived as positive, others may pose a significant threat to the adolescent's overall health and well-being. Most adolescents experience more stress when they perceive a situation as problematic, difficult or painful and they do not have the resources to cope. Some sources of stress for adolescents might include school demands and frustrations, negative thoughts and feelings about themselves, physical changes in their bodies, problems with friends and/or peers at school, separation or divorce of parents, moving or changing schools, taking on too many activities or having too high expectations. In India, one of the major sources of stress among adolescents stems from academic pressures. Every year, during examination times, newspapers and dailies are flooded with reports of adolescents succumbing to high levels of stress and committing suicide. Inadequately managed stress can lead to experience of high levels of anxiety, withdrawal, aggression, physical illness or poor coping skills such as drug and/or alcohol use. Although stress is uncomfortable, it is a manageable condition. Effective stress management involves developing helpful and more problem-focussed coping skills and can thereby lead to building resilience in an individual. There are many ways in which individuals can be taught to manage stress. Where stress seems to be a directly avoidable, adolescent can be trained to identify vulnerable situations and directly prevent their exposure to these states. Stress can also be avoided by learning effective communication skills, learning to say no, resolving conflicts effectively and managing time. Adolescents can also be taught to alter the stressors by practising various relaxation exercises and meditation to cope with stress. They can also learn to alter stressors by expressing their thoughts and feelings so as to maintain communication and avoid bottling up of feelings leading to distress. Another way of managing stress involves adapting to the stressor by changing one's reactions to stress and styles of thinking. Cognitive techniques such as identifying automatic thoughts, recognizing and correcting cognitive distortions, developing new ways of thinking more realistically, practising how to think positively, building an optimistic disposition, practising distraction techniques and learning effective problem-solving skills can help adolescents cope better and more effectively. Finally, where stress seems unavoidable, accepting the situations, maintaining friendships, practising regular physical exercise, taking time to enjoy life and building an overall healthy lifestyle may help combat the experience of stress.

References

Adams, J. D. (1980). *Understanding and managing stress: A workbook in changing lifestyles*. San Diego: University Associates.

Aggarwal, S., Prabhu, H., Anand, A., & Kotwal, A. (2007). Understanding and managing stress. *Indian Journal of Psychiatry, 24*, 96–102.

Ang R. P., Huan V. S. (2006) Academic expectations stress inventory (AESI): Development, factor analysis, reliability and validity. *Educational and Psychological Measurement, 66*, 522–539.

Arun, P., & Chavan, B. S. (2009). Stress and suicidal ideas in adolescent students in Chandigarh. *Indian Journal of Medical Sciences, 63*, 281–287.

Augustine, L. F., Vazir, S., Rao, S. F., Vishnu Vardhana Rao, M., Laxmaiah, A., & Nair, K. M. (2011). Perceived stress, life events & coping among higher secondary students of Hyderabad, India: A pilot study. *Indian Journal of Medical Research, 134*, 61–68.

Bhasin, S. K., Sharma, R., & Saini, N. K. (2010). Depression, anxiety and stress among adolescent students belonging to affluent families: A school-based study. *Indian Journal of Pediatrics, 77*(2), 161–165.

Biegel, G. M., Brown, K. W., Shapiro, S. L., & Schubert, C. M. (2009). Mindfulness-based stress reduction for the treatment of adolescent psychiatric outpatients: A randomized clinical trial. *Journal of Consulting and Clinical Psychology, 77*(5), 835–866.

Byrne, D. G., Davenport, S. C., & Mazanov, J. (2007). Profiles of adolescent stress: The development of the adolescent stress questionnaire (ASQ). *Journal of Adolescence, 30*, 393–416.

Coddington, R. D. (1972). The significance of life events as etiologic factors in diseases of children. A survey of professionals. *Journal of Psychosomatic Research, 16*, 205–213.

Cohen, S., Kamarck, T., & Mermelstein, R. (1983). A global measure of perceived stress. *Journal of Health and Social Behavior, 24*, 385–396.

Connor-Smith, J. K., Compas, B. E., Wadsworth, M. E., Thomsen, A. H., & Saltzman, H. (2000). Responses to stress in adolescence: Measurement of coping and involuntary stress responses. *Journal of Counseling and Clinical Psychology, 68*, 976–992.

Dinesh, S., & Syamakumari, S. K. (2010). Prevalence of stress among school children in Kerala. Available at: http://www.articlesbase.com/mental-health-articles/prevalence-of-stress-among-schoolchildren-in-kerala-1868702.html. Last accessed 8 March 2011.

Dohrenwend, B. S., & Dohrnwend, B. P. (1984). *Stressful life events: Their nature and effects* (1st ed.). New York: Wiley.

Fletcher, K. (1996). Psychometric review of Dimensions of Stressful Events (DOSE) ratings scale. In B. H. Stamm BH (Ed.), *Measurement of Stress, Trauma, and Adaptation* (pp. 144–151) Lutherville, MD: Sidran Press.

Insel, P., & Roth, W. (1985). *Core concepts in health* (4th ed.). Palo Alto: Mayfield Publishing Co.

Humphrey, J. H. (2004). *Childhood stress in contemporary society*. New York: Haworth.
Johnson, J. H. (1986). *Life events as stressors in childhood and adolescents*. Newbury Park: Sage.
Kabat-Zinn, J. (1990). *Full catastrophe living: Using the wisdom of your body and mind to face stress, pain and illness*. New York: Delacorte.
Kassam-Adams, N. (2006). The acute stress checklist for children (ASC-Kids): Development of a child self-report measure. *Journal of Traumatic Stress, 19*(1), 129–139.
Kessler, R. C. (1997). The effects of stressful life events on depression. *Annual Review of Psychology, 48*, 191–214.
Kisiel, C., Lyons, J. S. Blaustein, M., Fehrenbach, T., Griffin, G., Germain, J., et al. (2010). Child and adolescent needs and strengths (CANS) manual: The NCTSN CANS comprehensive—trauma version: *A comprehensive information integration tool for children and adolescents exposed to traumatic events*. Chicago, IL: Praed Foundation/Los Angeles, CA & Durham, NC: National Center for Child Traumatic Stress.
Lazarus, R. S., & Folkman, S. (1984). *Psychological stress and the coping process*. New York: Springer.
Lewinsohn, P., Hoberman, H., & Rosenraum, M. (1988). A prospective study of risk factors for unipolar depression. *Journal of Abnormal Psychology, 95*, 378–383.
Mehta, M. (2000). Stress in school children. Report submitted to Indian Council of Medical Research (ICMR), New Delhi.
Meichenbaum, D. (1985). *Stress inoculation training*. New York: Pergamon Press.
Monck, E., & Dobbs, R. (1985). Measuring life events in an adolescent population: Methodological issues and related findings. *Psychological Medicine, 15*, 841–850.
Newcomb, M. D., Huba, G. J., & Bentler, P. M. (1981). A multidimensional assessment of stressful life events among adolescents: Derivation and correlates. *Journal of Health and Social Behavior, 22*, 400–415.
Patterson, J. M., & McCubbin, H. I. (1987). Adolescent coping style and behaviors: Conceptualization and measurement. *Journal of Adolescence, 10*, 163–186.
Peacock, E. J., & Wong, P. T. P. (1990). The stress appraisal measure (SAM): A multidimensional approach to cognitive appraisal. *Stress Medicine, 6*, 227–236.
Pennebaker, J. W. (1985). Traumatic experience and psychosomatic disease: Exploring the roles of behavioural inhibition, obsession, and confiding. *Canadian Psychology, 26*, 82–95.
Rabkin, J. G., & Streuning, E. L. (1976). Life events, Stress and illness. *Science, 194*, 1013–1020.
Sahoo, S., & Khess, C. R. (2010). Prevalence of depression, anxiety, and stress among young male adults in India: A dimensional and categorical diagnoses-based study. *Journal of Nervous & Mental Disorders, 198*(12), 901–904.
Selye, H. A. (1978). *Stress without distress*. Philadelphia: Lipincott.
Sharma, J., & Sidhu, R. (2011). Sources of stress among students preparing in coaching institutes for admission to professional courses. *Journal of Psychology, 2*(1), 21–24.
Tharoor, H., Kar, N., & Jagdisha, S. (2002). Profile of childhood depression in a south Indian clinic population. *Indian Journal of Psychiatry, 44*, 9–11.
Vadakkekkara, E. (2003). Concern over high stress levels among students. The Hindu.
Waghachavare, V. B., Chavan, V. M., Dhumale, G. B., & Gore, A. D. (2013). A cross-sectional study of stress among junior college students in a rural area of Sangli district of Maharashtra. *Innovative Journal of Medical and Health Science, 3*(6), 294–297.
Wells, A. (2009). *Metacognitive therapy for anxiety and depression*. New York: Guilford Press.

Chapter 9
Pain Management

Anubha Dhal, Manju Mehta and Rajesh Sagar

9.1 Introduction

Pain constitutes a complex multi-dimensional phenomenon with physiological (etiology), sensory (intensity, quality), affective (emotional response), cognitive (thoughts about the experience), and behavioral (e.g., grimacing, avoidance) components. It affects various aspects of an adolescent's life including physical, psychological, and emotional states, disrupting daily activities, academic aspects as well as peer and family relationships (France and Krishnan 1988; Marks et al. 2006; Pradhan et al. 2000).

Acute pain has a short duration (less than 6 months), which is usually associated with tissue damage. It serves as a warning symptom for a person to get investigated or treated for an injury or pathology. Chronic pain refers to pain lasting more than 6 months, resulting from neurobiological changes in the nervous system. The emotions usually accompanying this kind of pain are despair, frustration, hopelessness, and depression.

Chronic and recurrent pain not associated with a disease is very common in childhood and adolescence. In a recent systematic review, the prevalence rates for types of pain were reported as follows: headache: 8–83 %; abdominal pain:

A. Dhal (✉)
Global Health Strategies Emerging Economies Pvt. Ltd., New Delhi, India
e-mail: anubha.dhal@gmail.com

M. Mehta · R. Sagar
Department of Psychiatry, All India Institute of Medical Sciences, New Delhi 110029, India
e-mail: drmanju.mehta@gmail.com

R. Sagar
e-mail: rsagar29@gmail.com

M. Mehta and R. Sagar (eds.), *A Practical Approach to Cognitive Behaviour Therapy for Adolescents*, DOI 10.1007/978-81-322-2241-5_9

4–53 %; back pain: 14–24 %; musculoskeletal pain: 4–40 %; multiple pains: 4–49 %; other pains: 5–88 %. Pain prevalence rates were reported to be higher in girls and increased with age for most pain types. Lower socioeconomic status was associated with higher pain prevalence especially for headache (King et al. 2011). Recent negative evidence for certain pharmacological approaches (Silva 2003; Silva et al. 2005) suggests that there is a growing need for management of pain and psychiatric disorders using non-pharmacological therapies such as cognitive behavior therapy. Cognitive behavior therapy is based on the inter-relationships between our thoughts, emotions, and behavior (Beck 1995).

9.2 Cognitive Behavioral Model of Pain

This model assumes that the symptoms and disability associated with chronic pain are perpetuated by psychological, behavioral, and social factors. The cognitive behavioral experience of pain can be conceptualized under the following heads (Brown 2007) (Fig. 9.1):

(a) Predisposing factors

These factors include the following:

- *Childhood trauma*—This constitutes physical, emotional, or sexual abuse by parents or caregivers as well as neglect or lack of care. Persons with a history of trauma in childhood are thought to focus on bodily symptoms such as pain as a means of avoiding the cognitive and emotional processing associated with the traumatic experiences.
- *Childhood experience of illness*—The children with a history of physical illness in childhood that is reinforced by anxious parents may increase the focus on bodily symptoms, anxiety, and illness behavior in adulthood as well as resorting to maladaptive coping behaviors.
- *Temperament/Personality*—Negative affectivity or neuroticism personality factors have been found to be associated with somatic preoccupation, illness behavior as well as symptom misinterpretation in persons with somatic complaints.

(b) Precipitating factors

These factors include the following:

- *Physical illness*—Recent physical illness may increase anxiety related to health, which may precipitate development of multiple somatic complaints such as recurrent headaches.
- *Life events*—Somatic symptoms such as pain may be preceded by life events such as trauma, interpersonal difficulties, or financial problems. This relationship between life events and development of somatic illness may be medicated by factors such as anxiety or depression or body focus to avoid unwanted cognitive and emotional processes associated with those life events.

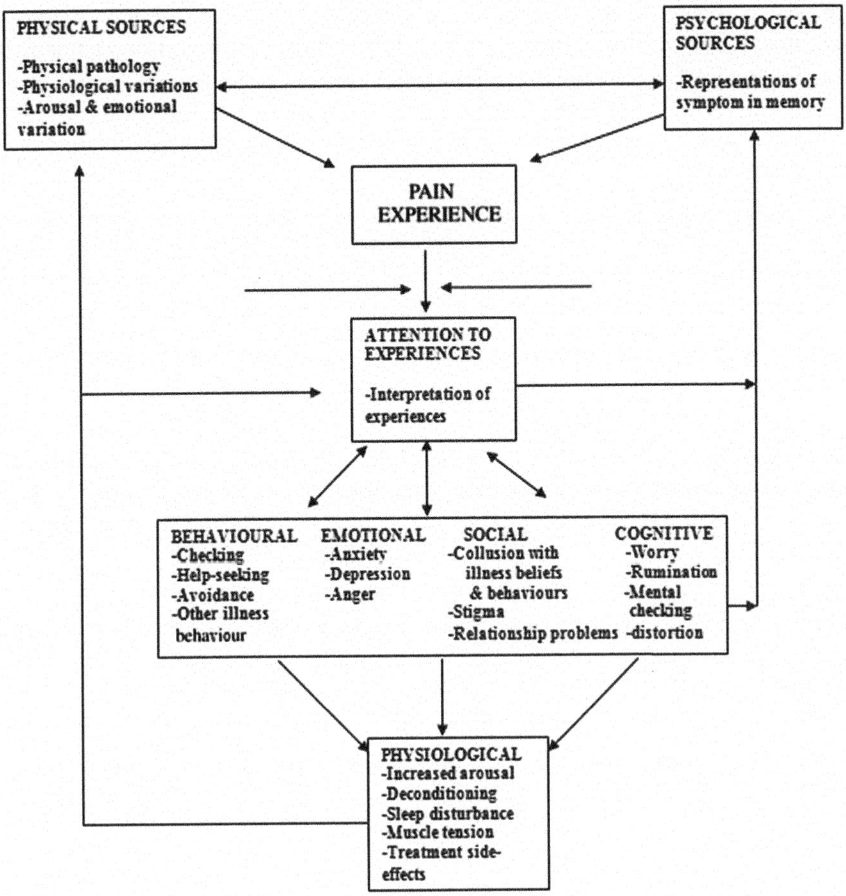

Fig. 9.1 Cognitive behavioral conceptualization of pain. *Source* Brown (2007)

(c) Maintaining factors

These factors include the following:

- *Illness beliefs*—Some beliefs about physical health and illness have been found to be associated with maintaining somatic complaints such as headaches. Example of such beliefs include those involving beliefs about inability to tolerate stress or having vulnerability to illness, beliefs about importance of maintenance of vigilance about symptoms, cost of illness or death, danger of anxiety as well as all or none beliefs about personal competence.
- *Illness behaviors*—Certain illness behaviors such as avoidance of certain stimuli or physical exercise, compensatory behaviors, repeated medical consultations, and body checkups may maintain somatic illness or symptomatic distress.
- *Cognitive factors*—Excessive rumination or worry about causes, implications, and treatment of symptoms, and physical health often maintain somatic complaints

experienced by persons. A selective attribution bias for information confirming symptoms has been found to be associated with maintenance of somatic symptoms.

- *Affective factors*—Emotional distress such as anxiety and depression has been associated with increase in rumination, catastrophizing, and worrying about the pain symptoms as well as increase in illness behavior and increase in other pain symptoms.
- *Social factors*—Excessive reassurance/care-seeking from significant others may increase somatic preoccupation. The stigma associated with emotional distress and psychological illness by others may reinforce assigning physical causes to symptoms as well as increase illness behaviors. Increase in visits to doctors may at times increase misattributions regarding symptoms especially if causal factors associated with somatic symptoms are explained in an ambiguous way to the patient.
- *Physiological factors*—Certain physiological factors such as sleep and appetite changes, organic illness, and medication overuse may maintain the illness behavior, associated emotional distress as well as cognitive misattributions and hence, exacerbate somatic symptoms.

9.3 Case Vignette

Ms. A, a 14 year old girl, student of class 9, belonging to middle socioeconomic family with no family history of psychiatric illness, presents with headache with nausea and vomiting. She reports having difficulty in attending school and concentrating on her studies due to the headaches. She has been diagnosed with having migraine by the physician and has been prescribed some medication. She has been referred to the consultant psychologist for non-pharmacological management.

9.4 Assessment

The goals of assessment include the following: firstly, to establish whether the possibility of any physical disease has been ruled out; secondly, to engage the patient in a therapeutic process; thirdly, to gain information regarding the cognitive behavioral formulation of the presenting complaints; and lastly, to understand the medical and psychological conditions that the adolescent is suffering from.

The assessment tools employed in assessing an adolescent with pain are discussed below:

(a) *Interview*—This involves interviewing the adolescent and informant regarding the symptoms, history of development of symptoms, personality/temperament of the child (easy going, difficult), any associated medical conditions, history

0 1 2 3 4 5 6 7 (8) 9 10

No Pain Moderate Pain Severe Pain

Fig. 9.2 Example of Visual Analog Scale

of psychiatric illness in family, and developmental history. A detailed account of the chief complaints pertaining to the site(s) of pain, duration as well as precipitating stressors associated with it is taken into account. The medical investigations as well as comorbid pathology should also be elicited. At times, a model, i.e., a caregiver with pain behavior may be present in the patient's environment. Information regarding that should be noted. This can also be supplemented with a mental status examination (appearance, perception, thought, mood, affect, thought, gait, attention and concentration, eye contact, higher mental functions, and insight).

(b) *Self-report measures*—Self-report measures can be considered as the most valid approach to pain measurement. Although self-report measures exist in verbal and nonverbal formats, both require sufficient cognitive and language development to understand the task and generate an accurate response. Verbal self-report measures include structured interviews, questionnaires, self-rating scales, and pain adjective descriptors. Nonverbal measures include facial expression scales, Visual Analog Scales (VASs) (Fig. 9.2), and drawings. Quantitative scales include the VAS and Colored Analog Scale (Barretto et al. 2004). Multi-dimensional pain measures help to assess pain experience, disability, and quality of life. These include the Bath Adolescent Pain Questionnaire (Eccleston et al. 2005). The McGill Pain Questionnaire (MPQ) may be used with older adolescents (Melzack et al. 1975).

(c) *Pain diary/ABC chart*—A pain diary or an ABC chart is a way to keep track of the situations, thoughts, and feeling. This helps to elicit the negative/automatic thoughts associated with pain sensations. This diary may be useful in identifying cognitive distortions and restructuring them. Example of the pain diary of Ms. A is as follows:

A (Activating event)	B (Beliefs)	C (Consequences)
Trying to finish homework	*I cannot understand anything*	*Headache, feeling irritated*

(d) *Observation* The adolescents' maladaptive patterns of emoting and behaving can be observed and recorded while he/she is at home or school (teacher and parent reports), while waiting for the therapy session, and during the therapy sessions. These can be useful in helping the adolescent learn adaptive coping patterns to cope with pain and any associated disability as well as for social skills training.

9.5 Pain Management Sessions

Cognitive behavioral therapy focuses on understanding the physiological, emotional, behavioral, cognitive as well as social factors involved in the precipitation and maintenance of symptoms, distress, and disability experienced by the child/adolescent. It emphasizes the role of negative thoughts and increased emotional distress in increasing maladaptive behavioral responses. It employs a range of cognitive and behavioral techniques such as relaxation, cognitive restructuring, and problem solving to reduce symptomatic distress (Lipchik et al. 2002). The contraindications for cognitive behavior therapy include mental retardation, organicity, severe emotional and thought disturbance, and developmental disorders.

The common goals of cognitive behavioral interventions targeted at managing pain symptoms usually fall into the following categories: (1) psycho-education, (2) addressing the lifestyle and personality factors associated with the vulnerability to develop a psychiatric illness, (3) provision of alternative, non-catastrophic interpretation of symptoms in cognitive behavioral terminology, (4) challenging catastrophic thoughts related to psychiatric symptoms, (5) modification of the dysfunctional beliefs associated with symptoms through behavioral experiments, (6) reversal of avoidance and maladaptive coping behaviors, (7) inculcating behavioral coping skills, and (8) instilling problem solving skills (Brown 2007).

Cognitive behavior management of pain disorders in adolescents is based on principles of agenda setting, guided discovery, and collaborative empiricism. The steps or techniques involved in the cognitive behavioral management of pain disorders in adolescence are discussed under the heads of initial, middle, and termination sessions.

9.5.1 Initial Sessions

The initial sessions involve establishing a rapport with the adolescent, explaining the relationship between thoughts, feelings, and pain behavior as well as establishing goals of therapy. The initial sessions take usually two sessions.

The first session is focused on forming a working therapeutic alliance with the adolescent and psycho-educating him/her regarding the nature and course of chronic pain as well as the role of stress and other psychological factors in precipitating and maintaining the illness. The adolescent is made aware of what cognitive behavioral therapy entails by explaining the model of cognitive behavior therapy using an example. This further involves making the adolescent aware of how physical symptoms can be maintained or worsened through certain thoughts and behavior patterns.

Example of an excerpt from the initial sessions:

Therapist: "…Hello A. My name is Dr. X. Would you like to tell me what problems you have been facing?…"

Adolescent: "…I have been having lot of headaches lately and have not been able to do anything…"

Therapist: "…When pain persists over time, you may develop negative thoughts about your pain or yourself (e.g., "I cannot do anything"). As a result of this, you may avoid doing activities (e.g., not going to school) for fear of increase in pain. (The therapist can draw a pain cycle diagram to show the adolescent the relationship between pain, distress, negative thoughts and avoidance behaviour.)

The treatment goals identified prior to therapy include objective and realistic goals. A contract regarding number of sessions can be negotiated at this stage with the adolescent as per the goals delineated.

Example of goals for the case vignette

The goals of therapy for the case of Ms. A would include the following:

- *To reduce the pain and reliance on pain medicine*
- *To learn skills to cope with pain*
- *To improve physical and emotional functioning (feeling better, going to school regularly, being able to concentrate on studies, etc.)*

9.5.2 Middle Sessions

The middle therapy sessions focus on teaching the adolescent cognitive behavioral techniques and giving homework assignments. Middle sessions usually range from 4 to 6 sessions. The cognitive behavioral techniques that are used for pain management include the following (Beck 1995):

(a) *Relaxation techniques*—Since pain is associated with emotions of stress and anxiety, simple relaxation techniques can be introduced in the third or fourth session of therapy. Relaxation techniques for pain may include the following:
   - **Muscle relaxation**—Pain often results in muscle tension. Muscle relaxation exercises involve a series of movements where participants actively tense and then relax different sets of muscles in a particular order, such as beginning with those in the head and working your way down to the feet.
   - **Guided imagery**—This involves imagining a peaceful, beautiful environment to refocus attention and divert the mind and feelings away from the pain sensations (Appendix IIb).
   - **Biofeedback**—This involves making changes to one's bodily functions through activities such as guided imagery. Through hand-held machines that provide audio and visual information, biofeedback can help to measure changes in heart rate, muscle tension and relaxation.

(b) *Distraction techniques*—This technique involves redirecting the focus from the pain sensation to another activity, such as listening to music, drawing, etc. (Appendix IIe). If the pain is mild or lasts for some minutes, the distraction technique may provide some relief. This technique can also serve as a temporary coping strategy for even the most intense pain.

(c) *Structured activity scheduling*—The adolescent is encouraged to increase his/her involvement in activities that he/she may be avoiding due to the fear of pain. Activity pacing and pleasant activity scheduling are used to help the adolescent increase the level and range of his/her activities. *Example*: *in the case described above, the adolescent may be at times avoiding school due to the fear of pain or in case of mild pain. Here, she may be encouraged to attend school on days when the pain is relatively mild. Further, she may be asked to include pleasurable activities such as drawing which would help the adolescent gain a sense of mastery and reduce avoidance behaviors.*

(d) *Cognitive restructuring*—Negative automatic thoughts may serve as precipitating and maintaining factors for pain, emotional distress, and pain-related avoidance behaviors (Appendix IIh). Adolescents suffering from acute or chronic pain often report cognitive distortions or errors in thinking. Some examples of common cognitive errors in the case described above are as follows:

- *All or none thinking*—when the adolescent sees things in all or none categories. E.g., "…I can't understand anything…"

- *Overgeneralization*—when a person generalizes one event to all events. E.g., since the adolescent is not able to complete her homework, she may report that "…I can't do anything properly…"
- *Catastrophizing*—predicting extreme or horrible consequences for events. E.g., due to constant difficulty in concentrating on studies due to headaches, the adolescent reports "…I will never be able to do well in school…"
- *Labeling*—attaching a negative label to self. E.g., "…I am a failure…"

Example of an excerpt from the session on cognitive restructuring:

Therapist: "…Let us review your ABC chart (*presented in the assessment section*). Here we can see that when you are trying to study or finish your homework, you feel irritated and get headaches due to the thought that you can't understand anything…"

Adolescent: "…Yes. I just don't feel that I can understand anything when I try to concentrate on my studies in class or am trying to finish my homework …"

Therapist: "…When pain persists over time, you may develop negative thoughts which may affect the way you feel and lead to headaches. You can change these negative thoughts into positive thoughts. Let us take the example of the thought that you can't understand anything. What evidence do you have that suggests that this thought is true?…."

Adolescent: "…I am not able to complete my homework and concentrate on my studies so that's why I feel that I can't understand anything…"

Therapist: "…Has there been any time when you may have had difficulty but were still able to complete your school work?…"

Adolescent: "…Yes. On some days I do find it difficult to understand the school work but I still am able to complete it…"

Therapist: "…So there may be some days when even though you find it difficult, you still are able to understand and complete your school work…"

Adolescent: "…Yes. I think so…"

Therapist: "…So then the thought that you can't understand is not true. Every time you get such a thought, you can change it to "…I have been able to complete my work in the past, and will be able to do so today also…"

9.5.3 Termination Sessions

The adolescent is encouraged to take more responsibility while ending therapy. The therapist discusses the possibility of minor setbacks involved when terminating therapy. The goals of therapy as well as the process of therapy are reviewed with the adolescent and practicing techniques which have proved to be effective for the adolescent is reinforced by the therapist. This is followed by follow-up sessions. Example of termination session is as follows:

Example of an excerpt from a session during the termination phase:

Therapist: "…Let us review the progress you have made since the first session. What are the changes that you have observed since the first session? …"

Adolescent: "…I feel much better now. My headaches have reduced and I am able to go to school more often. I am also able to complete my school work on time…"

Therapist: "…Keep up the good work and practice the coping methods that you have learnt. There may be times when you may face difficulty and fall back into negative thinking patterns. At that time motivate yourself and use the coping methods. Let us meet once a month till now instead of on a weekly basis…"

9.6 Follow-Up

After terminating therapy, the adolescent may be called on a monthly basis and then after 3 and 6 months, respectively. The follow-up sessions can be used to review the progress the adolescent has made and address the challenges that he/she may be facing. In case of a relapse, therapy may be resumed on a regular basis.

9.7 Barriers to Treatment and How to Overcome Them

There may be certain barriers which may interfere with successfully implementing cognitive behavior therapy as an approach to pain management. These barriers include the following:

- *Therapist's gender*—Most adolescents may be more comfortable with same gender therapists, particularly while dealing with issues pertaining to abuse, which may present as a significant factor in predisposing and maintaining pain behavior. Hence, it is important to address the factor pertaining to gender at the beginning of therapy.
- *Therapeutic relationship*—It is important to establish a working relationship with the adolescent during the therapeutic process to ensure successful therapeutic outcomes. This involves establishing a rapport with the adolescent and ensuring that adolescent understands the concepts being explained in therapy and complies with the homework assignments.

- *Mental illness and disability*—Certain comorbid psychiatric conditions with pain such as severe depression, psychosis, etc. may not respond to cognitive behavioral management as a first line treatment approach and may require pharmacological management. Hence, this factor needs to be explored during history taking and mental status examination.
- *Cultural factors and concept of cognition*—"Cognition" may be seen as a culturally based phenomenon, and some adolescents may be uncomfortable to separating their thoughts and feelings. They may also find the concept of challenging or disputing maladaptive thoughts a difficult one to grasp. Also, appropriate behavior may be defined as a culturally mediated phenomenon and may pose as a challenge in separating adaptive and maladaptive cognitions and disputing the same.
- *Other barriers* These may include lack of willingness or motivation on the part of the adolescent, language barriers, lack of training on the part of therapists, and inability to understand concepts and follow through with cognitive behavioral techniques, etc.

References

Barretto, E. P., Ferreira, E., & Pordeus, I. A. (2004). Evaluation of toothache severity in children using a visual analogue scale of faces. *Paediatric Dentistry, 26*, 485–491.

Beck, J. S. (1995). *Cognitive therapy: Basics and beyond*. New York: Guilford Press.

Brown, R. J. (2007). Medically unexplained symptoms. In N. Tarrier (Ed.), *Case formulation in cognitive behavior therapy: The treatment of challenging and complex cases* (pp. 263–292). New York: Routledge.

Eccleston, C., Jordan, A., McCracken, L. M., Sleed, M., Connell, H., & Clinch, J. (2005). The bath adolescent pain questionnaire (BAPQ): Development and preliminary psychometric evaluation of an instrument to assess the impact of chronic pain on adolescents. *Pain, 118*, 263–270.

France, R. D., & Krishnan, R. K. R. R. (1988). *Chronic pain*. Washington: American Psychiatric Press.

King, S., Chambers, C. T., Huguet, A., MacNevin, R. C., McGrath, P. J., Parker, L., et al. (2011). The epidemiology of chronic pain in children and adolescents revisited: A systematic review. *Pain, 152*, 2729–2738.

Lipchik, G. L., Holroyd, K. A., & Nash, J. M. (2002). Cognitive-behavioral management of recurrent headache disorders: A minimal-therapist-contact approach. In D. C. Turk & R. J. Gatchel (Eds.), *Psychological approaches to pain management: A practitioner's handbook* (2nd ed., pp. 365–389). New York: Guilford Press.

Marks, D. F., Murray, M., Evans, B., Willig, C., Woodall, C., & Sykes, C. M. (2006). *Health psychology: Theory, research and practice*. New Delhi: Sage.

Melzack, R. (1975). The McGill pain questionnaire: Major properties and scoring methods. *Pain, 1*, 277–299.

Pradhan, S. C., Anand, K. S., & Biswas, A. (2000). Chronic pain: An interface between neurology and psychiatry. *Indian Journal of Medical Sciences, 54*, 238–245.

Silva, R. R. (2003). Psychopharmacology news. *Journal of Child and Adolescent Psychopharmacology, 13*, 409–410.

Silva, R. R., Gabbay, V., Minami, H., Munoz-Silva, D., & Alonso, C. (2005). When to use antidepressant medication in youths. *Primary Psychiatry, 12*, 42–50.

Part III
Interventions

Chapter 10
Anxiety Management

Swati Kedia Gupta and Manju Mehta

10.1 Introduction

Anxiety is a natural response to any situation involving harm and therefore can be considered as a fundamental human survival response (Stein and Bouwer 1997). In that sense, most anxiety is functional, beneficial and inhibits excessive risk-taking. As a common psychological problem it usually manifests for the first time in childhood (Verhulst et al. 1997). In significant minority of young people, the natural anxiety system responds excessively or is misinterpreted leading to development of anxiety disorders. Moreover, it can be highly distressing for the person experiencing it and leads to significant social and personal impairment. It may also negatively affect the individual's overall development and personality. Figure 10.1 describes a model to explain the development of anxiety disorders (Rapee 2001).

According to the model, genetic, shared as well as non-shared environmental factors play an important role in the development of anxiety. Some individuals are born with a genetic vulnerability to develop anxiety, which is manifested through their temperament and is evident in high level of arousal, emotionality, and a coping style characterized by avoidance. The temperament is the guiding force behind choosing an environment that maintains their coping style and also elicits protective behavior from significant others' (i.e., parents). In turn, this "over-protectiveness" may exaggerate the individual's threat perception leading to development of symptoms of anxiety disorders.

S.K. Gupta (✉)
NIMHANS, Bangalore, India
e-mail: swatikedia80@yahoo.com

M. Mehta
Department of Psychiatry, All India Institute of Medical Sciences, New Delhi 110029, India
e-mail: drmanju.mehta@gmail.com

M. Mehta and R. Sagar (eds.), *A Practical Approach to Cognitive Behaviour Therapy for Adolescents*, DOI 10.1007/978-81-322-2241-5_10

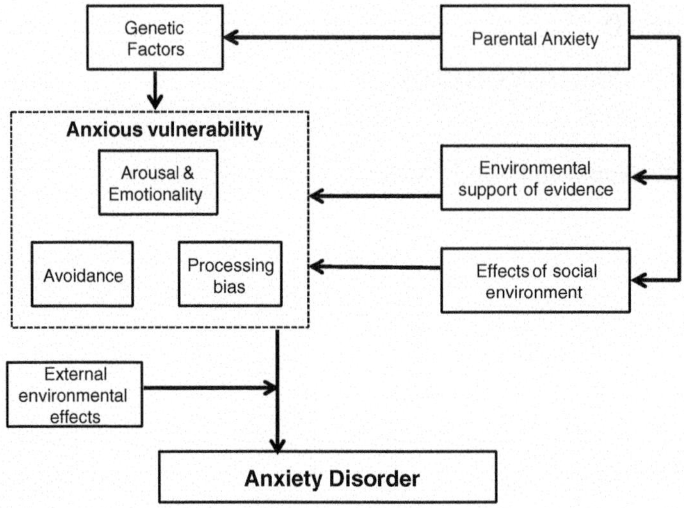

Fig. 10.1 Cognitive model of development of anxiety (Rapee 2001). Reproduced with permission from author

10.1.1 Presentation of Anxiety Symptoms

As mentioned earlier, anxiety is not always pathological; however, it is commonly accepted across cultures that it becomes maladaptive when it is persistent, severe, and frequent, gives rise to avoidance behaviors and interferes with functioning. In children and adolescents, the differentiation between normal and pathological anxiety is a particularly difficult task, as they tend to manifest many anxiety-like symptoms as a part of normal development.

Table 10.1 illustrates some of the normative anxiety in childhood and adolescence along with the corresponding anxiety disorders that the adolescent may develop (Beesdo et al. 2009; Muris et al. 1998).

Most commonly seen anxiety symptoms in adolescents, which can be highly debilitating are manifested in form of social anxiety and examination anxiety. Social anxiety can be typically seen in form of having less friends, difficulty in classroom activities participation, and avoidance of social interaction (e.g., initiating conversations). It is further associated with loneliness, dysphoria, and long-term functional impairment. Examination anxiety is seen in form of moderate to severe anxiety before tests/exams or in any situation where the adolescent would be evaluated. This can lead to decreased performance and poor self-esteem. Thus, it is important for the clinician to carefully assess for the presence of these syndromes and plan management accordingly.

Table 10.1 Normative and pathological anxiety in childhood and adolescence

Age	Development conditioned period of fear and anxiety	Psychopathological relevant symptoms
Toddler (12–18 months)	Separation anxiety	Sleep disturbances, nocturnal panic attacks, oppositional behavior
Toddler (2–3 years)	Fear of thunder, lightening, fire, animals, darkness, etc.	Crying, clinging, withdrawal, freezing, avoidance, secondary enuresis
Early childhood (4–5 years)	Fear of death or dead people	
Primary school (5–7 years)	Fear of specific objects, fear of germs, fear of natural disasters/ accidents, school anxiety	Withdrawal, timidity, extreme shyness to unfamiliar people, feelings of shame, avoidance
Adolescence (12–18 years)	Rejection from peers	Fear of negative evaluation, difficulty in forming interpersonal relationships

10.1.2 Comorbidity and Dysfunction

Usually presentation of anxiety symptoms in adolescence is complex and chronic. By late adolescence or early adulthood, decrease is seen in cases meeting the criteria for one anxiety disorder in favor of development of multiple anxiety disorders (Ollendick et al. 2008). It seems that the "load" of anxiety tends to contribute to the development of secondary complications. It has been consistently shown that anxious children are 8–29 times at risk of developing additional depression (Ford et al. 2003). Besides depression, alcohol and substance use and externalizing disorders, such as ADHD and conduct disorders are the most commonly co-occurring disorders (Bittner et al. 2007; Kendall et al. 2004; Ollendick et al. 2008).

Given these findings, it is important to work on the adolescent's coping skills and family's behavior early on to facilitate healthy development and possibly halt the transition to full-blown anxiety disorders. Thus, this chapter would highlight the role of cognitive behavior therapy or CBT with adolescents with anxiety symptoms as well as the need for involving their parents in the treatment process.

10.1.3 Cognitive Behavior Therapy

Various cognitive as well as behavioral factors are implicated in the development and maintenance of anxiety symptoms in adolescents. Therefore, it goes without saying that changes in approach/avoidance behaviors and cognitions are considered to be crucial for treatment change (Rapee et al. 2000), and therefore, CBT appears to be the obvious choice for management of anxiety symptoms.

The primary goals of CBT in adolescents with anxiety symptoms are to change the maladaptive learnings and thought patterns. It also involves skill-building in the session (use of role-plays and games, etc.) with an emphasis on generalizing these skills outside the sessions. As part of skill-building segments or as homework assignment, the adolescent is encouraged to practice the learnt skills in actual anxiety-provoking situations. The rationale behind exposure is that it helps the teenager in developing a sense of self-competence, which he/she also learns to acknowledge and appreciate. Additionally, an important component is involvement of parents or significant others who are not only made more sensitive to adolescent's condition, but also learn newer skills to reinforce positive coping behaviors (Rapee et al. 2009).

To facilitate the process of learning and skill-building, the therapist needs to play the role of a "collaborative coach" who generates treatment goals with the adolescent and his/her family and tailors the intervention to match the person's interest and ability. It has been seen that in most cases, 12–16 weeks of active treatment sessions are required, followed by spaced out "booster sessions" (Seligman and Ollendick 2011).

10.2 Assessment

Given the fact the anxiety can present as a normative developmental behavior in adolescents, its assessment and differentiating between normal, subclinical and pathological anxiety states becomes challenging as well as important.

Therefore, a thorough assessment is of utmost importance before embarking on the course of successful cognitive behavior therapy. The first and foremost step in assessment is a complete diagnostic evaluation, and efforts should be made to determine whether the presenting symptoms are clinically significant. Given the high rate of comorbidity, precautions should be taken to determine their presence and deciding which symptoms would form the primary target for interventions. Avoidance patterns, environment's reaction (for example, parents) to avoidance behaviors, and cognitive patterns of appraisals should be elicited in details so as to develop an individual case formulation. Information should be sought from as many sources as possible to have a full understanding of the person's symptoms and their context.

Assessment includes both interviews and rating scales. However, behavioral and cognitive assessment forms a crucial element in reaching an individualized formulation and tailoring of treatment to meet the needs, age, and ability of the individuals. See Appendix I for more details on assessment.

10.2.1 Interviews

The interview remains one of the most common methods for assessing anxiety symptoms in adolescents. Interviews can be structured or semi-structured, or they can be completely unstructured to elicit chief complaints, history of symptoms, temperament issues, ways of coping, and relationship patterns with significant others. A well-conducted interview should be able to provide glimpses into behavioral avoidance of fearful situations and the reinforcing factors for the same.

Apart from the adolescent, the family members should be interviewed as it would be useful in eliciting more information about adolescent's anxiety symptoms as well as to assess the concerns, coping strategies, and behaviors of the family members. It is often useful to interview the adolescent first and then talking to the family member as it can help the therapist becoming an ally of the adolescent.

10.2.2 Rating Scales

There are many rating scales that have been used for assessment of anxiety and anxiety disorders in children and adolescents. Moreover, administration of rating scales pre- and post-intervention can provide valuable information about changes in intensity of the symptoms. Although these tools have been developed in the Western countries and most of them have not been standardized for the Indian setting, they can be used to gain valuable information about the adolescent and his/her anxiety symptoms.

10.2.3 Cognitive and Behavioral Assessment

The rating scales and diagnostic schedules help the therapist to assess the presence or intensity of anxiety symptoms. However, to make a cognitive behavior formulation and subsequently plan CBT, the clinician needs to access the teen's thoughts, behaviors, and feelings in various situations and also his/her current repertoire of coping skills and abilities. The techniques for eliciting cognitions, emotions, and behavior patterns of the adolescent are as follows:

- Direct questioning
- Indirect assessment of anxiety
- Behavior analysis

Direct questioning: Once rapport has been established adequately, the therapist can engage the adolescent in direct questioning. Open-ended questions should be used to allow the adolescent to articulate freely. Some of the direct questions can be as follows:

- "*What are you thinking?*"
- "*What thought came to your mind when you first met me?*"
- "*What are the thoughts that run through your mind when you see a snake (or any particular animal the adolescent is afraid of)?*"
- "*What thoughts came to your mind when your friends asked you to talk to that girl/boy you really like?*"
- "*What are your thoughts when you are not able to wash your hands as often as possible?*"

Fig. 10.2 An anxious adolescent in a social situation

- *"How did you feel when you were left alone with a group of strangers in that party?"*
- *"How do you feel when you get up in the morning?"*

Assessing anxiety indirectly: If the rapport is well-established, most adolescent would be able to provide information with direct questioning. However, sometimes a reluctant, introvert, or unsure adolescent may answer with, "I don't know" or "I m not sure." With these kinds of individuals, eliciting information through other means might work better; for example, they may be more comfortable in telling what someone else might be thinking in the similar situation. This can be done with the use of series of stories or thought bubbles. The adolescent can be presented with a vignette and asked to describe what the characters were thinking and feeling (Fig. 10.2).

Behavior analysis: With slightly older children and adolescent, the therapist can make use of behavioral charts that can easily identify the thoughts, feelings, and behaviors of the person. This should be given as homework assignment that should be filled each time the individual feels anxious. An example of behavioral chart is given in Table 10.2.

Table 10.2 Example of Behavior chart

Day/Time	Situation	Thoughts	Emotions	Behavior
	What were you doing? Whom were you with? What exactly happened?	What were you thinking? Rate how much you believe them on a scale of 0–10	How did you feel? Rate your feelings on a scale of 0–10	What did you do? What happened after that?

10.3 Case Vignettes

Case Vignette 1: Juhi, a 16-year-old girl studying in class IX was bought for therapy by her parents. The main complaints were difficulty in talking to new people, feeling insecure, and feeling anxious in social situation. She had been experiencing these symptoms since a long time, but these had worsened in the past few months. Rapport was established, and diagnostic schedules were administered. Though she did not meet full criteria for social anxiety disorder, she was highly distressed by her symptoms. It was also seen that the primary caregiver who was the mother also exhibited anxiety symptoms during traveling alone in public transport, at high places and while undertaking long journeys. She would also be extra worried if Juhi was even 20–30 min late while coming from school or party.

10.4 Intervention

Skill-based CBT packages for management of anxiety symptoms in adolescents typically include psycho-education, affect recognition, cognitive restructuring, relaxation, and exposure. Additional areas may include assertiveness, social skill training, and problem-solving strategies. Most of these packages also include a parent component (Kendall and Hedtke 2006). Figure 10.3 delineates the various techniques to be used while intervening with anxious adolescents.

Initial Sessions

- Establishing rapport and assessment
- Psycho-education
- Recognition of anxiety and physiological affect associated with anxiety
- Managing Emotions

Middle Sessions

- Coping Skills: Recognizing and managing dysfunctional thoughts and schemas
- Coping Skills: Problem Solving
- Coping Skills: Social Skill Training
- Exposure based procedures
- Involvement of parents

Termination

Fig. 10.3 Session-wise CBT techniques

10.4.1 Establishing Rapport and Conducting Assessment

Some fundamental aspects of engagement in CBT are the motivation to change, capacity to learn, and use the skills. Developmental and social aspects tend to influence the adolescent's motivation to engage in therapy (Holmbeck et al. 2006). Some of these factors can be-being "bought" for treatment, fear of giving up established patterns of behaving, adolescent "egocentrism," reduced capacity for self-reflection, and need for autonomy and therefore conflict with adult figures (Stallard 2009).

A good rapport is the foundation stone of therapy. Thus, the first and most important step is establishing a rapport with the adolescent. Apart from assessing anxiety symptoms, the first couple of sessions should be dedicated to developing a good working alliance with the adolescent. Some of the ways of establishing rapport and boosting motivation can be as follows (Sauter et al. 2009):

(a) Engaging first with the adolescent and then family members
(b) Providing psycho-education to match the adolescent's cognitive level of understanding
(c) Providing facts and correct information while maintaining genuine interest in adolescent's welfare
(d) Boosting the adolescent's confidence in their ability to change
(e) Avoiding questioning and confrontations
(f) Orienting the adolescent to their personal goals
(g) Working collaboratively with the young person to set goals and have a say in the pace of treatment
(h) Encouraging adolescent to offer inputs for agenda of each session

Once rapport has been established, the therapist can conduct assessment of anxiety symptoms and comorbid conditions as discussed in the previous section. Although assessment is a continuous process, new information can arise at any point of time. However, an initial thorough assessment usually takes about 1–3 sessions after which interventions can be initiated.

10.4.2 Providing Psycho-Education

Psycho-education forms an important part of CBT as it provides the adolescent as well as the family with a wider perspective into what is happening, and it also helps them to prepare themselves for the treatment sessions. In the above-mentioned case (case vignette 1), the following components of psycho-education were incorporated (also see Fig. 10.4):

- She was made to understand nature of anxiety, the fact that is a common and natural response encompassing certain physiological reactions that are accompanied by negative thoughts, feeling anxious, and avoidance behaviors. The therapist then emphasized that some anxiety is helpful, but at times, it blows out of proportion, which can cause problems in daily living.

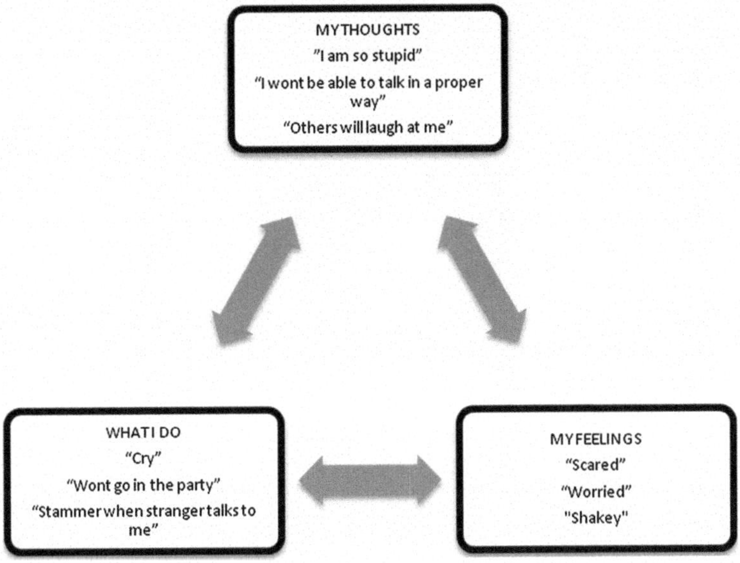

Fig. 10.4 Explanation for how thoughts, feelings, and behavior are related

- She was made to understand the basic premises behind cognitive behavior therapy, course of treatment, and how goals would be set.
- The role of family members and significant others in therapy process was delineated, and mother was made to understand that she needs to address her own thoughts and feelings, which may be acting as maintenance factors of anxiety in her daughter.

10.4.3 Recognition of Anxiety Symptoms and Associated Physiological Changes

It is imperative that the adolescent recognizes and is able to label the physiological changes that occur at the time of stress/anxiety. This is followed by an explanation of the purpose of these bodily changes. The final aim is to empower the adolescent to interpret his/her anxiety symptoms correctly and to take appropriate action to manage and reduce anxiety feelings. Figure 10.5 shows the worksheet that can be used to help the adolescent in identifying their bodily changes.

10.4.4 Managing Emotions: Relaxation Exercises

The aim of teaching relaxation exercises is to help the adolescent develop an awareness as well as control over their physiological reactions to anxiety. In treating anxiety symptoms, relaxation training is imperative as it can bring immediate

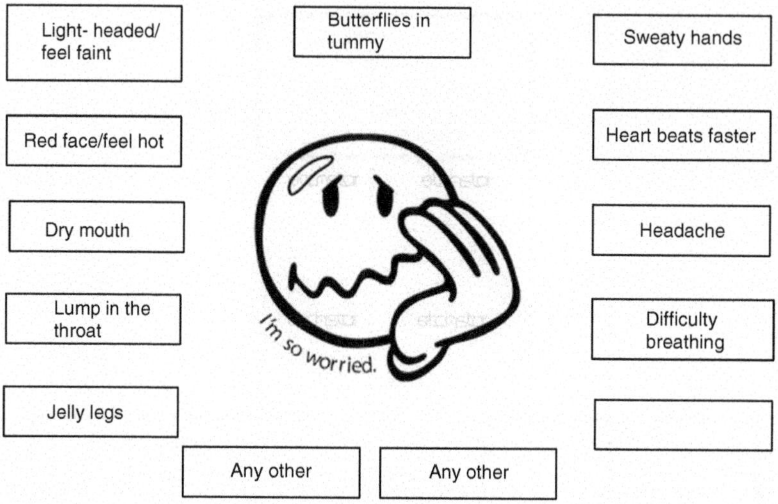

Fig. 10.5 Recognition of bodily symptoms associated with anxiety

relief. However, before teaching relaxation exercises to the adolescent, it is important to explain the rationale for the same. The therapist can either teach Jacobson Progressive Muscular relaxation (JPMR), which, in general, is found to be an efficacious form of treatment of generalized anxiety disorders and phobias. Another form of relaxation is controlled or deep breathing or its extension- cue- controlled relaxation.

Some of the other relaxation techniques, which have been found to be effective in management of adolescent anxiety disorders are mindfulness meditation (Broderick and Metz 2009; Kendall 2011) and yoga (Silva et al. 2009). Also, deep breathing or applied relaxation can be taught to adolescents with examination anxiety so that they can practice it before beginning the exam/test.

The therapist needs to reiterate to the adolescent that there is no one particular way of relaxing, and he/she needs to find out what works best for them. It is important to note that the therapist needs to make the adolescent practice these exercises in the session for a few times before they can do it without supervision. For more details on different ways of relaxation, please refer to Appendix II.

With respect to case vignette 1, Juhi was taught JPMR that was practiced for 3–4 sessions till she could do it on her own without guidance of the therapist. Then, she was also taught cue-controlled relaxation in which she voluntarily decided to pair the image of red light that had turned green with a state of relaxation. In two more sessions, she was able to relax herself using the cue. Before beginning each session, she was asked to rate her anxiety on a scale of 0–10 with 0 being no anxiety and 10 being "as anxious as she can be," then after JPMR/cue-controlled relaxation was administered, she was asked to rate her state of relaxation as well as anxiety from 0 to 10.

10.4.5 *Recognizing and Managing Dysfunctional Thoughts and Schemas*

CBT is based on the premises that emotional and behavioral dysfunction can be taken care of by helping the individual identify and challenge his/her distorted or unrealistic cognitions (thoughts). The process is also known as "cognitive restructuring" that involves identification of negative automatic thoughts ("hot" thoughts), identification of core beliefs, and finally, challenging thoughts and substituting them with alternative, positive thoughts. The other ways of dealing with negative thoughts are: positive self-talk and time-out.

Identifying Automatic Thoughts and Thinking Errors: One of the ways of identifying automatic thoughts is with the help of behavioral chart (Table 10.2). By describing the immediate thoughts that follow a situation, the adolescent can identify the negative automatic thoughts. Once the adolescent has learnt to identify his/her automatic thoughts, they can be introduced to the concept of "thinking errors," that is "the ways in which we try to look for evidence to prove that our 'automatic thoughts' were correct." Common example of thinking errors can be *magnification and minimization*—"I dropped my books and the **whole class** was looking at me and laughing" or "Doing well in dance class wasn't such a big deal. Anyone can do it" or *catastrophization*—"I m neither good in academics nor am I good at sports. I am good-for-nothing. I would never make any friends."

Using case vignette 1, Table 10.3 is an example of eliciting "negative automatic thoughts".

- Identifying Core Beliefs: The adolescent is made to understand that core beliefs are "fixed ideas that we have about ourselves that develop in childhood and are shaped and subsequently get crystallized due to early childhood experiences. These core beliefs affect the way we see ourselves, others, and future." The way of identifying core beliefs is called the "downward arrow technique" or simply the "SO WHAT" method. The idea is to take the negative automatic thought and keep asking "so what? If this was true, what would this mean about me?" till the core belief is reached. Using case vignette 1 above, Fig. 10.6 illustrates how core beliefs can be reached.
- Challenging Automatic Thoughts and Core Beliefs: Once the adolescent has learnt to identify their negative thoughts and core beliefs, they can be taught to challenge them. Following questions may be useful while challenging these thoughts and beliefs:

Table 10.3 Example of behavior chart using case vignette 1

Day/Time	Situation	Thoughts	Emotions	Behavior
18/11/2013 8:00 p.m.	A family friend who is very rich and fluent in English had come home for dinner, and everyone was talking and laughing	"I would never be able to talk like her" (7) "If I talk, I would mess up." (7)	Hopeless (6) Anxious (8)	I quickly finished my food and made an excuse to go to my room. I did not come out entire evening

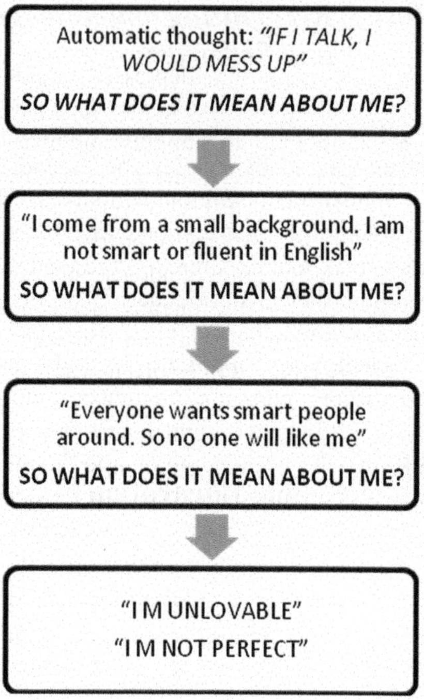

Fig. 10.6 Example of identifying core beliefs

- What evidence is there to **support** these thoughts?
- What would **my best friend/parent/teacher say** if they heard me thinking like that?
- What would **I say** to someone having these kinds of thoughts?
- Am I making a thinking error?

Again, using case vignette 1, Table 10.4 illustrates how thoughts or core beliefs can be challenged.

10.4.6 Coping Skills: Problem Solving

Another component of CBT is teaching the adolescent the steps in problem solving (D'Zurilla and Goldfried 1971). The goal is to train the adolescent in developing confidence in their own ability to help themselves meet challenges of daily lives. Before teaching the skill, the therapist emphasizes that problems are a part of everyday life and the adolescent needs to learn how to face them rather than avoiding them. Problem solving helps the adolescent become adept at generating alternatives in what may, at first, seem to be hopeless situations and therefore

Table 10.4 Challenging negative automatic thoughts using case vignette 1

Thoughts	Support	Challenge	Best Friends	New Thought
"I can never speak as fluently as her"	"In the last party I had gone to, I couldn't talk. When I tried to talk to another person, they did not show interest"	"Once I get comfortable, I can speak very well and no one laughs at me." "I got very good marks in English recitation in school"	What they would say—"You do speak well. Remember that class drama in which everyone appreciated your dialogue delivery." What would I say—"You don't have to compare yourself with others, you speak pretty well yourself."	"I have slight inhibitions in front of strangers. But once I get over that, I am able to speak pretty well"

anxiety provoking. In one session, the adolescent can be taught the technique using examples from his/her daily life, and then as a homework assignment, they can be asked to pick another problem bothering them and find a solution for it. Following are the stages of solving problems effectively.

Step 1 *Defining the problem*: The adolescent is encouraged to define and operationalize the problem so that it appears a 'workable' problem rather than something that is impossible to solve.

Step 2 *Generating alternatives*: Through use of brainstorming, all possible solutions, no matter how outlandish they may seem, are generated. The therapist needs to enable the adolescent to come with as many solutions as possible even if they do not seem viable. The therapist can model good brainstorming skills by generating both pragmatic and improbable alternatives, and encouraging the adolescent to follow.

Step 3 *Evaluating Alternatives*: The adolescent is asked to evaluate each alternative for its viability as well as positive and negative consequences.

Step 4 *Choosing the best solution and implementing it*: After weighing all possible solutions, the adolescent puts into action the best possible solution.

Step 5 *Re-evaluating*: The last stage involves evaluating the merits of the chosen action.

Figure 10.7 can be used as a worksheet for training the adolescent in problem-solving strategies.

Write down your exact problem.
Generate ideas and think about negatives, positives and feasibility of each idea.
It maybe a good idea to take help of others in the process.
Choose the best solution for your problem

My exact problem is:

Possible solutions	Positives	Negatives	Can it be done?

Fig. 10.7 Which solution should I choose?

10.4.7 Exposure-Based Procedures

A common occurrence in anxious adolescent is avoidance of any situation that is anxiety provoking. This not only leads to dysfunction at a various levels, it also hampers the individual's ability to learn adaptive coping and negatively affects his/her self-efficacy. Procedures involving exposure are helpful in decreasing avoidance behaviors and reinforcing the adolescent's belief in his/her ability to face anxiety-provoking situations. This technique is also very relevant in cases of social anxiety and specific phobias. At an initial stage, exposure itself may be an anxiety-provoking activity that may elicit resistance in the adolescent. Thus, it is of utmost importance to take **small steps** and reinforce the adolescent for every step that he/she takes.

Exposure can take place in vitro (in imagery) or in vivo (in real-life situations). It can also be done in a *gradual fashion* or by *flooding*. Which kind of technique would be followed should depend on the adolescent's preference, ability, and circumstances.

One of the most commonly followed techniques is of systematic or gradual exposure. The early exposure therapies were based on the principle of "reciprocal inhibition" that postulated that if a feared stimulus is paired repeatedly with a response incompatible with anxiety (i.e., relaxation), the stimulus would lose its ability to generate anxiety.

The technique of systematic desensitization followed this approach wherein the youth would be taught relaxation and a hierarchy of feared stimuli would be developed. Systematic exposure to feared stimuli would take place with the adolescent engaging in relaxation. However, recent research has strongly indicated that systematic exposure can be done without the relaxation training component as well (Stewart and Watt 2008). Thus, the exposure-based treatment generally have four phases: (1) instruction; (2) hierarchy development; (3) exposure proper, and (4) generalization and maintenance (Seligman and Ollendick 2011).

The exposure-based techniques would be explained with the use of following case vignette 2.

"Shanti, a 14 year-old girl, studying in class 6th presented with complaints of being fearful when asked to go out of the house alone since the past 2 months. Due to this, her mother had to accompany her to school. On days, when she wasn't able to do so, she skipped school. On further assessment, it was found that she started having physiological arousal the moment he stepped out of the gate alone. She would then start feeling anxious and would have the thought that she would die."

- Instruction: Rationale for treatment needs to be provided, which is often learning-based, "*We know that since a long time, you have always avoided any situation that was anxiety provoking. You would also understand that avoidance leads to decrease in anxiety (negative reinforcement) and therefore increases the likelihood that you would not attempt to face that or similar situation in the future. I want you to learn that you are capable of facing situations even if they are anxiety-provoking. The procedure we are going to begin now is called graded exposure. In this we both would gradually face the anxiety-provoking situations beginning from the least anxiety-provoking to the most till you are able to feel confident in all situations. Initially, it may increase your anxiety, but if you hold on, the discomfort would gradually reduce. We would be practicing this technique in-session, but it is of utmost importance that you practice it outside the sessions too.*"

- Development of Hierarchy: The therapist and adolescent create a hierarchy of feared situations and then rank them in terms of "subjective units of distress" from least feared to the most feared. The therapist should make sure that enough steps are generated so that each step represents a *gradual* progression, and it should also be ensured that adolescent has not skipped the most anxiety-provoking steps because of the fear of not being able to face them. An example of hierarchy created in case vignette 2 is given below. After each step is the subjective unit of distress with '0' being the lowest and '10' being the highest.

Example of hierarchy of feared situations

1. Stand by her front door for a couple of minutes (2)
2. Take a couple of steps out of the front door and then come back inside (2)
3. Walk in the garden inside house for 5 min (2)
4. Increase time spent in garden alone by 10 min (3)
5. Stand at the main door for a couple of minutes (3.5)
6. Take a couple of steps outside the main door and then return back (4)
7. Take a couple of steps outside the main door and stay there for 2–3 min (5)
8. Stay out of the main door for 8–10 min (5.5)
9. Go with mother to the nearby market (6)
10. Go alone to the nearby market (7)
11. Go with mother till the bus stop, and from there onward, her best friend would sit with her in the school bus (7.5)
12. Go alone to the bus stop and sit with her best friend in the bus (8)
13. Go alone to the bus stop and sit with an unknown person in the bus (8.5)

- Exposure—proper: The adolescent is exposed to each situation in the hierarchy till anxiety decreases. If possible, the therapist should model the desired behavior, but in case where in vivo exposure is not possible, then it can be done in the session by either using imagery or simulation programs. Each situation needs to be repeated till the anxiety has completely diminished for it. Then, he/she is encouraged to move to the next step. It is imperative that the therapist ascertains that the adolescent is NOT engaging in avoidance behavior and habituation is taking place both within and between sessions. At each stage, the adolescent is reminded to praise him/herself for the effort and accomplishment.
- Generalization and Maintenance: In order to generalize treatment gains across situations, the adolescent is usually given homework assignments to repeat exposures across similar situations outside the therapy room. This allows for solidification of the skills learned during the session.

10.4.8 Social Skill Training

Social skill training forms an important part of treatment especially for adolescent facing social anxiety. It is formed on the assumption that development of key social behaviors is often hindered due to inadequate socialization experiences. Social skill training is composed of the following components: listening to others, initiating a conversation, maintaining a conversation, expressing unpleasant feelings, ability to say No, ending a conversation politely, and resolving conflicts. For each skill, the counselor explains the rationale, and then using situations relevant to the particular adolescent, the counselor teaches each skill. Role-plays and behavioral experiments form the basis of teaching of these skills. Chapter 4 provides details of social skills training for adolescents.

10.4.9 Involvement of Family Members

As discussed earlier also, it has been strongly suggested that parental factors (e.g., over or under protectiveness; own anxieties and negative thoughts and modeling anxious behaviors) play a crucial role in the development and maintenance of anxiety symptoms in adolescents (Ginsburg et al. 2004). Given these factors, therapists are often faced with the dilemma of when and in what capacity to include parents in the treatment process.

Parents can be involved in the treatment in any of the three ways (Kendall et al. 2000):

- As "**consultants**": Parents provide information regarding nature of adolescent's anxiety. For example, the factors that exacerbate the child's social anxiety.
- As "**collaborators**": Parents help in carrying out treatment plan. For example, practicing relaxation at home, exposure to anxiety-provoking situations, etc.
- As "**co-adolescents**": Parents are involved in the treatment with the view that they are exhibiting behaviors that are believed to be contributing to maintenance of the child's anxiety. For example, an anxious parent might be encouraged to develop and implement a plan for managing his/her own anxiety in a social situation.

Whatever the role, at the outset, the therapist should psycho-educate parents about the nature of anxiety and how their child is affected by it. The parents should be given space to discuss their concerns, issues, and negative thoughts/feelings. However, when dealing with the family, the therapist must be careful not to breach the adolescent's trust by disclosing sensitive information that he/she may not want to share with parents. The parents can be taught to SUPPORT the adolescent:

S Show your child how to be successful (show your child how to successfully approach and cope with anxious situations. Model success)

U Understand that your child has a problem (remember that your child is not being willfully naughty or difficult. They have a problem and need your help)

P Patient approach (do not expect things to change quickly. Be patient and encourage your child to keep trying)
P Prompt new skills (encourage and remind your child to practice and use their new skills)
O Observe your child (watch your child and highlight the positive or successful things they do)
R Reward and praise their efforts (remember to praise and reward your child for using their new skills and for trying to face and overcome their problems)
T Talk about it (talking with your child shows them that you care and will help them feel supported)

10.4.10 Termination

Closure is a very sensitive issue especially when dealing with over anxious adolescents and therefore must be dealt with adequately. Since anxiety and stressful situations are a normal part of life, termination should be considered only when all treatment goals are achieved and anxiety appears to be within normal limits of the individual's developmental level. Termination should never be abrupt and should always be planned well in advance so that the adolescent is made more and more independent in handling their responses in various situations. Prior to termination, the therapist and adolescent must plan and prepare for potential stressful situations and review the individual's ability to deal effectively with them. Also, booster sessions must be planned to review the adolescent's progress and to help him/her deal with a new situation that was not anticipated.

10.5 Barriers to Treatment

Working with adolescent is a challenging issue, and the therapist may face certain barriers. Although, they are not impossible to deal with, but a therapist who is aware of these may deal with them more effectively when he/she encounters them. Some of the common barriers faced in therapy are enlisted below:

- Client related
  - Severe anxiety that may interfere with skill-building
  - Comorbid conditions that may complicate the issues at hand and require intensive intervention
  - Individual versus group interventions: Some adolescents may be more comfortable in individual sessions, while others may prefer groups

- Involving adolescent in treatment (treatment may be too "taxing" or too "kiddish" for the adolescent)
- Non-communicating adolescent
- Adolescent does not take responsibility for securing change (misses appointments, does not do homework)
- Limited cognitive or verbal abilities

- Family related
  - Noncooperative family members
  - Significant family dysfunction which warrants referral for family therapy
  - Psychiatric problems in significant others which may act as precipitating or maintaining factors for adolescent anxiety

- Therapist related
  - Inability to deal with adolescent issues due to lack of proper training
  - Personal biases (in terms of values and morality)
  - Lack of interest in dealing with adolescent population

10.6 Summary and Conclusion

To summarize, anxiety is a normal response to stressful situations and some anxiety is present at each developmental stage. However, problems stem up when anxiety symptoms blow out of proportion and start interfering with the individual's daily life. Moreover, since adolescence is a period of transition, anxiety symptoms can have long-lasting effects on individual's intrapersonal as well as interpersonal abilities. Therefore, treatment is crucial at an early stage.

Till date, cognitive behavior therapy for anxiety symptoms/disorders in adolescents has proved its efficacy over other treatment modalities in various randomized control trials. CBT in over anxious adolescent involves psycho-educating them about nature of anxiety and teaching them skills to identify and manage their thoughts and emotions. It also involves reducing anxiety with the aid of relaxation exercises and exposure-based procedures. The most crucial aspect of CBT is its emphasis on learning through games, role-plays, and modeling. Also, since CBT is a time-limiting treatment modality, most individuals benefit in a relatively briefer time.

Research proves that parents play a crucial role in not only maintenance of anxiety symptoms but also can become an aide in maintenance of treatment gains. Thus, it has been suggested that parents be involved in treatment as consultants, collaborators, or co-adolescents as required.

The therapist may face certain barriers to treatment, but by involving the adolescent and family members in a collaborative framework right from the beginning, many of these barriers can be overcome.

References

Beesdo, K., Knappe, S., & Pine, D. S. (2009). Anxiety and anxiety disorders in children and adolescents: Developmental issues and implications for DSM-V. *The Psychiatric Clinics of North America, 32*(3), 483–524.

Bittner, A., Egger, H. L., Erkanli, A., Jane Costello, E., Foley, D. L., & Angold, A. (2007). What do childhood anxiety disorders predict? *Journal of Child Psychology and Psychiatry and Allied Disciplines, 48*(12), 1174–1183.

Broderick, P. C., & Metz, S. (2009). Learning to breathe: A pilot trial of a mindfulness curriculum for adolescents. *Advances in School Mental Health Promotion, 2*(1), 35–46.

da Silva, L. T., Ravindran, L. N., & Ravindran, A. V. (2009). Yoga in the treatment of mood and anxiety disorders: A review. *Asian Journal of Psychiatry*, 2(1), 6–16. doi:10.1016/j.ajp.2008.12.002.

D'Zurilla, T. J., & Goldfried, M. R. (1971). Problem solving and behavior modification. *Journal of Abnormal Psychology, 78*(1), 107–126.

Ford, T., Goodman, R., & Meltzer, H. (2003). The British child and adolescent mental health survey 1999: The prevalence of DSM-IV disorders. *Journal of the American Academy of Child and Adolescent Psychiatry, 42*(10), 1203–1211.

Ginsburg, G. S., Siqueland, L., Masia-Warner, C., & Hedtke, K. A. (2004). Anxiety disorders in children: Family matters. *Cognitive and Behavioral Practice, 11*(1), 28–43.

Holmbeck, G., O'Mahar, K., Abad, M., Colder, C., & Updegrove, A. (2006). Cognitive-behavior therapy with adolescents: Guides from developmental psychology. In P. C. Kendall (Ed.), *Child and adolescent therapy: Cognitive-behavioral procedures* (pp. 419–464). New York: Guilford Press.

Kendall, P. C. (2011). *Child and adolescent therapy: Cognitive-behavioral procedures* (4th ed.). New York: Guilford Press.

Kendall, P. C., Chu, B., Pimentel, S., & Choudhary, M. (2000). Treating anxiety disorders in youth. In P. C. Kendall (Ed.), *Child and adolescent therapy: Cognitive-behavioral procedures* (pp. 235–287). New York: Guilford Press.

Kendall, P. C., & Hedtke, K. A. (Eds.). (2006). *Cognitive-behavioral therapy for anxious children: Therapist manual.* Ardmore, Pa.: Workbook Pub.

Kendall, P., Safford, S., Flannery-Schroeder, E., & Webb, A. (Eds.). (2004). Child anxiety treatment: Outcomes in adolescence and impact on substance use and depression at 7.4-year follow-up. *Journal of Consulting and Clinical Psychology*, *72*(2), 276–287.

Muris, P., Merckelbach, H., Mayer, B., & Meesters, C. (1998). Common fears and their relationship to anxiety disorders symptomatology in normal children. *Personality and Individual Differences, 24*(4), 575–578.

Ollendick, T. H., Jarrett, M. A., Grills-Taquechel, A. E., Hovey, L. D., & Wolff, J. C. (2008). Comorbidity as a predictor and moderator of treatment outcome in youth with anxiety, affective, attention deficit/hyperactivity disorder, and oppositional/conduct disorders. *Clinical Psychology Review, 28*(8), 1447–1471.

Rapee, R. (2001). The development of generalized anxiety. In M. Vasey & M. Dadds (Eds.), *The developmental psychopathology of anxiety* (pp. 481–503). Oxford: Oxford University Press.

Rapee, R. M., Schniering, C. A., & Hudson, J. L. (2009). Anxiety disorders during childhood and adolescence: Origins and treatment. *Annual Review of Clinical Psychology, 5*, 311–341.

Rapee, R., Wignall, A., Hudson, J. L., & Schniering, C. (2000). *Treating anxious children and adolescents: An evidence-based approach*. Oakland, CA: New Harbinger.

Sauter, F. M., Heyne, D., & Michiel Westenberg, P. (2009). Cognitive behavior therapy for anxious adolescents: developmental influences on treatment design and delivery. *Clinical Child and Family Psychology Review, 12*(4), 310–335.

Seligman, L. D., & Ollendick, T. H. (2011). Cognitive-behavioral therapy for anxiety disorders in youth. *Child and Adolescent Psychiatric Clinics of North America, 20*(2), 217–238.

Stallard, P. (2009). *Cognitive behaviour therapy with children and young people*. East Sussex: Routledge.

Stein, D. J., & Bouwer, C. (1997). A neuro-evolutionary approach to the anxiety disorders. *Journal of Anxiety Disorders, 11*(4), 409–429.

Stewart, S. H., & Watt, M. C. (2008). Introduction to the special issue on interoceptive exposure in the treatment of anxiety and related disorders: Novel applications and mechanisms of action. *Journal of Cognitive Psychotherapy, 22*(4), 291–302.

Verhulst, F. C., van der Ende, J., Ferdinand, R. F., & Kasius, M. C. (1997). The prevalence of DSM-III-R diagnoses in a national sample of Dutch adolescents. *Archives of General Psychiatry, 54*(4), 329–336.

Chapter 11
Depression

Paakhi Srivastava, Manju Mehta, Atul Ambekar and Rajesh Sagar

11.1 Introduction

Adolescence is a period enveloped by tensions of childhood, rapidly changing physical, emotional, and social changes, and apprehensions about adulthood. It is a critical affectively laden period for a developing self. More often than not, depressive mood is experienced during adolescence. The term "depression" can refer to an emotional state, or a cluster of signs and symptoms. The field of psychiatry and clinical psychology recognize depression as a disorder when it impacts the child with so much intensity, severity, and long duration that it causes a lot of personal distress to the adolescent; to the extent of hampering his physical, cognitive, social, emotional, occupational development and adjustments in different spheres of life.

P. Srivastava (✉) · M. Mehta · R. Sagar
Department of Psychiatry, All India Institute of Medical Sciences, New Delhi 110029, India
e-mail: paakhisrivastava@gmail.com

M. Mehta
e-mail: drmanju.mehta@gmail.com

R. Sagar
e-mail: rsagar29@gmail.com

A. Ambekar
National Drug Dependence Treatment Centre and Department of Psychiatry,
All India Institute of Medical Sciences, Ansari Nagar, New Delhi 110029, India
e-mail: atul.ambekar@gmail.com

M. Mehta and R. Sagar (eds.), *A Practical Approach to Cognitive Behaviour Therapy for Adolescents*, DOI 10.1007/978-81-322-2241-5_11

11.2 Epidemiology

Depression is one of commonest psychiatric disorders experienced by adolescents in India, and its prevalence is on rise (Malhotra et al. 2009; Chadda et al. 1994). Globally, depression has an estimated 1-year prevalence of 4–5 % in mid-to-late adolescence (Lochman et al. 2008). But the probability of depression rises from around 5 % in early adolescence to 20 % by the end of that time. In India, Nair et al. in 2004 found that among adolescents, depression was found in 11.2 % of school dropouts, 3 % among school going, and nil among college-going adolescents. In another study, it was found that out of 125 ninth-grade public school students, 18.4 % were depressed (Bansal et al. 2009). Of 964 adolescents belonging to X, XI and XII grade across 21 schools, Mohanraj et al. (2010) found that 37.1 % were mildly depressed, 19.4 % were moderately depressed, and 4.3 % severely depressed. A more recent study by Nagendra et al. (2012) found that prevalence of depression in their study was 57.7 %. The prevalence of suicidal ideation was higher among the depressed group (41.7 %) than the non-depressed group (11.4 %). There are, however, no surveys to report prevalence in a national sample.

Depression in adolescence tends to be a re-occurring disorder with an increased probability of depression and impairment in adulthood (Curry et al. 2006). Gender differences in the prevalence of depression manifest during adolescents with female being twice as likely to have depressive disorder as males (Essau et al. 1999). The course of depression varies widely in this population. The duration ranges from 2 weeks to 10 years (Lewinsohn et al. 1993). Depression in this age group often co-occurs with anxiety disorders, attention deficit hyperactivity disorder (Biederman 1992), conduct disorder (Harrington et al. 1998), and substance use (Rohde et al. 2004).

11.3 Common Signs of Depression Among Adolescents

Adolescents' depression often goes unrecognized for long and is brought to clinical attention only when a significant change is noticed to inform a steady decline in academic performance, increased conduct problems or argumentative behavior at home or school. Common signs that may be used for early recognition of depression are shown in Table 11.1.

Table 11.1 Common clinical features of depression

Domain	Features
Thinking	Negative thoughts about self, others, and the world. Preoccupation with past experience, inability to concentrate, unable to take decisions. Apprehensions about future. Thoughts of worthlessness, helplessness, hopelessness, and guilt
Mood/emotional state	Depressed and/or irritable mood, inability to experience pleasure, worry and anxiety
Behavior	Easily gets tired, appears lazy, does not talk or does not initiate talk, agitation at slight provocation, increased argumentative attitude, aggressive behavior, does not complete classwork or homework
Somatic complaints	Fatigue, disturbance of sleep, aches and pain, loss of appetite or overeating, change in weight, diurnal variation of mood (worse in morning)
Interpersonal adjustment	Withdrawal from peer groups, lack of participation in cocurricular activities, lack of interest in play, school refusal, reports feeling inferior to classmates, refusal to go to social events

11.4 Case Vignette

Master K is a 15-years-old male studying in class XI belonging to middle socioeconomic status and urban domicile presented with complaints of sadness of mood, anger outburst, decreased interaction, refusal to attend school, and decreased interest in studies. K was apparently well until 6 months back, when a girl of his class whom he liked mocked at his physical appearance in front of others. K could not respond to the comment at that time, but he reported thinking about the same even after two weeks. He reported feeling embarrassed while entering the class, or giving answer to the questions asked by the teacher. K did not discuss the incidence with anyone. Gradually, he stopped talking to anyone in his class and remained quiet. His parents reported that K would often seem sad and preferred to stay in his room. If his parents coaxed him to talk or study, he would react with anger and disobedience. K was angry at slightest of comment by parents for his decline of interest at academics. When he obtained results of a class test, he reported having severe headache and was relieved from the school. That day, K lied in his room and did not talk to anyone at home. He declared that he will not go to school. His parents were informed by his school counselor that since past few weeks, K was non-talkative in class, he was not attending sports or library period, his attention in class was declining, and he was often found eating his lunch alone. With these complaints, K was referred to a psychiatrist for identification and management of the problem. He was diagnosed as having moderate depression without somatic complaints using ICD 10 system of classification. He was given antidepressants and was sent to psychologist for further management.

Table 11.2 Box showing the information gathered while assessing a depressed adolescent

Current problem	Detailed description of the problem, triggers, thoughts, behaviors, affect, physical aspects, environment, current level of activity, changes in level of interest in activities
	Nature, pervasiveness, duration, and severity of depression
Behavior and psychosocial assessment	**Precipitating**: What caused the problem? What was happening in the adolescents' life when the depression was experienced? Stress at school, academic pressure, bullying, death in family, etc.
	Maintaining: What keeps the depression going? Avoidance behaviors (not going to school, not playing favorite games, not talking to parents), hopelessness, lack of social support, too much support, continuing stressors in environment
	Protective factors: Adequate social support, strengths of the adolescent—absence of previous episodes of depression, easy temperament, average intelligence
Case history	Sequential narrative account of the problem from beginning till present. History of the problem and associated life events at the time of start of depression were the stressors continuous or appeared suddenly?
Comorbid conditions	Assess for anxiety, ADHD, conduct disorder, substance use disorders, etc.
Family history	History of psychiatric illness in parents, family structure, and relationships
Developmental history	Early life history, temperamental constellation, medical history, school history, prepubertal and pubertal history, etc.
Expectations from therapy	What is it that the adolescent wants to gain from therapy, what are the goals that adolescent wants to achieve? Does he/she have any fears associated with therapy?

11.5 Assessment

Assessment is an essential and integral part of psychotherapy with adolescents as it provides clinical data and subsequently aids in planning and implementing appropriate intervention.

The cognitive behavior therapy assessment is a structured approach to identify issues to be addressed in therapy. Some relevant areas to be covered are in Table 11.2.

Assessment incorporates the application of ***inventories, rating scales, and self-report questionnaires*** to assess degree and severity of depression and other comorbid disorders.

Some assessment tools are given in Table 11.3.

Table 11.3 Box illustrating the various tools for assessment tools used in India for adolescent's depression

Assessment tools	Details
Childhood depression inventory	Developed by Kovacs and Beck in 1977
	27-item self-report instrument
	Adolescent version of the BDI
	Assesses change in symptoms and intensity
Depression self-rating scale	Developed by Birleson in 1981
	18-item self-report inventory
Centre for epidemiological studies depression scale revised	Created in 1977 by Laurie Radloff, and revised in 2004 by William Eaton and others
	The scale is well known and remains as one of the most widely used instruments in the field of psychiatric epidemiology
Children's depression rating scale	Developed by Pozanski et al. in 1984
	Reported by parents
	A child and adolescent version of the Hamilton Rating Scale. Useful in assessing change in symptom and their intensity
Beck scale for suicidal ideation	Developed by Beck and Steer in 1991
	A psychometric measure of suicidal ideation
Suicide interview schedule	Developed by Reynolds in 1991
	A semi-structured interview for assessing suicidal risk

Assessment of a depressed adolescent follows a developmental perspective incorporating the systematic, successive, and interdependent changes overtime in adolescent's mood, thoughts, and behavior.

Parents, teachers, and peers are important sources of information apart from adolescent himself. Use of verbal interaction and careful analysis of verbal reports appear to be a strong alternative to the standard test procedures. These ensure greater participation of adolescents and produce more valid information.

Later on, in the therapy, some measures may be used. These include ABC chart (see Appendix Ia) and Dysfunctional Thought Record (see Illustrations 11.1 and 11.6) which will be discussed in the intervention part.

11.6 Sample Illustration of Assessment

The assessment showed that K was having depression since past 6 months. K had teased his classmate for being over talkative. In turn, the girl had said that K looked like a monkey and that no girl would want to talk to him (situation). This happened in front of group of his friends who also laughed at him. His thoughts were, “They think I look like monkey. Nobody supported me. They all laughed at me” (thoughts). On most days, his mood was sad and he would avoid smiling or making eye contact with his classmates (avoidance behaviors). If his friends would ask him to play along, he would refuse. Gradually, his friends stopped asking him and this strengthened the idea that none of his friends really cared. Gradually, he started spending most of his time in thinking about what went wrong? (Ruminations). He could not pay attention in class as he would notice other classmates’ behavior toward himself. He realized that he had not understood anything in class and avoided asking his parents for help. He started feeling anxious at the thought of failing in his tests (worrying thoughts). On the day he obtained his test results, he had a thought that “They will laugh at me again. What all will they think about me?” (automatic thought). He had headache (somatic complaints) and he took leave that day.

K spends his day by sitting alone in his room. He rarely watches TV which he used to like earlier. If coaxed he reacts to his parents with anger. He refuses to go out and play. His grades are declining since past few months. He has completely stopped going to school since three weeks (socio-occupational functioning). His father constantly scolds him for disobedience and acting irresponsibly. His mother constantly keeps a check on him and attempts to talk to him about problems (reaction of parents).

There was nothing significant found in the birth and developmental history. There is absence of family history of any psychiatric illness.

11.7 Formulation of Problem and Communication

A complete assessment permits the evolution of a comprehensive case formulation. The CBT formulation has been illustrated in Fig. 11.1 with examples of some thought content in depressed adolescent.

11.8 Management

11.8.1 Cognitive Behavior Therapy for Depression in Adolescents

It is well known that a combination of pharmacotherapy and psychotherapy is effective for management of adolescent depression (Harrington et al. 1998; Lewinsohn et al. 1993). Cognitive behavior therapies represent a range of empirically supported psychotherapy for adolescents’ with depression (Kazdin et al. 1998). CBT is also recommended by NICE for the management of depression (National Institute for Clinical Excellence 2002).

Cognitive behavior therapy for adolescent is effective in management of depressive symptoms and comorbid conditions and tends to reduce the risk of relapse (Curry et al. 2006). Follow-up studies on effect of CBT on depressed adolescents report that at 3 months post-intervention, the moderate effect size of the treatment tends to be maintained (Curry et al. 1960).

This chapter will focus on management of mild and moderate depression in adolescents. CBT with depressed adolescents will be based on the development of case formulation. The total number of sessions range from 12 to 16 weekly sessions (minimum). The average number of sessions per week is once weekly of

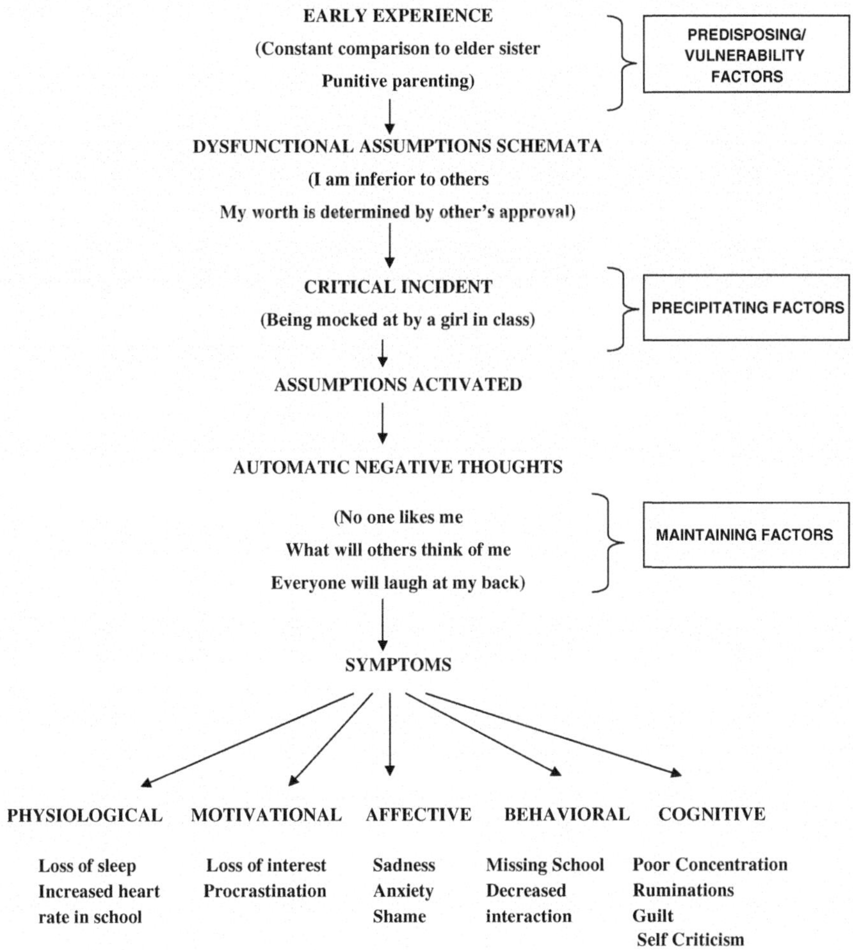

Fig. 11.1 Figure depicting the cognitive behavior conceptualization of adolescents' depression using master K's example

45- to 50-min duration. The therapist may take dyadic session with adolescents along with some sessions with parents. However, it is recommended that few minutes of every session to be held with parents. The usual flow of a CBT session may be as follows:

- Last week experience
- Review of HW
- Fresh concerns: adolescent and parents
- Difficulties in completing HW
- Goal of current session
- Imparting the skill
- HW assignment
- Tips to parents

Important

Depression in adolescents often occurs with other comorbid disorders such as anxiety, ADHD, and conduct disorders. The management of these disorders is important for recovery from depression. Refer to other chapters in the book to read about management of comorbid conditions.
This chapter does not focus on management of suicide. However, during assessment or therapy sessions, if adolescent reports thoughts of hopelessness, suicidal ideation, or attempts suicide; refer the adolescent to a psychiatrist.

11.9 The Therapeutic Relationship

The therapeutic alliance has been found in a meta-analysis to be significantly associated with outcomes in child and adolescent therapy (Shirk et al. 2003). ***Working alliance is formed from the point of meeting with the adolescent and goes beyond termination***. The essential characteristics of a therapist include accurate empathy, warmth, and genuineness (Brent et al. 1997). In CBT, the therapist serves as an active "coach," with an emphasis on a collaborative process.

11.9.1 Rapport Formation

Behaviors such as courtesy, timeliness, appearance, active listening, eye contact, tone of voice, and timing of verbalizations during sessions facilitate rapport formation. The therapist can ask the adolescent to discuss his or her interests, hobbies, or activities. During treatment, the therapist may explain the rationale for specific interventions, homework assignments, or shift in the agenda of sessions.

11.9.2 Collaborative Empiricism

The therapist may join with the adolescent in setting agenda for session, choosing activities or homework assignments, and looking for evidence against a thought.

11.9.3 Confidentiality

One of the important issues includes therapist balances the disclosing and withholding of information regarding the adolescent. Discussing the entire content shared by the adolescent with parents may hamper alliance with therapist. This gets inflated when there is an actual conflict with parents. However, parents may be informed and advised about suicidal ideation, impulse, or acts of the adolescent. Disclosure to parents of the content may be done only after taking consent from the adolescent.

11.10 Common Goals of CBT for Adolescents with Depression

Therapist may focus on setting goals for the management. The adolescent and the parents may be asked about their expectations from therapy. The goals then may be modified so that goals are as follows:

- Specific
- Achievable
- Possible

Some common goals may be in Table 11.4.

The intervention is guided by the case formulation specific to the depressed adolescent. The formulation informed by assessment sessions including self-report inventories, comorbid diagnosis, experiences in family or school environment.

11.11 Goal-Symptom Reduction

The following section will focus on reducing the core symptoms of depression. Refer to Table 11.4 for the goals and corresponding technique to be used across sessions.

Table 11.4 Boxes illustrating the common goals of CBT for adolescents' depression

Goals	Techniques
Symptom reduction	
Educating about depression	Psychoeducation
Motivating the adolescent for CBT	Presenting the CBT model
Involvement of parents	Educating and training parents
Increasing activity level of the depressed adolescent/externalization of interest	Behavioral activation
	Mood monitoring
Reducing ruminations	Imparting skills to modify pre hoc and post hoc evaluations
Identification and modifications of negative automatic thoughts	Direct and indirect techniques : Socratic questioning, downward arrow, Dysfunctional Thought Record and others
Identification and modifications of dysfunctional assumptions	Verbal challenging
	Reattribution
	Behavioral experiment, survey method
	Generating positive thoughts
	Survey method
Relapse prevention	
Management of stress	Stress management
Skills training	Assertiveness training, anger management, study skills
Relapse prevention	Education about relapse and steps to manage the same, booster sessions

11.12 Initial Phase

11.12.1 Sessions 1–4

11.12.1.1 Psychoeducation

The first step of intervention is psychoeducation, which is given early so that the adolescent and parents have common knowledge and understanding about depression. It is often repeated across sessions which aids in the adolescent and parents in:

- Recognizing and accurately understand the adolescent's behavior as manifestation of depression and see it as transitory
- To give an impression to adolescent that the changes are experienced as normal reactions of a depressed person, thereby normalizing the experience.

The components of psychoeducation include the following:

1. Depression as a psychiatric conditions with changes in mood, activity, and thoughts
2. The epidemiology, rates of relapse, precursors to relapse, and etiological factors in general and specific to the case

3. Role of predisposing, precipitating, and maintaining factors
4. Role and support of family in management
5. Possible treatments: pharmacotherapy and psychotherapy
6. Compliance to medication needs to be emphasized
7. Prognosis

11.13 Presentation of Cognitive Behavior Therapy Model

Collaborative empiricism is an important premise of CBT; hence, it is relevant to inform the adolescent about the nature, components, and course of CBT. Information that needs to be emphasized is as follows:

- CBT is an effective psychological intervention for managing depression
- Our thoughts, emotions, and behavior are interrelated so that each influences the other.
- In depression, the relationship between thoughts, feelings, and actions become negative.
- Change is possible by changing the nature of this association from positive to negative.
- It is difficult to change our emotions, but to change our behavior and thoughts is feasible.
- Change requires CBT sessions and active participation on part of therapist, adolescent, and parents both in and out of therapy.
- CBT is a structured intervention which would require multiple (12–16) weekly sessions, some fortnightly session followed by booster sessions
- The adolescent will acquire some skills and would practice them at home as HW assignments
- With CBT, the adolescent wills to know about new ways of handling his/her difficulties by way of looking at stress with more adaptive perspective or with use of newly acquired skills to deal with problems at hand.
- The therapy progress will be adolescent directed and can accommodate changes over the course of time.

11.14 Educating Parents

In India, family system is strong influencing agency on the adolescent. Family can be a protective, predisposing, or maintaining factor in depression. It is important to involve and work with families of depressed adolescents:

- Educating family about the actual cause of depression is important to alleviate misconceptions, anxieties and reduce strain within family (blaming each other for the adolescents' depression)
- Family needs to know how to respond to adolescent's depression.

- Family needs to understand its role in maintaining depression and may be advised to reduce certain communication patterns and reduce some overt behaviors that exaggerate depression
- Differential reinforcement techniques may be imparted to parents in order to reinforce positive behaviors of the adolescent. They may be asked to reduce some other behaviors like scolding or making critical remarks on adolescent's behavior. This will aid in boosting confidence and reducing stress for adolescent.

11.15 Behavioral Activation

While emphasizing the interrelationship between thoughts, feelings, and actions, instances may be elicited from the adolescent that reflect engaging in some activities lead to change in thoughts and mood. Small tasks including age-appropriate challenging and pleasant tasks tend to improve mood. The large, difficult, and uninteresting tasks lead to sadness, boredom, or thoughts of worthlessness. With this premise, behavioral actions aim to:

- Decrease avoidance of some tasks, situation, etc.
- Decrease non-depressive behavior
- Increase probability of positively rewarding behaviors
- Increase physical activity
- Lead to healthy distraction from depressive thoughts

These functions can be attained by scheduling:

- Graded tasks (breaking large activities into smaller parts and rewarding for each small completed task)
- Activity scheduling (activities assigned along pleasure and mastery principle, and specific activities are assigned to each hour of the day, Refer to Appendix Ib)
- Pleasant events (activities that give pleasure to adolescent)
- Remembering pleasant events (scheduling each day same time to discuss that activities completed and the associated mood change)
- Age-appropriate tasks (the activities that give sense of achievement and autonomy)
- Physical exercise (some daily physical exercise)
- Relaxation skills (diaphragmatic relaxation, rest time, or visualization)

Parents and adolescent can collaborate to identify each of these activities by:

- Identifying when adolescent feels or is observed to be less sad
- Activity that the adolescent does by himself more often or offers to participate in
- Activity that the adolescent used to like doing before being depressed
- The activity that the adolescent never used to refuse when asked to do
- Specific questions may be asked phrased differently on adolescent's interest in activities such as hobbies, outdoor activities, and indoor activities to more

specific like music, TV, peer interaction, games on computer, writing, and logging on social websites.

- Parents may be asked to encourage the adolescent by giving rewards (verbal praise, etc.), and for younger adolescents, star charts may be used (refer to Appendix Ic)

11.16 Barriers

- **Shoulds', Musts' and Perfectionism**: Discuss with the adolescent to defocus on shoulds' in terms of, "I should be able to feel better after completing task", "I should choose studies over leisure activities"; as an age-appropriate challenges. The focus should be on the process, for example, planning, attempting, and avoiding barriers.
- **Difficulty in getting started**: Motivation to start a task may be low. The parents might be asked to break the tasks into further small steps or to use contingency management technique.
- **Not-Feasible**: Adolescent may often choose impractical tasks like completing few chapters from a textbook which may changed in doable tasks during depression

11.17 Mood Monitoring

An important component of CBT is imparting the skill of mood monitoring. In this session, the rationale for mood monitoring is explained with emphasis on interrelationship between thoughts, mood, and behavior. Following skills may be imparted:

1. Rationale: Mood monitoring is a skill of paying attention to mood changes associated with situations. It may also be used to gain knowledge about what activities or situation bring positive changes in mood. Benefits of the same may be highlighted.
2. Mood monitoring: The skill involves labeling emotion correctly and rating its strength on a scale of 0–10 or 0–100.
3. Practice in session and homework assignment: Therapist may ask the adolescent to recall events of past day and fill out details of changes in the mood on a paper for practice. Feedback may be given and homework may be assigned.

11.18 Barriers in Treatment

- **The adolescent may not do mood monitoring**: Factors such as fatigue, preoccupation with rumination, and low motivation may be assessed and intervened.
- **Procrastination, inability to decide:** Setting specific time and place every day and setting specific goal like "my mood in morning, in evening and at night or

SITUATION	MOOD
Mom asked me why I am was sitting alone in my room	Irritation (9%)
Dad was comparing my test result with my classmate	Anger (10%) Sadness (9%)

Illustration 11.1 Illustration showing two-column dysfunctional thought record form

at home, school etc" may help to avoid confusion and overcome obstacles posed by decision making (Illustration 11.1).

11.19 Middle Phase

11.19.1 Sessions 5–12

11.19.1.1 Follow-up from Previous Session

- Reinforce the adolescent for partially completed or completed activities
- Attribute the act of completion of the task to the adolescent
- Elicit and discuss about obstacle (a thought, a mood state, etc.) for incompletion

11.20 Management of Negative Automatic Thoughts and Ruminations

Across sessions, certain patterns of thinking in adolescent may be observed. One of the manifestations of depression is depressogenic cognitions, which if not handled in therapy may lead to maintenance of depression or relapse. Identification and modification of maladaptive thoughts are necessary. A gradual transition to this part of therapy may be done in case of Indian adolescents.

One strategy may be to not disrupt the flow of the session as directed by the adolescent and use reflective reasoning to pave way for modification of cognitions.

Some cues for initiation of cognitive techniques may be as follows:

- Thoughts or self-talk leading to procrastination or avoidance of graded assignments.
- Planning about any task during session
- Discussion around sibling or parents' behavior at home
- Interpersonal difficulties faced at school.

11.20.1 Identification

During therapy, some thoughts that the adolescent can readily access on little probing are "Automatic thoughts". Some methods to elicit these thoughts could be as follows:

(a) **Direct Questioning**: "*What was going through your mind when you felt distressed?*" *or* "*What were you thinking while reading your textbook?*"
(b) **In Direct Questioning**: "*What could a adolescent in this situation think?*" or "*What could normally strike a person he faces this difficulty?*"
(c) **Guided Discovery or Socratic Questioning Technique**: The therapist poses a series of questions to guide the adolescent to access the automatic thoughts like "*what does this mean to you?*" This approach demands good listening skills, an understanding of the adolescent's style of thinking, and a formulation of the problems which acts as a guide or a map.
(d) **Downward Arrow Technique**: It is a method to explore the relationship between conscious cognition and dysfunctional assumptions. Therapist "repeatedly asks" (with appropriate variations in phrasing) to thoughts of a adolescent associated with a dysphoric state (Burns et al. 1980).
(e) **Mental Imagery**: The therapist can use ask adolescent to visualize as vividly as possible, with all the sensory inputs which might be involved. This method helps in triggering strong emotions and the accompanying automatic processing which might have taken place.
(f) **Role-Plays**: These may be used to elicit automatic thought during an interpersonal situation, or the thoughts may manifest as a consequence of practicing social skills.

11.21 Techniques of Self-monitoring

Another strategy commonly utilized to assess negative automatic thoughts is **Self-Monitoring** such as the daily record of dysfunctional thoughts (Beck et al. 1979). Adolescents are required to recognize unpleasant emotions by recording their occurrence, the situation, or thoughts that triggered them and associated automatic thoughts.

11.21.1 Dysfunctional Thought Record

The Dysfunctional Thought Record is used to identify automatic thoughts of the adolescent. This involves teaching the adolescent to add third column in the mood monitoring table in which the adolescent may record the thoughts/images triggered by a situation (Illustration 11.2).

SITUATION	THOUGHTS	MOOD
Mom asked me why I am was sitting alone in my room	'Why does she have to know everything about me? I want some private space'	Irritation (9%)
Dad was comparing my test result with my classmate	'I am tired of parents comparing me with others, my life is so hard'	Anger (10%) Sadness (9%)

Illustration 11.2 Illustration showing the three-column dysfunctional thought record

11.22 Barriers to Treatment

- **Adolescent may avoid recording**: A common phenomenon observed with Indian adolescents. Explaining the rationale, benefits of the thought recording may be emphasized. Motivation may be assessed and addressed. Specific time and brief period each day may be set aside for the adolescent to record thoughts. Parents may be involved to remind adolescent to complete homework.
- **Adolescent reports having no thoughts**: If the adolescent reports that he has no automatic thoughts, the adolescent may be probed in the session (with two-column dairy) to describe the situation, what it means to him/her or what it would mean to any other adolescent in the same situation. This would yield the dysfunctional thought of the adolescent.

11.23 Modification: Cognitive Techniques

11.23.1 Distraction

Some techniques may be imparted to the adolescent to cut down on time spent on ruminations. Distraction techniques are particularly useful in the early stage of treatment when the adolescent is not skilled at identifying and modifying negative automatic thoughts. These tools may equip the adolescent to:

1. Reduce personal distress,
2. Reducing the frequency of negative thoughts,
3. Focus on other productive activities and subsequently lead to
4. Change of mood.

These include the following:

1. **Focus on Object**
   The adolescent may be trained in a session to focus on an object of choice. The object chosen must be of adolescent's preference, and he/she is asked to describe it. Cue questions may be asked like, "What is its color? How big is it?

Where is it kept?" After sufficient practice in session, the adolescent may practice it at home to distract from negative thoughts

2. **Sensory Awareness**
   The adolescent may be taught to focus on his/her surrounding. The focus may shift from outside to oneself. The cue questions may be, "what can you see in the surroundings? What can you hear? What else? Can you feel your clothes? Can you feel your hair?"
3. **Mental Exercises**
   These include some activities such as counting backwards and imagining a relaxing scene
4. **Pleasant Memories**
   The adolescent may directed to recall a pleasant memory and visualize it as vividly as possible. In session, he/she may be asked to rate the vividness on a scale of 0–10 and may then be facilitated to imagine more clearly by the use of cue questions
5. **Absorbing Activities**
   The adolescent may be asked to select activities that may be mentally occupying such as
   - Solving sodoku, crossword, or puzzles
   - Reading novel
   - Creating own scrap book
   - Surfing Internet

Refer to Appendix IIe to learn more distraction techniques.

To begin with, these activities may be included for brief periods as decreased concentration may obstruct in focusing on these activities. It is important that ruminations may be managed by imparting the cognitive technique mentioned below as distraction is only a temporary solution to management of rumination.

11.24 Barriers

- **Adolescent does not engage in distraction**: The rationale of distraction and the benefits may be discussed elaborately with adolescent. If the adolescent does not have good imagination capacity, switch to a more structured activity. For example, he/she may be recommended to use absorbing activity rather than pleasant memories or imagining a scene. More practice may be given in session.
- **Thoughts as barriers**: Some adolescents may attempt to control their thoughts; this may be addressed in session. The goals of distraction and expected outcomes may be collaboratively discussed and revised. Cognitive technique to manage rumination may be imparted.
- **Ruminations are frequent and intense**: Rumination is a common symptom of depression. It may be managed by teaching metacognitive skills mentioned below. The source of ruminations may be identified and modified. In India, stress from family/parents may produce ruminations. The parents in such cases may be educated and asked to reduce stressful interaction patterns.

11.25 Management of Ruminations

Negative automatic thoughts may increase in frequency and intensity due to pre- and post-event processing of situation, thoughts, or behavior. The role of the anticipatory and post-event processing in maintaining sad mood may be discussed with the adolescents, and the negative consequences of the same may be emphasized. The depressed adolescents tend to ruminate before encountering a situation and also brood over the negative aspects once it s over. The adolescents may be informed that such evaluations of the situations contribute in overemphasizing negative aspects of a situation (selective abstraction) and prolong the sad or anxious mood. With the help of examples, the adolescent may be aided to focus on the actual situation by shifting attention to information that was initially disregarded.

11.26 Verbal Challenging

The goal of verbal challenging (Fennell 2004) is to re evaluate the thoughts. It is done through careful questioning to guide the adolescent to consider various alternatives to their original, automatic processing and to adopt more adaptive alternatives that they can test and come to believe in. Such a questioning may take the form of:

(a) What is the evidence for this interpretation?
(b) Are there alternative interpretations which may be more realistic?
(c) What is the effect of thinking on me, on others?
(d) What are the consequences of thinking in this manner?

Disconfirmatory maneuvers to falsify beliefs are also necessary, which may be done using behavioral tests. Other techniques include the following:

(1) **Alternative Interpretations**: More realistic and adaptive interpretations can be sought, and the probability of these alternatives can be assessed. The alternative interpretations are more realistic. It is beneficial to emphasize that one interpretation is not necessarily correct, so that the degree of belief in the distressing interpretation gets automatically reduced.
(2) **Reattribution**: In the process of revaluation, a negative event or outcome may be reattributed to external instead of internal, less global, and less stable causes (Abramson et al. 1978). **Pie chart drawing** is quite useful, and **verbal and behavioral reattribution** may be considered. It may also be aimed at changing attributions from internal, stable, and global to external, unstable, and specific ones. The alternatives are then plotted on a pie chart divided by percentage, to visually present the different causes that may be responsible for an event, thereby reducing the increased sense of personal responsibility.

(3) **Behavioral Experiments**: These are activities which are carried out to check the validity of personal rules or to collect evidence against a thought. ***Behavioral tests*** of the new interpretation can be devised collaboratively to check whether the new interpretation is indeed more probable. This technique has been discussed in detail below

(4) Drawing on past experiences and survey method.

To consolidate the adolescent's revaluation of their automatic thoughts, several methods can be used, for example, ***rehearsal, role-plays, and behavioral tests.***

11.27 Behavioral Experiment

Verbal challenging may be followed by experiments designed to:

- Test the validity of dysfunctional thoughts (predictions)
- Assessing new ideas
- Trying out new learned behaviors.

The adolescent may be aided to carry out behavioral experiment by introducing following steps:

1. Making a prediction: specify the thought or consequence that will follow.

   "***If I ask Aditya for his notebook, he will refuse***"

2. Review existing evidence for or against the prediction: This involves listing out evidence both for the prediction and disconfirmatory evidence.
3. Devise a specific experiment: The experiment should be stated out clearly with details. In some cases, role-play may be used to practice the behavior.
4. Note the results: The results may be recorded. If the results are positive, reinforcement and attribution to adolescent may be made. If results are negative, reasons for the same may be sought.
5. Draw conclusions: Inferences drawn may be used to develop new formulations.

11.28 Survey Method

An effective way to deal with negative interpretations is gained more perspectives on the situations. The adolescent is taught to find alternative interpretations to the situation by seeking perspective of others. This may be carried out with instructions in Illustration 11.3.

"Whenever you feel upset, write the situation, your thoughts, and reactions. Then identify and ask three different people who were in the situation to give their interpretation and reaction to the situation".

K's Case Example: Low marks in Unit Test

Person	Perspective	Emotions	Reaction
Self	I am a total academic failure	Sadness	Crying
Friend A	I would not take it personally it was the question paper that was made tough	Little disappointed	Putting more efforts
FRIEND B	Teachers are going to intimidate us so that we prepare harder for boards	Not concerned	Preparing with more efforts
FRIEND C	It is pre boards after all teachers are going to be strict in checking papers	Not concerned	Putting more efforts

Illustration 11.3 Table illustrating the use of survey method using a case example

11.29 Generating Positive Alternative Thoughts

In depression, our perspective tends to be negatively biased build on rigid, maladaptive assumptions. The adolescent may be given an analogy of remarks by an encouraging teacher or a discouraging teacher to point difference between critical or encouraging thoughts or self-talk.

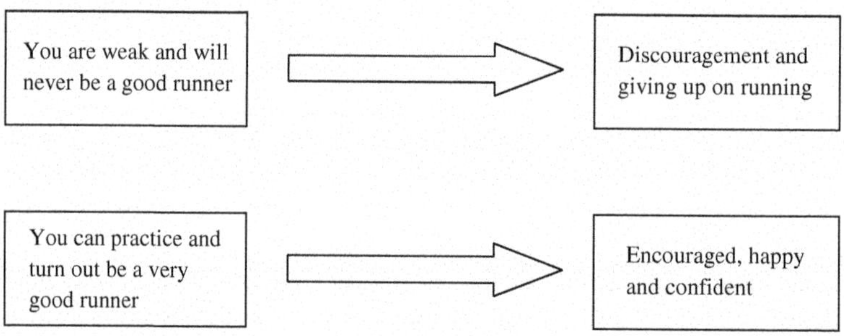

The adolescent may be encouraged to talk back to himself/herself with positive encouraging and counter thoughts. Few examples may be as follows:

I can perform better.
Failure to perform in test does not mean that I will fail in final exams.

Some techniques that may be used to reinforce the counter positive thoughts:

Distancing: The adolescent may not be able to think of counter thoughts specific to their own situation, so they may be given multiple common adolescent agers' problem and may be facilitated to generate counter thoughts.

Use other person's perspective: Asking the adolescent to imagine what he/she would have been told by significant others.

Role-plays: The therapist may generate counter thoughts to depressive thoughts by adolescent and then may reverse position with adolescent. Some of the negative automatic thoughts occur because of the presence of cognitive distortions. The cognitive distortions are important maintaining factors of depression and need intervention. However, in order to avoid repetition, the section on cognitive distortions and their management (already covered in this chapter and also in Appendix IIh) are not discussed here.

11.30 Dysfunctional Assumptions

An important component of preventing relapse, a step forward, includes identification and modification of dysfunctional assumptions. The identification is difficult to extract, and the therapist may look for following characteristics:

- They are rigid, overgeneralized, and extreme: An assumption that that does not take into consideration the variability of a phenomena and is rather taken as absolute. For example:

  I must always know all the answers to teacher's question

- They are associated with strong emotions: If the assumptions are violated, then they lead to strong negative emotions
- They often impede goal attainment
- They do not accommodate human fallibility and vulnerabilities

Some assumptions may be identified along the themes of self, the world, and others as illustrated in Illustration 11.4.

If I don't have 100% concentration then studying is a waste **(Rigid, extreme, overgeneralized, does not take into account the ordinary human experiences like fatigue etc and the adolescent may ruminate more than actually study)**

Illustration 11.4 Illustration showing an example of dysfunctional assumptions

11.30.1 Cognitive Triad

The dysfunctional thoughts may be inferred across therapy sessions. This may be facilitated by paying attention to:

1. **Themes across sessions**: During sessions, some dominant themes may emerge that seem repetitive across sessions (Fig. 11.2).
2. **Changes in mood**: Low mood may occur if the assumptions are violated and elevated mood may be related to fulfillment of assumption.
3. **Association of assumptions with past experiences**: imitation of an adult in family or internalization of family stereotypes. For example:

   If I do not study then I will be wasting my life as did my uncle

4. **Global Judgments**: judging situations, people, and experiences into categories of white and gray

A technique to identify the assumptions is downward arrow technique (Burns 1980). An illustration of downward arrow technique has been given in Chap. 10, Fig. 10.6

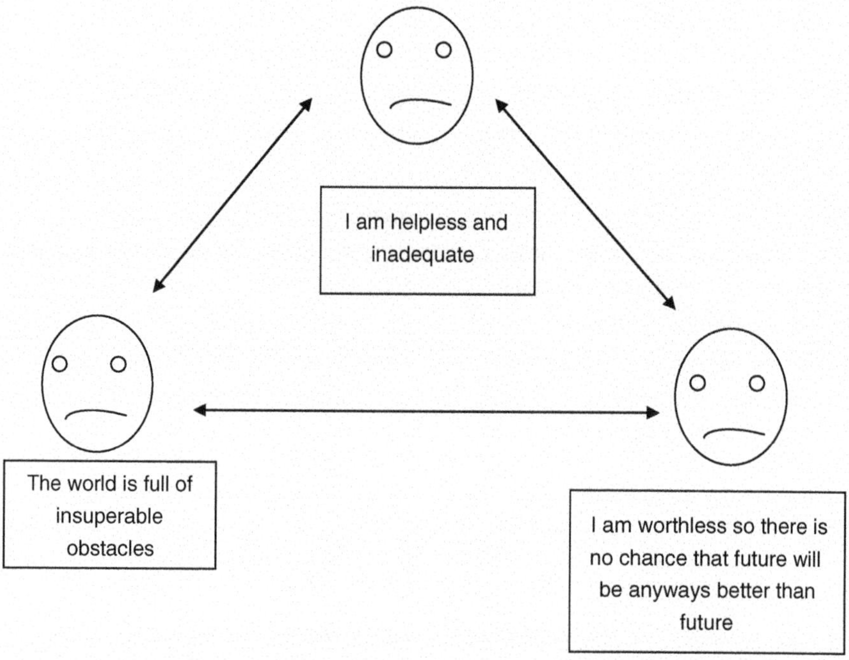

Fig. 11.2 Image showing the cognitive triad often present among depressed adolescents. The dysfunctional thoughts and assumptions may be elicited along the themes of self, others and the world

11.31 Modification of the Dysfunctional Assumptions

The tools for modification of assumptions include Socratic questioning and downward arrow, and the techniques lead to insight in most adolescents. Some other techniques include verbal challenging, positive talk, behavioral experiments, and survey method.

11.32 Verbal Challenging

Some questions may be asked in non-confrontational way to find evidence against the assumptions, gather new ideas, and develop moderate rules. These may be as follows:

- Has the assumption ever failed? What happened then? Is it same consequences that you anticipated?
- Has holding on to this assumption ever put you in trouble? What are some disadvantages of this assumption?
- Can we think of any ways in which this assumption has loopholes? Or is unreasonable?
- How has the assumption formed? Any memories that you can relate this thought to in the past?
- How can we synthesize all this information we just gathered against your assumption? Can we think of reframing the assumption in some way?

In addition, common thinking errors such as personalization and over generalization are handled using cognitive restructuring by facilitating reasoning with the adolescent. This may in turn be facilitated by asking the following techniques:

(a) Contrasting the short- and long-term utility of personal rules
(b) Examining the validity of the conclusions drawn at the time when the basic schemata were arrived at in childhood
(c) Collecting evidence contrary to the thought

If the adolescent is capable of completing the Dysfunctional Thought Record, a fourth column may be added which will make the record look like the illustration given on next page.

This may be augmented with POSITIVE TALK. The adolescent may be taught to generate positive statements alternative to the dysfunctional thoughts/assumptions. The thoughts may be written and verbally or nonverbally repeated. They may be as follows:

- Alternative to negative thought/assumptions
- Positive attributions to self: attributing positive outcomes to one's own internal abilities
- Positive self-affirmations: Statements that boost confidence or are encouraging (Refer to Appendix IId for learn more on positive self-affirmations) (Illustrations 11.5 and 11.6)

Behavioral experiments and survey method have already been explained.

"It's good to be able to have 100% concentration but sometimes it is humanly not possible, so when I can concentrate well its good, when I cannot I can still keep going" "I completed a chapter of English today" "Going with this pace, I will be study consistently"

Illustration 11.5 Illustration showing an example of rational response to a dysfunctional thought

SITUATION	MOOD	THOUGHTS	RATIONAL RESPONSE	CONSEQUENCE
Dad was comparing my test result with my classmate	Anger (10%) Sadness (9%)	'I am tired of parents comparing me with others, my life is so hard'	He does that with my brother as well so he is not picking on me only My friend told me that his mom does the same, so only my parents are not bad If this is happening everytime after results, Dad is normal after scolding it may not be that bad	Decreased Irritation (60%) No arguments with dad (90%) Reduced Tension (75%) Better concentration at the task at hand (65%)

Illustration 11.6 Illustration showing an example of five-column dysfunctional thought record including rational response to a dysfunctional thought

11.33 Termination Phase

11.33.1 Session 13–16

11.33.1.1 Relapse Prevention

An important source of relapse may skill deficit in adolescent, which may precipitate another depressive episode. The sessions focusing on skills training are important, and skills relevant to the case may be chosen and imparted.

11.34 Problem Solving

Sessions with adolescents demand focus on issues and incidents that occur as the therapy takes place. The therapist often picks a theme from the narrative of the adolescent and may use guidance, support, or reassurance. Few important skills may be imparted (e.g., goal setting, study skills, and problem-solving skills) on the journey through therapy.

Techniques such as problem solving, study skills, goal setting, and social skills are given elsewhere (refer to Chap. 15 for detailed knowledge about problem-solving skills training).

In these sessions, instances from daily life, adolescents are personal experiences and his/her participation in imparting the skills may be done. Constant encouragement and reinforcement may go a long way in sustaining motivation. (Refer to Appendix IIg to learn more on problem solving)

11.35 Skills Training

The commonest precipitating, maintaining, and a symptom of depression are dysfunction in interpersonal functioning. The problems occur either due to skill deficits or as a manifestation of depression.

Social problem-solving skills are skills which are used to analyze, understand, and prepare an individual to respond to everyday problems, decisions, and conflicts (Elias and Clabby 1988). Learning these skills helps adolescents to improve their ability to cope with stress (Dubow and Tisak 1989; Elias and Clabby 1988), handle interpersonal situations (Elias and Clabby 1988), experience more positive social adjustment, improve academically, and show improvements in behavior (Dubow and Tisak 1989; Gootman 2008; Nelson et al. 1996). Segrin (2007) hypothesized that deficits in social skills were positively related to depression among children and adolescents. In their randomized control trail study, they found that imparting skills such as assertiveness training, anger management, problem solving, and conflict resolution were associated with decrease in scores on CDI-II (Segrin 2007).

Refer to Part 2 "Building Skills" in this book to gain more knowledge about skills training.

11.36 Relapse Prevention

Relapse is a common phenomenon in psychiatric disorders. The session on relapse prevention needs to be carried out jointly with adolescent and parents. Pertinent issues to be discussed while conducting session on relapse prevention include the following:

- Relapse is reoccurrence of persistent and pervasive depressive symptoms that may be differentiated from slip or lapse, which is reappearance of one or more symptoms during the course of recovery.
- Identification of a slip or lapse: mild irritability, decreased interest in otherwise pleasurable activities, or occasional thoughts of hopelessness or worthlessness
- Reasons for lapse or relapse:
  1. Poor compliance
  2. Stress: examination, familial conflict, death of closed ones, etc.
  3. Medical conditions: hypothyroidism
  4. Seasonal changes: depression tends to occur in winters known as seasonal affective disorder.

Management of a Lapse or Relapse may be discussed with parents, which may include the following:

1. Early identification of lapse or relapse
2. Not panicking or catastrophizing at the appearance of the lapse or relapse
3. Seeking professional help
4. Identifying the skills both behavioral and cognitive that helped the most while in intervention
5. Identification and removal of stressors
6. Increasing social support
7. Practicing skills that helped to adolescent earlier during intervention to overcome depression

A session on relapse prevention helps the family to be prepared for handling variability in recovery process or manage a complete recurrence of symptoms.

11.37 Termination Process

Termination process is important with adolescents. The termination is planned with adequate preparation of the adolescent, with a protocol, with focus on adequate timings. Termination is generally planned when the goals of therapy are achieved. With adolescents, it is suggested that therapist should not be satisfied with the relief of symptoms. Therapist must evaluate adolescents' dependency over himself and the work through to foster independence and proceed to the termination phase. Termination encompasses the discussion over the review of the course of therapy, closure of therapist–adolescent relationship, discussion of adolescent's future, and post-therapy plans. Additionally, the affective response of the adolescent about the end of therapy and problematic termination reactions of the adolescents require adequate handling. Psychotherapy goes beyond a cross-sectional interaction, and booster sessions with adolescent need to be scheduled every once in a month or once in three months to maintain the well-being in future.

11.38 Barriers to Treatment

Barriers to treatment may occur in therapy because of poor preparation and planning of therapy, poor quality of therapeutic relationship, non-facilitative family and parental characteristics. In particular in depressed adolescent, drop outs may occur if activity scheduling is initiated too early and the adolescent has marked anhedonia, avolition and is prone to thoughts of worthlessness and guilt if tasks are not completed. In such a case, graded task assignment with contingency management may be used.

An important barrier to treatment is non-compliance to medication. The parents and adolescent may stop the medication without the psychiatrist's advice, and this leads to poor prognosis. The need for compliance to medication and regular follow-ups with psychiatrist may be emphasized. The efficacy of a combination of pharmacotherapy and CBT is more than efficacy of CBT alone (Harrington et al. 1998; Lewinsohn et al. 1993).

The issue of sexuality is a reason why the adolescents of both the genders do not want to stick to psychotherapy on one-to-one sessions. They want other ways through which they can tackle their concerns without direct discussions.

The critical events include those instances in which the therapist perceives difficulty dealing with. Extremely high expectations of the parents, parents hiding important facts of their life, parents being indirectly uncooperative, and unexpectedly extreme behavior of the adolescents may be some reasons for drop outs.

11.39 Recent Trends in Management of Adolescents' Depression with CBT

Literature is replete with reviews, guidelines, longitudinal and meta-analytic studies on cognitive behavior therapy for adolescents with depression. Recent trends include revision in existing cognitive behavioral models in understanding depression and other psychiatric disorders among adolescents. These include incorporation of social and contextual models, parent–child interactions, and cognitive vulnerabilities to depression

A pertinent trend is the bidirectional linkage between biological and social factors warranted by research that shows that CBT affects brain metabolic activities in ways similar to that of psychotropic drugs (Goldapple et al. 2004). Similarly, Caspi et al. (2003) found that specific genes may determine depression and suicidality among adolescents upon interaction with specific stressful environment.

There is an increasing evidence for the effectiveness of CBT for management of child and adolescent emotional problems. It is deemed debatable then whether empirically supported CBT module be followed or guided by broader, case specific, free of therapist preference ad biases approach. Perhaps in India, the latter is more required which, however, does not rule out the need to adapt and generate evidence for a culturally specific intervention for depressed adolescents. Briefer CBT modules are a new trend in the field, with a potential of brief CBT in reducing the number of hospital visits and days' supply of all medications maintained over 1-year follow-up for depressed adolescent (Clarke et al. 2005).

With the advent of manualized and evidence-based therapies, given the structured nature of CBT, it lends itself to be translated into a computerized cognitive behavior therapy (cCBT) (Cavanagh and Shapiro 2004). cCBT has been developed for anxiety disorders (Camp Cope a Lot, Khanna and Kendall 2008) and depression for adolescent (Sparx, Fleming et al. 2011; Stressbusters, Abeles et al. 2009). The aim of cCBT is to improve access to CBT. With the same objective, the Department of Psychiatry, AIIMS, is developing cCBT module for adolescents with depression (Smart Teen, Srivastava et al. 2013).

Finally, investigations about development of personality disorders and prevention programs have been attempted (Freres et al. 2002; Garber 2006). Similar programs are carried out in India which include imparting interventions at school and community level to students (Srikala and Kishore 2010).

Conclusively, CBT for depressed adolescents is effective and recommended. CBT is structured and can be carried out by a professional at school and hospital, individually or in groups. Clinical population, specifically adolescents, have high rate of comorbidity. Attempts to incorporate culturally adapted, case-sensitive and developmentally appropriate techniques may be instrumental in changing the trajectory of a depressed adolescents.

References

Abeles, P., Verduyn, C., Robinson, A., Smith, P., Yule, W., & Proudfoot, J. (2009). Computerized CBT for adolescent depression ("stressbusters") and its initial evaluation through an RCT. *Behavioural and Cognitive Psychotherapy, 37*(2), 39–44.

Abramson, L. Y., Garber, J., Edwards, N. B., & Seligman, M. E. (1978). Expectancy changes in depression and schizophrenia. *Journal of Abnormal Psychology*, *87*(1), 102.

Anand, U., & Sharma, M. P. (2012). The Effect of a mindfulness-based stress reduction (MBSR) program on stress and well-being in adolescents: A pilot study. *Indian Journal of Applied Research, 1*(6), 216–218.

Bansal, V., Goyal, S., & Srivastava, K. (2009). Study of prevalence of depression in adolescent students of a public school. *Industrial Psychiatry Journal, 18*(1), 43–46.

Beck, A. T., Rush, A. J., Shaw, B. F., & Emory, G. (1979). *Cognitive therapy of depression*. New York: Guilford Press.

Brent, D.A., Holder, D., Kolko, D., Birmaher, B., Baugher, M., Roth, C., Iyengar, S. & Johnson, B.A. (1997). A clinical psychotherapy for adolescent depression comparing cognitive, family, and supportive therapy. *Archives of General Psychiatry*, *54*, 877–885.

Biederman, J., Faraone, S. V., Keenan, K., Benjamin, J., Krifcher, B., Moore, C., & Tsuang, M. T. (1992). Further evidence for family-genetic risk factors in attention deficit hyperactivity disorder: patterns of comorbidity in probands and relatives in psychiatrically and pediatrically referred samples. *Archives of General Psychiatry*, *49*(9), 728–738.

Burns, D. D. (1980). *Feeling good*. New York: Avon.
Caspi, A., Sugden, K., Moffitt, T. E., Taylor, A., Craig, I. W., Harrington, H., & Poulton, R. (2003). Influence of life stress on depression: moderation by a polymorphism in the 5-HTT gene. *Science, 301*(5631), 386–389.
Cavanagh, K., & Shapiro, D. A. (2004). Computer treatment for common mental health problems. *Journal of Clinical Psychology, 80*(3), 239–251.
Chadda, R. K. (1994). Pattern of psychiatric morbidity in children attending a general psychiatric unit. *The Indian Journal of Pediatrics, 61*(3), 281–285.
Clarke, G. N., Eubanks, D., Reid, E., Kelleher, C., O'Connor, E., DeBar, L. L., et al. (2005). Overcoming depression on the internet (ODIN) (2): A randomized trial of a self-help depression skills program with reminders. *Journal of Medical Internet Research, 7*, 16.
Curry, J. F., & Reinecke, M. A. (2006). Modular therapy for adolescents with major depression. In M. A. Reinecke, F. M. Dattilio & A. Freeman (Eds.), *Cognitive therapy with children and adolescents: A casebook for clinical practice*. New York: Guilford Press.
Dubow, E. F., & Tisak, J. (1989). The relation between stressful life events and adjustment in elementary school children: The role of social support and social problem-solving skills. *Child Development, 60*(6), 1412–1423.
Elias, M. J., & Clabby, J. F. (1988). Teaching social decision making. *Educational Leadership, 45*(6), 52–55.
Essau, C., & Dobson, K. (1999). Epidemiology of depressive disorders. *Depressive disorders in children and adolescents: Epidemiology, course and treatment*, 69–103.
Fennell, M.J.V. (2004). Depression, low self-esteem and mindfulness.*Behavior Research and Therapy, 42*, 1053–1067.
Fleming, T., Dixon, R., & Merry, S. A. (2011). Pragmatic randomized controlled trial of computerized CBT (SPARX) for symptoms of depression among adolescents excluded from mainstream education. *Behavioural and Cognitive Psychotherapy, 73*, 1–13.
Freres, D. R., Gillham, J. E., Reivich, K., & Shatté, A. J. (2002). Preventing depressive symptoms in middle school students: The Penn Resiliency Program. *International Journal of Emergency Mental Health, 4*(1), 31–40.
Garber, J. (2006). Depression in children and adolescents: linking risk research and prevention. *American journal of preventive medicine, 31*(6), 104–125.
Goldapple, K., Segal, Z., Garson, C., Lau, M., Bieling, P., Kennedy, S., & Mayberg, H. (2004). Modulation of cortical-limbic pathways in major depression: treatment-specific effects of cognitive behavior therapy. *Archives of general psychiatry, 61*(1), 34–41.
Gootman, M. E. (2008). The caring teacher's guide to discipline: helping students learn self-control, responsibility, and respect, K-6. CA: Corwin Press.
Harrington, R., Woo, A., & Verduyn, C. (1998). Clinically depressed adolescents. In Graham (Ed.), *Cognitive-behaviour therapy for children and families*. Cambridge: Cambridge University Press.
Kazdin, A. E., & Weisz, J. R. (1998). Identifying and developing empirically supported child and adolescent treatments. *Journal of Consulting and Clinical Psychology, 66*, 19–36.
Khanna, M. S., & Kendall, P. C. (2008). Computer-assisted CBT for child anxiety: The coping cat CD-ROM. *Cognitive and Behavioral Practice, 15*, 159–165.
Lewinsohn, P., Hops, H., Roberts, R., Seeley, J., & Andrews, J. (1993). Adolescent psychopathology: I. Prevalence and incidence of depression and other DSM-IIIR disorders in high school students. *Journal of Abnormal Psychology, 102*(1), 133–144.
Lochman, J. E., & Pardini, D. A. (2008). Cognitive–Behavioral Therapies. *Rutter's Child and Adolescent Psychiatry* (5th ed, pp. 1026–1045).
Malhotra, S., Kohli, A., Kapoor, M., & Pradhan, B. (2009). Incidence of childhood psychiatric disorders in India. *Indian Journal of Psychiatry, 51*(2), 101–107.
Mohanraj, R., & Subbaiah, K. (2010). Prevalence of depressive symptoms among urban adolescents of South India. *Journal of Indian Association for Child and Adolescent Mental Health, 6*(2), 33–43.

Nagendra, K., Sanjay, D., Gouli, C., Kalappanavar, N. K., & Kumar, C. S. V. (2012). Prevalence and association of depression and suicidal tendency among adolescent students. *International Journal of Biomedical and Advance Research, 3*(9), 714–719.

Nair, M. C. K., Paul, M. K., & John, R. (2004). Prevalence of depression among adolescents. *Indian Journal of Pediatrics, 71*(6), 523–524.

National Institute for Clinical Excellence. (2002). Full guidance on the use of computerised cognitive behavioural therapy for anxiety and depression. Health Technology Appraisal Monologue, 156.

Nelson, J. R., Dykeman, C., Powell, S., & Petty, D. (1996). The effects of a group counseling intervention on students with behavioral adjustment problems. *Elementary School Guidance and Counseling, 31*, 21–33. [384]

Rohde, P., Kahler, C. W., Lewinsohn, P. M., & Brown, R. A. (2004). Psychiatric disorders, familial factors, and cigarette smoking: III. Associations with cessation by young adulthood among daily smokers. *Nicotine & Tobacco Research, 6*(3), 509–522.

Segrin C., & M. Taylor. (2007). Positive interpersonal relationships mediate the association between social skills and psychological well-being. *Personality and Individual Differences, 43*: 637–646.

Shirk, S. R., & Karver, M. (2003). Prediction of treatment outcome from relationship variables in child and adolescent therapy: A metaanalytic review. *Journal of Consulting and Clinical Psychology, 71*, 452–464.

Sinha, U. K. (2001). Psychotherapy with emotionally disturbed children and adolescents in Nepal. In M. Kapur & P. Bhola (Eds.), *Psychological therapies with children and adolescents*. Bangalore: Nimhans Publications.

Srikala, B., & Kishore, K. V. V. (2010). Empowering adolescents with life skills education in schools: School mental health program: Does it work? *Indian Journal of Psychiatry, 52*(4), 344–349.

Srivastava, P., Mehta, M., Sagar, R., & Ambekar, A. (2013). Conceptualizations guiding a computerized cognitive behavior therapy for adolescents with depression. *Proceedings of 41st International Conference of British Association of Cognitive and Behavior Therapists* (pp. 32–33).

World Health Organization. (2008). *ICD-10: International statistical classification of diseases and related health problems* (10th ed.). New York: Author.

Chapter 12
Obsessive-Compulsive Disorder

Sneh Kapoor, Manju Mehta and Rajesh Sagar

12.1 Overview

Obsessive-compulsive disorder, from the subset of anxiety disorders, is primarily characterized by repetitive, unwanted, and intrusive thoughts, and the resultant repetitive behavior or acts performed to neutralize this distress. Obsessions, and the associated compulsions, are highly distressing to the individual and interfere significantly with the person's social and occupational functioning and/or relationships.

An obsession may be a thought, image, impulse, or a sensation. The common and defining factor among all these being that an obsession is a mental event. A compulsion is a conscious, standardized, and recurrent act or behavior, which may in certain cases be a mental act. Compulsions, both overt and covert, are performed to neutralize the distress or anxiety caused by obsessions. For a diagnosis of Obsessive Compulsive Disorder (OCD), it is essential that the individual recognizes that this behavior is excessive and irrational, as also a product of his/her own mind.

Commonly, the OCD cycle proceeds in the following fashion (Fig. 12.1).

S. Kapoor (✉) · M. Mehta · R. Sagar
Department of Psychiatry, All India Institute of Medical Sciences,
New Delhi 110029, India
e-mail: sneh.kapoor@gmail.com

M. Mehta
e-mail: drmanju.mehta@gmail.com

R. Sagar
e-mail: rsagar29@gmail.com

M. Mehta and R. Sagar (eds.), *A Practical Approach to Cognitive Behaviour Therapy for Adolescents*, DOI 10.1007/978-81-322-2241-5_12

Fig. 12.1 The OCD cycle

12.2 Epidemiology

OCD is estimated to be the fourth most common psychiatric diagnosis, preceded by phobias, substance abuse, and major depressive disorder. The World Health Report 2001 estimates the burden of OCD to 2.5 % of the total global YLDs. Weissman et al. (1994) examined the prevalence of OCD in diverse cultures (Cross-National Collaborative Study) and reported lifetime prevalence of 1.9–2.5 %.

Onset of OCD is generally in late adolescence and adulthood, though in some cases symptoms may begin in childhood. When onset is in adolescence, boys are more likely to be affected than girls—about 60 % of patients are male possibly due to the earlier age at onset in males (Reddy et al. 2000). OCD typically appears to be a chronic disorder with a waxing and waning course. Demal et al. (1993) differentiated five courses of OCD: continuous and unchanging (27.4 %); continuous with deterioration (9.7 %); continuous with improvement (24.4 %); episodic with partial remission (24.2 %); and episodic with full remission (11.3 %).

OCD frequently co-occurs with other disorders. Most often, OCD is found to co-occur with major depression. Comorbidity with panic disorder, phobias, and eating disorders is also observed fairly commonly. Studies have also found a striking comorbidity between OCD and Tourette's syndrome.

12.3 Clinical Features

Obsessions and compulsions are the primary features of OCD. Most people with OCD report both obsessions and compulsions, with some studies reporting figures as high as 90 % (Foa 1995). Another key feature is the distress that accompanies

Table 12.1 Common types of obsessions

Common types of obsessions	
• Contamination fears	• Fears of harming self or others
• Pathological doubt	• Sexual obsessions
• Religious/moral obsessions	• Concerns about symmetry and order

the obsessions—this distress may manifest itself in the form of anxiety, dread, disgust, or guilt among others. Compulsions serve as a means to reduce this distress and generally seem to the individual to be "beyond control." Both obsessions and compulsions are viewed as irrational and excessive by most affected individuals, even when intense and vivid, and are known to be a product of his/her own mind. Though this is true for most cases, in some cases, OCD may be associated with poor insight.

Contamination fears may include intense anxiety or concern regarding germs or dirt, bodily fluids (saliva, urine, blood, etc.), contact with certain places, surfaces, people, or animals. They may fear coming in contact with germs or other contaminants for fear of contracting an illness and/or passing it on to others. In some cases, this fear of contracting an illness may be replaced by a generalized and overwhelming feeling of disgust or "being dirty." What constitutes a "contaminant" may vary from individual to individual—while some may show fear of germs or dirt and some may extend this fear to other substances such as sticky substances such as glue, bodily fluid, and household items such as cleaning agents among others (Table 12.1).

Fears of harming self or others may include intense anxiety or concern regarding harming other people without seriously intending to, being responsible for harm caused to others, not doing anything to prevent harm to self or others, and excessive concerns regarding certain unlucky numbers/dates.

Pathological doubt involves intense anxiety or concern that something terrible may happen because they have not completed an act thoroughly or completely.

Sexual obsessions may include intense anxiety or concern regarding perverse sexual ideas, repetitive forbidden sexual topics, perverse/unwanted sexual images, doubts regarding sexual orientation, and fear of committing sexual aggression (rape, etc.).

Religious and Moral Obsessions, or Blasphemous thoughts, involve repetitive blasphemous ideas—abuses/perverse imagery related to God, excessive concerns about morality or scrupulousness and ideas of right and wrong, excessive concerns about sin and punishment.

Excessive need for *symmetry and order* involves intense anxiety or concern regarding exactness/sameness, order and arrangement and excessive attention to, and concern regarding even or odd numbers (Table 12.2).

Apart from these common types of compulsions, some people may experience a compulsion to perform routine activities extremely slowly, a phenomenon known as primary obsessional slowness. In other cases, an individual may be compelled to not throw away things that are not necessary or to collect things thrown away by others with the belief that they may belong to them, in what is known as hoarding.

Table 12.2 Common types of compulsions

Common types of compulsions
Checking—repeatedly checking locks, gas stoves, keys, money, etc.
Counting—counting associated with routine activities, e.g., counting the number of stairs being descended, counting the number of times a switch is turned off, counting until ten before descending every step, etc.
Ordering/arranging—fixing everything over and over again until it feels "just right," such as fixing paintings on walls properly, and arranging and rearranging one's own cupboard or table
Cleaning—washing hands, taking excessively long time in the shower, repeatedly cleaning objects around the house such as clothes constantly cleaning the house
Repeating—this may involve repeating routine activities, repeating what is being said by self or others, etc.

In recent years, the concept of mental compulsions and rituals is also coming to light. For example, an individual may not perform an outward, overt act to neutralize his anxiety but may silently repeat prayers a fixed number of times to do the same. The prayer then comes to serve as a covert compulsion or mental ritual. Often, an individual may not engage in the compulsion directly but may insist on family members or significant others performing the act. For example, an individual who has been instructed to refrain from excessive cleaning may insist that his family members clean all items thoroughly before they are handed over to him, thereby reducing his anxiety while not engaging in the compulsion directly. This phenomenon of transferring responsibility for the compulsion, known as proxy compulsions, is especially important in therapy along with that of mental compulsions.

12.4 Cognitive Behavioural Conceptualization of OCD

Many cognitive behavioural theories now emphasize that the problem of OCD is not limited to thoughts, but is the result of a set of reactions to what would otherwise be considered normal intrusive thoughts. These reactions could range anywhere from anxiety to guilt and heightened responsibility and personal significance, with consequent efforts at suppression. The crucial difference between normal intrusive thoughts and obsessions lies in the meaning attached by the adolescent to these thoughts and their intrusive nature.

12.4.1 Cognitive Biases in OCD

Personal meaning/significance of thoughts: Many individuals with OCD believe that their intrusive thoughts hold personal significance to them or are reflective of their character. For example, blasphemous thoughts are especially intrusive to those who may believe themselves to be god loving/fearing people and may generate distressing thoughts about these beliefs such as "If I have such thoughts about God, it means I am a bad person," "Having such thoughts about God reflects on my true character," etc.

Thought–action fusion (Rachman 1993): This refers to the belief that having a thought about doing something is equal or equivalent to having performed that action and that thoughts of possible dreaded consequences/misfortunes increase the likelihood of their occurring. For example, a woman having thoughts about harming her child believes that it is as bad as actually harming the child and that such thoughts increase the likelihood that she will harm her child.

Inflated sense of responsibility (Salkovskis 1985): The idea that the probability of a disaster is higher if they are responsible, even if they have no control over the outcome. For example, an adolescent suffering from OCD may believe that harm may come to his family if he does not wash his hands repeatedly—this sense of inflated responsibility for his family's well-being drives him to perform the compulsive acts.

Non-specific cognitive biases: Other biases may include:

- Overestimation of the likelihood that harm will occur
- Belief in being more vulnerable to danger
- Intolerance of uncertainty, ambiguity, and change
- The need for control
- Excessively narrow focusing of attention to monitor for potential threats
- Excessive attentional bias on monitoring intrusive thoughts, images, or urges
- Reduced attention to real events.

12.4.2 Behavioral Perspectives

Put simply, the paradigm of operant condition can be used to explain compulsions. Following the anxiety produced by obsessive thoughts which is experienced as distressing, compulsions serve to neutralize the anxiety and this relief is experienced as reinforcing. Therefore, viewed classically, this negative reinforcement maintains the compulsive behavior.

Mowrer's two process theory (1960) is a more elaborate account of acquisition and maintenance of compulsion and avoidance behaviors. According to this theory, classical conditioning explains how a neutral event acquires the capacity to induce arousal or anxiety by means of pairing with aversive event, thought, or impulse. As explained, compulsions act as negative reinforcers and are therefore maintained. The theory also accounts for avoidance, and since the triggers are actively avoided, the individual never gets the opportunity or required exposure to learn that anxiety relief may also be experienced without performing the compulsions; hence, extinction of the responses becomes difficult. Also, avoidance limits any opportunities for habituation of anxiety.

12.4.2.1 Case Vignette

A is a 13-year-old male belonging to middle socioeconomic strata and studying in class IX in a private school in urban setting. He was brought to the therapist with complaints of prolonged hours spent taking bath and repetitive washing of his hands and feet since past one and a half years. They also reported that he appears distressed and preoccupied at all times, yet does not share his troubles on being asked.

A was maintaining well until one and a half years back. Parents noticed a change in his behavior when he refused to attend the diwali puja held at his home and became agitated when his parents insisted on the same. They noticed that he did not take part in the festivities at all and remained aloof from family members. Gradually, he started interacting with family members as before but continued to appear distressed. They noticed that after some time, he started spending long hours in the shower which escalated to 3–4 h at the time of intake. He was also observed to continually wash his hands 7–8 times over a number of times per day. Sometimes they would see him mumbling something to himself. This is when they got worried and brought him for a referral.

On interview, A reported that he had experiences great distress during the puja before diwali. He felt "uncomfortable" looking at pictures and idols of God, and abusive words kept coming into his mind no matter how much he tried to block them or distract himself. He became very scared and refused to participate in the prayers the following week. He was too scared to tell his parents as he thought they would reprimand him for his bad thoughts. However, he was constantly troubled by the idea that he had those thoughts, and after a while, the bad words about God kept coming into his mind even without looking at pictures or participating in prayer. He felt that he had committed a terrible sin and thus felt that he needed to cleanse himself. He started spending long hours in the shower and would go wash his hands and feet every time an abusive word came to mind. He noted that the frequency and intensity of cleaning had increased over time, and the distress due to these words had also increased. He lived in constant fear that he would be punished and frequently apologized verbally to God and prayed for forgiveness—what his parents had observed as mumbling.

As a result of his troubles, he stopped participating in family prayers and going to temples, kept a close watch on himself to avoid meeting priests or accidentally viewing pictures of God, and kept a constant vigilance on his thoughts in an attempt to control them. He reported that all this left him exhausted and he was always tired and anxious, and that his school work was beginning to suffer.

12.4.3 Cognitive Behavioural Formulation

See Fig. 12.2.

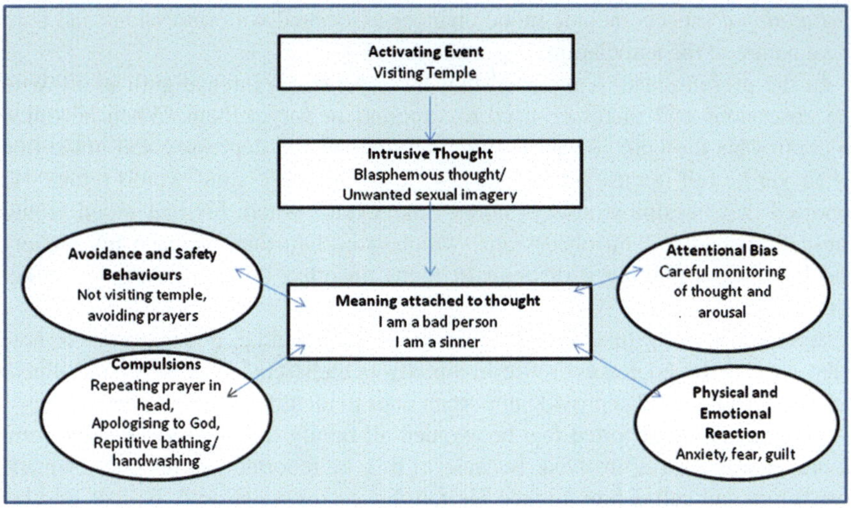

Fig. 12.2 Cognitive behavioural formulation in OCD

12.5 Assessment

Assessment in OCD involves a detailed procedure that goes beyond general intake and administration of clinical scales. Key components to be evaluated in the clinical interview include cognitive, behavioral, and emotional aspects.

Cognitive aspects include form and content of obsessions, cognitive neutralizing, and avoidance.

In the presented case, for example, the form and content of sexual imagery—whether thought, impulse, or action—is to be determined. Triggers for the obsessions such as visiting temples, seeing idols and pictures of God, attending prayers, etc. are explored. Cognitive neutralizing is seen in the form of repeating prayers and apologizing to God mentally.

Beliefs relating to the obsessions are explored. For example, in the present case, A's beliefs about the obsession, and his idea about why he has them and why they persist is discussed. The personal meaning of his obsessions is explored, that is, what he thinks it means when he has these obsessions and what they reflect about him. The distress associated with his evaluations of these beliefs or his misinterpretations is explored.

Behavioral aspects include triggers for obsessions, avoidance, ritualizing, reassurance seeking, and proxy compulsions.

In the present case, these can be seen in the form of triggers such as going to the temple, avoidance of prayer and temples, and overt compulsions such as constant cleaning to "remove sin." It is also essential to note if the adolescent is indulging in any proxy compulsions such as asking the family to pray/clean, etc.

Emotional aspects include mood changes associated with obsessions and temporal nature of the association.

In the present case, A reported that he experiences intense guilt along with the obsessions and therefore tried to suppress or forget them. When he failed to control his thoughts, he started feeling anxious and depressed and noted that whenever he felt intense anxiety or low mood, his obsessions would return. He reported that he almost always noted this "cycle" where his bad mood would cause him to dwell on obsessions, which would further increase his anxiety and low mood, making it difficult to focus on other things or carry out other activities.

Assessment of dysfunction due to illness is also essential. It is important to note what area of the adolescent's life is directly or indirectly affected by the illness behavior. This may also provide important cues to identifying *avoidance*.

For example, A reported that he avoided all family functions since some form of prayer was always involved. Because of this, he reported that his cousins made fun of him and called him a loner. He felt that he was constantly bullied, and his family thought he was just being dramatic to get away from prayers because he thought they were boring. His studies were starting to get affected as he felt that he would not be able to do well in exams without praying, and because he was now a sinner, God would punish him by making him fail his examinations, so why should he study.

Some common clinical scales used for assessment, specifically in OCD, are enumerated below.

- Yale-Brown Obsessive Compulsive Scale (Y-BOCS), Goodman et al. (1989)
- Children's version of the Yale-Brown Obsessive-Compulsive Scale (CY-BOCS), Scahill (1997)
- Maudsley Obsessive Compulsive Inventory (MOCI), Hodgson and Rachman (1977)
- Padua Inventory, Burns et al. (1996)

Self-monitoring tools are further elaborated in the section on intervention, as part of exposure–response prevention.

12.6 Interventions

Traditionally believed to have poor prognosis, OCD and its management have now been vastly researched. A two-pronged approach is generally employed for the management of obsessive compulsive disorder, incorporating both pharmacological and psychological interventions. A large number of studies have found pharmacotherapy, behavior therapy, or a combination of both effective in reduction of obsessive compulsive symptoms.

12.6.1 Evidence for Efficacy of CBT for OCD

Gava, Barbui et al. (2007), in a systematic review of randomized trials, compared the efficacy of psychological treatments (CBT) for OCD with treatment as usual and found that patients receiving any variant of cognitive behavioural treatment exhibited significantly fewer symptoms post-treatment than those receiving treatment as usual. A meta-analytic comparison study of OCD treatments found that clomipramine, SSRIs, and ERP all had comparable results (Kobak et al. 1998). Studies suggest that behavior therapy not only provides long-lasting gains but also results in greater short-term improvement in symptoms (Foa et al. 2005; Greist 1996). CBT using exposure and ritual prevention can lead to a significant reduction in OCD symptoms in patients who remain symptomatic despite an adequate trial of an SRI (Simpson et al. 1999). ERP is, therefore, currently the treatment of choice for OCD.

12.6.2 The Module

The following section focuses on the key principles to be incorporated into therapy, preceded by a temporal sequencing of sessions. It is important to note that number and duration of symptoms may vary depending on the symptom severity and number of different symptoms that each individual presents with.

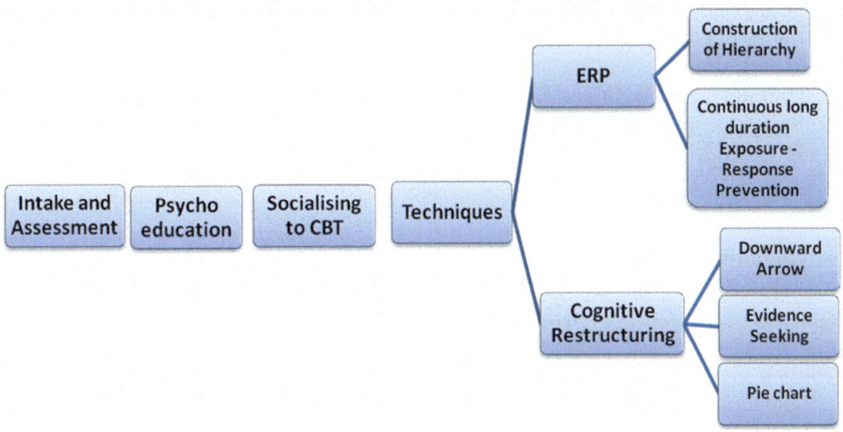

12.6.2.1 Initial Phase (Session 1–3)

Goals:

- Intake
- Detailed clinical history

- Assessment
- Psychoeducation

The initial sessions should focus on a thorough intake, incorporating the elements mentioned in the section on assessments, along with detailed clinical history as well as administration of the relevant scales. A detailed behavioral analysis is essential for planning therapy.

It is essential at this stage to psychoeducate the adolescent and family about OCD and help clarify doubts and questions about the illness. Sharing the case formulation and familiarizing the adolescent with key principles and techniques of cognitive behavioural therapy are the first steps to beginning the therapy sessions.

Psychoeducation would include dissemination of information about OCD and its symptoms; clarification of, and differentiation between, obsessions and compulsions; and nature, course, prognosis, and possible treatment modalities. It is also advised to introduce the CBT model, explaining the association between thought, emotion, and action and to share the cross-sectional formulation with the adolescent at this stage—making him/her aware of the various precipitating and maintaining factors in the illness.

12.6.2.2 Middle Phase

Goals:

- Exposure and response prevention
  - Psychoeducating regarding ERP
  - Preparing adolescent for ERP
  - Monitoring
  - Hierarchy construction
  - Practicing ERP in session
  - Homework assignments
- Cognitive techniques
  - Cognitive restructuring

Exposure and Response Prevention

Session 4

Preparing for Exposure and Response Prevention (ERP): ERP, being an anxiety inducing technique, requires the adolescent to be fully aware of its steps and prepared to provide consent for participation. It is essential to psychoeducate the adolescent and caregiver and obtain informed consent before initiation of therapy.

A key point to be kept in mind during educating regarding ERP is to provide a detailed rationale regarding using ERP. The therapist may explain principles of habituation, extinction of compulsions, and Mowrer's two process theory as models of explanation. The steps involved need to be explained in detail, and the adolescent is prepared to experience intense anxiety at the beginning of treatment. They are also educated about an "extinction burst." that is, a sharp increase in obsessions and compulsions at the outset.

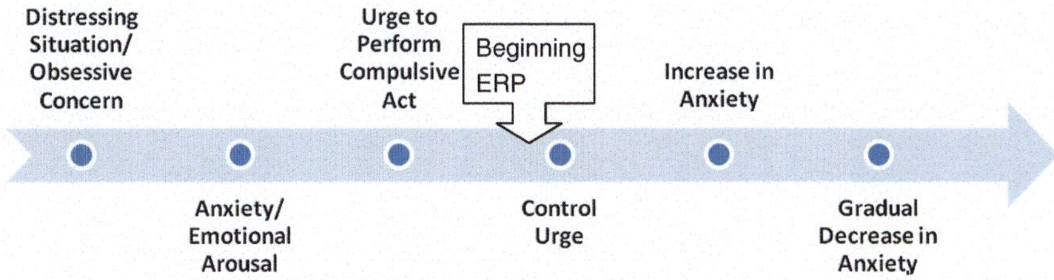

As can be seen on the figure above, the adolescent needs to be made aware that at the initial stages after exposure, there will be increases in anxiety before any reductions take place.

Further, they also need to be educated about the trajectory of anxiety that takes place with and without compulsions. The following graphs may be used for the same.

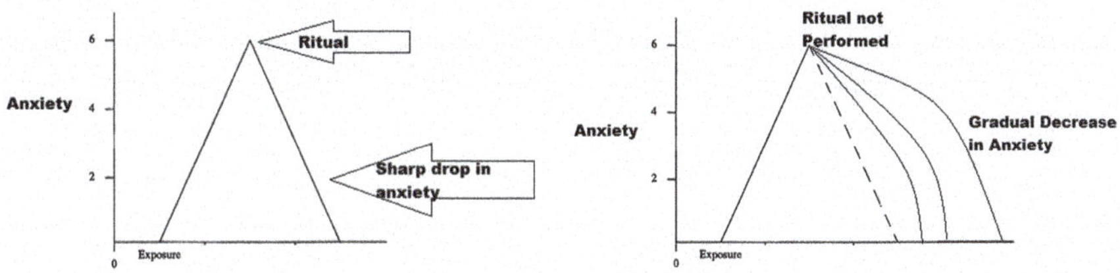

As can be seen from the first graph, adolescents can be educated that though performing the compulsion results in a sharp reduction in anxiety over a short period of time, it is counterproductive in the long term as each subsequent trigger will produce more anxiety and would require larger frequency/intensity of compulsions to be performed with lesser consequent relief. The second graph, which is the key principle of ERP, illustrates how waiting out the period of anxiety is beneficial as it also produces reduction in anxiety, albeit slowly, without performance of the compulsion. However, this is beneficial in the longer run as the process of avoidance and conditioning of triggers and compulsion is terminated over time.

Session 5

Hierarchy Construction: This session begins with identifying the key symptoms vis a vis obsessions and compulsions from the assessment data, followed by hierarchy construction in the following steps:

- Listing out of all obsessions and compulsions and enumerating subjective units of distress (SUD) for each on a scale of 0–100 %. This involves asking the adolescent to identify how much distress—that may be anxiety, guilt, or generalized arousal—he/she experiences on being exposed to a trigger for obsession or compulsions.

For example, one sample list could look like this:

Problem	SUD (0–100)
Going to temple	90
Seeing image of God	80
Hearing prayers	70
Not washing hands and face after such thoughts	70
Not apologizing	50
Not reciting special prayer	60

- This is followed by creating a hierarchy of symptoms in ascending order of SUDs, with lowest distress at the bottom of the hierarchy.

Going to temple	90
Seeing image of God	80
Hearing prayers	70
Not washing hands and face after such thoughts	70
Not reciting special prayer	60
Not apologizing	50

Monitoring: At this stage, monitoring of the identified symptoms is also initiated, either by means of an ABC chart or a daily record of dysfunctional thoughts (DRDT).

For example, if the target symptom is washing hands, the ABC chart may look as follows.

Activating event	Belief	Consequence
An abusive word came to mind when I went to the temple this morning	"I am a bad person and a pervert for thinking such things in a holy place" "I should be punished"	Anxiety, guilt

Session 6

Initiating ERP: Once the adolescent has been educated and the hierarchy constructed, he/she is instructed on ERP. ERP is generally started targeting a symptom at the lower end of the hierarchy, at around 30–40 % SUD—too high a level of anxiety may be overwhelming, and starting at a level too low is counterproductive as the adolescent may not observe the change in anxiety that is essential for any significant change.

One target is set per session and ERP practiced on it. The adolescent is advised to continue practicing the same at home. The next symptom in the hierarchy is targeted only when the individual is habituated to the previous target symptom.

ERP essentially involves continuous, high duration exposure to the trigger and prevention of the associated response. For example, adolescent A is instructed in the session to refrain from washing his hands. At this time, he is instructed not to indulge in compulsions, distractions, or any form of mental neutralizing or avoidance as well as from proxy compulsions. At this time, anxiety and urge to perform compulsion over time are monitored by means of a visual analog scale.

This exercise is terminated only when anxiety and urge to perform compulsion have reduced to more than half of baseline level, that is, at first exposure.

An example of a visual analog scale could be the following.

Time	Baseline	5 min	10 min	15 min	20 min	25 min	30 min
Anxiety (%)	50	80	80	75	60	60	45
Urge to neutralize (%)	70	80	90	80	70	60	50

12.6.3 Cognitive Techniques (Simultaneously with ERP Sessions)

Some cognitive techniques that are used in dealing with obsessions are briefly below. They have been elaborated in previous sections. Cognitive restructuring is used to address magical thinking, catastrophic misinterpretations of obsessive thoughts, thought–action fusion, and inflated sense of responsibility. Common techniques used are briefly described below.

- ***Downward Arrow/Vertical Descent Technique***: This technique is used to arrive at the core dysfunctional belief and work toward modifying it. The therapist begins with an instance/event and through a downward process of finding what the event/thought/feeling means to the adolescent, and what would happen next; the adolescent and therapist together arrive at the dysfunctional belief that needs to be addressed.
- ***Evidence Seeking***: The adolescent is asked to seek evidence in support of and against the current dysfunctional thought, by means of behavioral experiments, past experience, judgement or surveys, etc., and to generate alternative, more adaptive interpretations of those dysfunctional thoughts.

For example, taking the case of adolescent B who feels that his brother would meet with an accident if he did not shut the door ten times every time he left the room. B is asked to collect evidence from the past wherein something bad happened when he did not shut the door multiple times. He finds that bad events are not directly correlated with his actions, and this learning combined with adequate psychoeducation is used to test his beliefs.

- ***Pie Chart Technique***: Generating alternative explanations for events that the adolescent takes excessive and undue responsibility for. The alternatives are then plotted on a pie chart divided by percentage, to visually present to the patient the different causes that may be responsible for an event, thereby reducing the sense of responsibility that he/she feels.

For example, adolescent B is asked to first list out the possible reasons for people having accidents in general.

*careless driving on part of driver *fog *sudden distraction
*careless driving on part of others *faulty car *poor driving skill

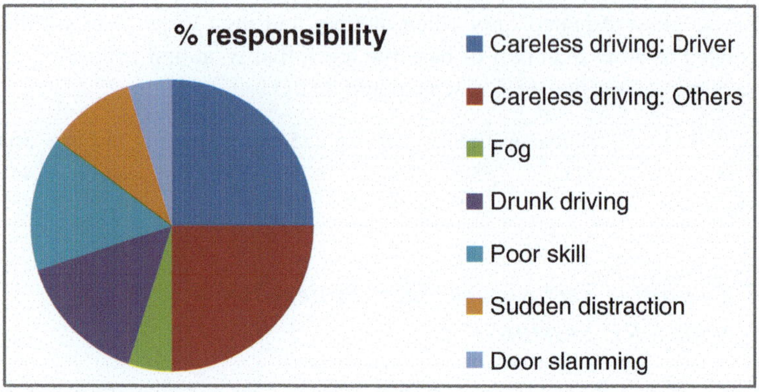

Fig. 12.3 The pie chart technique

The adolescent is then asked to put them in a pie chart according to proportion of responsibility, along with the percentage of responsibility that his slamming the door has (Fig. 12.3).

The adolescent is then made to see the relative lower percentage of responsibility that he has for the event and that other more real events may be responsible for accidents.

12.6.3.1 Termination Phase

Goals:

- Relapse prevention
- Maintenance of improvement
- Continued use of ERP and cognitive techniques
- Family member/co-therapist training

This phase is focused on relapse prevention, anxiety management, and stress management. Parent/family members are also psychoeducated and directed as co-therapists to help in facilitation of continued practice to enable maintenance of therapeutic gains. Practical tips to help adolescents increase efficacy of ERP may be shared to facilitate independent practice and management of future concerns.

12.6.4 Increasing Efficacy of ERP

- Make ERP Gradual
  - Make sure you begin with tasks that are lower in the list, i.e., less disturbing and then move upward to the more difficult ones
  - Do not take on too much or more than you can handle at a time

- Daily practice
  - Practice for a brief duration every day
  - It is better to have few short sessions than one long session in a day
- Accept rather than fight
  - Accept that you have certain thoughts and let them be. Do not try to consciously suppress or stop those thoughts, or feel upset if they occur
- Tolerate and habituate to anxiety rather than avoid
  - Instead of always distracting yourself, or running away from anxiety, face it
  - Learn that anxiety will gradually decrease with time and make an effort to notice this change
- Start with situations that are SIMILAR to your feared situation before you actually move on to the feared situation
  - Practice in situations that are a lot like your feared situation and get used to those first and then move on to the difficult ones
- Do not distract/rationalize/reassure yourself
  - Do not tell yourself everything will be ok, my hands are not dirty, the money is fine, etc., repeatedly
  - Do not seek reassurance from others about your concerns or ask them to perform compulsions for you

12.7 Barriers to Treatment

A large number of barriers to treatment exist in carrying out cognitive behavior therapy for OCD. First and foremost, the anxiety-inducing nature of ERP in itself may act as a barrier for many adolescents. Suffering from an anxiety disorder of such debilitating nature, many adolescents may not be prepared to deal with the intense anxiety and discomfort that they may feel at the start of therapy. Hence, symptom severity acts as an important variable in therapy. Level of insight also acts as an important predictor of motivation—where magical thinking is a common phenomenon among children and adolescents, and some therapists may find it challenging to bring about the desired level of insight into their problems and challenge the dysfunctional beliefs.

Beliefs about OCD, its prognosis, nature, and causes also influence progress in therapy. Beliefs about therapy—beliefs about therapy procedures, treatability of OCD, past experiences with therapy, etc., are important predictors of involvement in therapy and may act as barriers where the adolescent believes OCD is either not treatable or "a figment of the mind." Poor experience with therapy in the past or lack of desired outcomes from such experiences may also act as impediments.

Comorbid conditions such as depression, bipolar disorder, etc., may also impede treatment progress and are required to be addressed in the early stages of therapy. Lack of access, poverty of resources, geographical barriers, long waiting periods, and poor homework compliance is also important barriers to be considered. Homework compliance, as mentioned before, may become an important factor owing to the nature of therapy. Hence, it is advisable to assign a co-therapist to facilitate and monitor compliance with assigned tasks and to support and motivate the patient in the practice of ERP. Performing mental compulsions/covert neutralization during exposure exercises that result in a sudden drop in anxiety impedes the process of habituation/conditioning and decreases the efficacy of ERP and therefore, must be looked out for.

Finally, poor communication with therapist is an important barrier to treatment and impedes progress in therapy. It is important for both therapist and the adolescent to maintain open communication regarding difficulties in treatment as well as progress.

12.8 Future Directions

Newer approaches to management of OCD using the basic CBT principles are being explored. Danger ideation reduction therapy (DIRT), a variant of CBT, uses a variety of techniques to decrease patient estimates of the probability of dangerous outcomes. DIRT procedures include cognitive restructuring, filmed interviews, corrective information, microbiological experiments, a probability of catastrophe estimation task, and attentional focusing. Mindfulness-based CBT is another upcoming approach to the treatment and management of OCD. CBT has been rigorously studied as a treatment for adult OCD. Studies have varied some in terms of number of sessions provided, session format (group vs. individual, and intensive vs. weekly), reliance on cognitive restructuring, and in combination with pharmacotherapy.

The realm of therapy for OCD is progressing by leaps and bound, yet treatment accessibility is vastly hampered by a large number of barriers. Geographical barriers, stigma, paucity of therapists' time and resources, and long waiting periods have reduced treatment seeking and dissemination over the years. Therefore, foremost, steps need to be taken to increase treatment dissemination and provision of CBT/ERP. In this regard, research is now being carried out to incorporate technology into the therapy module of OCD (Morgan et al. 2010). A number of computer-based, telephone-based, and other self-help approaches to treatment of OCD are being developed and researched. Telemental health applications have been found to be effective as a low-threshold, efficacious, time-effective, and economic treatment for patients with OCD (Herbst et al. 2012). Computer-based/Internet-assisted therapy modules have also been found to bring out about statistically and clinically significant improvement (Anderson et al. 2011; Greist et al. 2002). The area of self-help manuals for CBT/ERP has also been explored as an independent therapy module and found to be effective in bringing about significant improvement on OCD symptoms (Robinson 2012; Tolin et al. 2007). Self-guided therapy is, therefore, not only proving to be an adjunct to therapy or as part of a stepped care approach, but is also being explored as an independent modality of psychotherapy.

References

American Psychiatric Association. (1987). Diagnostic and statistical manual of mental disorders (3rd ed., rev.). Washington, DC: Author.

Andersson, E., Ljotsson, B., Hedman, E., Kaldo, V., Paxling, B., Andersson, G., et al. (2011). Internet-based cognitive behavior therapy for obsessive compulsive disorder: A pilot study. *Biomed Central Psychiatry, 11*, 125.

Demal, U., Lenz, G., Mayrhofer, A., Zapatoczky, H. G., & Zitterl, W. (1993). Obsessive compulsive disorder and depression: a retrospective study on course and interaction. *Psychopathology, 26*, 145–150.

Foa, E., Liebowitz, M., Kozak, M., et al. (2006). Randomized, placebo-controlled trial of exposure and ritual prevention, clomipramine, and their combination in the treatment of obsessive-compulsive disorder. *American Journal of Psychiatry, 162*, 151–161.

Foa, E. B., & Kozak, M. J. (1996). Obsessive compulsive disorder: long term outcome of psychological treatment. In M. Mavissakalian & R. Prien (Eds.), *Long term treatments of anxiety disorders: Psychological and pharmacological approaches* (pp. 285–309). Washington, DC: American Psychiatric Press.

Foa, E. B., Liebowitz, M. R., Kozak, M. J., Davies, S., Campeas, R., et al. (2005). Randomized, placebo-controlled trial of exposure and ritual prevention, clomipramine, and their combination in the treatment of obsessive-compulsive disorder. *American Journal of Psychiatry, 162*, 151–161.

Gava, I., Barbui, C., Aguglia, E., Carlino, D., Churchill, R., et al. (2007). Psychological treatments versus treatment as usual for obsessive compulsive disorder (OCD). *Cochrane Database of Systematic Reviews, 2*.

Goodman, W. K., Price, L. H., Rasmussen, S. A., Mazure, C., Fleischmann, R. L., et al. (1989). The yale-brown obsessive compulsive scale, I: Development, use, and reliability. *Archives of General Psychiatry, 46*, 1006–1011.

Greist, J. H. (1996). New developments in behavior therapy for obsessive compulsive disorder. *International Clinical Psychopharmacology, 11*, 63–73.

Greist, J. H., Marks, I. M., Baer, L., et al. (2002). Behavior therapy for obsessive compulsive disorder guided by a computer or by a clinician compared with relaxation as a control. *Journal of Clinical Psychiatry, 63*(2), 138–145.

Herbst, N., Voderholzer, U., Stelzer, N., Knaevelsrud, C., Hertenstein, E., et al. (2012). The potential of telemental health applications for obsessive-compulsive disorder. *Clinical Psychology Review, 32*(6), 454–466.

Hodgson, R. J., & Rachman, S. (1977). Obsessional-compulsive complaints. *Behaviour Research and Therapy, 15*(5), 389–395.

Janardhan Reddy, Y. C., Srinivas Reddy, P., Shobha, S., Khanna, S., Sheshadri, S. P., et al. (2000) Comorbidity in juvenile obsessive-compulsive disorder: A report from India. *Canadian Journal of Psychiatry, 45*, 274–278.

Kaplan, H. I., Sadock, B. J., Grebb, J. A. (Eds). (1994). Synopsis of Psychiatry (7th ed., pp. 598–606). Baltimore: Williams and Wilkins.

Kobak, K. A., Greist, J. H., Jefferson, J. W., & Katzelnick, D. J. (1998). Behavioral versus pharmacological treatments of obsessive compulsive disorder: a meta-analysis. *Outcomes Management, 136*, 205–216.

Morgan, J., Lack, C., & Storch, E. A. (2010). The utilization of technology in the treatment of obsessive compulsive disorder. In L. V. Berhardt (Ed.), *Advances in medicine and biology* (pp. 161–176). Hauppauge, NY: Nova Science Publishers.

Rachman, S. (1993). Obsessions, responsibility and guilt. *Behaviour Research and Therapy, 31*, 149–154.

Rasmussen, S. A., & Eisen, J. L. (1998). Phenomenology and clinical features of obsessive-compulsive disorder. In M. A. Jenike, L. Baer, & W. E. Minichiello (Eds.), *Obsessive compulsive disorders: Practical management* (3rd ed., pp. 12–43). St. Louis, MO: CV Mosby.

Robinson, S., Turner, C., Heyman, I., & Farquahrson, L. (2013). The feasibility and acceptability of a cognitive-behavioural self-help intervention for adolescents with obsessive-compulsive disorder. *Behavioural and Cognitive Psychotherapy, 41*, 117–122.

Salkovskis, P. M. (1985). Obsessive—compulsive problems: A cognitive behavioural analysis. *Behaviour Research and Therapy, 23*(5), 571–583.

Simpson, H. B., Gorfinkle, K. S., & Liebowitz, M. R. (1999). Cognitive-behavioral therapy as an adjunct to serotonin reuptake inhibitors in obsessive-compulsive disorder: An open trial. *Journal of Clinical Psychiatry, 60*, 584–590.

Sternberger, L. G., & Burns, G. L. (1990). Obsessions and compulsions: Psychometric properties of the Padua inventory with an American college population. *Behaviour Research and Therapy, 28*(4), 341–345.

Tolin, D. F., Hannan, S., Maltby, N., Diefenbach, G. J., Worhunsky, P., et al. (2007). A randomized controlled trial of self-directed versus therapist-directed cognitive-behavioral therapy for obsessive-compulsive disorder patients with prior medication trials. *Behaviour Therapy, 38*, 179–191.

Weissman, M. M., Bland, R. C., Canino, G. J., Greenwald, S., Hwu, H. G., et al. (1994). The cross national epidemiology of obsessive compulsive disorder. The Cross national collaborative group. *Journal of Clinical Psychiatry, 55*, 5–10.

World Health Organization (WHO). (2008). *The global burden of disease: 2004 update*. Geneva: World Health Organization.

Chapter 13
Somatoform Disorders

Suparna Kailash, Manju Mehta and Rajesh Sagar

13.1 Introduction

In reality, no illness is purely physical or psychological. Physical and psychological symptoms interact, and one cannot separate the body from the mind. It is vital to consider underlying psychological distress in children who repeatedly present with physical symptoms that are medically unexplained as children and adolescents often find it difficult to express their feelings and emotions through words. Medically unexplained symptoms refer to those bodily symptoms that do not have a recognized medical illness explanation. These symptoms may lead to distress, impairment in functioning, and healthcare-seeking behaviour, as in somatoform disorders.

13.2 Diagnostic Features

DSM-IV describes ***somatoform disorders*** as having

1. Physical symptoms suggesting a medical condition; however, no medical disease, substance misuse, or another mental disorder can be found to account for the symptoms.

S. Kailash (✉)
Connecticut, USA
e-mail: kailashpanna5@yahoo.co.in

M. Mehta · R. Sagar
Department of Psychiatry, All India Institute of Medical Sciences, New Delhi 110029, India
e-mail: drmanju.mehta@gmail.com

R. Sagar
e-mail: rsagar29@gmail.com

M. Mehta and R. Sagar (eds.), *A Practical Approach to Cognitive Behaviour Therapy for Adolescents*, DOI 10.1007/978-81-322-2241-5_13

2. The symptoms cause significant distress or impairment in social, occupational, or other areas of functioning.
3. The physical symptoms are not intentionally produced.
4. No diagnosable medical condition can fully account for the symptoms.

The same diagnostic criteria are used for adults as well as children. DSM-IV subdivides somatoform disorders into *somatization disorder*, *undifferentiated somatoform disorder*, *conversion disorder*, *pain disorder*, *hypochondriasis*, *body dysmorphic disorder*, and *somatoform disorder not otherwise specified.* The most commonly seen in children and adolescents are *persistent somatoform pain disorder and dissociative/conversion disorder*.

13.3 Clinical Features (DSM-IV)

Persistent somatoform pain disorder

1. Abdominal pain, headaches, joint pains and other aches and pains constitute persistent somatoform pain disorder.
2. Pain is characterized as being persistent, severe, and distressing.
3. It is associated with psychosocial stressors.
4. It tends to be worse during the day and does not occur at night or in school holidays.
5. There may be accompanying altered bowel habit, vomiting, headache, and fatigue.

Conversion disorders

1. These disorders involve partial or complete loss of bodily sensations or movements; loss or disturbance of motor function; and pseudo-seizures being the most common presentations.
2. Less frequently, they may present in children with loss of sight, hearing, sensation, consciousness, fugue or mutism.
3. The symptoms are often brought on by abuse, traumatic event.
4. They usually remit after a few weeks or months.
5. *La belle indifference*, which refers to a lack of concern about the symptoms, is not particularly common in children.

Pseudo-seizures

1. These seizures do not have the typical features of an epileptic fit and are not accompanied by an abnormal EEG.
2. Pseudo-seizures and epilepsy can coexist, but those with both conditions form a small proportion of patients with epilepsy.
3. Pseudo-seizures can be similar to epileptic seizures leading to delays in diagnosis.

13.4 Etiology

Somatoform disorders are likely to be caused by a combination of factors. A variety of child, family, and environmental factors have been proposed as predisposing, precipitating, or maintaining factors.

Predisposing factors	Precipitating factors	Maintaining factors
Family	*Child*	Current family relationship difficulties
Genetic component	Anxiety, depression	Family model of serious illness
Physiological vulnerability	Life stresses	Current parental anxiety and somatisation
Verbal communication about emotional issues limited	Physical illness	School problems
Conditional caretaking	Peer group problems	High achievement orientation
Suspicious attitude to medical expertise	Academic problems	Conflict avoidance
Parental history of somatoform illness, anxiety, or depression	Cognitive limitations	Benefits of sick role
Problems with boundary setting for children	Low self-esteem	
Child	*Parent*	
Temperamental factors, including sensitive, conscientiousness, emotional labiality, vulnerability, + worthlessness	Life crises	
Earlier emotional abuse		
Low IQ		
Social-relating difficulties		
Physical illness		

13.5 Burden

Children with somatoform disorders tend to present repeatedly to doctors because their presenting symptoms are physical and families tend to attribute the symptoms to medical, not psychological causes. The medical help-seeking behaviour that accompanies the symptoms often leads to various unnecessary painful medical investigations and treatments before their psychological nature is identified. These investigations tend to reinforce the belief in the child and family that there is an underlying physical cause Domenech-Llaberia et al. (2004). All of this can result in a huge burden on patients in terms of time, money, and effort as well as wastage of resources. Children often miss school to attend multiple appointments, and parents may need to take time off work to care for their child and take them to appointments. Further, it may result in parents having decreased leisure time, having to take time off work and subsequent financial implications. Families may need to reorganize themselves in their activities of daily living to accommodate caring for the sick child, which may increase overall family stress.

13.6 Assessment

Steps involved in assessment

1. Ascertaining the child and parents' views of the illness is important since most of them have come after meeting several doctors. Many parents may still be pursuing organic causes; therefore, it is important to address all the physical symptoms, find out what medical disorders have been excluded, explore possible physiological explanations, and be aware of the possibility for physical and psychological causes to coexist.
2. Psychiatric assessment should include developmental and psychiatric history and mental state examination.
3. Psychometric assessments may be helpful in determining the child's cognitive level, and any disparity between child's educational expectations and actual abilities, school history, and family functioning is assessed.
4. Engaging the family early in the assessment process, explain the formulation to them and engage them in therapy. The intervention module is an adaptation of the work done previously (De Shazer (1985); Gureje et al. (1997); Knapp et al. (2006); Keiling et al. (2011); Kozlowska et al. (2007); Lieb et al. (2000); Pehlivanturk and Unal (2002) and Robins et al. (2005)).

13.7 Intervention

13.7.1 Integrated Eclectic Intervention Module for Children with Somatoform Disorder and Their Parents

Outline of Module

- Number of sessions: 6
- Frequency of sessions: 2 per week
- Duration of each session: 50–60 min
- Setting: Hospital
- Type of session: Individual sessions or with parents
- Who delivers: Clinical psychologist

13.7.2 Instructions for Therapists

- Use this module as a guide. It presents the fundamental areas you should focus on during the sessions. The content worked on in each session should be integrated and build upon in subsequent sessions. Become familiar with the module and use it based on each child/adolescent's particular symptoms, circumstances, and your own personal style. The psychiatrist is consulted for any comorbid condition.

Session 1: Preintervention assessment and Psychoeducation
Participant: Child and parent
Objective of the session

- Understand the child's problem
- Increase child's and parent's understanding of somatoform disorders
- Form a rapport with child and parent.

Duration: 60–90 min
Tasks

(i) Semi-structured interview
(ii) Preintervention study measures (child and parent)
(iii) Psychoeducation
(iv) Providing reassurance, support, reattribution
(v) Functional analysis.

Homework: ABC charting

13.7.3 Task (I) Semi-structured Interview

- The therapist should administer the semi-structured interview Performa and generate information from the child on the following areas: School, Academics, Teachers, Peer group, Family, Parents, Siblings
- The therapist starts the session by asking the child, "What is your name, age? What class do you study in?"
- The therapist inquires from the parents about their relation with child, their family setup, support, and any family stress. "Do you have a joint family or do you live with your parents, any stress the family is currently undergoing?"

13.7.4 Task (II) Preintervention Study Measures (Child)

- The therapist instructs the child and tells the child, "This is a list of 35 items assessing bodily difficulties you experienced in the last 2 weeks. You have to tell me how much you were bothered by each symptom rating from 0 which means not at all, 1 Some-what, 2 Often, 3 Quite a lot, 4 a whole lot."
- The child is given some time to complete the Childhood Somatization Inventory. Any queries are simultaneously answered.

- Following which the child is given the Coping Scale for Children and Youth. The therapist explains to the child, "During problems, how much do you make use of the following methods. You have to tick the option that you find most appropriate."
- The Children's Global Assessment of Functioning was filled by the therapist, in consultation with the parent, by rating the child's most impaired level of general functioning for the specified time period by selecting the lowest level which describes his/her functioning on a hypothetical continuum of health illness.

13.7.5 Task (II) Preintervention Study Measures (Mother)

- The mother is given the DASS and asked to fill the questionnaire, "Please read each statement and circle a number 0, 1, 2, or 3 which indicates how much the statement applied to you over the past week. There are no right or wrong answers. Do not spent too much time on any statement."
- Then, she is given the coping checklist to complete, "This is a list of commonly used methods of handling stress and reducing stress. You have to answer yes if it applies to you and no if it doesn't."
- Following which the GAF is administered.
- The therapist starting at the top level evaluates each range by asking "Is your symptom severity OR level of functioning worse than what is indicated in the range description? Keep moving down the scale until the range that best matches your symptom severity OR the level of functioning is reached, whichever is worse."

13.7.6 Task (III) Psychoeducation

- The therapist can use the following information for psychoeducating the parents.
- The parents are psychoeducated by telling them, "Your child may sometimes respond to stressful or painful experiences with somatic symptoms without having a serious medical illness. Although these symptoms are referred to as psychological, but it does not mean that the child is mentally handicapped. The child is not intentionally producing these symptoms and is not malingering."

Predisposing factors

- It is further explained to them, "Both personal and factors based on context may predispose children to developing somatic complaints. Genetic, physiological vulnerability to a particular somatic condition, a high level of suggestibility, difficult temperament and low self-esteem may predispose children to somatoform disorders. A family culture that is illness-oriented may predispose children and adolescents to develop somatic problems through a process in which the children observe that sick-role behaviours of other family members elicit excessive care and distress is communicated through somatic complaints."

Precipitating factors

- The therapist explains the role of precipitating factors, "Biological factors such as personal illness or injury or illness, injury in a family member, major stressful life events, such as bereavement or abuse, and a build-up of small stressors may also precipitate somatoform disorders."

Maintaining factors

- The therapist further educates the parents by telling them, "Somatic complaints may be maintained by the belief that they are un-controllable. Also, it permits the child to avoid anxiety-provoking issues which would have to be faced if the symptoms were resolved. Poor coping strategies and cognitive distortions involving catastrophizing about the symptoms may contribute, by increasing autonomic arousal and reducing the efficiency of the immune system. Family, school, peer-group and health-care may give the child secondary gains associated with the sick role. Poor coping strategies of parents, high levels of stress and limited support to family may compromise their resourcefulness in managing their children's difficulties."

13.7.7 Task (IV) Reassurance, Support

- The therapist reassures and gains the parents' confidence by telling them, "The child would be followed until full recovery and even later to make sure that no possible organic cause is overlooked."
- The child is told, "You will get fine soon and we completely understand your problem and it can be overcome."

13.7.8 Task (V) Functional Analysis

- The therapist explains to the parent, "You need to record information regularly about the child's symptoms, the circumstances surrounding its occurrence and treatment adherence. The Intensity of the symptoms will be rated from 0 to 10, with 0 not present being and 10 being maximum intensity, frequency counts i.e. the number of times the child reports of symptoms during the day and how long do they last."
- For child's age <10, parents will record.
- For child's age ≥10, the child records.

The following chart is used for recording:

Day/date/time	Intensity 0–10	Antecedents	Behaviour	Consequences	Duration

The child and parents are asked whether they have any further questions and they are told to come for the next session.

Session 2: Symptom management
Participant: Child and parent
Objective of the session

- Engage parents in active management of symptoms
- Encourage child to take control of symptoms by teaching cognitive and behavioural skills.

Duration: 50–60 min
Tasks

(i) Review charting
(ii) Teach parents to limit secondary gains from sick behaviour
(iii) Activity scheduling
(iv) Teach child symptom control using relaxation, distraction, and cognitive restructuring.

Homework: Practice relaxation, chart self-statements

(i) Review charting
(ii) The therapist must review before beginning the next session. Revise the previous session and the homework assignment. Ask child and parent whether they have any questions from the previous session.

13.7.9 Task (I) Review Charting

- The therapist must review before beginning the next session. Revise the previous session and the homework assignment. Ask child and parent whether they have any questions from the previous session.

13.7.10 Task (II) Help Parent Limit Child's Secondary Gains from Sick Behaviour

- *The therapist educates the parent about the removal of reinforcement for symptomatic behaviour by explaining to them that,* "You might be reinforcing illness behaviour in your child by giving excessive attention to the child whenever he displays illness behaviours. You should try and limit giving too much attention to your child, limit frequent visits from visitors, phone calls, gifts, recreational privileges whenever the child displays symptomatic behaviour. You are advised to ignore non-verbal illness behaviours and use children's complaints about symptoms as an opportunity to prompt them to use symptom-management skills."

- *The therapist educates the parent about reinforcement of well behaviours by explaining to them that*, "When the child does not display any symptomatic behaviour for sometime (define based on the kind of symptoms) and engages in positive productive activities you have to praise the child, allow them to watch TV, give food of their choice, let them engage in other recreational activities."

Breathing exercises

- The therapist starts by telling the advantages of breathing exercises to the child.
- "Relaxation exercises have advantages and some of them are:
  - It helps us in taking more oxygen in our brain. The more oxygen reaches our brain, the more alert we feel. It helps us to bring our mind to here and now and helps us see the situations more objectively and then work on it.
  - Our mind may be full of thoughts that prevent us from seeing the true nature of problem. Therefore, through relaxation our mind becomes clear."

- The therapist sits on a chair and demonstrates the instructions before asking the child to follow them. Once the child starts practicing the breathing exercise, the therapist should ensure that the child keeps their eyes closed during the session and check whether the child is doing it correctly.
- Additionally, they should be instructed that, "The exercises can be done as many times as possible and remember to give a gap of about 1 h for eating a meal before and after the breathing exercises."

For the breathing exercise, the child is instructed to

- "Sit comfortably and assume a relaxed posture with your arms loosened and placed on your thighs, your back against a support, and your feet firmly placed on the ground, parallel to each other
- In case you wear spectacles, take them off
- Loosen your neck ties or belts
- Let your body feel loose and comfortable
- Now take a deep breath, inhale through your nose, and as you inhale feel your stomach expanding
- Hold it for a second or two
- Now exhale slowly, and as you exhale feel you stomach contracting
- Keep breathing in slowly through your nose, experience your stomach gently expand while you inhale air and gently contract while you exhale
- Now concentrate on the movement of your stomach and take 10 deep breaths while concentrating on your stomach
- Now, while breathing in the similar manner, concentrate on the movement of your chest and take 10 deep breaths
- Now, while breathing in the similar manner, bring your focus on your nose and while concentrating on your nose take 10 deep breaths
- All through-out breath in slow and deep"

13.7.11 Task (III) Teach Relaxation Exercise

- The therapist sits on a chair and demonstrates the instructions for the imagery exercise before asking the child to follow them. Once the child starts practicing the breathing exercise, the therapist should ensure that the child keeps their eyes closed during the session and check whether the child is doing it correctly.
- For imagery exercise, the therapist explains by giving an example, "Imagine a beach with clear blue water everywhere, sun just about to rise in the sky. Feel the cool touch of the air on your skin, imagine walking bare feet on the water, feel the water under your feet, smell the fragrance in the air, hear the soothing sounds of the waves."

For positive imagery, the child is instructed to

- "Sit comfortably in a quiet place
- Close your eyes
- Breathe slowly and as you inhale your stomach expands and as you exhale your stomach goes inside
- Deep breathe four times
- Create a mental image of a pleasant scene where you have been. It could be a park, mountain, sea beach
- Make the mental image as real and in as much detail as possible
- Involve all your senses such as sight, hearing, smell, touch and taste
- While imagining the scene clearly and in detail, relax yourself more deeply and feel it
- As you relax, use positive statements in your mind to reinforce the relaxation response. Use statements such as: I am deeply relaxed; my body is relaxed and my mind is calm; I am peaceful, calm and relaxed
- When you feel relaxed and calm you can gradually open your eyes"

The therapist should ask the child about their experience of the exercise. Clear any doubts regarding any difficulty or uneasiness in practicing the exercises.

13.7.12 Task (IV) Activity Scheduling

Steps involved

- Child is encouraged to return to school.
- Child is encouraged to engage in normal activities, for example, dressing, bathing, self-care, eating meals at regular times, peer interaction, recreational activities, and helping parent in household chores.

13.7.13 Task (V) Teach Distraction

- The therapist gives the rationale for distraction technique, "Distraction involves directing attention away from the present situation to something more pleasurable or engaging. This would help to bring your anxious feelings under control."

- The child is told, "You can distract yourself by listening to music, reading a book or newspaper, playing some game or talking to someone, listening to personal stereo whenever you feel uneasy or feel the symptoms coming."

13.7.14 Task (VI) Cognitive Restructuring

The therapist asks the child to

- Write down their negative thoughts.
- The therapist evaluates these thoughts in an objective way with the child.
- The child is encouraged to adopt a more balanced view based on information or evidence which has previously been ignored.
- The number of alternative explanations is generated at any one time.
- Link is made between somatic symptoms, affects, cognition, and behaviour.
- Modify their negative thoughts.

Session 3: Family-based treatment
Participant: Parent and child
Duration: 50–60 min
Objectives

- Teach parents relaxation exercises
- Improve parental coping
- Improve family communication.

Tasks

(i) Manage parental stress
(ii) Teach parental coping strategies
(iii) Teach family communication skills.

13.7.15 Task (I) Relaxation Exercises for Parents

For the breathing exercise, the parent is instructed to

- "Sit comfortably and assume a relaxed posture with your arms loosened and placed on your thighs, your back against a support, and your feet firmly placed on the ground, parallel to each other
- In case you wear spectacles, take them off
- Let your body feel loose and comfortable
- Now take a deep breath, inhale through your nose, and as you inhale feel your stomach expanding
- Hold your breath for a second or two
- Now exhale slowly, and as you exhale feel you stomach contracting

- Keep breathing in slowly through your nose, experience your stomach gently expand while you inhale air and gently contract while you exhale
- Now concentrate on the movement of your stomach and take 10 deep breaths while concentrating on your stomach
- Now, while breathing in the similar manner, concentrate on the movement of your chest and take 10 deep breaths
- Now, while breathing in the similar manner, bring your focus on your nose and while concentrating on your nose take 10 deep breaths
- All through-out breathe in slow and deep"

13.7.16 Task (II) Teaching Parent Coping Strategies

The therapist explains to the parents how to handle various kinds of stresses when managing a child with somatoform disorder:

- *Internal Stress*: Expectations of parents about their child. When expectations about parenting are not met, the first thought that comes to the parents' mind is that, "What they did wrong?" Therefore, parents are taught how to develop realistic expectations and how to recognize when negative self-talk defeats effective coping.
- *Management Strategies*: Identify their self-defeating assumptions and think of alternative messages. The parents are told to be kind to yourself and accept yourself and child as fallible.
- *External Stress*: The therapist explains that the neighbors, friends, and relatives don't understand why such a normal-acting child is having problems. Teachers frequently don't fully understand the ramifications of a child's problem. Parents are called upon by the school to help make decisions about the child's education, but often feel helpless because of their own lack of understanding. External stressors are those that are situational and often involve relationships with others.
- *Management Strategies*: Know your limits and be realistic about what you can accomplish. Say no to unreasonable demands. Learn about your child's problems and needs.

The therapist presents the following list to the parent and asks them to

- "Below is a short list of coping behaviours that has been extracted from studies of coping styles and from reports by parents and others. It is intended to help you reflect upon your coping behaviours and hopefully benefit from the positive (and negative) attributes and behaviours that have been reported by others."

Coping behaviours: thinking negatively

- Deny the problem ("It's just a matter of time before he'll grow out of it…")
- Hide ("I know, but I am so embarrassed that…")
- Become overwhelmed ("I feel helpless because…")
- Blame yourself ("I feel so guilty; if only I had…")
- Blame others ("If only his teacher had…")

- Panic ("We need to change everything right now…")
- Worry ("I can't help thinking that…")

Coping behaviours: thinking positively

- Listen carefully and ask for clarification ("Are you telling me that…")
- Take good notes ("When last we spoke, we agreed that…")
- Seek information ("What I need to know is…")
- Focus on the problem ("My specific concern is about…")
- Seek social support ("Who can I turn to when I need to talk about…")
- Become a self-advocate ("What I need you to provide for my child is…")
- Become an advocate for change ("The system needs to adjust by…")
- Reduce tension ("It feels good just to…")
- Focus on the positive ("One good thing is that…")
- Seek professional guidance ("With her help, I realized that…")
- Share your wisdom ("What I now know is…")

13.7.17 Task (III) Family Communication

Steps to building effective family communication

- *Communicate frequently*

Families should spend time together. Make time to communicate. Talk in the car turn the TV off and eat dinner together, and talk to your children at bedtime.

- *Communicate clearly and directly*

Families should communicate their thoughts and feelings in a clear and direct manner. This is especially important when attempting to resolve problems that arise between family members (e.g., spouse, parent–child).

- *Be an active listener*

Listen to what family members and the child are saying. Being an active listener involves trying your best to understand the point of view of the other person. It is important to pay close attention to their verbal and non-verbal messages. As an active listener, you must acknowledge and respect the other person's point of view. For example, when listening, you should nod your head or say, "I understand," which conveys to the other person that you care about what he or she is saying. Another aspect of active listening is seeking clarification if you do not understand the other family member. This can be done by simply asking, "What did you mean when you said…?" or "Did I understand you correctly?"

- *Openness and honesty*

Individual family members must be open and honest with one another. This openness and honesty will set the stage for trusting relationships.

- *Think about the person with whom you are communicating*

Not all family members communicate in the same manner or at the same level. This is especially true of young children. When communicating with young children, it is important for adults to listen carefully to what the children are saying without making unwarranted assumptions. It is also important to take into consideration the ages and maturity levels of children. Parents cannot communicate with children in the same way that they communicate with their spouse because the child may not be old enough to understand.

- *Pay attention to non-verbal messages*

Pay close attention to the non-verbal behaviours of other family members. It is important to find out how the person is really feeling.

- *Be positive*

It is very important for family members to verbally compliment and encourage one another.

- *Speaking skills*

Clearly articulating what you want to communicate. Often communication, particularly disagreements, between two people can escalate to conflict.

- *Roadblocks to communication*

Sometimes when communicating, roadblocks appear that get in the way of really hearing what your family member is saying or that hinder your ability to communicate what you are thinking and feeling.

- *Deployment communication*

Communication between two people usually involves not just the words that are used but also the listener's interpretation of the speaker's words, the body language of the speaker and listener, and the tone of voice. These factors change depending on the medium being used (i.e., face to face, phone, e-mail, video chat, letters). Families who have a member deployed or away from the other(s) for periods of time require an additional skill set to enhance these relationships.

- *Listening skills*

It describes how to use "I statements" to accurately convey what you are saying and start the conversation off well, how to respond, and how to have more productive and positive conversations.

Session 4: Stress management and problem-solving
Participant: Child
Objective of the session

- Help the child understand and handle stress-inducing situations
- To help child improve decision-making by eliciting and evaluating all possible solutions and choosing the best alternative to resolve their problem.

Duration: 50–60 min
Task

(i) Managing stressful situations
(ii) Finding solutions to problems.

13.7.18 Task (I) Managing Stress

Stress management steps for children under 10
Acknowledging their feelings

- It is important that children understand what they are feeling, that we teach the word "stress" by letting them know what they may feel that they may feel.
- Let the child know that it is all right to feel angry, alone, scared, or lonely.
- Teach children names or words for their feelings and appropriate ways to express them.
- The therapist shows more interest in the child's experience and feeling than in the behaviour that results.

Promote a positive environment

- Praise children for the acceptable things that they do also explain to the parents to do so.
- The experience of stress and tension can serve to defeat an individual's concept and confidence. Help the child sees and understands the positive things about themselves and that they are worthwhile persons.
- Listen without judging the child or the situation; that is, if the child chooses to tell you about the situation that produced the stress.
- Help the child feel comfortable in expressing feelings. Assist the child in clarifying his or her feelings. Correct any misconceptions that the children may have about themselves or their feelings.

Set a good example

- Children learn lessons from the family and other adults around them, whether these lessons are positive or negative.
- Children are imitators and may cope with stress in the same way they see adults handle their stress. In some cases, it is appropriate to explain why something is being done. This explanation can often ease the child's reaction.

Stress management for children above 10 years
The child is taught how to
Prepare for the stressor

- You can develop a plan to deal with it.
- Just think about what you have to do.
- Just think about what you can do about it.
- Worrying won't help anything.
- You have lots of different strategies you can call upon.

Confronting and handling the stressor

- You can meet the challenge.
- One setup at a time; you can handle the situation.
- Just relax, breathe deeply, and use one of the strategies.
- Don't think about the problem, just do what you have to do.
- That's right; it's the reminder to use your symptom management skills.

Coping with feelings at critical moments

- When pain comes, just pause; keep focusing on what you have to do.
- Don't try to eliminate the pain totally; just keep it under control.
- Just remember, there are different strategies; they'll help you stay in control.
- When the pain mounts, you can switch to a different strategy; you're in control.

Reinforcing self-statements

- Good, you did it.
- You handled it pretty well.
- You knew you could do it!

13.7.19 Task (II) Problem-Solving

The steps involved are as follows:
Stressors experienced

- Discuss about the stressors which the child is experiencing in their day-to-day life. Ask them, "What kinds of stress do you experience in your lives?"
- "What are the stressful situations that you experience over which you have absolutely no control?"
- "What are the stressful situations that you experience over which you do have some control?"

Finding solutions to problems

- Tell the child, "We would learn about these steps by using an example."
- Give child a situation.
- Encourage responses from the child and write them down.

General orientation

- Explain to the child that they need to accept that problem situations are a normal part of life and that one can cope with such situations.
- To deal with their problems, they need to prepare a list of all the problems that need fixing them and start working on solving them.

Problem definition, formulation, and goal setting

- Definition of the problem in concrete terms.
- Decide the time frame for solving the problem and accomplishing goal.
- Specify a desirable outcome by deciding what you would like to have happen instead of what did happen.
- What is the situation right now that is upsetting me?
- How would I like the situation to be?
- How would things be if I weren't upset?
- What are the obstacles?

Generation of alternatives

- Brainstorming all possible solutions without judging whether solutions are good or bad
- Come up with as many solutions as possible to deal with the problem situation
- Seek help of others if need to be

Decision-making

- Evaluating each alternative in terms of its likelihood of solving a problem.
- Going back through the list of alternatives generated and predict the consequences of each alternative behaviour.
- Each alternative may have several possible consequences all of which need to be considered.
- Both immediate and long-term consequences should be examined in determining the costs and benefits of a given solution.
- The following questions can be asked:
  - "Will this solution help me reach my goal and solve my problem?"
  - "If I choose this solution, how good or bad am i going to feel?"
  - "How much time and effort does this situation involve?"
  - "Does this solution have more benefits than costs if I choose it?"

Choosing a solution and putting solution into action

- It consists of two tasks
- Decision regarding which alternative has the most probable benefits and least probable cost in light of original problem and the stated goal
  - If you are given what you want to happen, which one of these alternatives would be the best for you?
  - Which one would be most likely to help you get what you want and avoid what you don't want?

- Need to identify the specific manner in which the chosen solution is to be carried out. For example, for a problem encountered in a social situation, one can ask:
  - What will be said?
  - What will the non-verbal behaviour be like?
  - What will the setting be?
  - When will it be done?
  - What might the reaction of others be and how will I deal with these reactions?
- Using this method, the best possible option is chosen. The strategies and behaviours should then be rehearsed by means of imagery, behavioural rehearsal/role-play, and graduated practice

Evaluation

- Evaluation is done after one has carried out the chosen solution
  - "Did i do what i set out to do?"
  - "Did i accomplish what i said i wanted to accomplish?"
  - "Am i satisfied with the results?"
- If you are satisfied with the results, then the solution was implemented effectively.
- If solution doesn't seem to be working, then ask yourself.
- "Did i define my problem correctly?"
- "Were my goals unrealistic?"
- "Was there a better solution?"
- "Did I carry out the solutions properly?"

Rewarding self for successfully solving the problem

- Once the implemented solution proves to be effective in solving the given problem, reinforce/praise yourself.

Session 5: Coping skills and assertiveness training
Participant: Child
Duration: 50–60 min
Objectives

- Teach child coping skills
- Teach assertiveness skills.

Tasks

(i) Coping practice exercise
(ii) Assertiveness exercise.

13.7.20 Task (I) Coping Skills

Steps involved:

- Write down experiences because of which you become stressed or upset
- Coping skills practice for getting over each above upset

For each upsetting experience, write down your answers to these questions:

- Name which types of upset your experience might be called. Is it a loss; rejection; betrayal, or humiliation?
- What does this upset make me feel like inside?
- How does this upset make me feel about myself? Usually, this answer shows what you really want and need that is the opposite of the upsetting experience you've had. So write down what positive thing you've found out about yourself by going through this upset and coping exercise.

13.7.21 Task (II) Assertiveness Skills

The steps are as follows:
Creating an assertiveness hierarchy

- You need to write down 10 situations in which you would like to be more assertive. This can be at home, at work, with friends, or out in public.

Work out the order of difficulty

- To do this, first give each situation a rating of how hard or difficult you think the task would be. Another way of thinking about it is to ask yourself how anxious would it make you. You give each situation a rating from 0 to 100. A rating of zero would mean the task wasn't difficult at all. A rating of 100 would mean it was the most difficult thing you could imagine doing. Using the ratings, you can then work out which task would be the easiest and which would be the hardest. You can then give each task a rank going from the easiest to the hardest. The therapist asks this to child:

   1. What is the situation in which you want to become more assertive?
   2. What unhelpful beliefs are maintaining the unassertive behaviour?
   3. What are more assertive beliefs?
   4. What unassertive behaviours are you using?
   5. What are more assertive behaviours you could use?

Identify and change any unhelpful thinking

- There is usually some unhelpful thinking underneath non-assertive behaviour.
- Use a thought diary and come up with more assertive thoughts. Once they have come up with this new thought, they were able to do that task and move on to the next task.

Identify and change any unhelpful behaviour

- Change unhelpful behaviours with more helpful behaviours

Rehearse and practice

Session 6: Relapse management
Participant: Parent and child
Duration: 60–90 min
Objectives

- Assess progress
- Reinforce gains
- Prepare for continued coping
- Relapse management.

Tasks

(i) Completing post-intervention measures
(ii) Review relaxation and behavioural, cognitive, and distraction techniques.
(iii) Prepare for minor setbacks and a plan of action to manage them.

13.7.22 Task (I) Completing post-intervention measures

- The child is given the post-intervention measures consisting of Coping Scale for Children and Youth, Children Somatization Inventory, and Children Global Assessment of Functioning using the same set of instructions.
- The parent is given the post-intervention measures consisting of DASS, coping checklist, and Global Assessment of Functioning.

13.7.23 Task (II) and (III) Review and relapse management

- All the doubts are clarified whether the child and the parent have any.
- It is explained to the parents that the symptoms might reappear, which might be just a phase. They can manage them with the above-explained strategies or can come back to us.
- All the skills taught are reviewed.

13.8 Barriers to Treatment

The belief system of the people that it is God's wish and nothing can be done about it or that it is black magic is a major barrier to families seeking treatment for their children. Poverty and lack of knowledge makes these patients vulnerable to taking treatment from people not specialized to handle such issues. There is a dearth of trained professionals to meet the mental health needs of children and adolescents, and barriers to care include poor identification and lack of specialized personnel. Hence, attention needs to be focused on the training and supervision of professionals.

13.9 Conclusion and Future Directions

Unexplained physical symptoms are common in children and adolescents. These symptoms when severe, impairing, associated with psychological factors and result in frequent medical help seeking they form the basis of somatoform disorders. In some cultures, families may explain the physical symptoms in religious ways. Psychiatric comorbidity also commonly occurs. Medical examination and investigation, acknowledging parental and child attitudes and management strategies to reduce impairment, are essential to successful management. The best evidence of treatment comes from involving the family. Involving families during assessment and treatment is important and will aid recovery. Psychoeducation may be an effective means of preventing and managing these disorders across different countries and cultures.

References

De Shazer, S. (1985). *Keys to solution in brief therapy*. New York: Norton.

Domenech-Llaberia, E., Jané, C., Canals, J., et al. (2004). Parental reports of somatic symptoms in preschool children: Prevalence and associations in a Spanish sample. *Journal of the American Academy of Child and Adolescent Psychiatry, 43*, 598–604.

Garralda, M. E. (1996). Somatisation in children. *Journal of Child Psychology and Psychiatry, 37*, 13–33.

Garralda, M. E. (2005). Functional somatic symptoms and somatoform disorders in children. In C. Gillberg, R. Harrington, & H. C. Steinshausen (Eds.), *A clinician's handbook of child and adolescent psychiatry* (pp. 246–268). Cambridge: Cambridge University Press.

Gledhill, J., Garralda, M. E. (2009). The relationship between physical and mental health in children and adolescents. In M. G. Gelder, N. C. Andreassen, J. J. Lopez- Ibor et al. (Eds.), *New Oxford Textbook of Psychiatry* (2nd ed., pp. 1740–1746). Oxford: Oxford University Press.

Gureje, O., Simon, G. E., Ustun, T. U., et al. (1997). Somatization in cross-cultural perspective: A world health organization study in primary care. *American Journal of Psychiatry, 154*, 989–995.

Knapp, M., Funk, M., Curran, C., et al. (2006). Economic barriers to better mental health practice and policy. *Health Policy and Planning, 21*, 157–170.

Keiling, C., Baker-Henningham, H., Belfer, M., et al. (2011). Child and adolescent health worldwide: evidence for action. *The Lancet, 378*, 1515–1525.

Kozlowska, K., Nunn, K. P., Rose, D., et al. (2007). Conversion disorder in Australian pediatric practice. *Journal of the American Academy of Child and Adolescent Psychiatry, 46*, 68–75.

Lieb, R., Pfister, H., Mastaler, M., et al. (2000). Somatoform syndromes and disorders in a representative population sample of adolescents and young adults. Prevalence, comorbidity and impairments. *Acta Psychiatrica Scandinavica, 101*, 194–208.

Pehlivanturk, B., & Unal, F. (2002). Conversion disorder in children and adolescents. A 4 year follow up study. *Journal of Psychosomatic Research, 52*, 187–191.

Robins, P. M., Smith, S. M., Glutting, J. J., et al. (2005). A randomised controlled trial of a cognitive-behavioural family intervention for pediatric recurrent abdominal pain. *Journal of Paediatric Psychology, 30*, 397–408.

Chapter 14
Headache—A Transdiagnostic Approach

Pragya Sharma, Manju Mehta and Rajesh Sagar

14.1 Introduction

14.1.1 Headache

Headaches are very common in children and adolescents. According to the International Headache Society (IHS), headaches are divided into primary and secondary headaches. Primary headaches do not have an underlying disease, and the most common types are migraine, tension-type and cluster headaches. Secondary headaches are part of a syndrome, and underlying causes of these headaches are organic disorders or physical diseases.

14.1.1.1 Diagnostic Classification

See Table 14.1.

P. Sharma (✉) · M. Mehta · R. Sagar
Department of Psychiatry, All India Institute of Medical Sciences, New Delhi, India
e-mail: pragya.cp@gmail.com

M. Mehta
e-mail: drmanju.mehta@gmail.com

R. Sagar
e-mail: rsagar29@gmail.com

M. Mehta and R. Sagar (eds.), *A Practical Approach to Cognitive Behaviour Therapy for Adolescents*, DOI 10.1007/978-81-322-2241-5_14

Table 14.1 Diagnostic criteria for three types of primary headache (IHS 2004)

Episodic tension-type	Migraine	Cluster
Headache lasting 30 minutes to 7 days	Headache lasting 4–72 h	Headache lasting 15–180 min
At least **two** of • bilateral location • non-pulsating quality • mild to moderate pain intensity • not worsened by routine physical activity	At least **two** of • unilateral location • pulsating quality • moderate to severe pain intensity • worsened by routine physical activity	**Both** of • unilateral location • severe to very severe pain around and/or above the eye and/or temple
Neither of: • nausea and/or vomiting • photophobia and phonophobia (but may have one or the other)	At least **one** of: • nausea and/ or vomiting • photophobia **and** phonophobia	At least **one** of: • conjunctival injection and/or lacrimation • nasal congestion and/or rhinorrhoea • eyelid oedema • forehead and facial sweating • constricted pupil and/or drooping of the upper eyelid • restlessness or agitation (On the same side of the face as the headache pain)
	without aura: at least 5 attacks *with aura*: at least 2 attacks	At least 5 attacks: from one attack every other day up to 8 attacks a day

14.1.1.2 Epidemiology

The prevalence rate of headache increases with age in children, with female predominance, after the age of 13 years (Russell et al. 2006). It ranged from 37 to 51 % in those who were at least seven years of age and gradually rose to 57 to 82 % by age 15 (Karli et al. 2006). Frequent episodic tension-type headache was the most common (25.9 %) headache followed by migraine (14.5 %) (Karli et al. 2006). The prevalence of adolescent migraine varies from 3 to 22 % in different populations (Laurell et al. 2006).

In India, Gupta et al. (2009) found 57.5 % adolescents to be suffering from recurrent headaches. Migraine was the most prevalent (17.2 %) followed by unspecified (14.9 %) and tension headache (11 %). Average age of headache onset was 11 years.

14.1.1.3 Social Functioning in Adolescents with Headache

Migraine causes significantly reduced school attendance. Collin et al. (1985) reported that over a time span of twelve weeks, the prevalence of school absence due to headache for children 5 to 19 years of age was 3.7 %.

Caring for a child with a physical disease puts a strain on the child's family. School absence and frequent somatic complaints due to frequent headache or migraine may lead to 'perceived role restriction' in the parents which is defined as 'the extent to which a person feels unable to pursue one's own personal interests due to the responsibilities involved with raising a child with a chronic physical condition' (Breslau et al. 1982). Thus, though tension headache and migraine are not regarded as disabling physical diseases, these disorders may lead to a perceived role restriction in the family to the same degree as a disabling disease.

14.1.2 Headache and Comorbid Disorders

According to *The International Classification of Headache Disorders-2nd Edition (ICHD-II)* (IHS 2004), primary headache disorders in adolescence are often comorbid with psychiatric disorders. Girls with anxiety disorder had a significantly greater prevalence of headaches than girls without an internalizing disorder (Egger et al. 1998). Cross-sectional investigations of psychiatric disorder prevalence in migraine samples found an increased risk of anxiety disorders, particularly panic disorder and phobias (IHS 1998). Breslau et al. (1991) found an association between migraine and obsessive–compulsive disorder as well as generalized anxiety disorder. Thirty-five percent of youths with chronic headaches had anxiety disorders (Liakopoulous-Kairis et al. 2002). Emiroglu et al. (2004) found 94 % adolescents suffering from unexplained neurological symptoms (such as headache) to be suffering from at least one mental disorder, most frequent being depressive disorders (40 %). High rates of anxiety and depressive symptoms among adolescents with headaches have been found by Fritz et al. (1997). For more information on anxiety or depression, refer to Chaps. 11 and 12.

14.1.3 Cognitive behavioral therapy

The CBT model for headache is based on the belief that thoughts influence feelings which influence our behaviors/experience (including pain). CBT has been successfully applied to pediatric headaches (Palermo et al. 2009, 2010; Trautmann and Kroner-Herwig 2010). There is increasing evidence for the short- and long-term efficacy of CBT for anxiety-related difficulties in childhood and adolescence (Silverman et al. 2008). Cognitive behavior therapies represent a range of empirically supported psychotherapy for adolescents with depression (Kazdin and Weisz 1998).

14.1.4 *Transdiagnostic Cognitive behavioral therapy (TCBT)*

Transdiagnostic treatments are those that apply to the same underlying treatment principles across mental disorders, without tailoring the protocol to specific diagnoses (McEvoy et al. 2009). According to Mansell et al. (2009), less time is spent on selecting the right therapy, there is no problem with comorbidity in an individual, the stigma attached to a diagnostic label can be avoided and it fosters a more idiographic approach to treatment. It helps the continued generalization of knowledge from established models of psychological disorders to new disorders that are yet to be fully investigated. It further leads to development of treatment components that are effective across a wide range of disorders (Mansell 2008).

14.1.5 *Transdiagnostic CBT for Headache and Comorbid Disorders*

Headache frequency is significantly associated with externalizing and internalizing problem behaviors (Virtanen 2008). Comorbidity of headache with other disorders renders it suitable for application of TCBT as TCBT focuses on all aspects of problem behavior.

14.2 Case Vignette

Master N is a 13-year-old male studying in class IX belonging to middle socioeconomic status and urban domicile presented with complaints of frequent, recurring headache and feeling anxious in social situations. N had always been a shy child, but the situation had intensified in the last six months after he changed school owing to a change in residence. He had been in the previous school since kindergarten, every teacher knew him, and thus, his anxiety symptoms went unnoticed to some extent. With the new school, he had to start all over again. This was distressing for him. Unable to hold a conversation, he could not make friends, and even when he tried, he stammered. This lead to his being made fun of by classmates and further drew him away from everyone. These situations at school distressed him, and he was unable to concentrate on studies resulting in poor performance. He began feeling sadness of mood, lost interest in earlier pleasurable activities, and had low self-esteem. It was also at this time that the headaches started and gradually increased in intensity and duration. He reported significant physiological (e.g., sweating excessively, having a dry mouth, heart racing), cognitive (e.g., 'I will say something wrong and embarrass myself'), and behavioral (e.g., blushing, stammering) symptoms of anxiety when forced to face social situations. At best, he liked to avoid all social interactions. He reported 'freezing up' when talking to others and often felt that he was not able to respond despite wanting to, which he found very distressing. His mind went 'blank' and he stopped trying to talk. Even while narrating these symptoms, N was seen struggling with anxiety and it was difficult for him to talk. He used compensatory behaviors to communicate across settings by asking others to do things for him (e.g., parents ordering food at restaurants). Further, recurring headache episodes made it difficult for N to concentrate on anything. School being a consistent stressor due to its social demands led N to refuse to go to school leading to several absences each week. His 'silent' instances in the class (not asking questions in class, not answering when asked of, not talking to peers, or remaining silent during group work) prompted teachers to complain to his parents. N's concerned parents brought him to a psychiatrist for identification and management of the problem. He was diagnosed as having tension headache (IHS classification), social phobia, and mild depressive episode (ICD-10 classification). He was given medication and sent to psychologist for further management.

14.3 Assessment

Before initiating intervention, an in-depth assessment is an integral part of the treatment process and helps in deciding the treatment module to be followed. Assessment involves a detailed case history focusing on current problems, factors leading to and maintaining current problems, family history, and any comorbid conditions. Further assessment includes the application of inventories, rating scales, and self-report questionnaires to assess degree and severity of headache, anxiety, and other comorbid disorders. Some of the important tools to measure headache and anxiety are listed in Table 14.2. For information on tools to measure depression, refer to Chap. 11.

Parents, teachers, and peers are important sources of assessment apart from adolescent himself. Assessment is an ongoing process and continues into therapy where tools such as ABC chart (see Appendix) and self-monitoring form (see Appendix) will be used.

14.3.1 Sample Illustration of Assessment

N's initial assessment included semi-structured diagnostic interviews, clinical interview, questionnaires, and self-monitoring. Parent and adolescent report on ADIS-IV indicated that N met the criteria for a diagnosis of social phobia. Parent and adolescent report on RCADS indicated clinically elevated sub-scales for social phobia and borderline elevation on major depression. On Youth Self Report, clinical elevations were seen on the scales of Withdrawn/Depressed and Anxiety problems.

Table 14.2 Assessment tools

Name of the test	Measures	Description
Headache history and diary	Frequency, duration, and intensity of headache	Questions to assess history, visual analogue scale (0–10), record frequency and duration
Youth self report (Achenbach and Rescorla 2001)	Behavioral and emotional functioning	2 sub-areas: (a) 20 competence items (b) 112 items that measure eight sub-scale symptoms
Anxiety disorder interview schedule-IV child/parent (Silverman and Albano 1996)	Assesses and diagnoses presence or absence of anxiety disorders	Structured interview
Revised children's anxiety and depression scale (Chorpita et al. 2000)	Report of symptoms	47-item self-report questionnaire
Revised children's manifest anxiety scale-2 (Reynolds and Richmond 1978)	Measures the level and nature of anxiety	Yes/no response format, self-report
State trait anxiety inventory (Spielberger et al. 1973)	Indicates intensity of feeling of state and trait anxiety	40-item self-report questionnaire
Beck anxiety inventory (Beck 1993)	Measures severity of anxiety	21 items multiple choice questionnaire
Hamilton anxiety rating scale (Hamilton 1959)	Assesses severity of anxiety symptoms	14-item rating scale

14.4 Intervention

Intervention includes therapy sessions for headache and comorbid disorders such as depression and anxiety.

Important

Headache in adolescents occurs with comorbid disorder such as anxiety and depression. This chapter will focus on management of headache and anxiety. For elaboration on management of depression, refer to Chap. 11.

The total number of sessions range from 10 to 16 weekly sessions (minimum). The average duration of a session is 45–50 min. The sessions may either be with the adolescent alone or parents or a single session involving a separate time for both. A brief look at the various therapy phases is given in Table 14.3.

Table 14.3 Therapy phases

Initial phase (Sessions 1–3)
Establishing rapport and assessment
Psychoeducation
Relaxation
Guided imagery
Middle phase (Sessions 4–12)
Hierarchy development
Identifying automatic negative thoughts
Cognitive restructuring
Exposure-based procedures
Problem-solving skills training
Stress management
Assertiveness skills training
Termination phase (Sessions 12–14)
Relapse prevention
Termination

14.4.1 Session 1: Rapport Formation and Psychoeducation

14.4.1.1 Rapport Formation

Rapport with the parent and adolescent is crucial to management. Establishing trust with an adolescent can be difficult because adolescents are going through dramatic biological and emotional changes. Seeking mental health care may seem challenging to them because the normal changes of adolescence affect their self-confidence, relationships, social skills, and general thinking. It might need repeated assurance and discussion by the therapist to put the adolescent at ease regarding the issue of confidentiality. Some activities can be carried out with the adolescent in order to encourage expression, such as drawing, journaling, or interacting with them about their hobbies.

14.4.1.2 Psychoeducation

Once the rapport is formed, therapist should proceed to educating the adolescent and the parents about the nature and causes of headache and comorbid disorders. The purpose of psychoeducation is to help the adolescent and their families understand how the illness affects them and what kind of activities or treatment might help. Psychoeducation helps them understand that there are others who have similar problems and that there are treatments that work. This type of education helps them understand what will happen in the treatment sessions and how long the treatment might take. They will also learn what role the parent, the therapist, and the adolescent will play in the treatment and that they will be a team that will work on problems together.

Correct information presented in developmentally appropriate terms is essential for decreasing family anxiety and increasing acceptance of a multifaceted approach. Reassurance that headache does not signify a lethal illness while expressing understanding of the significant disability the pain is causing allows both the adolescent and the families to feel reassured and validated. They need to be psychoeducated that pain results from multiple biological and psychological factors and is not either/or.

The meaning of anxiety is discussed as an emotional state experienced when a person anticipates threat or is threatened in some way. It is explained that the type of threat can vary from situation to situation and from person to person. How anxiety is a normal part of everyday life is explained by examples like when one is appearing for an exam. It is further explained that anxiety is experienced by all individuals when they feel there is some type of threat and it is unpleasant but not unmanageable and decreases once the fear is faced. The positive side of anxiety is shown in how it motivates the individual to prevent the threat or protect himself/herself from being physically or emotionally harmed.

After the normalization of anxiety, therapist moves on to explaining when is it that anxiety becomes a problem. The difference between typical and problematic anxiety is explained with the help of case examples of two people, like one who is afraid of water and the other who moderates necessary caution but is otherwise not fearful. The adolescent is then encouraged to come up with things and situations that seem to trigger anxiety for him/her but not for other people. He/she is also asked what he/she would like to accomplish in treatment. The adolescent is asked to explain how his/her anxiety interferes with his/her life (school/home/social life). The importance of this is emphasized in the process of identification of goals and the measurement of progress.

The causes of problematic anxiety are further explained as a combination of genetic factors, early learning, and important life experiences. The goal of this discussion is to discourage the adolescent from assuming the role of a single determining factor and to view his/her anxiety difficulties more objectively and scientifically.

Once the adolescent reflects learning of all the previous concepts, he is made aware of the three components of anxiety with the help of a case example. Physiological component includes bodily feelings and sensations an individual experiences when anxious. Cognitive component is what people think about and pay attention to when anxious. N thought he would say something wrong and will be embarrassed. Finally, the behavioral component refers to the actions the individual engages in when anxious. These behaviors can be of three types: nervous behaviors, such as tapping your feet, avoiding eye contact, checking your watch, and playing with your hair; escape/avoidance behaviors such as escaping or avoiding anxiety-provoking situations; and coping behaviors which include learning how to minimize anxiety by engaging in certain actions. Coping behaviors, such as escape/avoidance behaviors, are also effective in short-term anxiety reduction, but counterproductive in the long term. Once sufficient understanding of the three components has been built up, the therapist goes on to explain how the

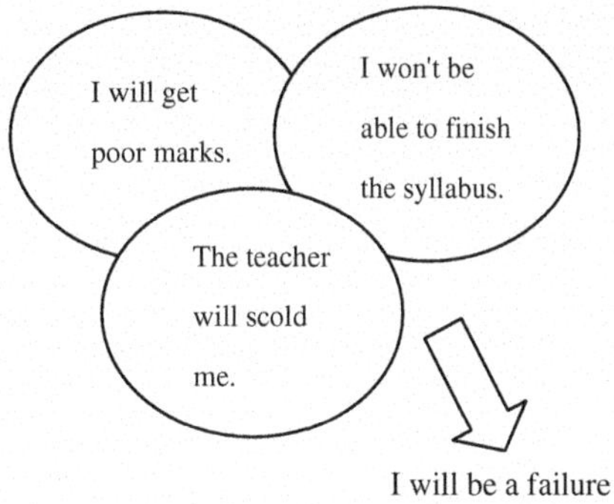

Fig. 14.1 Downward spiral of anxiety

three interact with each other to create a downward spiral of anxiety (Fig. 14.1). The adolescent is then asked to look at how the components interact in case of his anxieties.

14.4.1.3 Treatment Components

After having psychoeducated the adolescent, a brief discussion of the treatment components takes place. It is further emphasized that each component of treatment will require work both in session and at home. The importance of completing the assigned homework exercises is stressed as they help the adolescent apply the skills they learn in the session to the real-life situations they encounter.

14.4.1.4 Homework

Toward the end of the session, the adolescent is given homework including self-monitoring which will be done throughout the course of treatment. It includes keeping a headache diary in which the adolescent should note down the date and time of headache instances, its intensity on a scale of 0–10 (with 1 being the lowest and 10 being the maximum), what he/she did before and during a headache episode, and how did the headache got relieved (Table 14.4). For anxiety, he/she needs to monitor anxiety on a daily basis by rating the average level of anxiety and stress for that day on a scale of 0–100, with higher numbers meaning more severe anxiety or stress (Table 14.5). The adolescent is further explained how level of anxiety needs to rate severity of anxiety with regard to his/her fears that day,

Table 14.4 Headache diary

Date and time when headache started	Before headache behavior	Intensity (0–10) and efforts to relieve	Total duration of headache and how did it get relieved
.	.	.	.

Table 14.5 Anxiety self-monitoring form

Date	Average anxiety (0–100)	Average stress (0–100)	Notes
.	.	.	.

Table 14.6 Monitoring anxiety components

Date:		
Describe anxiety-provoking situation briefly		
Physiological component	Cognitive component	Behavioral component
What I *felt* was…	What I *thought* was…	What I *did* was…

while stress rating reflects daily general stress level, irrespective of the specific fears. The benefits of self-monitoring are then discussed including its importance in identifying patterns, themes or unexpected headache and anxiety triggers, tracking progress throughout treatment, and providing encouragement or motivation. The final monitoring task involves looking closely at one or two anxiety episodes and breaking it down into specific components of anxiety as experienced during these episodes (Table 14.6).

The adolescent is also asked to think about and make a list of fearful or anxiety-provoking situations that he/she will be working on in the subsequent sessions with the therapist.

At the end of the session, the adolescent is thanked for coming to the session and congratulated for having begun the treatment process. He/she is given a brief overview of the next session which will focus on discussion of fears and relaxation training.

14.4.2 Session 2: Education, Relaxation, and Hierarchy Development

The focus of the second session is on reviewing self-monitoring homework in order to decode possible problematic situations for headache and causes of anxiety. Further, analyzing the possible headache triggers, the adolescent feels in control of the symptom once he learns to control his reactions to the situation. Relaxation training and development of hierarchy are to be taught to the adolescent for the management of headache and anxious responses.

14.4.2.1 Homework Review

Some time is spent in reviewing the self-monitoring homework given to the adolescent in the previous session. Graphing of the daily monitoring activity is taught to him/her and practiced in the session (Fig. 14.2).

Fig. 14.2 Self-monitoring graph

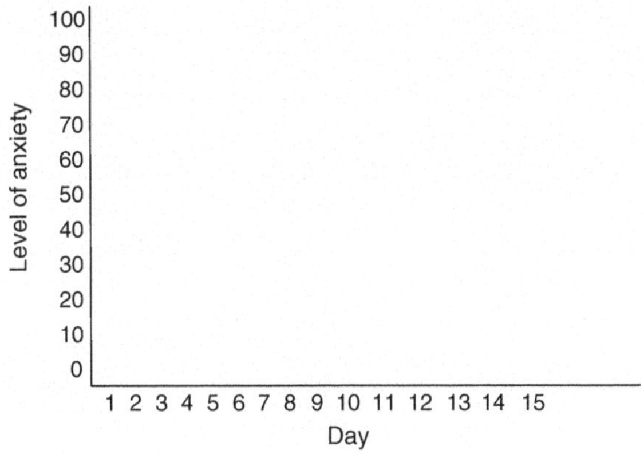

14.4.2.2 Adaptive Basis of Anxiety Components

Looking at the headache diary, the frequency and intensity of headache in the last few days can be ascertained. The stress and anxiety ratings further give an understanding of what affects the adolescent the most, gives an overview of anxiety-/stress-provoking situations, and sets a task for the therapist to handle these situations in further sessions.

The therapist goes on to elaborate more on the anxiety components. Firstly, the therapist takes a look at the physiological symptoms that the adolescent has jotted down in response to the anxiety-provoking situations in the last week. He/she is then asked to think of how these may be useful in protecting us when facing a dangerous situation.

The therapist then moves onto the cognitive component of anxiety. The adolescent's homework is reviewed, and he/she is further assisted to come up with other possible list of cognitions. It is explained that when we are anxious, our minds focus on the threat and its potential consequences and all other thoughts vanish from our mind. The adolescent is encouraged to think why we focus our attention onto the threat and start assessing the possible consequences immediately. The importance of this particular attentional shift is discussed with an emphasis on the fact that this shift in thinking occurs to help us identify, avoid, or escape from the threat if it actually occurs.

Lastly, talking about the behavioral component of anxiety, it is restated that these are the things we do or are motivated to do when anxious or fearful. It is explained that in the face of a threat, we either try to avoid or escape the dangerous situation.

The components of anxiety are reaffirmed as natural and normal processes experienced by everyone and that they are designed to be helpful and save us from harm.

14.4.2.3 Discussion of Fears

From the homework done during the last week, the adolescent is asked to discuss his list of fears and anxiety-provoking situations that he/she would like to work on in the subsequent sessions. These fears might be fear of heights, water, social situations, contamination, etc.

Once the list has been reviewed in general and some details have been elicited, it is explained to the adolescent that you will be developing an anxiety hierarchy in accordance with him/her. It is elaborated that an anxiety hierarchy is a list of situations to which you react to with varying degrees of anxiety. The most disturbing item is placed at the bottom of the list and the least disturbing at the top. In working on the hierarchy, we begin with the top item on the list and work step by step through the hierarchy to the last item.

14.4.2.4 Development of Hierarchy

Reviewing the list of situations that provoke fear or anxiety, the adolescent is then encouraged to make a list of some of the variables that affect his/her anxiety level. Once these have been listed, the adolescent should be given an example of a sample hierarchy and asked to identify variables affecting the amount of anxiety in them, for example, fear of speaking in class (see Table 14.7).

Once the adolescent seems to have developed a good understanding, he/she is asked to build his/her own hierarchy. Most people include 10–20 items beginning with very mild items in order to ease into the process.

14.4.2.5 Relaxation Training

Relaxation training is to be taught to the adolescent for help with the relieving of headache as well as to desensitize him/her to the anxiety-evoking items on the hierarchy. Instructions for relaxation training can be found in the Appendix.

Table 14.7 Sample hierarchy

Target behavior: Fear of speaking up in class	
1	At home, the night before I go to class
2	Driving to school before the class
3	Walking to my class
4	Walking inside the classroom
5	Looking around at the people in the room
6	Walking in and saying hello to someone in the room
7	Sitting down in the front row
8	Catching the professor's eye and smiling
9	Nodding or agreeing with a comment made in class
10	Asking the professor a question from the front of the room
11	Asking the professor a question from the back of the room
12	Answering a short question from the front of the room
13	Answering a short question from the back of the room
14	Answering a longer question
15	Making a comment on a particular point to the class

The adolescent is asked to practice this relaxation technique for 10 min each in the morning and evening in order to gain mastery and make a habit of it. Also, it is to be done when he/she suffers from headache. When he/she is able to relax himself/herself completely in three to four minutes by briefly running through the relaxation exercises, then he/she is ready to begin the desensitization sessions.

14.4.2.6 Homework

Toward the end of the session, the adolescent is given homework regarding daily practicing of relaxation exercises and making hierarchies for each target behavior. Self-monitoring is to be done similar to last week (headache diary, anxiety monitoring).

At the end of the session, the session summary is given and any doubts addressed. He/she is given a brief overview of the next session.

14.4.3 Session 3: Automatic Negative Thoughts and Guided Imagery

The focus of the third session is on addressing any problems the adolescent might have faced in developing hierarchy and practicing relaxation technique. Further, importance of thoughts is discussed with an emphasis on identifying and monitoring automatic negative thoughts, and guided imagery is taught and practiced.

14.4.4 Homework Review

Headache diary and anxiety monitoring diary are seen and any pattern to it analyzed. Effect of relaxation is enquired about. Progress made is noted.

14.4.4.1 Importance of Thoughts

Adolescent's thoughts from last week regarding anxiety-provoking situations are reviewed. The therapist goes on to explain how it is the interpretation of the event that is causing anxiety and not the actual situation itself.

14.4.4.2 Cognitive Restructuring

The adolescent is told that one of the components of treatment involves looking at one's thoughts and to learn ways to analyze and evaluate them. This process is termed cognitive restructuring. It involves paying attention to one's thoughts and interpretations, learning to identify which of our thoughts and interpretations may be incorrect or irrational interpretations of the situation one is in and to logically challenge the assumptions underlying these thoughts.

14.4.4.3 Automatic Thoughts

The concept of negative automatic thoughts is then introduced to the adolescent, explaining how they seem to automatically come to mind and are usually incorrect interpretations of the situation.

14.4.4.4 In-Session Exercise

When the adolescent displays an understanding of the concept of negative automatic thoughts, an in-session exercise is begun. The adolescent is asked to remember an anxiety-provoking situation. When he/she is describing the situation, the therapist looks for the presence of automatic thoughts and comes up with questions to ask of the adolescent in order to elicit these thoughts. At this stage, the therapist should refrain from countering or challenging the validity of the thoughts.

14.4.4.5 Guided Imagery

Guided imagery is effective in providing relief from headache and is a relaxing activity by nature. There are three principles of guided imagery. First principle is the mind–body connection which says that to the body, images created in the mind can be almost as real as actual, external events. The second principle says that in the altered state, we are capable of more rapid and intense healing, growth, learning, and performance. We have a heightened sensitivity to the object of our attention and a decreased awareness of other things going on around us, things we would ordinarily notice. The third principle is the 'locus of control' factor. When we have a sense of being in control, that, in and of itself, can help us to feel better and do better. Relaxation can allow us to influence automatic physical responses such as blood flow and muscle tension, primary causes of migraine headaches and tension headaches. By reversing these, it is possible to achieve headache relief through relaxation. An in-session exercise is done. The instructions for the same can be found in the Appendix.

14.4.4.6 Homework

Toward the end of the session, it is reminded to the adolescent that identifying automatic thoughts is a very important part of the treatment. The homework of

Table 14.8 Thought monitoring form

Date
Describe trigger that made you feel anxious or fearful
List automatic thoughts you recall having

practicing monitoring and identifying automatic thoughts is given wherein the adolescent needs to identify an anxiety-provoking situation, pay attention to the automatic thoughts, and record them on a form (Table 14.8). If this happens to be an anxiety-free week, he/she is to fill the form using memory of a recent anxiety-provoking experience. The adolescent is given a guided imagery audio CD in order to be able to practice it at home. At the end of the session, he/she is given a brief overview of the next session.

14.4.5 Session 4: Cognitive Restructuring

This session is an extension of the last one as far as thought-challenging skills are concerned. Its focus is on helping the adolescent realize that his/her assumptions and beliefs may not be accurate reflection of true degree of threat. The original assumption and these alternative possibilities are further evaluated during subsequent exposures in upcoming sessions.

14.4.5.1 Homework Review

It is ensured that the adolescent is doing self-monitoring and putting it up on a graph. Also, it is to be asked if he/she is indulging in relaxation training and guided imagery. Further automatic thoughts that the adolescent had over the past week are discussed. He/she is asked to briefly describe the situation and list the thoughts he/she has identified.

14.4.5.2 Thinking Errors

If the adolescent seems comfortable with the concept of automatic thoughts, spend some time reviewing it with an example. Then, introduce some critical errors in logic or thinking errors. It is to be explained that these errors fall into three categories: (1) overestimation, where one overestimates the likelihood of a negative outcome; (2) catastrophizing, exaggerating how terrible or negative something will be; and (3) maladaptive thinking, engaging in unhelpful thoughts. In overestimation, the person takes an unlikely negative outcome and assumes that it is guaranteed to happen. In catastrophizing, the worst possible outcome is assumed to happen or the worst possible meaning is thought of as true. Maladaptive thoughts are technically correct and not thinking errors, but they are not helpful and make the person anxious. Once the adolescent displays an understanding of these errors, he/she is encouraged to look at some of his/her thoughts from last week that he recorded and to find any thinking errors in them. The goal of this exercise is to help the adolescent begin to see his/her thoughts as incorrect interpretations of the situation which leads to fear or anxiety.

14.4.5.3 Challenging Automatic Thoughts

The rationale for cognitive restructuring is briefly reviewed, emphasizing that the second part is to challenge erroneous thoughts. The adolescent is told that he/she will be learning how accurate his/her current thoughts are and will be developing a set of more accurate or neutral interpretations of an anxiety-provoking situation. Questioning the accuracy and probability of the automatic thoughts will be done using 'disputing questions.' The key to using it effectively is to both *ask* and *fully answer* a disputing question.

14.4.5.4 In-Session Exercise: Asking and Answering Disputing Questions

An automatic thought is selected from the adolescent's form. For example, 'I am a loser because I have never had a girlfriend. I am undesirable.' During the last activity, this thought was found to have an error of catastrophization. His thought of being undesirable is an exaggerated negative outcome of the event. Then, the adolescent is asked what would be a good disputing question he could ask of himself, what would be his response to that question, and what disputing question would be a good follow-up to that answer. He might respond in the manner below and helped during the process (Table 14.9).

This process needs to continue until an effective challenge has been developed.

14.4.5.5 Rational Responses

Once disputing questions have been developed to challenge an automatic thought, the concept of rational responses is introduced. A rational response summarizes

Table 14.9 Sample of disputing questions and answers

Disputing question	Answer
Does never having a girlfriend equal being a loser?	No. I have many positive qualities that contradict the label of loser
Does never having a girlfriend mean I am undesirable?	Though it might be possible that women find me undesirable, there can be other explanations for my never having a girlfriend like the fact that I have never asked someone out on a date

Table 14.10 Cognitive restructuring practice form

Describe trigger that made you anxious
List major automatic thoughts you experienced
Pick a strong automatic thought and identify thinking error in that
Use disputing questions to challenge the automatic thought
Disputing question
Disputing answer
Develop a rational response

the main ideas developed while asking and answering disputing questions and reduces them down into a single short statement (Table 14.10).

At this point, the therapist returns to the disputing questions and answers that the adolescent developed. They are briefly reviewed, and the adolescent is asked to identify what he/she thinks is the most important point to remember. For example, a rational response in the last example may be 'I have many desirable characteristics and can have a girlfriend if I make an attempt for it.'

14.4.5.6 Full Cognitive Restructuring Practice

Once all the steps have been discussed and demonstrated, the adolescent is asked to walk through the entire cognitive restructuring process while you will be there to help.

14.4.5.7 Homework

Toward the end of the session, the client is asked to continue with the previous homework of self-monitoring, relaxation, and guided imagery and to start doing the complete cognitive restructuring procedure for as many anxiety-provoking situations that come up during the week. At the end of the session, the session summary is given and any doubts addressed. He/she is given a brief overview of the next session.

14.4.6 Session 5: Problem-solving Skills Training and Distraction

This session focuses on problem-solving skills training and distraction. Although adolescents who experience anxiety may worry about things in general, sometimes there is a need to deal with problems and difficulties in a practical way. Further, distraction techniques are useful to cut down time spent on rumination.

14.4.6.1 Homework Review

Progress on guided imagery is asked about. The cognitive restructuring process the adolescent has done over the past week is discussed.

14.4.6.2 Problem-Solving Skills Training

The purpose of problem-solving skills training is to assist the adolescent to develop better coping strategies and a feeling of being able to manage his/her own life. Some of the problems being faced by the adolescent are discussed before following it up with the training.

Techniques of problem solving are given in detail in the Appendix and are to be followed out within the session. Role play may be enacted with the adolescent for a better understanding of the process as a whole.

14.4.6.3 Distraction

Distraction simply involves trying to take your mind off uncomfortable symptoms or thoughts. Distraction techniques can be a useful way to manage anxiety symptoms in the short term. The adolescent is explained about distraction and that it works by providing something other than the feared object to think about, providing an increased sense of control over anxiety and by showing that one is able to cope in the face of anxiety. Also, distraction helps in keeping the headache from becoming severe by distracting the brain from focusing on pain signals. Distraction types and techniques are explained to the adolescent (see Appendix for details).

Downside: The distraction techniques are useful in the short term but are not the best techniques to be used in the longer term. They prevent the person from participating fully in exposure. It does nothing to reduce the fear, and sometime people use it so much that they do not use other more powerful techniques to assist them in overcoming their fears.

14.4.6.4 Homework

Toward the end of the session, the client is asked to continue with the previous homework and include distraction and problem solving with relation to headache and anxiety and in general in their day-to-day lives. At the end of the session, he/she is given a brief overview of the next session.

14.4.7 Sessions 6–8: Exposure and Cognitive Restructuring

These sessions focus on exposure and advanced cognitive restructuring. There is a graduated exposure to anxiety-provoking stimuli, and the adolescent is encouraged to continue self-directed exposures.

14.4.7.1 Homework Review

Self-monitoring homework is taken account of. It is ensured that the adolescent is utilizing techniques so far learned in his/her daily life. Further five to ten minutes are spent on discussing the application of problem solving the adolescent has done over the past week.

14.4.7.2 Exposure

Exposure therapy is directed toward having the adolescent confront or face his/her fears. Exposure therapy works through two mechanisms: habituation and disconfirming evidence. Habituation refers to the fact that the more often you encounter something that causes an emotional reaction, the less intense the reaction will be. Providing disconfirming evidence happens when participating in exposures, the person begins to unlearn the belief that the stimulus he/she fears is dangerous in reality and is able to accommodate new evidence that it can be safe. The rationale and procedure of exposure is explained to the adolescent. The procedure is elaborated in Chap. 12.

14.4.7.3 Homework

The adolescent is assigned a homework exposure to be conducted before the next session. He/she is to record the procedure in the appropriate form. He/she should continue with the self-monitoring homework and practice techniques learned in the last few weeks. The adolescent is reminded that the next session will involve continuing the graduated exposure exercises, slowly moving up the hierarchy.

14.4.8 Session 9–10: Advanced Cognitive Restructuring

14.4.8.1 Homework Review

Exposure homework is reviewed. The adolescent is encouraged to adopt an exposure lifestyle whereby he/she should see every anxiety-provoking situation as an opportunity to employ cognitive restructuring skills and do exposure exercises. Self-monitoring data graphs are reviewed to highlight the progress so far made.

14.4.8.2 The Transfer of Therapeutic Effects to Real-life Situations

The completion of an item on the hierarchy in desensitization sessions indicates that the adolescent is making progress toward the alleviation of his/her problem.

If the progress on the hierarchy is good but does not lend itself to a significant transfer to real-life situations, it indicates that the items are not being desensitized completely. This can often be remedied by spending a full session on relaxation between each group of 5–8 desensitizing sessions.

14.4.8.3 Role Playing

While working on desensitization, another technique that will help the adolescent get rid of the fears will be role playing. Role playing, here, means acting out an anxiety-provoking behavior with the therapist or another person you feel comfortable with. Using this technique, the adolescent is to act out each step on the hierarchy.

14.4.8.4 Advanced Cognitive Restructuring

The aim of the current and subsequent sessions is to focus broadly on the general anxious style rather than specifically targeting a fear. It is reiterated to the adolescent that in the initial sessions, we talked about how anxiety develops, involving genes and learning. This leads to an anxious style which puts them at a greater risk for developing anxiety and even depressive problems. The rationale for returning to cognitive restructuring is briefly reviewed for the adolescent elaborating that these same skills will help in counteracting this anxious style and reduce future lapses.

14.4.8.5 Anxious Style and Automatic Thoughts

The adolescent is helped to see that dysfunctional thoughts underlie the negative reactions characteristic of the anxious style and are manifested as automatic thoughts. The adolescent is encouraged to think of daily life situations which make him worried or get him into a negative mood. Some of these automatic thoughts are then recorded. It is to be ensured that the adolescent sees these thoughts as biased or irrational interpretations of the real situation. He/she is then asked to categorize the recorded thoughts into the thinking errors previously discussed.

14.4.8.6 Disputing the Anxious Style

It is explained to the adolescent that process of asking and answering questions is also involved in challenging automatic thoughts of daily life. It is emphasized that to restructure these habitual thinking patterns will require effort and practice. The adolescent is appreciated for the disputing so far and encouraged to continue with the same. The process is briefly revised as follows:

- Becoming good at noticing when he/she is reacting more negatively to a situation or event that is necessary.
- Identifying automatic thoughts.

Table 14.11 Daily self-monitoring form

Date	Avg. anxiety (0–100)	Avg. stress (0–100)	Avg. depression (0–100)	Avg. other negative emotion (0–100)	Describe stress or depression trigger. Identify automatic thoughts
.	.	.	.	.	.

- Challenging them using disputing questions.
- Developing a new rational interpretation of the situation.

An in-session exercise is then put forth taking up from a recent situation in the adolescent's life. The cognitive restructuring steps are followed one by one.

14.4.8.7 Homework

The adolescent is to continue with self-monitoring along with doing the homework exposure to be conducted in real-life situations (a variety of different settings) in order to generalize to all possible situations (Table 14.11). He/she is to practice cognitive restructuring for daily events that lead to negative/anxious thoughts. At the end of the session, the session summary is given and any doubts addressed. He/she is given a brief overview of the next session.

14.4.9 Session 11–13: Cognitive Restructuring, Stress Management and Assertiveness Skills Training

This session focuses on continuing with cognitive restructuring. Further, the adolescent is taught skills training in stress management and assertiveness.

14.4.10 Homework Review

Self-monitoring, exposure, and cognitive restructuring homework are taken account of. It is ensured that the adolescent is utilizing techniques so far learned in his/her daily life. The adolescent is told that the monitoring and reevaluating homework will not be assigned again but need to be continued whenever a suitable situation arises.

14.4.10.1 Advanced Cognitive Restructuring

After the monitoring and reevaluating of homework have been reviewed, the major goal of stopping the negative reactions from occurring in the first place is

Table 14.12 Commonly observed core themes

'Bad things always happen to me'	'Everything should be a certain way or it is wrong'
'People always reject me'	'I must be perfect or else I'm a failure'
'I'm an unlovable person'	'I am inadequate'
'I cannot cope with it all'	'The future is hopeless'

discussed with the adolescent. In order to stop the negative reaction as soon as one detects the trigger or knows he/she may encounter the trigger is to find out what triggers the negative reactions. Looking at the adolescent's self-monitoring forms, he/she is asked to find any common themes from his/her automatic thoughts. It is emphasized that there might be just one theme or several others. Certain commonly observed themes are then showed to the adolescent (Table 14.12).

Once the adolescent has identified a common theme, he/she is guided through the cognitive restructuring process. The adolescent's core beliefs are worked with by demonstrating the process of reevaluating them and generating alternate possibilities. He/she is asked to practice using rational responses by intentionally putting oneself in such situations in order to become more comfortable with challenging core themes.

14.4.11 Stress Management

Since headache and anxiety sometimes both stem from stress, it is important to teach the adolescent how to manage his/her stress better. Adolescent may experience stress everyday and can benefit from learning stress management skills. For further details on stress management, refer to Chapter 8.

14.4.12 Assertiveness Training

The adolescent needs to be trained for assertiveness in order to be able to stand for his/her rights to be treated fairly and be able to say no where required. This means tactfully, justly, and effectively expressing one's preferences, needs, opinions, and feelings. The adolescent is explained how *being assertive* is distinguished from being unassertive (weak, passive, compliant, self-sacrificing) or aggressive (self-centered, inconsiderate, hostile, arrogantly demanding). He/she is further told about the ways to become assertive in his/her daily interactions with others. These are listed in the Appendix.

14.4.12.1 Homework

The adolescent is asked to continue to practice cognitive restructuring and confront situations that may trigger the common themes. He/she is asked to practice techniques of stress management when such situations arise. He/she is also asked to indulge in situations where he/she might have a chance to be assertive. Finally, it is explained that the following session will be the last one and will focus on strategies to maintain gains, continue improvement and to deal with lapses and avoid relapses.

14.4.13 Session 14: Relapse Prevention and Termination

The final session will involve discussion and planning for how adolescents can maintain their gains. Also, plans for dealing with stressors and lapses are introduced and emergency plans for relapses are developed. Finally, treatment conclusion issues are discussed and post-treatment assessments are scheduled.

14.4.13.1 Homework Review

The adolescent is asked about how he/she is doing in terms of experiencing headache and anxiety. The adolescent is asked if he/she has been able to identify and work on core themes which are further discussed. He/she is also enquired about managing stress and being more assertive in situations of daily living. Also, review weekly reduction in anxiety as depicted by the graph.

14.4.13.2 Maintaining Gains and Continuing Progress

The adolescent is made aware of the fact that it is sometimes easier to slip back into old habits once the treatment is over and no one looks over your homework. The adolescent is strongly encouraged not to do that. He/she is given some tips to follow. These include approaching anxiety by seeing it as an opportunity to gain more control by doing exposure exercise, not to give into avoidance or compulsions; practicing and using cognitive restructuring skills with one's fears, negative thoughts and core themes; and rewarding oneself for a work well done by doing something one would like to or something that one has not been able to do due to anxiety previously. The adolescent is asked about his/her ideas for rewarding himself/herself.

14.4.13.3 Dealing with Stressors and Lapses

The adolescent is prepared regarding situations and stressors where lapses may occur like before an exam. He/she is further told about the distinction between a lapse and a relapse. A lapse is avoiding something you should be doing or doing something you should not be. A relapse occurs when the anxiety takes control. In the situation of a relapse, the adolescent is instructed to start with cognitive restructuring and exposure. However, if things get out of hand and the anxiety is unmanageable, the adolescent is told to schedule a session.

14.4.13.4 Concluding the Treatment

The therapist gives a run through of the last 14 weeks of sessions describing in brief what happened during these sessions. The adolescent is then asked to give feedback on what does he think of different aspects of therapy and which ones he/she found more useful to manage headache and anxiety. Further, he/she is asked why he/she found that aspect more helpful. Then, the adolescent is asked to mention which component was the least helpful and why did he/she feel so. Finally, the adolescent is asked to discuss what lessons and new perspectives he/she might have learned about himself/herself and his/her problems. The adolescent is congratulated for completing the treatment and thanked for his/her participation.

Any post-treatment assessments may then be carried out or another session scheduled for the same.

14.5 Barriers to Treatment

Working with adolescents poses many challenges. Right from rapport formation to sustaining their interests, the therapist has to put in more effort than is needed when working with an adult. There are many barriers to treatment. These include difficulty in rapport formation with the adolescent, gaining his/her trust, non-completion of homework, high dropout rates, missing sessions, difficulties on the family front, non-cooperative or uninvolved parents, and lack of time.

14.6 Conclusion and Future Directions

Adolescence is a sensitive period and any problems faced during this time should be acted upon immediately to avoid it from becoming worse. Headache is becoming a common ailment afflicting adolescents with an increase in stress levels. Also, they suffer from a variety of anxiety and depressive disorders. In order to seek treatment, the adolescent, parents, and teachers need to be vigilant and able to identify that there resides a problem. Once the identification has been done, the next step is to consult a health professional. The therapist assesses the adolescent and moves onto the appropriate treatment module.

TCBT comes across as very effective when there is more than one diagnosis to deal with. A single module thus made can work with adolescents suffering from various types of anxiety disorders.

Headache, depression, and anxiety disorders have some common ground to cover as they all in some manner involve the presence of stress, whether it be a causal or worsening factor.

The intervention module has been designed to not only treat headache and comorbid disorders but go a step ahead in order to prevent similar problems in the future. As an upcoming therapy, TCBT has a long way to go especially looking at its benefits for the treatment of mental disorders.

References

Achenbach, T., & Rescorla, L. (2001). *The Manual for the ASEBA School-Age Forms & Profiles*. Burlington: University of Vermont, Research Center for Children, Youth, and Families.

Beck, A. T. (1993). Cognitive therapy: past, present, and future. *Journal of consulting and clinical psychology, 61*(2), 194.

Breslau, N., Davis, G. C., & Andreski, P. (1991). Migraine, psychiatric disorders, and suicide attempts: an epidemiologic study of young adults. *Psychiatry research, 37*(1), 11–23.

Breslau, N., Strauch, K., & Mortimer, E. (1982). Psychological distress in mothers of disabled children. *American Journal of Diseases in Children, 136*, 682–686.

Collin, C., Hockaday, J. M., & Walers, W. E. (1985). Headache and school absence. *Archives of Disease and Childhood, 60*, 245–247.

Chorpita, B. F., Yim, L., Moffitt, C., Umemoto, L. A., & Francis, S. E. (2000). Assessment of symptoms of DSM-IV anxiety and depression in children: A revised child anxiety and depression scale. *Behaviour research and therapy, 38*(8), 835–855.

Egger, H., Angold, A., & Costello, E. J. (1998). Headaches and psychopathology in children and adolescents. *Journal of the American Academy of Child and Adolescent Psychiatry, 37*, 951–958.

Emiroglu, F. N., Kurul, S., Akay, A., Miral, S., & Dirik, E. (2004). Assessment of child neurology outpatients with headache, dizziness and fainting. *Journal of Child Neurology, 19*(5), 332–336.

Fritz, G. K., Fritsch, S., & Hagino, O. (1997). Somatoform disorders in children and adolescents: A review of the past 10 years. *Journal of American Academy of Child and Adolescent Psychiatry, 36*(10), 1329–1338.

Gupta, G., Bhatia, M. S., Dahiya, D., Sharma, S., Sapra, R., Semalti, K., & Dua, R. P. S. (2009). Recurrent headache in Indian adolescents. *The Indian Journal of Pediatrics, 76*(7), 733–737.

Hamilton, M. A. X. (1959). The assessment of anxiety states by rating. *British journal of medical psychology, 32*(1), 50–55.

Headache Classification Committee of the International Headache Society. (1988). Classification and diagnostic criteria for headache disorders, cranial neuralgias and facial pain. *Cephalalgia, 8*(7), 1–96.

Headache Classification Subcommittee of the International Headache Society. (2004). The international classification of headache disorders. *Cephalalgia: an international journal of headache, 24*, 9.

Karli, N., Akis, N., Zarifoglu, M., Akgoz, S., Irgil, E., Ayvacioglu, U., et al. (2006). Headache prevalence in adolescents aged 12 to 17: A student-based epidemiological study in Bursa. *The Journal of Head and Face Pain 46*(4), 649–655.

Kazdin, A. E., & Weisz, J. R. (1998). Identifying and developing empirically supported child and adolescent treatments. *Journal of consulting and clinical psychology, 66*(1), 19.

Laurell, K., Larsson, B., Mattsson, P., & Eeg-Olofsson, O. (2006). A 3-year follow-up of headache diagnoses and symptoms in Swedish schoolchildren. *Cephalalgia, 26*, 809–815.

Liakopoulou-Kairis, M., Alifieraki, T., Protagora, D., Korpa, T., Kondyli, K., Dimosthenous, E., et al. (2002). Recurrent abdominal pain and headache- psychopathology, life events and family functioning. *Eurpopean Child Adolescent Psychiatry, 11*(3), 115–122.

Mansell, W. (2008). Keep it simple—the transdiagnostic approach to cognitive behavioral therapy. *International Journal of Cognitive Therapy, 1*, 179–180.

Mansell, W., Harvey, A., Watkins, E., & Shafran, R. (2009). Conceptual foundations of the transdiagnostic approach to CBT. *Journal of Cognitive Psychotherapy, 23*(1), 6–19.

McEvoy, P. M., Nathan, P., & Norton, P. J. (2009). Efficacy of transdiagnostic treatments: A review of published outcome studies and future research directions. *Journal of Cognitive Psychotherapy, 23*(1), 20–33.

Palermo, T. M., Eccleston, C., Lewandowski, A. S., Williams, A. C., & Morley, S. (2010). Randomized controlled trials of psychological therapies for management of chronic pain in children and adolescents: An updated meta-analytic review. *Pain, 148*(3), 387–397.

Palermo, T. M., Wilson, A. C., Peters, M., Lewandowski, A., & Somhegyi, H. (2009). Randomized controlled trial of an internet-delivered family cognitive-behavioral therapy intervention for children and adolescents with chronic pain. *Pain, 146*(1–2), 205–213.

Reynolds, C. R., & Richmond, B. O. (1978). What I think and feel: A revised measure of children's manifest anxiety. *Journal of abnormal child psychology, 6*(2), 271–280.

Russell, M. B., Levi, N., Šaltytė-Benth, J., & Fenger, K. (2006). Tension-type headache in adolescents and adults: A population based study of 33,764 twins. *European Journal of Epidemiology, 2*, 153–160.

Silverman, W. K., & Albano, A. M. (1996). *Anxiety Disorders Interview Schedule for DSM-IV.: Parent interview schedule* (Vol. 1). Oxford University Press.

Silverman, W. K., Pina, A. A., & Viswesvaran, C. (2008). Evidence-based psychosocial treatments for phobic and anxiety disorders in children and adolescents. *Journal of Clinical Child and Adolescent Psychology, 37*(1), 105–130.

Spielberger, C. D., Sharma, S., & Singh, M. (1973). Development of the Hindi edition of the State-Trait Anxiety Inventory. *Indian Journal of Psychology.*

Trautmann, E., & Kroner-Herwig, B. (2010). A randomized controlled trial of Internet-based self-help training for recurrent headache in childhood and adolescence. *Behaviour Research and Therapy, 48*, 28–37.

Virtanen, R. (2008). *Epidemiological studies of childhood and adolescence headache (Unpublished doctoral dissertation).* Finland: Institute of Clinical Medicine.

Chapter 15
Attention-Deficit/Hyperactivity Disorder

Monica Mongia, Manju Mehta and Rajesh Sagar

15.1 Introduction

Attention-deficit/hyperactivity disorder is a neuro-developmental disorder that begins in childhood and affects individuals across the life span (American Psychiatric Association 1994). About 80 % of children diagnosed with ADHD continue to have the disorder in adolescence (Antshel et al. 2012; Ingram et al. 1999).

Although the primary manifestations of ADHD in adolescence are similar to those in childhood involving symptoms of hyperactivity, impulsivity, and inattention, adolescents experience a reduction in hyperactivity compared to children (Faraone et al. 2006). In adolescence, ADHD may be associated with high rates of impairments, e.g., cognitive, social, and emotional (Fischer et al. 2002) as well as high rates of comorbidity, e.g., anxiety, depression, and conduct disorder (Barkley et al. 2007), all of which drastically affect the adolescent's self-esteem (Harpin 2005).

Interestingly, while symptoms such as poor sustained attention, impulsivity, and restlessness continue during adolescence, hyperactivity tends to be less pervasive compared to childhood (Young and Amarasinghe 2010). Adolescents with ADHD are at a higher risk for negative outcomes including academic problems, substance use, interpersonal problems, and criminal offenses. New comorbid problems also

M. Mongia (✉)
Lady Shriram College, University of Delhi, New Delhi, India
e-mail: drmonicamongia@gmail.com

M. Mehta · R. Sagar
Department of Psychiatry, All India Institute of Medical Sciences, New Delhi 110029, India
e-mail: drmanju.mehta@gmail.com

R. Sagar
e-mail: rsagar29@gmail.com

M. Mehta and R. Sagar (eds.), *A Practical Approach to Cognitive Behaviour Therapy for Adolescents*, DOI 10.1007/978-81-322-2241-5_15

tend to emerge during this period. Even though a lot is known about ADHD as a lifelong disorder, research on the adolescent stage of ADHD in general is relatively sparse. The majority of what is known, especially relating to adolescent treatment, is based on assumptions derived from research on child and adult samples.

15.2 Need for CBT in Adolescents with ADHD

Unfortunately, despite suffering from ADHD and associated problems, adolescents are poorly represented in the ADHD literature with only 10–30 % receiving attention from mental health services (Jensen et al. 1999). This discrepancy may reflect changes in adolescents' attitudes toward treatment (e.g., desire for autonomy, identity issues), but it is also likely related to the dearth of research into effective treatments. Some adolescents with ADHD may not benefit significantly from medication and that others may experience adverse side effects that may prevent them from continuing pharmacotherapy. Even if the teens somehow struggle with the side effects, the delay in the manifestation of the positive effects of the ADHD medication as well as the inability to fulfill increased parental expectations after a period of sustained medication regime may force them to give up pharmacotherapy in the longer run. Thus, many teens may refuse to stay on ADHD medication and adherence to medication may be a big issue that the professionals and the parents of ADHD teens may encounter.

Since medication, which is the mainstay of treatment for ADHD, is effective only in the short term (Jensen et al. 1999) and also since studies report about 95 % non-compliance in individuals up to 21 years of age (McCarthy et al. 2009), it is understood that medication adherence may be problematic when adolescents perceive medication as an impediment to their independence or when they are not fully informed regarding ADHD and its treatment. In addition, literature points to the fact that medications do not teach skills such as organizational skills, study skills, or interpersonal skills that are required by individuals with ADHD for coping with their problems (Waxmonsky 2005). CBT interestingly teaches these skills to individuals with ADHD that help them deal with problem situations.

Finally, it is important to train individuals with ADHD to manage their dwindling sense of self-esteem due to the various difficulties they face in social, interpersonal, and academic realms. Skill-building exercise, such as cognitive behavior therapy, that has proven to be an effective strategy for adults with ADHD as well as individuals with other psychiatric disorders is presumably helpful for adolescents with ADHD as well.

Considering that the chronicity of the disorder of ADHD leads to significant public health burden, it is important that intervention is initiated early in life; thus, late childhood and adolescence being the right developmental phases to understand the nuances of CBT, it is suggested that CBT be started around that time (Quinn 2001).

CBT could be a promising intervention for the treatment of the core symptoms of ADHD in children (Safren et al. 2005). In adults, however, the literature provides support for CBT as a useful adjunct to medication that may help improve ADHD symptoms, self-esteem, depressive symptoms, anxiety, anger expression, and global functioning (Greenfield and Hechtman 2005; Wilens et al. 1999; Stevenson et al. 2002; Safren et al. 2005). Theoretically, due to higher cognitive maturity in adolescents compared to children, adolescents would better comprehend the idea behind CBT and would communicate their needs and understand their deficits better. Thus, a CBT intervention that focuses on academic, interpersonal, and coping skills would hold promise for improving the quality of life of adolescents with ADHD. Adolescents may develop a clear sense of ownership when they are actively involved in their own ADHD treatment process (Smith et al. 2000). Adolescents and their families may have the best sense of which symptoms and skill deficits contribute the most to impairment in their lives; their input should be solicited for program development. Such an intervention could build on components that have been successful for adults with ADHD. Strategies must be put in place to ensure that adolescents acquire skills and practice them outside the treatment time, as generalization of skills is crucial to treatment success. The use of coaches to encourage skill maintenance in individuals with ADHD has received support (Quinn 2001).

Further, diversion of stimulant medication has become a real problem and teens may do it often for want of money or favors from their peers in the form of drug, sex, or other things/behaviors that their parents may not approve of and thus need to be adequately informed.

Although the efficacy of CBT for adolescents with anxiety and mood disorders is well supported (Compton et al. 2004), there is a dearth of studies on CBT with adolescents with ADHD (Young and Amarasinghe 2010). Research supporting the efficacy of CBT for adolescent ADHD, therefore, is scarce. Results of the available studies suggest that CBT can be effective in addressing some of the unique needs of adolescents with ADHD (Antshel et al. 2012; Mongia and Hechtman 2014 [submitted]).

Compared to children, the cognitive abilities that develop during adolescence in theory should allow them to understand the purpose of therapy and better implement the various strategies taught.

It may be that employing a strict cognitive behavioral focus is an ineffective approach to adolescent ADHD treatment (Chronis et al. 2006). Therapies including both medication and psychosocial treatments may be able to control ADHD symptoms as well as help treat secondary problems and comorbid disorders. Waxmonsky (2005) suggested that CBT may be a helpful adjunct for adolescents (and adults) with ADHD.

Recent adolescent studies have begun to include more of a focus on combined treatments. Antshel et al. (2012) ran an intervention on 68 adolescents which was based on an empirically validated CBT protocol for adults (Safren 2006). Adolescents with ADHD alone as well as those who were only comorbid for depression or anxiety improved across several symptoms and improved on functional measures according to parent and teacher ratings. Those with ADHD who were comorbid for CD or ODD did not make the same gains. Unfortunately, those who did improve were still impaired on at least one domain and therefore continued to perform sub-optimally. The strengths of this study include structured CBT and use of standardized outcome measures; limitations include inclusion of individuals with high motivational levels, lack of blinding, possible low inter-rater reliability, and lack of actual placebo control group.

In a recent study, by Mongia and Hechtman (2014; submitted), demonstrating the efficacy of CBT for 18 adolescents with ADHD on stable medication. Intervention consisted of 14 weekly group sessions and individual coaching 3 times per week. The areas addressed were organization and time management skills, anger management, social skills, and self-esteem. Baseline to post-treatment improvements in restlessness and impulsivity dimension (Conners' Global Index—self-report and parent report), self-esteem (Rosenberg Self-Esteem Scale), level of disability (Sheehan Disability Scale—independent blind clinician rated), and severity of ADHD (Clinical Global Impression Scale—independent blind clinician rated) were noted. These improvements were maintained at 3-month follow-up. Subjective improvements in ADHD symptoms, motivation, and level of disability were reported by adolescents, their parents, and the independent blind clinician. Treatment gains were maintained 3 months post-intervention. On CGI–independent blind clinician report, no improvements were noted from baseline to post-treatment. However, from post-intervention to follow-up, improvement in restlessness, impulsivity (CGI—independent blind clinician report), and disability (Sheehan Disability Scale (SDS)—self report) was observed. No improvements were noted on CGI (teacher report). No improvements were observed on SDS—parent report. The methodological limitations of this study include small sample size, low power, lack of actual control group, short duration of follow-up (i.e., 3 months), and no control over other treatments during follow-up. Despite these limitations, this study is one of the first studies assessing the efficacy of CBT in adolescents with ADHD. Standardized outcome measures were used for assessment to make the assessment more objective. Blinding served as an effective method for reducing bias.

In another study, a component of CBT, i.e., mindfulness meditation (8 weeks) was studied in 24 adults and 4 adolescents by Zylowska et al. (2008) that led to improvements in self-reports of ADHD symptoms, anxiety, and depression as well as attention and cognitive inhibition tasks after. An absence of evidence in favor of CBT for adolescents with ADHD, however, does not mean that CBT is ineffective for this population but does stress the need for more research.

To conclude, although the findings from studies examining CBT in adolescence to date are mixed, research should be continued into this type of treatment.

15.3 Process of CBT in Adolescents with ADHD—Practical Steps

This section describes the psycho-educational training process that all the adolescents and their parents enrolled in a CBT-based skill training program must undergo. After each skill training session, handouts are provided detailing the skill taught in the session. In addition, homework is given to enable the adolescent to practice, in real-life settings, the skills learnt in therapy. Also, individual coaching is provided by trained individuals who may assist the adolescents during the group CBT sessions and may remain in once a week telephonic contact with the adolescents. Retention of skills taught in the last session is checked before beginning the new session, and also, homework given in the last session is reviewed. Barriers in completing homework are addressed.

Case vignette
"A 14 year old adolescent, 'X', with complaints of persistent restlessness, inability to concentrate on any task, poor performance at school, inability to maintain friendships is referred to the clinic by his school teacher. Even though 'X' has a normal IQ, he is unable to perform academically as well as socially at par with his peers. In addition, he has problems in learning such as inability to remember concepts taught at school, poor handwriting, incomplete work, slowness etc. Despite repeated requests, 'X' is unable to organise his belongings and loses them frequently as a result. He has shown aggressive behaviour in social settings in the past and has no friends. 'X' is shy and has poor self esteem and therefore, does not like to attend social gatherings. He has recently started experimenting with drugs and feels he is better accepted by his peers when he uses them. His parents report that he has been extremely active and fidgety since childhood and has never been able to complete his work on time. 'X' has intermittently been on stimulant medication for ADHD since childhood and lacks social skills as well as takes a lot of time for adjusting to a new settings. He cannot deal with failures as well as feels upset that he is so different from his peers. 'X' and his parents reported feeling isolated from the social setting and extremely burdened by his symptoms and their consequences."

15.4 Sessions 1 and 2: Introduction, Interview, and Assessment

In the first two sessions, after forming a rapport with the adolescent and his/her parents, the adolescent's as well as the parent's subjective problems are recorded. These may relate to excessive activity, impulsivity, and inability to attend and concentrate on tasks. In addition, behavioral and self-esteem problems may be noted. Parental stress and anxiety impact on their lives due to ADHD in their adolescent as well as burden of caring for an offspring with ADHD may be understood. Visual analog scale may be used to record the subjective level of distress due to ADHD. Positive and negative coping strategies may also be recorded. Subjective account of the impact of ADHD on various aspects of the adolescent's as well as parent's lives is also noted (Tables 15.1 and 15.2).

In addition, objective account of the adolescent's ADHD symptoms, their performance at school, and behavior in general, using standardized scales such as Malin's Intelligence Scale for Indian Children (MISIC), Child behavior checklist

Table 15.1 Aims: Sessions 1 and 2

Aims
• Forming rapport with adolescents and his/her parents
• Recording the adolescent's as well as parent's difficulties using semi-structured interview technique as well as standardized scales
• Noting the subjective and objective impact of ADHD on the adolescent and their family
• Assessing willingness for CBT
• Informing adolescents and their parents about the process of CBT

Table 15.2 Aims: Session 3

Aims
• Normal developmental course of children and adolescents
• Distinguishing normal development from pathological development
• Hyperactivity that is abnormal
• Subjective assessment of parents' knowledge of ADHD
• Psycho-education about ADHD
• Clarifying misconceptions

(CBCL), Conners' Parent Rating Scale (CPRS), Conners' Teacher Rating Scale (CTRS), and ADD Evaluation Scale (ADDES)—Home and School versions— are used. In addition, historical treatment and therapy reports are analyzed.

Further, both the parties are informed about the process of CBT structure, duration, techniques, and levels of expected involvement and their willingness to participate is assessed informally. Perceived barriers in participation may be discussed. Consent and assent for CBT is finally sought after clarifying misconceptions and discussing barriers.

15.5 Session 3: Psycho-education for Adolescents and Their Parents

The psycho-educational element of giving information by discussion supplemented with fact sheets is crucial to CBT. This may help in improving compliance to treatment and is genuinely appreciated by the child, family, school, and often the referring general physician.

Educating adolescents and parents about ADHD as a disorder, its symptoms, course, types, comorbidity, causes, impact, role of parental disciplining, and resources available to deal with it may help them understand from a scientific point of view.

In addition, clarifying misconceptions associated with this disorder such as ADHD is an intentional behavior on the part of the child that these children are absolutely normal or on the other hand are absolutely abnormal and can never function normally and that they are absolutely handicapped, among several others may be essential to initiating effective management. Parents who feel that their child is malingering symptoms may attribute resultant problems to adolescent's behavior, whereas those who understand it as being caused by uncontrollable biological factors and maintained by environmental factors may work in collaboration with the adolescent sufferer and may support him/her in dealing with their symptoms. Misconceptions are thus addressed, and a balanced view of ADHD is presented to the parents.

15.6 Session 4: Stress and Coping

In this session, after assessing the adolescent and parents' subjective stress levels on a visual analog scale, they are educated about stress: what is stress, how stress build up, what factors may maintain it, what happens when it continues beyond a point, and how ADHD and associated problems may cause and maintain stress in them. Further, adolescents and their parents are asked about ways in which they cope with problems. They are then educated about the different types of coping such as positive coping (adaptive and constructive coping) viz. anticipation or proactive coping (anticipating what the problem situation will be like and preparing the steps to cope with it), social coping (seeking social support), and meaning focussed coping (understanding the meaning of stress causing situation), temporary avoidance of thoughts or circumstances that cause stress and getting back to them when calm, relaxation exercises, physical exercises, healthy nutrition and adequate sleep, and humor. The adolescent and their parents also receive an understanding of how these positive ways of coping help in improving overall functioning (Table 15.3).

They are further taught about the negative or maladaptive coping strategies that may provide temporary relief from symptoms or problem but may maintain it in the long term. Ways of coping negatively include dissociation (the ability of the mind to separate and compartmentalize thoughts, memories, and emotions), sensitization (seeking to learn about, rehearse, and/or anticipate fearful events in a protective effort to prevent these events from occurring in the first place), safety behaviors (relying on something, or someone, as a means of coping with excessive anxiety), anxious avoidance (avoiding anxiety-provoking situations by all means), and escape (fleeing the situation at the first sign of anxiety).

Table 15.3 Aims: Session 4

Aims
• Addressing adolescent and parental stress
• Assessing current level of (subjective) stress using a visual analog scale
• Addressing coping strategies of adolescents and parents
• Psycho-education about stress and coping

Thus by the end of this session, the adolescents and parents are able to identify the various ways in which they cope with different situations and whether their ways of coping help them in overcoming or maintaining their distress.

15.7 Session 5: Stress Management and Coping Training

This session is a continuation of the last session in that it teaches some coping strategies to deal with specific symptoms of ADHD. Relaxation techniques such as deep breathing and imagery are taught to adolescents with ADHD. In addition, distraction techniques such as writing a diary, talking out to a friend, engaging in a hobby, reading books for pleasure, going out for a walk, praying, yoga, an elastic band around the wrist, holding an ice cube in the hand, or stroking a pet while distracting may actually help the adolescent in bring back his trail of thoughts to the point where he got distracted. Some mental strategies such as learning a rhyme, memorizing motivational quotes, or tongue twisters such as 'she sells seashells on the sea shore' may also challenge the distracting stimuli and remind the adolescents to divert back their focus to the task at hand. Similarly, self-use of memo or flash cards can also help in distracting adolescents with positive messages or memories of happy experiences such as holidays or personal achievements, reminding you that things will improve again (Table 15.4).

Further, adolescents are taught an important technique in cognitive behavior therapy, i.e., cognitive restructuring which is a set of techniques for becoming more conscious of one's thoughts and for modifying them whenever they are distorted or unrealistic. Adolescents are taught to use cognitive restructuring technique to use reason and evidence to replace the distorted thought patterns with more accurate, believable, and functional ones.

For helping the adolescents identify their thought distortions as well as restructure them after brief evaluation, the adolescents are introduced to the following worksheet (Tables 15.5 and 15.6):

Table 15.4 Aims: Session 5

Aims
To educate parents about
• Relaxation exercises: breathing exercises and imagery
• Distraction techniques
• Cognitive restructuring
• Effective communication
• Problem solving
• Planning and management

Table 15.5 Cognitive restructuring worksheet

Situation	Emotions (ratings)	Automatic thoughts (rating)	Evaluate and modify thoughts

Table 15.6 Example of cognitive restructuring technique for dealing with self-esteem issues in adolescents with ADHD

Cognitive restructuring worksheet example

1. Situation	2. Emotions and ratings	3. Automatic thoughts and ratings	4. Evaluate and modify thoughts
Thought of being a loser because I have ADHD	Discouraged/ashamed (rating before = 90; rating after = 70) New emotion = not that ashamed	I'm a loser because I have these symptoms (magnifying negative, minimizing positive, overgeneralizing)	Does having ADHD mean I am a loser? • No it is a distortion in my thinking. I have many positive qualities that I am ignoring by calling myself a loser

Ratings Both before and after you complete column 4: (A) in column 2, rate the intensity of the emotions (0–100 %); and (B) in column 3, rate your degree of belief (0–100 %) in the automatic thoughts. Cognitive distortions (detailed in appendix at the end of this book): in column 3, identify any cognitive distortions in automatic thoughts

Next, the adolescents are taught the technique called problem solving which involves the following steps:

1. Identify and define problem area/issue or problem definition
2. Generate and list all possible solutions/options
3. Evaluate alternatives in terms of their advantages and disadvantages
4. Decide on a plan in terms of action, steps, who, when
5. Implement plan
6. Evaluate the outcome and seek answers for questions such as 'how effective was the plan?' and 'does the existing plan need to be revised or would a new plan be needed to better address the problem?'

   If you are not pleased with the outcome, return to Step 2 to select a new option or revise the existing plan, and repeat Steps 3 to 6.

All these techniques are also taught to the parents to help adolescents (who are comfortable involving their parents in the therapy process) understand and implement these strategies. For those parents whose adolescent children are not comfortable in involving them in the therapy process as well as for others, it is advisable to implement these strategies to deal with their own day-to-day problems.

The last technique that is taught in this session is planning and management. The adolescent is taught to maintain a daily routine such that adequate time is allotted to each activity. Each activity must be followed by a small break. The important thing is to get to the next task after the break time is over. Planning for unexpected events is important to avoid frustration later on.

15.8 Session 6: Working with Adolescents with ADHD (I)

This session begins with teaching adolescents the technique called ABC charting. This involves educating them about (Table 15.7):

A = Activating Event

- What do you think happened?
- What would a camera see?

B = Beliefs about Activating Event

- What did you tell yourself?

Table 15.7 Aims: Session 6

Aims
• ABC charting
• Star chart method
• Clarity and brevity of instruction
• Time-out
• Reinforcement
• Consistency

Table 15.8 ABC charting

A—Activating event	B—Beliefs	C—Consequences
My teacher asks me if I have completed a piece of homework	I think • 'She thinks I am not working hard enough' • 'She is trying to catch me out'	*Actions* I say defensively that I have nearly finished the homework, although in fact I still have some way to go *Emotions* I feel annoyed, angry, and resentful

C = Consequences

- How did you act?
- How did you feel (Table 15.8)?

Using this technique, the adolescent can make sense of the situations that give rise to a certain kind of beliefs in him or her and the negative or positive consequences those beliefs lead to.

Understanding such patterns would be crucial to changing ones beliefs and therefore one's reactions in stressful or intimidating situations.

15.9 Session 7: Working with Adolescents with ADHD (II)

Techniques such as token economy may help adolescents in modifying their behavior. Parents or significant others may need to be involved in this process as per the convenience of the adolescents. Negotiation with the adolescent may form the first step before this technique can be implemented. Tokens must be used as reinforcers to be effective. A token may be any object or symbol that can be exchanged for material reinforcers, services, or privileges such as a bag of chips, breakfast in bed, or extra pocket money, whatever way they have been negotiated to serve the adolescents. Tokens may be in the form of coins, checkmarks, stars, smileys, etc (Table 15.9).

Parents or significant others such as peers or a close relative may model desired behavior such as waiting for turn and speaking only when asked to, and the

Table 15.9 Aims: Session 7

Aims
Educating about
• Token economy
• Modeling
• Attention strategies
• Study skills training
• Knowledge of feedback
• Consistency (reviewed)

adolescent with ADHD may imitate that behavior following the demonstration and be appropriately rewarded for it.

Attention strategies such as beading, counting, or canceling all 'p's on a newspaper front page or subtracting 4s from 100 and going backwards to zero may help adolescents with ADHD in building their attention span. Parents can use various strategies such as grain sorting, vegetable sorting, cutting pictures and using them as picture completion test, and pattern tracing on sand or with pencil.

For dealing with academic issues, the adolescents are taught studying skills. Study skills training helps them in managing large chapters by breaking them into smaller, achievable targets and by reinforcing themselves for achieving each small target.

The significant others are then taught to provide immediate, clear, precise, and short-sentenced feedback about the performance of the adolescent with ADHD.

The importance of being consistent in using these techniques is highlighted as using them frequently in similar problem situations may help them in getting habituated to these techniques and thereby sustaining their motivation and building their confidence in themselves.

15.10 Session 8: Working with Adolescents with ADHD (III)

This session also focuses on teaching-specific skills to the adolescent with some involvement of the parent or significant other (Table 15.10).

Since adolescents with ADHD face difficulty in managing their time effectively, they are taught to set long-term goals. After having set long-term goals, they are instructed to envisage the time it would take them to reach that goal. The long-term goal is then viewed in term of several short-term goals that must be reached in stipulated time period to be able to reach the long-term goal in time. They are taught to use timelines, set deadlines for themselves for finishing a certain task and adequately reinforce themselves (self-reinforcement) for doing so. Further, the adolescents are taught self-instructional training ('stop, look, listen, and think') which includes the following steps: watching a trainer model and talk through a

Table 15.10 Aims: Session 8

Aim
To impart training about
• Time management
• Self-instructional training
• Self-reinforcement
• Star chart method
• Thought diary
• Dealing with comorbid factors self-esteem issues, drug abuse, defiance, conduct problems, etc.

task, including planning and talking through possible difficulties (cognitive modeling); carrying out the task, prompted by a trainer; carrying out the task, prompting themselves aloud; carrying out the task, prompting themselves by whispering; and finally, carrying out the task silently using covert self-instruction/self-talk.

In order to reinforce themselves or for their parents to reinforce them, the adolescents as well as the parents are taught to use the star chart method. A star chart is a behavior change program that involves the delivery of a sticker or star to a child as a reward for engaging in an appropriate or desired behavior. The sticker or star is typically placed on a chart that is visible to the child. The chart commonly displays descriptions of the specific behaviors that have been identified for improvement. Sticker/star charts are typically designed to increase the frequency of desired behaviors by rewarding desired behaviors that do not occur frequently enough. For example, behaviors identified for improvement might include doing chores, completing homework, remembering to wait for turn, so on and so forth.

Finally, in this session, the adolescents are taught to use a thought diary to keep their thought patterns under check for which the following instructions may be given (Table 15.11):

Instructions are as follows:

1. In the above diary, keep a note of when you feel any of the following: anxiety, fear, hurt, anger, shame, guilt, and depression in the feelings column. Rate how strongly you experience the feeling on a scale of 0 % (low) to 10 % (high).
2. Note what you were doing at the time in the situation column.
3. Think about what you were saying to yourself about the situation and identify any unhelpful thoughts. Write these into the thoughts column.
4. Try to generate more helpful, realistic, and supportive thoughts in the alternative thoughts column.
5. Practice thinking these new alternative thoughts next time you are in or entering a similar situation.
6. Monitor what new feelings you experience and rate these on a scale of 0–10 %. More helpful feelings can include annoyance, concern, regret, sadness, and remorse.

Finally, the therapist may suggest strategies to deal with associated problems such as low self-esteem, defiance, conduct problems, and drug abuse. These may be done for specific cases in which these problems are highly intense in nature and negatively impact functioning.

Table 15.11 Thought diary

Day	Situation	Thoughts	Feelings	Alternative thoughts	New feelings
	What were you doing?	Anxious, negative, pessimistic	0 (low)–10 (high)	Helpful thoughts	0 (low)–10 (high)
					.

Table 15.12 Aims: Session 9

Aim
• Identifying social skill deficits
• Distinguishing between skill acquisition and performance deficits
• Selecting intervention strategies
• Implementing intervention
• Assessing and modifying intervention as necessary

15.11 Session 9: Social Skills Training

In this session, the adolescents are taught to identify the deficit social skills such as not greeting friends, not making eye-to-eye contact, and using abusive language. Then, they are taught to distinguish between difficult in skill acquisition, i.e., whether they possess the skill or have difficulty in learning a certain social skill such as verbal or non-verbal, and performance deficits wherein they already possess the skill but are unable to implement it in the social setting, for example, knowing that one must exchange greetings when one meets his or her friends and also knowing what to use as a greeting and how to say it but still not doing it in the real-life setting. Based on the kind of settings and skill deficit or performance deficits, intervention strategies are custom made for each adolescent, e.g., different for shy adolescent from that for an abusive or overtalkative adolescent. The strategies may include explicitly teaching social skills by using say board games about friendships and appropriate behavior, using peer mentors for mediation say for social initiation, thoughts, and feelings activities involving recognition of the other's feelings and thoughts a different from those of the self-using stories and picture cards, facilitating reciprocal interactions, using social stories to teach social concepts, and finally, role plays for addressing basic interaction skills. The mutually worked out intervention plan is then implemented in real-life settings, and the adolescents' performance in these setting is adequately and appropriately reinforced. Finally, the intervention is evaluated and modified as necessary (Table 15.12).

15.12 Session 10

The final CBT session is usually meant for summarizing the training program, post-intervention assessment using the same objective measures as in the initial sessions to evaluate the change due to intervention as well for obtaining subjective perception of the participants regarding the effectiveness of the training sessions. A gist of the pertinent information taught is presented to the participants. An open discussion about the barriers in implementing the CBT techniques learnt is held and issues are clarified.

15.13 The CBT Process Addresses More Than the Adolescent with ADHD

A number of pertinent issues must be addressed in the therapeutic formulation when working with adolescents with ADHD:

15.13.1 The Family

The therapist needs to engage both the parents and the adolescent. The younger the adolescent is, higher is the need for the parents to be included in the cognitive behavioral model.

Specific instruction in management techniques, such as using positive reinforcement for compliance with a child with a conduct disorder, may help parents deal with various ADHD-related issues. Using excerpts from their own settings may help them understand their child's illness in a perspective, and implementing the CBT strategies for dealing with their adolescent's issues may then become easier.

The therapist must be aware of the family's structure and its belief system, as well as the systemic implications of any intervention.

Additionally, crucial information for parents for adolescents with oppositional defiant disorder, conduct disorder, specific learning disability, interpersonal issues, or drug addiction may be provided.

Parent training enhances problem-solving skills training for adolescents, reduction in aggressive behavior problems at home and at school, better adjustment, and reducing parental anxieties. Parents may feel better sharing their problems with similar others and therefore must be introduced to ADHD support groups. Information about resources available for ADHD as well as advocacy may also be provided.

NICE, 2006, guidelines suggest that parent training may prove to be an effective intervention for children and adolescents up to 13 years old who have been diagnosed with ADHD. For older adolescents, however, considering their high need for autonomy and independence, parental involvement may jeopardize the process of CBT and therefore, caution must be exercised and adolescent's approval must be sought before involving their parents in therapy. Initial interview may therefore be conducted with the adolescent alone.

15.13.2 The School

The adolescent's school, with due permission from the adolescent as well as the parents, may also need to be informed of the disorder as well as the treatment that the adolescent is currently undergoing. Reports on historical and current performance and behavior at school may be requested from the school, and periodic feedback on performance, post-therapy, may be sought. The adolescent's assets and weaknesses may well be provided by the teachers. Support from teachers as well as peers may be invited for facilitating management of the adolescent with ADHD.

15.13.3 The Adolescent

Published materials such as self-help books, workbooks, and manuals may be supplemented by individual tailor-made charts or materials prepared by the therapist for the purpose of improving adolescent's understanding of their symptoms as well as the therapeutic process. These materials may also help in practising the skills learnt in the CBT sessions in the real-life settings.

The therapist provides a guiding role, teaches various skills to deal with ADHD symptoms, provides appropriate and clear feedback to increase the adolescent's motivation, and provides support throughout. The therapist appreciates effort at first and gradually focuses on the outcome of those efforts, for example, initially a therapist may say: 'Well done! Even though it was difficult to continue to work on the math problem for ten minutes, I can see how hard you've tried.' Later in therapy, this may be substituted by 'You have followed five out of ten steps correctly to solve your math problem, this is indeed great progress!' Progress must be demonstrated on a visual analog scale, and barriers to implementing strategies must be discussed in detail.

For adolescents with ADHD, 13–18 years of age, with moderate impairment, tailor-made CBT intervention involving social skills training may work better than structured interventions provided in group.

Psychological interventions may additionally help in the holistic management of older adolescents with comorbid behavioral problems such as risky sexual behaviors, drug addiction, and interpersonal issues. In addition to focusing on symptom management and dealing with issues associated with ADHD, these individuals may be better assisted by training in specific skills in prosocial competence, emotional control, problem solving, and conflict resolution.

15.14 Barriers to Cognitive Behavioral Treatment of Adolescents with ADHD

15.14.1 Developmental Issues

While a highly intelligent and highly motivated adolescent with ADHD may grasp the adult CBT principles or programs easily and feel motivated to implement the strategies, however, younger adolescents may have difficulty making sense of the adult program, for example, thought diaries and time management strategies; these and other complex techniques may need further simplification for them.

It may help if the adolescents are taught to distinguish between feelings, thoughts, and behavior at the outset, these concepts being the crux of CBT. Thus, practical exercises that help them relate emotions with situations, thoughts, and behavior may help, for example, feeling 'anxious' in an examination setting while thinking 'I may not pass' and therefore not attempting a number of difficult questions due to the fear of failure.

Thus, abstract concepts such as setting up a hypothesis and gathering evidence for and against one may be a difficult proposition for younger adolescents to understand but not so much for older adolescents. Since CBT entails forming a number of hypotheses about various situations and gathering evidence around it, it is imperative that adolescents at a lower cognitive stage of development be explained these concepts in sufficient details and with the use of pragmatic examples.

15.14.2 Generalization to Real-Life Settings

Issues of transportability (bridging the gap between the research intervention and the clinic), adherence to 'manualized treatments' (treatments based on manuals) and the integrity of the therapy have become more prominent recently and must be addressed when doing CBT for adolescents with ADHD.

15.14.3 Therapist Factors

Updating own knowledge base for therapist is important besides being supportive and guiding throughout without making the client dependent on himself or herself.

15.14.4 Overall Conclusion

CBT for adolescents with attention-deficit/hyperactivity disorders can be looked upon as an efficacious psychosocial treatment approach. CBT may work best when used in combination with medication for ADHD, especially for older adolescents as well as those with intense symptoms. CBT strategies such as psycho-education, skill-based training in attention strategies, maintaining a thought record, cognitive restructuring, planning and management, self-instruction, time and relationship management, self-reinforcement and consistency, social skills training, and working with self-esteem may help improve ADHD symptoms, adherence to

Table 15.13 Key learning points

CBT with adolescents with ADHD
• Helps manage functional impairments in social, emotional, and academic arenas
• Can address poor academic performance, relationship issues, and antisocial behavior
• Common CBT strategies used: psycho-education, skill-based training in attention strategies, maintaining a thought record, cognitive restructuring, planning and management, self-instruction, time and relationship management, self-reinforcement and consistency, social skills training, and working with self-esteem
• Common outcomes assessed: ADHD symptoms, social skills, self-esteem, organizational skills, comorbidities, and medication adherence
• Unique needs of adolescents viz. independence, poor social skills, and developing identity must be addressed

treatment, academic performance, interpersonal relationships, and self-esteem in adolescents with ADHD. In addition, associated problems such as defiance, conduct problems, and drug abuse may also be addressed through CBT in adolescents with ADHD (Table 15.13).

References

American Psychiatric Association. (1994). *Diagnostic and statistical manual of mental disorders* (4th ed.). Washington, DC: American Psychiatric Association.

Antshel, K. M., Faraone, S. V., & Gordon, M. (2012). Cognitive behavioral treatment outcomes in adolescent ADHD. *Journal of Attention Disorders*, May 24, epublication.

Barkley, R. A., Murphy, K., & Fischer, M. (2007). *ADHD in adults: What the science says.* New York: Guilford Press.

Chronis, A., Jones, H., & Raggi, V. (2006). Evidence-based psychosocial treatments for children and adolescents with attention deficit hyperactivity disorder. *Clinical Psychology Review, 26*(4), 486–502.

Compton, S. N., March, J. S., Brent, D., Albano, A. M., Weersing, R., & Curry, J. (2004). Cognitive-behavioral psychotherapy for anxiety and depressive disorders in children and adolescents: an evidence-based medicine review. *Journal of American Academy Child and Adolescent Psychiatry, 43(8)*, 930–959.

Faraone, S. V., Biederman, J., & Mick, E. (2006). The age-dependent decline of attention deficit hyperactivity disorder: A meta-analysis of follow-up studies. *Psychological Medicine, 36*(2), 159–165.

Fischer, M., Barkley, R. A., Smallish, L., & Fletcher, K. (2002). Young adult follow-up of hyperactive children: Self-reported psychiatric disorders, comorbidity, and the role of childhood conduct problems and teen CD. *Journal of Abnormal Child Psychology, 30*, 463–475.

Greenfield, B., & Hechtman, L. (2005). Treatment of attention deficit hyperactivity disorder in adults. *Expert Review of Neurotherapeutics, 5*(1), 107–121.

Harpin, V. A. (2005). The effect of ADHD on the life of an individual, their family, and community from preschool to adult life. *Archives of Disease in Childhood, 90*(1), i2–i7.

Ingram, S., Hechtman, L., & Morgenstern, G. (1999). Outcome issues in ADHD: Adolescent and adult long-term outcome. *Mental Retardation and Developmental Disabilities Research Reviews, 5*, 243–250.

Jensen, P. S., Kettle, L., Roper, M. T., Sloan, M. T., Dulcan, M. K., Hoven, C. et al. (1999). Are stimulants overprescribed? Treatment of ADHD in four US communities. *Journal of the American Academy of Child and Adolescent Psychiatry, 38*(7), 797–804.

McCarthy, S., Asherson, P., Coghill, D., Hollis, C., Murray, M., Potts, L., et al. (2009). Attention deficit hyperactivity disorder: Treatment discontinuation in adolescents and young adults. *The British Journal of Psychiatry, 194*(3), 273–277.

Mongia, M., & Hechtman, L. (2014). Cognitive behaviour therapy in adolescents with attention deficit hyperactivity disorder: A pilot study (Submitted).

Quinn, P. O. (2001). *ADD and the college student: A guide for high school and college students with attention deficit disorder*. Washington DC: Magination Press/American Psychological Association.

Safren, S. A. (2006). Cognitive-behavioral approaches to ADHD treatment in adulthood. *Journal of Clinical Psychiatry, 67*(8), 46–50.

Safren, S. A., Otto, M. W., Sprich, S., Winett, C. L., Wilens, T. E., & Biederman, J. (2005). Cognitive behavioral therapy for ADHD in medication-treated adults with continued symptoms. *Behavior Research and Therapy, 43*(7), 831–842.

Smith, B. H., Waschbusch, D. A., Willoughby, M. T., & Evans, S. (2000). The efficacy, safety, and practicality of treatments for adolescents with Attention-Deficit/Hyperactivity Disorder (ADHD). *Clinical Child and Family Psychology Review, 3*(4), 243–267.

Stevenson, C. S., Whitmont, S., Bornholt, L., Livesey, D., & Stevenson, R. J. (2002). A cognitive remediation programme for adults with attention deficit hyperactivity disorder. *Australian and New Zealand Journal of Psychiatry, 36*(5), 610–616.

Waxmonsky, J. G. (2005). Nonstimulant therapies for attention-deficit hyperactivity disorder (ADHD) in children and adults. *Essential Psychopharmacology, 6*(5), 262–276.

Wilens, T. E., McDermott, S. P., Biederman, J., Abrantes, A., Hahesy, A., & Spencer, T. J. (1999). Cognitive therapy in the treatment of adults with ADHD: A systematic chart review of 26 cases. *Journal of Cognitive Psychotherapy International Quarterly, 13*(3), 215–227.

Young, S., & Amarasinghe, J. M. (2010). Practitioner review: Non-pharmacological treatments in ADHD: A lifespan approach. *The Journal of Child Psychology and Psychiatry, 51*(2), 116–133.

Zylowska, L., Ackerman, D. L., Yang, M. H., Futrell, J. L., Horton, N. L., Hale, T. S., et al. (2008). Mindfulness meditation training in adults and adolescents with ADHD a feasibility study. *Journal of Attention Disorders, 11*(6), 737–746.

Chapter 16
Treatment of Substance-Abusing Adolescents

Renu Sharma, Manju Mehta and Anju Dhawan

16.1 Introduction

Substance use among adolescents is recognized as a serious public health problem. The hazardous use of chemicals involves both licit and illicit substances. The common substances abused by adolescents are alcohol, tobacco, marijuana, opioids, inhalants, and other stimulants. Alcohol and other drugs have the most serious impact on developing children and youth. Drug use in an early age can have far-reaching physical, psychological, social, and developing consequences. Youth are more vulnerable to threatening situations like accidents and injuries, impulsive and risk-taking behaviors, illegal activity, physical complications, and cognitive dysfunctions.

R. Sharma (✉) · M. Mehta
Department of Psychiatry, All India Institute of Medical Sciences, New Delhi, India
e-mail: agastyarenu@yahoo.com

M. Mehta
e-mail: drmanju.mehta@gmail.com

A. Dhawan
National Drug Dependence Treatment Center, All India Institute of Medical Sciences, Ghaziabad, India
e-mail: anjudh@hotmail.com

M. Mehta and R. Sagar (eds.), *A Practical Approach to Cognitive Behaviour Therapy for Adolescents*, DOI 10.1007/978-81-322-2241-5_16

16.2 Types of Drugs Abused by Adolescents

A number of drugs are abused by adolescents that can alter the user's mood, cognition, and behavior. Drugs are classified under different categories like depressants, stimulants, and hallucinogens. WHO has listed substances under the following classes:

- Alcohol
- Opioids
- Cannabis
- Sedative Hypnotics
- Cocaine
- Hallucinogens
- Volatile solvents
- Tobacco

A brief description of common substances is given below:

Alcohol: Alcohol is one of the oldest and most popular psychotropic substances. Alcoholic drinks are available in various forms like whisky, rum, sura, and brandy and are measured in standard units. One standard unit of alcohol is equivalent to 10 ml of absolute alcohol.

Opioids: An opioid is a naturally occurring substance (morphine) or semi-synthetics such as heroin. When an opioid is given to an individual for the first time, they produce an unpleasant feeling. Heroin which is popularly known as smack or brown sugar is one of the common forms to be used. Heroin may be smoked, chased, or injected (IV/IM).

Cannabis: Cannabis is available in various forms: bhang, ganja, charas, or hashish. At low dose, cannabis will produce a sense of high and a dreamy state followed by a period of drowsiness. At higher doses, confusion and mental/behavioral problems may occur. Bhang is used in various festivals in India and is legal.

Nicotine: Nicotine is the main active chemical in tobacco and is very popular. It is a commonly used legal substance in India and is socially accepted also. It is used in wide variety of ways including smoking, chewing gutka and sucking.

Sedative/Hypnotics: These are prescribed medicines that reduce anxiety and produce sleep. These drugs are also abused by adolescents as they are cheap and easily available. Certain medications like diazepam, nitrazepam, and pheniramine are widely used.

Hallucinogens: These are also called **Psychedelics.** These drugs alter a person's cognitions and will cause auditory and verbal hallucinations.

Inhalants: These are substances that produce a rush and sense of well-being. They are mostly petroleum products: glue thinners, petroleum, solvents, etc., on regular use; they can damage brain and are associated with liver and lung problems.

Injecting Drug Use (IDU): Injectable drugs are commonly used among adolescents specially opioids with or without sedative/hypnotics. It poses serious risk for an individual such as skin infection, HIV and thrombosis.

Some of these substances are well known by their street names only (see Table 16.1).

Table 16.1 Types of drugs and their street names

Depressants	Stimulants	Hallucinogens
Alcohol (whisky, rum, brandy, wine, beer, sura, tadi, vodka, etc.)	Amphetamine	LSD
Cannabis (charas, ganja, bhang)	Cocaine	Dextromethorphan
Opiods (smack, brown sugar, afeem, proxyvon, dodda, maal, morphine, norphine, etc.)	Tobacco (bidi, cig, gutka, pan masala, khanni, etc.)	
Volatile solvents (fluid, solution, iodex, petrol)	Caffeine (coffee, codeine)	
Sedative hypnotics (diazepam, nitrazepam, alprazolam		

16.3 Consequences of Drug Use

Substance use is having a number of consequences including physical, social, psychological, familial, occupational, and legal consequences.

Physical Consequences: Physical consequences include health-related problems like lung disease, heart problems, cancer, viral hepatitis, HIV, skin infections, seizures, and psychiatric illnesses.

Social Consequences: Stigma and isolation or rejections from society are the common consequences. Apart from this, loss of sober friends and limited interaction with relatives and friends also occur.

Psychological Consequences: Among these guilt feelings, lack of attention and concentration, loss of memory, academic difficulties, and forgetfulness are common. A person can also have adjustment difficulties along with behavioral problems.

Familial Consequences: Substance users are often in conflict with family members. The physical fights among family members, neglect, loss of trust, and critical attitude by parents are common. These adolescents will have less interaction with family members and sometimes are rejected by them.

Economic Consequences: Apart from the direct economic loss of money, adolescents will have other serious consequences like stealing of money and household goods, snatching, borrowing money from others, and debts.

Legal Consequences: Substance users are always at conflict with law. They will often engage in physical fights, vandalism, and illegal activities like robbing, rash driving, and drug paddling (Fig. 16.1).

16.4 Stages of Drug Use

Adolescent substance use is having 4 basic stages of the drug dependence syndrome. In each stage, the pattern of use and the progression of signs and symptoms resulting from drug use are observable (Fig. 16.2).

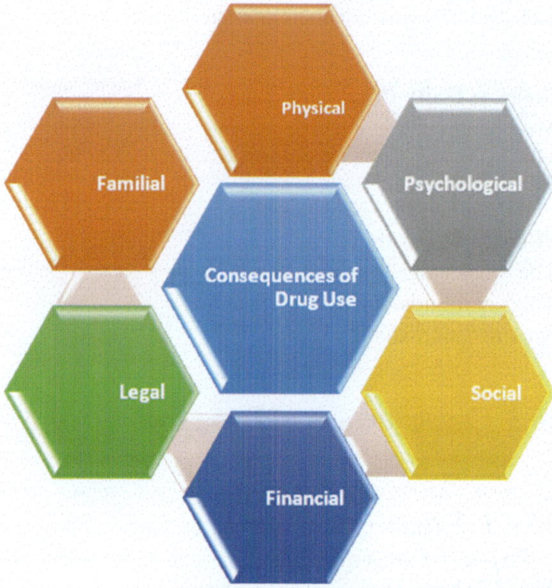

Fig. 16.1 Consequences of drug use

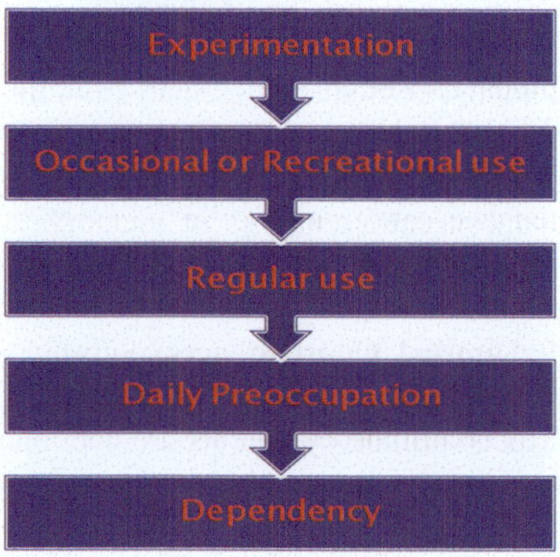

Fig. 16.2 Stages of drug use

Stage 1: Experimentation

During this stage, the initial use often begins with peer group or in social setting. This usually occurs at home, at party, school, or hanging out. In this stage, the small amount of drug is needed to get high and the person will usually return to a normal mood with no problems.

Stage 2: Occasional or Recreational Use

The second stage is occasional or recreational use in which the adolescent uses the drugs occasionally like in a party with some friends or on special occasion only.

Stage 3: Regular Use

At this stage, regular use of drugs become common and the person develops tolerance. More drugs are used to get the desired effect. Different drugs are tried, and person will perceive no undesirable consequences. Problems such as missing school, low grades, and not performing well in sports are common.

Stage 4: Daily Preoccupation
More regular use results in preoccupation with drugs and their euphoric effects. More serious problems develop that may involve stealing, breaking of laws, lying, and violence. Physical problems may also develop.

Stage 5: Dependency
The final stage of addiction is dependency. The person becomes dependent on drugs and finds it difficult to remain without drugs. Use gets out of control, and life becomes unmanageable in many areas—physical, psychological, social, family, school, and legally. In the absence of drugs, the person develops withdrawal symptoms also.

16.4.1 Stages of Change

16.4.1.1 Overview of the Model

The Trantheoretical Model (TTM; Prochaska et al. 1997) is an integrative, biopsychosocial model for behavioral change. One of the key constructs of the TTM is the stages of change. The TTM posits that individuals move through six stages of change: precontemplation, contemplation, preparation, action, maintenance, and termination. Termination was not part of the original model and is less often used in application of stages of change for health-related behaviors. For each stage of change, different intervention strategies are most effective for moving the person to the next stage of change. The stages of change are as follows:

Precontemplation: In this stage, people are often unaware that their behavior is problematic or produces negative consequences. They do not intend to take action in the foreseeable future (defined as within the next 6 months). People in this stage often underestimate the pros of changing behavior and place too much emphasis on the cons of changing behavior.

Contemplation: In this stage, people recognize that their behavior may be problematic, and a more thoughtful and practical consideration of the pros and cons of changing the behavior takes place. People intend to start the healthy behavior, but they still feel ambivalent toward changing their behavior.

Preparation (Determination): In this stage, people are ready to take action within the next 30 days. People start to take small steps toward changing the behavior and believe that changing their behavior can lead to a healthier life.

Action: People have recently changed their behavior (defined as within the last 6 months) and intend to keep moving forward with that behavior change. People may exhibit this by modifying their problem behavior or acquiring new healthy behaviors.

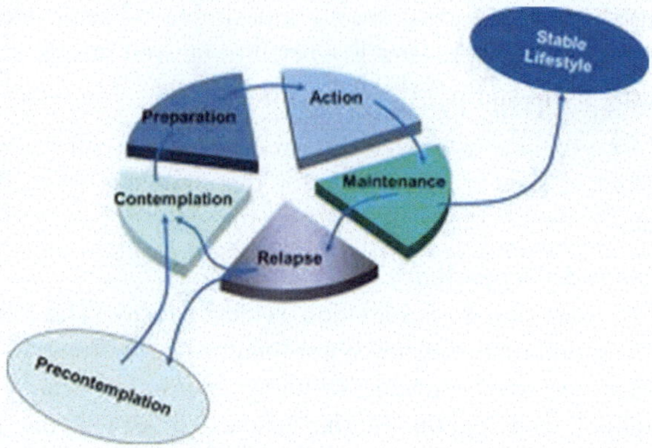

Fig. 16.3 Transtheoretical model of change

Maintenance: In this stage, people have sustained their behavior change for a longer period of time (more than 6 months) and intend to maintain the behavior change. They also work to prevent relapse.

Termination: People have no desire to return to their unhealthy behaviors and are sure that they will not relapse. Since this is rarely reached, people tend to stay in the maintenance stage (Fig. 16.3).

16.4.2 Comorbid Psychiatric Conditions

Among the comorbid psychiatric conditions, disruptive behavior disorder is common which includes conduct disorder, oppositional defiant disorder, and attention deficit hyperactivity disorder (Bukstein et al. 1989). In the MECA study, 32 % adolescent reported current mood and 20 % reported having comorbid anxiety symptoms (Kandel et al. 1982). Eating disorders are another type of psychiatric disorder often associated with adolescent substance abuse. Studies point to a high incidence of substance abuse among bulimic patients as opposed to anorexia nervosa.

16.4.3 Epidemiology

The purpose of epidemiology, broadly stated, is the "study of the distribution and determinants of health related states of events in specified populations, and the application of this study to control of health problems". When this definition has been applied to drug use and drug use disorders, epidemiology has historically served as a foundation for understanding the nature and extent of drug use, abuse, and dependence in the population, for informing basic, clinical, treatment, and services research, and for developing prevention strategies.

Estimates of "Illicit drug use" reported from NSDUH showed that in 2006, an estimated 20.4 million Americans aged 12 or older were current (past month) illicit drug users. Marijuana was the most commonly used illicit drug (14.8 millions past month users). In 2006, marijuana was used by 72.8 % of current illicit drug users and was the only drug used by 52.8 % of them. An estimated 5.2 million persons were current nonmedical users of prescription pain relievers in 2006, which is more than the estimated 4.7 million in 2005. There were 2.4 million current cocaine users, the same as in 2005 (2.4 millions). The number of current heroin users increased from 136,000 in 2005 to 338,000 in 2006, and the corresponding prevalence rate increased from 0.06 to 0.14 %. Hallucinogens were used in the past month by 1.0 millions persons (0.4 %) in 2006.

Among youths aged 12 to 17 years of age, 9.8 % were current illicit drug users: 6.7 % used marijuana, 3.3 % engaged in nonmedical use of prescription-type drugs, 1.3 % used inhalants, 0.7 % used hallucinogens, and 0.4 % used cocaine. As in prior years, males were more likely than females among persons aged 12 or older to be current illicit drug users in 2006 (10.5 vs. 6.2 %, respectively). Among youths aged 12–17, the types of drugs used in the past month varied by age group. Among 12- or 13-year-olds, 2.0 % used prescription-type drugs nonmedically, 1.2 % used inhalants, and 0.9 % used marijuana. Among 14- or 15-year-olds, marijuana was the dominant drug used (5.8 %), followed by prescription-type drugs used nonmedically (3.1 %), and then by inhalants (1.7 %).

Prevalence rates among 12- to 17-year-olds were lower in 2006 than in 2002 for current use of illicit drugs other than marijuana; nonmedical use of psychotherapeutics, pain relievers, and tranquilizers; and use of hallucinogens, LSD, and ecstasy. The rate for illicit drugs other than marijuana declined from 5.7 % in 2002 to 4.9 % in 2006, nonmedical use of psychotherapeutic drugs decreased from 4.0 to 3.3 %; nonmedical use of pain relievers declined from 3.2 to 2.7 %; and nonmedical use of tranquilizers decreased from 0.8 to 0.5 %. Adolescents' current use of hallucinogens declined from 1.0 % in 2002 to 0.7 % in 2006, reflecting decreases in current use of ecstasy (from 0.5 to 0.3 %) and LSD (from 0.2 to 0.1 %).

The 32nd Annual Monitoring the Future survey of 50,000 8th, 10th, and 12th graders in more than 400 schools nationwide which is the percentage of US adolescents who use illicit drugs or drink alcohol have showed a decade-long drop in 2006. This year's survey reveals that a fifth (21 %) of today's 8th graders, over a third (36 %) of 10th graders, and about half (48 %) of all 12th graders have ever taken *any illicit drug* during their lifetime.

The proportion saying they used any illicit drug in the prior 12 months continued to decline in 2006, and the rates (15, 29, and 37 % in 8th, 10th, and 12th grades, respectively) are now down from recent peak levels in the mid-1990s by about one-third in 8th grade, one quarter in 10th grade, and one-eighth in 12th grade.

16.4.4 Indian Scenario

The magnitude and dynamics of drug abuse at the national level have not been well researched in India. This deficiency of data is contributed by the lack of awareness on the one hand and the sheer vastness of the country on the other. "The extent, pattern and trends of drug abuse in India- National Household Survey" attempts to minimize the potential error of any single technique and provide a comprehensive picture depicting the data obtained from various components of the national survey Ray and Mandal (2004).

Information on drug abuse among youth is available from the following: (a) National Household Survey (NHS); (b) Rapid Assessment Survey (RAS); and (c) Drug Abuse Monitoring System (DAMS). The data from NHS revealed that among current alcohol, cannabis, and opiates users, about 21 and 0.1 %, respectively, were below 18 years. The mean age of onset of various drugs was during youth, between 21 and 23 years.

Among treatment seekers, there were a few young subjects (below 15 years and between 16 and 20 years) being reported from the DAMS component. Overall, 0.4 and 4.6 % of total treatment seekers in various states belonged to the above age groups, respectively. Among users of heroin, cannabis, and propoxyphene, 0.5–0.8 % were in the group below 15 years. The proportion of opium and alcohol users in this age group was considerably low. The proportion of users of various drugs belonging to the age group 16–20 years varied between 2.7 and 18.8 %, the percentage of users of propoxyphene being the highest. It was noted that young people reporting to treatment were more often users of propoxyphene, heroin, and cannabis.

Some information on drug abuse by youth is also available from the data obtained from NGO (Children) and NYKs who participated in the DAMS component. Profile of drug users shows that alcohol was the commonest drug of abuse followed by cannabis and opiates. About 25 % reported use of "other drugs", i.e., mostly tobacco products. The proportion of alcohol users was higher among subjects from NYKs. Most were introduced to drugs at young age (below 15 years). Some information on drug abuse by young and very young subjects is available from the data from the Rapid Assessment Survey (RAS). A total of 368 out of 2,831 subjects were below the age of 20 years. It clearly showed that street children use a variety of substance including inhalants, cannabis, alcohol, and heroin. Some of these children were involved in drug dealing.

16.4.5 Effectiveness of CBT with Adolescent Substance Users

The clinical trials for adolescent substance abuse treatment that were reviewed provide support for the benefits of cognitive–behavioral interventions. Consistent with literature reviews (Catalano et al. 1990–1991; Weinberg et al. 1998), these results show that outpatient CBT treatment can be effective in reducing adolescent substance use and related problems. However, some variation in outcomes was observed. For example, while Liddle et al. (2001) and Waldron et al. (2001) both found greater evidence for the immediate benefits of family therapy, they also found marked substance use reductions, although delayed, for the cognitive–behavioral group interventions. However, Dennis et al. (2004) did not find evidence that family-based treatments had superior outcomes. Both group and individual CBT outcomes were as favorable as those of the family interventions and were significantly more cost-effective. Similarly, Kaminer et al. (1998a, b) found consistent evidence for the efficacy of group CBT interventions. Overall, the outcomes appear better (Simpson et al. 1987; Hubbard et al. 1985). The empirical support for the efficacy of CBT with adolescents is also similar to evidence found for treatment studies for adult drinking and drug use (Woody et al. 1993; Graham et al. 1996; Marques and Formigoni 2001). The results of these recent clinical trials for adolescents are particularly important because of their enhanced design and methodological features that represent significant improvements over previous studies.

Box 16.1 Evidence-based approaches for adolescent substance users

- Family systems approach
- Brief motivational interventions
- Cognitive–behavioral skills building treatments
- Assertive aftercare programs
- Community-based treatment models
- Guided personal change programs
- Pharmacotherapy for psychiatric comorbidity

By contrast, research evaluating CBT for other behavioral problems and disorders associated with adolescent substance abuse, such as conduct problems (Kendall et al. 1990; Kazdin 1995), depression (Clarke et al. 1992; Wood et al. 1996; Birmaher et al. 2000) and anxiety (Barrett et al. 2001) for adult substance abuse and dependence, and behavioral approaches for preventing substance use in high-risk youths (Botvin and Botvin 1992) is well established. Given the success of CBT for other populations, especially for adolescents diagnosed with disorders known to co-occur with substance abuse, the newly emerging support for CBT with substance-abusing youths represents significant progress in the field.

16.4.6 Evidence-Based Approaches for Adolescent Substance Users

At present, several evidence-based, developmentally sensitive approaches are emerging for addressing alcohol, nicotine, and other drug use problems among adolescents (Wagner and Waldron 2001). These include family systems approaches (Liddle and Hogue 2001; Waldron 1997), brief motivational interventions, guided personal change programs, cognitive–behavioral skill-building treatments, and assertive aftercare programs (see Box-16.1). Moreover, there has been increasing attention devoted to community-based treatment models (e.g., treatment provided in neighborhood clinics, schools, and/or the home), which have greater ecological validity and impact, and fewer barriers to treatment access than more traditional treatment models for adolescent substance abuse. Finally, given the high rates of psychiatric comorbidity among adolescents with alcohol or other drug problems, an effective treatment "package" for substance-abusing teenagers may include medication. Group therapy and 12-step programs are commonly used with adolescents, but recent reports suggest that these interventions should be approached with caution.

16.5 Assessment

The clinical assessment of substance use and substance-related disorders are an important part of treatment process. The rate of substance use, abuse, and dependence varies among individuals and may depend on the sociodemographic factors like age, social class, gender, and type of family. A detailed assessment is required to determine the level or intensity of care required and the need for the specific treatment.

16.5.1 Eliciting the History

History taking is an important part of assessment procedure. The patients with substance use disorders may not easily give a reliable report about their substance use. It should not be surprising that these patients will attempt to protect their ability to continue to use by minimizing, denying, or even lying about the extent of use and the problems resulting from it. While eliciting the history, the clinician should be alert to these characteristic defenses and should have a nonjudgmental attitude toward the patient. The patients should be encouraged to share the information without any hesitation. Sometimes, the patient's reluctance to disclose sensitive information can be lessened by a frank discussion about how this information will be used and assuring about the confidentiality.

16.5.1.1 Case Vignette

Master x a 13-year-old boy was brought to the National Drug Dependence Treatment Centre by his parents for the treatment of substance abuse. He is an inhalant user and is abusing drugs from the last 2 years. Patient is a student of 7th class and coming from a lower middle-class urban Hindu family. The patient started using inhalants while was 10 years old and was introduced to this by his school friends. Initially, he was using gutka only and then started taking white fluid with his friends. Initially, he used it intermittently, once in 4–5 days with his friends only, and after some time (2 months), he started taking it regularly. He used to inhale 2 bottles in a day, and frequency increased to 7–8 times in a day.

The patient reported having a pleasant feeling after taking it. In case he will not take it for few hours, then he will start having irritability, uneasiness, and an intense desire to take it. Gradually, he started missing his classes and used to spend most of his time away from family. There were complaints from school regarding his studies, and the performance fell down. He started stealing money from his home to purchase the substance and sometimes will borrow money from his friends and neighbors too. He will often lie to his parents and remained tired most of the time. He stopped playing with his sober friends and will take less interest in other household responsibilities.

When parents came to know about his condition, he was brought to the treatment Centre. The patient when brought to the Centre was unaware of the harmful consequences of inhalant use. Patient's general physical examination was within normal limits. The mental status examination revealed no significant psychopathology except memory problems and difficulty in attention and concentration.

The patient fulfilled the ICD-10 criteria for *Inhalant Dependence* in the form of persistent desire and inability to stop the substance, spending most of the time in substance use only and social and other activities being given up. The patient was managed on outpatient basis and was on regular follow-up over a period of two months.

(For detailed management, see session wise treatment process)

After this general overview, a parallel chronology of the patient's use of alcohol and drugs can be obtained and specific questions can be asked about the drug use behavior. As part of the assessment, the patients should be asked about their lifetime use, recent or current use, age of onset, progression, frequency, length and pattern of use, and mode of ingestion. Specific questions should be asked about the pattern of use, tolerance, and withdrawal and treatment history.

Finally, attention needs to be directed to any medical, psychological, emotional, social, and legal complications of use and any family history of substance or other psychiatric disorders.

16.5.2 Physical and Mental Status Examination

A detailed physical and mental status examination is required. Physical examination is essential because of the wide range of medical disorders associated with tobacco, alcohol, or other drug use. The clinician should refer the patient to primary care or internal medicine physicians for a complete physical examination.

A detailed mental status examination, including assessment of cognitive functioning, is required for the accurate diagnosis of substance dependence, comorbid psychiatric disorders, and cognitive dysfunction. Assessment of cognitive function should include evaluation of attention and concentration, recent and remote memory, perception, abstract reasoning, and problem-solving ability.

16.5.3 Screening Instruments and Structured Interviews

The objective assessment can be grouped in 3 main categories: (1) self-report measures/structured semi-structured interviews, (2) direct behavioral observation, and (3) physiological measures.

Self-Reports Self-report measure or self-monitoring is one of the most universal methods of addictive behavior assessment. The use of structured or semi-structured interviews can yield an accurate, realistic understanding of the teenager and the problems he is experiencing.

Although self-reports are practical and easy to obtain, their reliability and validity must be assessed. This is usually done by obtaining reports from friends, family members, and relatives. There are numerous well-researched, self-report-based screening and comprehensive assessment tools available to clinicians. For a detailed description of assessment instruments, see Table 16.1.

Direct Behavioral Observations While direct behavioral observation of drug use is not as practical as self-reports, they provide detailed information on consumption and pattern that is highly reliable. Direct observations are obtained either through simulated analog system or in the natural environment. Observation of drug-consuming behavior in a naturalistic setting would probably add greater to our knowledge regarding the relationships among these habit patterns.

Physiological Monitoring Techniques to assess physiological correlates of substance abuse have greatly enhanced the objectivity of assessment. Urine screening for drugs has proven to be a practical, reliable, and inexpensive assessment tool. Urine specimens are collected and analyzed either on a daily basis or randomly. Analysis of blood/alcohol concentration via breath tests has also been found to be a useful measure for alcoholism (Table 16.2).

Table 16.2 Adolescent screening and assessment instruments

Instrument	Description	Developer
Adolescent drug involvement scale (ADIS)	12-item research and evaluation tool, adaptation of Mayer & Filstead's adolescent alcohol involvement scale (AAIS)	D. Paul Moberg
Drug and alcohol problem (DAP) quick screen	30-item test with 4 key items	Richard H. Schwartz, M.D.
Drug use screening inventory—revised (DUSI-R)	159-item instrument	Ralph E. Tarter
Personal experience screening questionnaire (PESQ)	40-item questionnaire	Ken Winters
Problem-oriented screening instrument for teenagers (POSIT)	139-item questionnaire	National institute on drug abuse (NIDA)

Table 16.2 (continued)

Instrument	Description	Developer
Teen addiction severity index (T-ASI)	Interview instrument covering 7 dimensions	The adolescent drug abuse and psychiatric treatment program editor: Kaminer Y., Bukstin O. & Tarter, R.
Adolescent drug abuse diagnosis (ADAD)	150-item instrument, provides a 10-point severity rating for each of the 9 life problems	Alfred S. Friedman & Arlene Terras
Adolescent diagnostic interview (ADI)	Provides diagnostic and level of functioning information for adolescents suspected of drug use and to screen for mental/behavioral problems	Ken Winters & George Henly
Adolescent self-assessment profile (ASAP)	225-item self-report instrument comprising 20 basic scales and 15 supplemental scales	Kenneth Wanberg
The American drug and alcohol survey (ADAS)	Self-report inventory of drug use and related behaviors. Two versions: The Children's Form (4th–6th grade) and the Adolescent Form (6th–12th grade) are available	E.R. Oetting, Ruth W. Edwards, & Fred Beauvais
Personal experience inventory (PEI)	PEI consists of two parts—the chemical involvement problem severity section (CIPS) and the psychosocial section (PS)	Ken Winters

16.5.4 Treatment Approaches

A number of *evidence-based, developmentally sensitive* treatment approaches are available for adolescent substance users including the following:

- Family system approaches
- Brief motivational interventions
- Cognitive–behavioral skills building
- Assertive aftercare programs
- Community-based treatment models
- Guided personal change programs
- Pharmacological agents

Among these family-based treatments is the most thoroughly studied treatment modality for adolescent substance misuse. An integrative cognitive–behavioral therapy and family therapy model (Waldron et al. 2001), a family empowerment intervention, and multidimensional family therapy (Liddle 2001) have been developed, tested, and yielded promising findings.

16.5.5 Motivation Enhancement Therapy and Psycho Education

Motivational enhancement therapy is a therapeutic approach based on the premise that patients will best be able to achieve change when motivation comes from within themselves rather than being imposed by therapist. Motivational interviewing, the primary element of MET, was developed by Miller and Rollnick. Prochaska and DiClemente described five stages of change in modifying problem. The primary goals of this treatment are to enhance participants' motivation to change their substance use and to develop basic skills needed to achieve abstinence or gain control over substance use. Psycho education about the harmful consequences of use is given, and the therapist explores the participant's reasons for seeking treatment, prior treatment attempts, readiness for treatment, problems associated with substance use, and patient's perception toward their life.

16.5.6 Cognitive–Behavioral Therapy

Cognitive–behavioral therapy (CBT) is designed to help participants coping with relapse and to remediate deficits due to substance use. The goal of this intervention is to provide some basic alternative skills to cope with situations that might otherwise lead to substance use. Skill deficits are viewed as central to the relapse process; therefore, the major focus of the technique will be on identifying cues that signal high-risk situations, development of effective coping skills, and rehearsal of these newly learned skills in day-to-day life.

Cognitive–behavioral treatment for substance abuse requires the active participation, as well as patient's assumption of responsibility for using the new self-control skill to prevent future abuse. CBT is generally effective because it helps patients recognize the situations in which they are likely to use substances and cope more effectively with the variety of situations, feelings, and behavior related to drug use. Active practice with positive, corrective feedback is the most effective way to modify self-efficacy and create long-lasting behavior change.

16.5.7 Family Counseling

Family-based treatment is the most thoroughly studied treatment modality for adolescent substance misuse. A number of family-based interventions have been developed, tested, and shown promise in treating substance-misusing teens. The parental involvement during treatment process increases the chances of better recovery and long-term abstinence. Reviews of formal clinical trials of family-based treatments have consistently found that more drug-abusing adolescents enter, engage in, and remain in family therapy than in other treatments and that family therapy produces significant reductions in substance use (Waldron 1997).

16.5.8 *Overview of Treatment Module*

16.5.8.1 Treatment Goals and Objectives

The goal of the treatment is abstinence and preventing relapse. With this perspective, the treatment module is administered while keeping in view the following objectives:

- To identify the high-risk situations associated with drug use
- To teach adolescents about the signs and symptoms of cravings and how to challenge the thoughts, cravings, and urges associated with substance use
- To teach adolescents a broad spectrum of coping strategies to deal with problem behavior
- To teach adolescents social skills for helping them deal with poor decision making and teaching them effective problem solving.

The overall goal of abstinence are to teach adolescents, first to abstain from substances and then to maintain the abstinence for a longer period of time. During the treatment, the subject's ambivalence about the possibility of stopping the drug use is considered normal. The therapist is encouraged to normalize ambivalence and concerns about quitting the drugs.

16.5.8.2 Target Population

The treatment module is designed for the treatment of adolescents between ages 11 and 19 who are exhibiting problems related to substance use as indicated by one of the following:

- Meeting criteria for substance abuse or dependence
- Experiencing problems (including emotional, physical, legal, social, economic, and academic problems) associated with substance use
- Having comorbid conditions like conduct disorder and anxiety etc.

Contradictions for the treatment are the following:

- Mental retardation
- Severe psychological problems like psychosis, bipolar disorder, seizures, and neurological problems

16.5.9 *Need for the Treatment*

Adolescent users differ from adults in many ways. Their substance use often stems from different causes and has different consequences. In treatment, adolescents must be approached differently than adults because of their unique developmental issues; differences in their values and belief systems; and environmental considerations (e.g., strong peer influences). Treatment programs for adolescents should make every effort to involve the adolescent patient's family to change the youth's environment.

Adolescent substance use occurs with varying degrees of severity. The degree of substance involvement is an important determinant of treatment. Apart from this, the family, peer environment, and the individual's stage of mental and emotional development should also be considered in planning appropriate treatment. A session wise description of adolescent substance users is given below:

16.5.10 Session 1: Motivation Enhancement and Psycho Education

Objectives of the session

- Take history and build rapport with the patient
- Begin the process of assessing and building the patient's motivation to address his or her substance problem
- Introduce functional analysis
- Provide a rational for extra-session tasks

16.5.11 Strategies of Motivational Enhancement Therapy

Miller and Rollnick have described five main strategies that are used in applying motivation enhancement. For effective sessions, therapist should have good listening skills and an empathetic attitude toward patients. Therapist should avoid behaviors like lecturing, criticizing, labeling, ordering, and judging. Therapist should give unconditional acceptance to the patient, and any kind of analytical judgment should also be avoided at this moment.

16.5.12 MET Strategies

16.5.12.1 Express Empathy

Therapist needs to express empathy in order to convey acceptance of the patient's current situation. It acknowledges that changing behavior is difficult and involves feelings of ambivalence. Respectful listening and reflection of feelings are two key communication skills for this task. Therapist should use paraphrasing here for reflecting. For example:

Th: *Tell me something about your substance use*
P: *I started it in 12th class. I wanted to experiment. I wanted to see what it is all about. Moreover I was tensed at that time. Actually my result was about to come. So I was tensed and I had it for the first time.*
Th: *So you want to say that you started because of curiosity and because you were under stress. Am I right?*
P: *Yes*

16.5.12.2 Identify Discrepancy

This is accomplished by identifying and amplifying incongruities between the patient's present behavior and his stated personal goals. Therapist should show the patient the apparent discrepancy between his present situation and his future goals and should suggest the ways through which patients could reach their goals.

16.5.12.3 Avoid Arguments

Therapist should avoid arguments with a patient. Arguing with a patient tends to evoke resistance. As a result, both the therapist and the patient are likely to come away feeling dissatisfied. While motivational counseling is confrontational in its goals, it is not confrontational in style. Therapist should roll with resistance.

16.5.12.4 Clarify Free Choice

Therapist should clarify to patient that it is his choice whether he wants to quit or not. There is nothing I or anyone else can do to make you stop using drugs, what you do is really up to you. You can decide to take this now or wait until another time.

16.5.12.5 Review Consequences of Action and Inaction

Patient should be suggested to always review the consequences of using drugs or always think about pros and cons of using. For example:

What do you see happening if you don't stop using drugs?
What do you think will happen if you don't use it?

16.5.12.6 Support Self-efficacy

This is the only possible path to change. Therapist should encourage the patient to believe in him and supports the idea that patient can change himself. Patients are suggested to make use of positive self-verbalization for change. For example:

> I would not take it. I have left it earlier also and I will make it again. This time I will quit forever.

16.5.13 Other Techniques

16.5.13.1 Use Positive Incentives to Reinforce Treatment Participation

One of the most powerful strategies to increase treatment involvement and establish treatment engagement is to use incentives and other tangible positive reinforcers to reward progress in treatment. The specific reinforcers include appreciation and any materialistic thing like money.

16.5.13.2 Call No Shows

Therapist should routinely telephone patients who fail to show up for scheduled clinic visits.

16.5.13.3 Establish Daily Schedule

Time planning and scheduling should be promoted as an important way to engage a patient or to avoid spending lot of time alone. Patients should be vigorously encouraged to schedule and plan each day, especially during this early phase of treatment.

16.5.13.4 Address Secondary Substance Use

Most adolescents also use some other substances, such as bidi, cig, and gutka. They often do not perceive their use of a secondary substance as problematic. Patients need help to identify the connections between the use of other substances and their primary drug of use. Patients should learn that using another substance increases the likelihood of relapse to primary drug use.

16.5.14 Psycho Education

Psycho education means educating a patient about the nature of problem and giving information about lapse/relapse, duration of medicines, and effects of drug use and negative consequences resulting from it. Patients with substance use disorders do not understand many of the things that they have experienced as a result of their drug use, such as impulsive behaviors, anger and hostility, and cognitive deficits. They require education to help them understand the learning and conditioning factors associated with drug use. Similarly, they need information about the impact of drugs on the brain and behavior, such as cognitive impairment and forgetfulness.

16.5.15 Relapse Prevention

Relapse prevention is a cognitive–behavioral treatment that combines cognitive intervention techniques with behavioral skill training procedures to assist individuals in maintaining desired behavioral changes. RP uses a self-management approach to substance abuse and helps patients in developing new coping responses. It helps to modify maladaptive beliefs and expectancies regarding substance use and helps in changing faulty patterns of behavior and lifestyles. Next three sessions are a part of RP.

16.5.16 Session 2: Identification of High-risk Situations

Objectives of the session

1. Identify common warning signs and high-risk situations/factors associated with relapse
2. Help patient anticipate dangerous situations by identifying his personal relapse risk factors

We assume that the individual will have a perceived sense of control while maintaining abstinence. This perceived sense of control will continue until the individual encounters a high-risk situation which will pose a threat to individuals' sense of control and increases the risk of potential relapse. According to Marlatt and Gorden (1985), almost 75 % of all the relapses are associated with three primary high-risk situations:

1. **Negative Emotional States** (35 % of all relapses in the sample): situations in which the individual is experiencing a negative or unpleasant emotional state, mood, or feeling such as frustration, anger, anxiety, depression, or boredom prior to or occurring simultaneously with the first lapse.
2. **Interpersonal Conflict** (16 % of the relapses): Interpersonal conflicts arise in the form of arguments and confrontations between friends, family members, employer, and employee. These conflicts seriously affect the interpersonal relationship and work as risky situations for relapse.
3. **Social Pressure** (20 % of the relapses): Social pressure in the form of peer pressure or the influence of another individual or group of individuals who

Fig. 16.4 Important high-risk situations for relapse

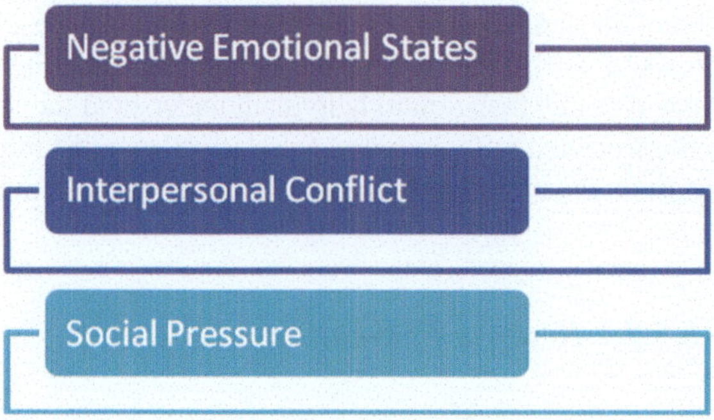

exert pressure on the individual to engage in the proscribed behavior play an important role in the relapse process. Social pressure may be either direct (e.g., verbal persuasion from others) or indirect (e.g., watching others using the drugs, even though no direct pressure is involved).

Other high-risk situations include positive emotional states (party mood), negative physical states (withdrawal), testing personal control, and responsivity to substance cues (craving, urges). An individual who copes successfully with high-risk situations will develop a sense of mastery or perceived self-control. A detailed account of techniques is given in the next session which will describe the management of high-risk situations with adolescent substance users (Fig. 16.4).

16.5.17 Strategies

16.5.17.1 Anticipate/Identify High-risk Situations

The first step in the prevention of relapse is to teach the patient to recognize and identify the high-risk situations that may precipitate or trigger a relapse. Therapists should ask patients to think what might be the possible stressors that might arise over the next few months, or what might be the possible high-risk situations which might lead to relapse. For each of these situations or circumstances, therapist and patient should develop concrete coping plans. This can be achieved using the following techniques:

1. **Self-Monitoring Procedures**: Keeping a record of strong urges or cravings along with situations can provide useful data.
2. **Reviewing list of relapse risk factors**: Reviewing lists of common relapse risk factors to identify personal potential relapse precipitants is another useful way to assess the patient's perceptions of high-risk situations.

Therapist should point out that although patient will find it helpful to recognize, avoid, and cope with high-risk situations, life is unpredictable, and not all high-risk situations can be anticipated. Crises, negative stressors, and even positive events can result in high-risk situations.

16.5.18 Session 3: Craving Management

Substance use becomes strongly associated with certain people, places, objects, activities, behaviors, and feelings. Because patients with substance use disorders may have engaged in drug use hundreds or thousands of times, their daily life is filled with numerous reminders or cues that can trigger substance craving and substance use. Accordingly, it is important for therapists to help patients to acknowledge and identify the cluster of cues unique to their lives. In this section, we will discuss the strategies designed to manage the cravings that may precipitate a lapse and to modify the cognitions and other reactions to prevent a full-blown relapse.

Objectives of the Session:
1. Teach how conditioning factors can elicit drug cravings.
2. Develop action plans for cravings
3. Identify strategies to cope with social pressures and cravings to use substances

16.5.19 Teach Basic Conditioning

Patients should be taught about the conditioning nature of drug cravings and urges. They should be taught that these cravings and urges are conditioning in nature and is a natural part of early abstinence (see Table 16.3).

16.5.20 Develop Action Plans for Cravings

Stopping substance use requires specific plans of action that can decrease the likelihood of encountering reminders of substance use. Because there are numerous reminders of substance use in the environment, the chances of experiencing drug

Table 16.3 Conditioning factors in substance use

Craving occurs as a result of long-term substance use and typically continues long after the substance use is stopped
Cravings can be triggered by people, places, situations, things, and feelings that were previously associated with substance use
Cravings and urges are always temporary and tend to disappear quickly
Cravings are typically strong in the beginning of abstinence period and become less frequent and severe over time
Specific techniques and actions must be taken to counteract cravings and urges whenever they occur

thoughts, triggers, and cravings are common. It is essential to take specific steps to avoid them. The following steps can be taken to reduce the drug craving:

1. **Getting rid of drugs and paraphernalia**

    - Get rid of all the drugs, paraphernalia, objects, or things which were used when taking drugs. Collect and throw all these objects away.

2. **Stopping contact with drug users**

    - Stop contact with people with whom you were having substances and from where used to obtain substances.

3. **Avoiding high-risk areas**

    - Avoid all those settings, neighborhoods, streets, houses, or other locations that are specially associated with obtaining or using substances? What are your specific plans to avoid them?

4. **Teach Functional Analysis of drug Use**

Functional analysis probes the situations surrounding the patient's substance abuse. Specifically, it examines the relationship between stimuli that trigger use and consequences that follow. The core components of a functional analysis are as follows:

1. Teaching patients to examine the types of circumstances, situations, thoughts, and feelings that increase the likelihood that they will use substances,
2. Counseling patients to examine the positive, immediate, but short-term consequences of their substance use, and
3. Encouraging patients to review the negative and often delayed consequences of their substance use.

    - Ask the patient to identify strategies that he has used in the past or could use in the future to manage drug craving or resist social pressures to use substances.

In case of the example given in the beginning of this chapter, functional analysis can proceed as follows.

> Functional analysis allows you to identify the immediate causes of your inhalant use. You might have noticed that in certain situations you will inhale fluid while in other situations you do not. The situation around us can powerfully control substance use. Particularly if we are unaware of its influence. Some of the situations that can influence inhalant use are:
>
> - The people you are with.
> - The place you happen to be
> - The hour of the day.
> - How much money you have
> - How much fluid you have consumed
> - What you are doing beside inhaling fluid
> - How are you feeling

The first step in understanding your inhalant use is to identify the types of situations in which you are likely to inhale fluid. Your first assignment will be to identify these situations and what made you to use substance. These are called triggers.

You will also need to identify the consequences of your use. There are two kinds of consequences: the immediate and often the positive consequences such as sense of high, or having fun and the delayed often negative consequences, such as spending all money on it only.

As you identify triggers and consequences, you will discover that there are certain patterns to your use. These patterns will become important for your intervention.

16.5.21 Cognitive and Behavioral Strategies for Managing Craving

Some of the cognitive and behavioral strategies for managing craving are given (see Figs. 16.5 and 16.6).

16.5.22 Session 4: Coping Skills

Patients should learn ways to cope with high-risk situations, persons, and feelings. The strategies or techniques used by patients to deal with high-risk situations are known as coping strategies.

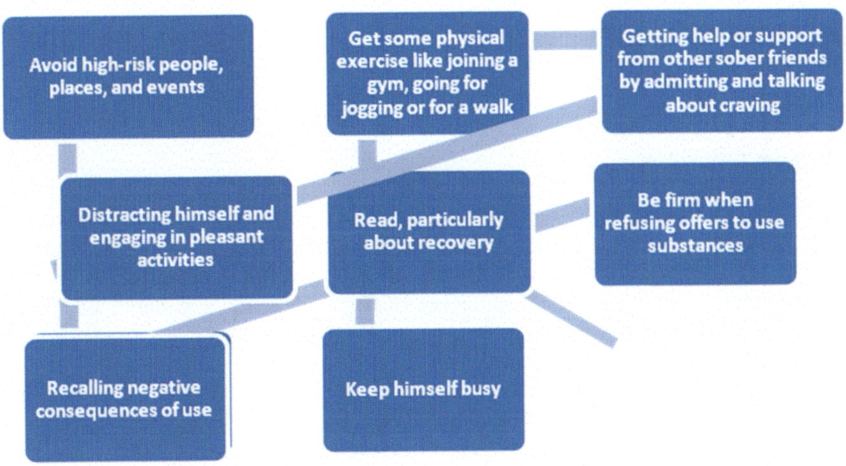

Fig. 16.5 Behavioral strategies

Fig. 16.6 Cognitive strategies

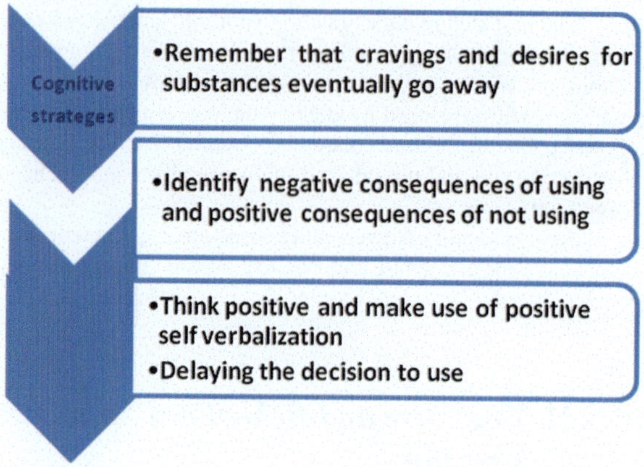

Objectives of the Session

1. Review of progress
2. Help patient to develop coping strategies to manage his high-risk situations to reduce the chances of relapse

Activities to reduce the chances of drug use These are some of the activities a patient should indulge in when trying to stay away from drug use:

- Staying away from drug-using friends
- Leaving money at home, carrying very little money with oneself
- Telling yourself of the consequences of drug use
- Handling feelings of anger and frustration directly
- Talking to parents
- Being in company of sober friends
- Going for a walk
- Not keeping drugs at home
- Keeping oneself busy
- Distraction
- Having a positive attitude
- Regular follow-up
- Change of place

When patients are most stressed, they may feel vulnerable and be more likely to use old, familiar coping strategies than to use the healthier strategies they have practiced during sessions. It is important to try to develop a generic, foolproof coping strategy that can be used in the event of any major crisis. This should include, at minimum, the following:

- A set of emergency phone numbers of supportive others who can be relied on
- Recall of negative consequences of returning to use
- A set of positive thoughts that can be substituted for high-risk drug thoughts

- A set of reliable distracters
- Positive self-verbalization

16.5.22.1 Counteract Euphoric Recall and the Desire to Test Control

Euphoric recall is the act of remembering only the pleasure associated with substance use and not the adverse consequences. Euphoric recall is a potent relapse risk factor because it minimizes clients' perceptions of substance danger, promoting ambivalence about quitting. Patients should be taught that urges to test their control over substance use are a powerful relapse warning sign.

16.5.22.2 Enhance Self-efficacy Regarding High-risk Situations

Once patients learn to identify, manage, and avoid high-risk situations, the therapist and patient should try to determine whether the patient is confident in his ability to use those skills in the real world. CBT posits that low levels of self-efficacy are related to substance use and an increased likelihood of relapse after having achieved abstinence (Marlatt and Gordon 1985). A model of relapse that is based on the role of self-efficacy and coping is depicted in Fig. 16.5 (Fig. 16.7).

16.5.22.3 Decision Matrix

A decision matrix allows patients to examine both the immediate and the delayed consequences of substance use, which may help counter the tendency of patients to think about only the pleasant short-term effects.

16.5.22.4 Relapse Rehearsal Methods

In this procedure, the patient is allowed to imagine as being involved in an actual high-risk situation and using a more adaptive coping skill. The patient is thus encouraged to visualize that he or she is successfully handling the difficult situation through effective coping skill (Fig. 16.8).

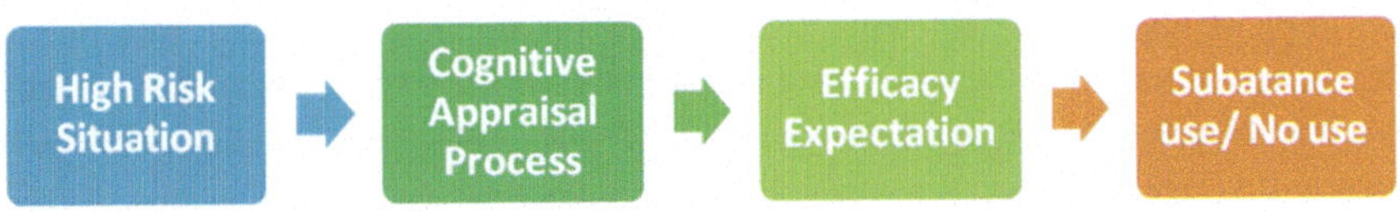

Fig. 16.7 A model of relapse that is based on the role of self-efficacy

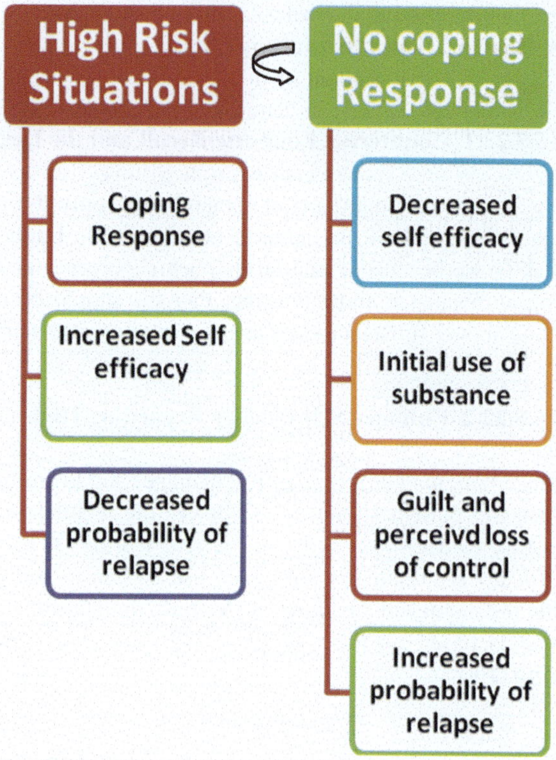

Fig. 16.8 Cognitive–behavioral model of the relapse process

16.5.23 Session 5: Social Skills Training

16.5.23.1 Remedial Skill Training

Remedial skill training is necessitated by identification of coping skill deficits and is an important part of treatment program. Going beyond that, we also need to modify the patient's lifestyle and give them skill training. The content of skill training program is variable and will depend on the *needs* of the individual. Possible content areas include assertiveness (see box 16.2), stress management, relaxation training, problem solving, decision making, and communication skills.

Practitioners working in the area typically prefer to develop a tailor-made program of techniques for each patient. We recommend the individualized approach for implementation of RP with most patient problems. Particular techniques should be selected on the basis of careful examination and assessment. A need-based approach is encouraged based on the patient's substance abuse problem and general lifestyle pattern.

Box 16.2

Assertiveness Training
The patient is encouraged to express and disclose his emotions and needs, to stand up for his rights, to do what is best for him, and to express negative emotions constructively. As a person becomes more assertive, he will be better able to refuse the offer and control his impulses as well as environmental factors that may lead to relapse.

Stress Management
The patient must be taught about the ways that will help him to reduce stress, including relaxation techniques, distraction planning in advance for a potentially stressful situation, and cognitive strategies.

16.5.23.2 Changing Lifestyle

As a part of treatment process, a global lifestyle change is also required to improve the patient's overall capacity to cope with more pervasive stress factors that are antecedents to high-risk situations. Marlatt and Gordon (1985) posit that one source of possible relapse risk has to do with the degree of stress or daily hassles that the patient experiences. They suggest that when the demands and obligations a patient feels (should) outweigh the pleasures the individual can engage in (wants), his life is out of balance. This often results in feelings of resentment, and the person begins making decisions that gradually lead toward possible relapse. The goal is to find a better balance, increasing involvement in pleasant and rewarding activities while reducing the level and sources of stress. *Therapist should emphasize upon the lifestyle changes in social and recreational areas.*

For example master x in the beginning of this chapter is suggested that Social and recreational activities are important in most people's lives. They provide

- A source of enjoyment
- A way to reduce boredom when you have free time
- A way to feel physically fit/healthy
- Increase your confidence/self esteem
- Provide you a chance to be with people you like to develop friendship

These activities are important for you to maintain abstinence. When you give up drugs, you have to do something else during that time you were using. If you don't do anything pleasurable, you will sit around and feel lonely and bored which can further cause relapse.

16.5.24 Drug Refusal Skills

Here, the patient has to learn the drug refusal skills. He has to learn to say no to the offer made by other drug-using friends. *In the earlier example, the refusal skills can be taught to the patient by giving the following instructions:*

> Remember that those persons who offer you the fluid are not thinking of your good interest they may be your friends but once you have decided to quit, it is important for you to discourage them politely, but firmly. Saying NO is the first thing. When refusing you have to take care of the following things:
>
> - No should be the first thing you say.
> - Tell the person not to ask you now or in the future.
> - Use appropriate body language:
> - Make good eye contact. Look directly in the eyes of the person
> - Your expression and tone should clearly indicate that you are serious
> - Offer an alternative (if you want to do something with that person) that is incompatible with inhalant use.
> - Change the subject or lave the setting.

16.5.25 Session 6: Family Counseling

A family counseling session with parents aims to decrease parental distress and anxiety and maximize parental involvement in treatment. It is expected that parents of these drug-using adolescents are having a lot of expectations from patients and are concerned about their drug use, behavioral aspects, social aspects, and work area. Helping the family members solve problems together in the therapeutic setting enables them to learn strategies that can be applied with the adolescent in the home. Such maneuvers in therapy decrease family conflicts and improve the effectiveness of communication.

While counseling parents, they should be given an opportunity to share their anxieties and doubts with therapist (catharsis). Parents should be taught how to provide age-appropriate monitoring of their teenager (e.g., to know their friends, to know how they spend their time), set limits, rebuild emotional attachments, and take part in activities with the adolescent inside and outside the home.

A detailed family session is required in which parents are trained or given advice about how to deal with their children to keep their youth drug free. Here are few suggestions for parents to follow:

16.5.25.1 Get Involved in Your Child's Life

Young people are much less likely to use drugs when they have positive activities to do and when caring adults are involved in their lives. Parents are suggested to get involved in their child's life by participating in his activities and praising his accomplishments. Following suggestions are given to parents:

- Spend at least 15 min a day in a child's activity. It is expected that doing something with child for at least 15 min a day is essential to build a strong parent–child relationship. Examples include the following:
- Identify at least one opportunity each week for you and your child to do something special together. Some possibilities are given in box: 16.3

Box 16.3

- Going for a walk
- Playing cards, board games, or video games
- Searching on the Internet to learn about each other's interest
- Going on a special outing, such as the park, playground, or ice cream stand
- *Recognize good behavior consistently and immediately.* Praise him for things you might ordinarily take for granted, such as getting up on time, helping to set the table, or finishing his homework without being asked. Give regular positive reinforcements in the form of praise or something else.

16.5.25.2 Handling Peer Pressure

- Explain to the family that peer pressure is an important risk factor in relapse
- Parents must be informed about their role in keeping their children away from drug-using friends and keeping them busy and distracted.

Examples

- Discussing a general topic
- Having dinner together
- Watching T.V. together
- Discuss about activities in school
- Ask for his viewpoint in home decisions
  Discuss the family matters

Handling Craving Explain to the family that parental role is important in helping their adolescents manage the craving. The family members can help by

- Encouraging the individual to express the craving and talking it through
- Teaching adolescents that the process is temporary
- Distracting them or engaging them in some pleasurable activities

16.5.25.3 Be a Positive Role Model

Children like to imitate adults. A parent or caregiver using alcohol, tobacco, or illegal drugs may increase a child's chances of using and becoming dependent on a substance.

16.5.26 Barriers to Treatment

A number of factors serve as barriers to treatment and affect the overall treatment outcome. Barriers to treatment include following:

Denial Even after being presented with a diagnosis, some individuals do not believe that they have a problem. Denial runs deep which is an important barrier to treatment.

Stigma Substance abuse is having a stigma attached to it. During intake procedures, which involve many personal questions, clients may react defensively, due to feelings of vulnerability.

Fear Fear is closely associated with substance abuse treatment. Fear is exhibited in many ways. Fear of being found out. Fear of facing the truth. Fear of what others will think. Fear of losing one's employment. And the list goes on.

Lack of Support Lack of social supports is another barrier to treatment. It has been shown that having a viable support system, addicts are better able to maintain abstintnce, whether it is in the form of family support, formal counseling, school counseling, or any other kind of social support.

References

Barrett, P. M., Shortt, A. L., & Wescombe, K. (2001). Examining the social validity of the FRIENDS treatment program for anxious children. *Behaviour Change, 18*(2), 63–77.

Birmaher, B., Brent, D. A., Kolko, D., Baugher, M., Bridge, G., Holder, D., et al. (2000). Clinical outcome after short-term psychotherapy for adolescents with major depressive disorder. *Archives of General Psychiatry, 57*, 29–36.

Botvin, G., & Botvin, E. (1992). Adolescent tobacco, alcohol and drug use: Prevention strategies, empirical findings, and assessment issues. *Journal of Developmental and Behavioral Pediatrics, 13*, 290–301.

Bukstein, O. G., Brent, D. A., & Kaminer, Y. (1989). Co-morbidity of substance abuse and other psychiatric disorders in adolescents. *American Journal of Psychiatry, 146*, 1131–1141.

Catalano, R. F., Hawkins, J. D., Wells, E. A., Miller, J., & Brewer, D. (1990). Evaluation of the effectiveness of adolescent drug abuse treatment, assessment of risks for relapse, and promising approaches for relapse prevention. *The International Journal of the Addictions, 25*, 1085–1140.

Clarke, G. N., Hops, H., Lewinsohn, P. M., Andrews, J. A., Seeley, J. R., & Williams, J. A. (1992). Cognitive-behavioral group treatment of adolescent depression: Prediction of outcome. *Behavior Therapy, 23*, 341–354.

Dennis, M., et al. (2004). The Cannabis Youth Treatment (CYT) study: Main findings from two randomized trials. *Journal of Substance Abuse Treatment, 27*(3), 197–213.

Graham, K., Annis, H. M., & Brett, P. J. (1996). A controlled field trial of group versus individual cognitive behavioral training for relapse prevention. *Addiction, 91*, 1127–1139.

Hubbard, R. L., Cavanaugh, E. R., Craddock, S. G., & Rachal, J. V. (1985). Characteristics, behaviors and outcomes for youth in the TOPS. In A. S. Friedman, G. M. Beschner (Eds.), *Treatment services for adolescent substance abusers* (pp. 49–65). Rockville, MD: National Institute on Drug Abuse, National Institutes of Health.

Kaminer, Y., Blitz, C, Burleson, J. A., Sussman, J., & Rounsaville, B. J. (1998a). Psychotherapies for adolescent substance abusers: treatment outcome. *Journal of Nervous and Mental Disease, 186*, 684–690.

Kaminer, Y., Blitz, C., Burleson, J. A., Kadden, R. M., & Rounsaville, B. J. (1998b). Measuring treatment process in cognitive behavioral and interactional group therapies for adolescent substance abusers. *The journal of Nervous and Mental Disorders, 186*(7), 407–13.

Kandel, D. B. (1982). Epidemiological and psychosocial perspectives and adolescent drug use. *Journal of the American Academy of Child and Adolescent Psychiatry, 21*, 328–347.

Kazdin, A. E. (1995). *Conduct disorder*. Newbury Park CA: Sage.

Kendall, P. C., Reber, M., McCleer, S. E. J., & Roman, K. R. (1990). Cognitive-behavioral treatment of conduct-disordered children. *Cognitive Therapy and Research., 14*, 279–297.

Liddle, H. A., Dakof, G. A., Parker, K., Diamond, G. S., Barrett, K., & Tejeda, M. (2001). Multidimensional family therapy for adolescent drug abuse : Results of a randomized clinical trial. *American Journal of Drug and Alcohol Abuse, 27*(4), 651–688.

Marlatt, G. A., & Gordon, J. R. (1985). *Relapse prevention: Maintenance strategies in the treatment of addictive behaviors*. New York: Guilford.

Marques, A. C., & Formigoni, M. L. (2001). Comparison of individual and group cognitive behavioral therapy for alcohol and or drug dependent. *Addiction, 96*, 835–846.

Prochaska, J. O., Diclemente, C. C., & Norcross, J. C. (1997). In search of how people change: Applications to addictive behaviors. In G. A. Marlatt & G. R. VandenBos (Eds.), *Addictive behaviours: readings on etiology, prevention and treatment*. Washington, DC: American Psychological Association.

Ray, R., & Mandal, A. B. (2004). The extent pattern and trends of drug abuse in India. National survey. Ministry of Social Justice and Empowerment, Government of India & United Nations Office on Drugs and Crime, Regional Office for South Asia.

Simpson, D. D., Savage, L. J., & Lloyd, M. R. (1987). Evaluation of drug abuse treatments: Based on first year follow-up. National Institute on Drug Abuse Monograph no. 78. Bethesda MD: National Institute of Health.

Wagner, E. F., & Waldron, H. B. (Eds.). (2001). *Innovations in adolescent substance abuse intervention*. Oxford, UK: Elsevier.

Waldron, H. B. (1997). Adolescent substance abuse and family therapy outcome: A review of randomized trials. In T H O R J. Prinz (Ed.), *Advances in clinical child psychology* (Vol. 19, pp. 199-234). New York: Plenum.

Waldron, H. B., Miller, W. R., & Tonigan, J. S. (2001). Client anger as a predictor of differential response to treatment. In: R. Longabaugh (Ed.) *Client treatment matching*. Rockville, MD: National Institutes of Health, National Institute on Alcohol Abuse and Alcoholism Research Monograph.

Weinberg, N. Z., Rahdert, E., Colliver, J. D., & Glantz, M. D. (1998). Adolescent substance abuse: A review of the past 10 years. *Journal of the American Academy of Child and Adolescent Psychiatry, 37*, 252–326.

Wood, A., Harrington, R., & Moore, A. (1996). Controlled trial of a brief cognitive-behavioural intervention in adolescent patients with depressive disorders. *Journal of Child Psychology and Psychiatry and Allied Disciplines, 37*, 737–746.

Woody, G. E., Luborsky, L., & McLellan, A. T. (1993). Psychotherapy for opiate addicts: Does it help? *Archives of General Psychiatry, 40*, 639–645.

Chapter 17
Intervention for Internet Use: Current Understanding and Perspective

Manoj Kumar Sharma and P. Thamil Selvan

17.1 Introduction

With the advancement of technologies, the Internet has revolutionized how we communicate and its flow has enabled and opened up entirely new forms of social interaction, activities, and organization, with its widespread usability and access. The emergence of social networking websites, such as Facebook®, Twitter®, and Orkut®, has not only made it possible to find existing acquaintances via net and renew communication but also has created newer patterns of socialization and interaction in the virtual world. Thus, the metaphor "global village" is often used to describe how the Internet has shortened distances between people and facilitated the flow of information. Researchers have associated Internet addiction to addictive syndromes similar to impulse-control disorders on the Axis I scale in the DSM, and pathological gambling was viewed as most akin to this phenomenon.

The term Internet addiction has generally being used to describe a variety of behaviors regarding computer use that are dysfunctional in nature; or in other words, it is characterized by excessive or poorly controlled preoccupations, urges, or behaviors regarding computer use and Internet access that leads to impairment or distress.

When Internet addiction was first conceptualized as a separate psychiatric disorder in 1996 by Kimberly Young, it sparked a controversial debate among both clinicians and academicians. While some researchers have conceptualized it as an "Addiction" and classified it along with alcohol, drug, and other substance abuse (Griffiths 1999), others have modeled it on obsessive-compulsive disorder

M.K. Sharma (✉)
Department of Clinical Psychology, NIMHANS, Bangalore, India
e-mail: mks712000@yahoo.co.in

P. Thamil Selvan
NIMHANS, Bangalore, India
e-mail: thamil.selvan04@gmail.com

M. Mehta and R. Sagar (eds.), *A Practical Approach to Cognitive Behaviour Therapy for Adolescents*, DOI 10.1007/978-81-322-2241-5_17

or impulse-control disorders. The first formal attempt to develop the identifying symptoms for Internet addiction was proposed by Young (1996) who modified the pathological gambling criteria from DSM-IV to develop an eight-item questionnaire, to screen for Internet addition, which she diagnosed on the basis of at least 5 of the 8 characteristic symptoms present in the preceding 6 months.

Young's eight item Diagnostic Questionnaire of Internet Addiction

1.	Do you feel preoccupied with the Internet (think about previous online activity or anticipation of next online session)?
2.	Do you feel the need to use the Internet with increasing amounts of time in order to achieve satisfaction?
3.	Have you repeatedly made unsuccessful efforts to control, cut back, or stop Internet use?
4.	Do you feel restless, moody, depressed, or irritable when attempting to cut down or stop Internet use?
5.	Do you stay online longer than originally intended?
6.	Have you jeopardized or risked the loss of a significant relationship, job, educational or career opportunity because of the Internet?
7.	Have you lied to family members, therapist, or others to conceal the extent of involvement with the Internet?
8.	Do you use the Internet as a way of escaping from problems or of relieving a dysphoric mood (e.g., feelings of helplessness, guilt, anxiety, depression)?

Young's criteria have been criticized by Beard and Wolf (2001) on the grounds that they are weighted too heavily on self-report and the characteristic symptoms appear to be more consistent with an impulse-control disorder rather than a true addiction. At least one of the last three criteria is required for diagnosis, as these criteria impact the person's ability to cope and function. Criteria for identifying Internet addiction (Beard and Wolf 2001) are as follows

1. Is preoccupied with the Internet (think about previous online activity or anticipate next online session).
2. Needs to use the Internet with increased amounts of time in order to achieve satisfaction.
3. Has made unsuccessful efforts to control, cut back, or stop Internet use.
4. Is restless, moody, depressed, or irritable when attempting to cut down or stop Internet use.
5. Has stayed online longer than originally intended.

17.2 Clinical Features

Internet addiction is not recognized as a formal mental health disorder. However, mental health professionals who have written about the subject note symptoms or behaviors that, when present in sufficient numbers, may indicate problematic use. These include the following:

Preoccupation with the Internet: User often thinks about the Internet while he or she is offline.

Loss of control: Addicted users feel unable or unwilling to get up from the computer and walk away. They sit down to check e-mail or look up a bit of information, and end up staying online for hours.

Inexplicable sadness or moodiness when not online: Like any other substance, there occur mood altering side effects when the addicted user is refrained from using the Internet.

Distraction (Using the Internet as an antidepressant): One common symptom of many Internet addicts is the compulsion to cheer oneself up by surfing the Web.

Dishonesty in regard to Internet use: Addicts may end up lying to employers or family members about the amount of time they spend online, or find other ways to conceal the depth of their involvement with the Internet.

Loss of boundaries or inhibitions: While this often pertains to romantic or sexual boundaries, such as sharing sexual fantasies online or participating in cyber sex, inhibitions can also be financial or social.

Creation of virtual intimate relationships with other Internet users: Web-based relationships often cause those involved to spend excessive amounts of time online, attempting to make connections, and dating via the Net.

Loss of a significant relationship due to Internet use: When users spend too much time on the Web, they often neglect their personal relationships. Over time, such relationships may fail as partners simply refuse to be treated badly and break off from relations with the addicted individual.

17.3 Types of Internet Addiction

Researchers have attempted to identify subtypes or sub-categories of Internet addiction, and various such proposals have been given till date, but they are yet to reach some common consensus. One of the first such attempts was made by Young (1999), who categorized it into five specific subtypes:

Cyber-sexual addiction: Compulsive use of Internet pornography, adult chat rooms, or adult fantasy role-play sites impacting negatively on real-life intimate relationships.

Cyber-relationship addiction: Addiction to social networking, chat rooms, and messaging to the point where virtual, online friends become more important than real-life relationships with family and friends.

Net compulsions: Net compulsions encompass a broad category of behaviors including obsessive online gambling, shopping, or stock-trading behaviors.

Information overload: Compulsive web surfing or database searching, leading to lower work productivity and less social interaction with family and friends.

Computer addiction: Obsessive playing of offline computer games, such as Solitaire or Minesweeper, or obsessive computer programming.

A brief description of the widely used and commonly observed types in the context of Internet addiction is as follows:

Cyber-sexual addiction: Internet sex addiction typically involves viewing, downloading, and trading online pornography.

17.4 Psychiatric Comorbidities with Internet Addiction

Liu and Potenza (2007) studied and suggested that Internet addiction is frequently associated with DSM-IV Axis I and Axis II disorders. Several cross-sectional studies show that comorbidities are norm rather than exception in case of Internet addiction. Block (2008) had noted that nearly 86 % of the individuals with Internet addiction have at least one comorbid psychiatric condition, in some cases with multiple comorbidities.

The most common psychiatric comorbidities that are found are mood disorders, anxiety disorders, attention deficit/hyperactivity disorder, impulse-control disorders, and substance dependence.

Shapira et al. (2000) reported DSM-IV Axis I diagnosis in all 20 problematic Internet users they assessed. In all, 70 % met the criteria for a current bipolar disorder and the figure jumped to 80 % when a lifetime diagnosis was considered. It was also noted that 35 % met the criteria for an impulse-control disorder, including intermittent explosive disorder (10 %), kleptomania (5 %), pathological gambling (5 %), and compulsive buying (20 %).

Bernardi and Pallanti (2009) found ADHD (14 %), hypomania (7 %), generalized anxiety disorder (15 %), social anxiety disorder (15 %), dysthymia (7 %), obsessive-compulsive personality disorder (7 %), borderline personality disorder (14 %), and avoidant personality disorder (7 %) to be associated with comorbidities. The same study also found that Internet addicts had higher mean score on the Dissociative Experience Scale, suggesting that dissociative symptoms were related to the severity and impact of Internet addiction.

Yen et al. (2009) noted an association between Internet addiction and harmful alcohol use. Comorbidity with other psychiatric conditions is also common among addictive disorders clouding the actual awareness that a client may suffer from a computer-related problem. While self-referrals for Internet addiction are becoming more common, often the client does not present with complaints of computer addiction. The client initially may present with signs of clinical depression, bipolar disorder, anxiety, or obsessive-compulsive tendencies, only for treating professional to later discover signs of Internet abuse upon further examination. Even when confronted by the therapist, a client may actively minimize the addictive behavior justifying his or her need to be online.

17.5 Tools Used for Assessment

Multiple assessment instruments have been developed by researchers from the west and the east. They are derived from different theoretical underpinnings and do not agree on the underlying dimensions that constitute problematic Internet use (Beard 2005). The most widely used instruments are the Diagnostic Questionnaire (DQ) (Young 1996) and the Internet Addiction Test (IAT) (Young 1998). Caplan (2002) has described the Generalized Problematic Internet Use Scale (GPIUS), which was reliable and valid in a preliminary study. Davis et al. (2002) described the Online Cognition Scale (OCS), a 36-item questionnaire they recommended for clinical assessment and pre-employment screening. Other instruments include Brenner's Internet-Related Addictive Behaviour Inventory (IRABI) (Brenner 1997) and the Pathological Internet Use Scale (PIUS) (Morahan-Martin and Schumacher 2000).

17.5.1 Psychotherapy

When it comes to psychotherapeutic interventions for Internet addiction, no particular form of psychological intervention can be suggested as being the gold standard for its treatment. Treatment includes a variety of inventions and a mix of psychotherapy theories to not only treat the behavior but to address underlying psychosocial issues that often coexistent with this addiction (e.g., social phobia, mood disorders, sleep disorders, marital dissatisfaction, job burnout). However, the most frequently investigated approaches had been cognitive behavioral therapy (CBT) and motivational interview (Wieland 2005; Young 1999).

The psychotherapeutic intervention can also be done under two contexts—total abstinence and controlled use. Given the Internet's numerous advantages and positive uses in day-to-day life, it is impractical to try the total abstinence model (as in treatment of substance addictions), even in those who are addicted to the Internet. The guiding principle should primarily be "moderate and controlled use." In the abstinence model, the individual abstains from a particular Internet application (e.g., using chat rooms or playing games) and uses other applications in moderation. This model of abstinence is recommended for those who have tried and failed to limit their use of a particular application (Murali and George 2007). The intervention starts with collecting information about the initiating factor as well as the maintaining factors:

17.5.2 Case Vignette

Ms 16-year-old female, educated up to 11th std presented with the complaints of increase use of social networking sites for the last four years. Temperamentally, easy-going child and extrovert. Personal history revealed normal developmental milestones, average in studies and attained puberty at the age of 12 and absence of high-risk behaviors presented with the complaints of increase use of social networking sites for the last four years. She spent on an average 6–7 h per day on social networking sites and started neglecting other works and academic works. Initially, it was used at home, subsequently on objections of family members, she started surfing at cyber café. Stealing and lying in form of excuse present to support her habit. The content shared on the social networking sites was to have chat with friend. She had currently 350 online friends. She attributed the usages to feeling of enjoyment, free time and boredom. She met some of these online friends. She disliked sexual comments/gesture during offline meeting/cheating happen due to fake status.

Behavioral analysis allows us to collect the information on following domains: "On what days do you typically get connected to the Internet? What time of the day do you usually sign into the Internet? How long do you usually stay connected in a typical login? Where do you usually use the computer?". Whether the users are dependent on a specific function of the Internet, because constant and frequent use of a particular function may trigger Internet addiction and it can also serve as an indication for the interventions (Is it a specific Internet addiction or a general one?). To do this, the answers to the following questions are evaluated: "What functions of the Internet/social networking sites are you using? How many hours on average do you allocate for each function in a week? Can you list the functions you use from the most important one to the least important one? What aspect of each function do you like the most?" (Young 1999).

Other useful questions for eliciting for usages includes

Reason for Initiation: How did your social networking sites start and continue? (may have started after a loss) and What are the others factors affecting the continuity of usages of social networking sites.

Perception of Problems: What do you think your problem exactly is, how do you interpret it? ; What are the effects of social networking sites on your living environments?;

Motivation for Treatment: Why did you come for treatment at this moment? (at his/her own will, directed by his/her relatives, changed social roles, coincidence) ; How long can you keep away from getting connected to the social networking sites when you feel the desire/urge to get connected to it? (how long he/she can tolerate boredom).

Assessment: Readiness to change questionnaire can be used to assess the motivation to change the current behaviors (Heather et al. 1999).

Motivation Enhancement: A general term for any part of the hypothetical psychological process which involves the experiencing of needs and drives and the behavior that leads to the goal which satisfies them. Before recovery is possible, clients must be motivated to enter treatment. Often, a loved one, a friend, a spouse, or a parent has pushed the individual into seeking help. The client may feel resentful and deny the extent that use of the Internet is a problem.

Like substance use disorders, motivational enhancement therapy (MET) is a systematic intervention approach for evoking change in Internet addicts. It is based on principles of motivational psychology and is designed to produce rapid, internally motivated change. This treatment strategy does not attempt to guide and train the client, step by step, through recovery, but instead employs motivational strategies to mobilize the client's own change resources.

Motivational interviewing is assisted by motivational balance exercise. To help a person make the decision of change, it would be a useful exercise to encourage him/her to consider the advantages and disadvantages of changing and continuing to use of Internet. This will help him/her understand the need for change after weighing the costs and benefit. To facilitate change from using to not using the Internet, you have to tip the balance so that the positives of quitting outweigh the negatives of continuing Internet use. This could, in turn, enhance the person's commitment to change

The process of change

1. Healthy does not happen in one step—people progress through five stages on the way to successful change.
2. Movement through the stages occurs as people utilize distinct (virtually universal) processes of change.
3. Progress through the early stages is dependent on particular shifts in the person's decisional balance, i.e., how they see the pros and cons of quitting.
4. Initiating and maintaining healthy use requires a sufficient sense of confidence—self-efficacy—in one's ability to actually carry out the actions required to change. People change as they progress through five stages.
5. There are five stages of change:
   - Precontemplation: Not thinking about healthy use in the foreseeable future
   - Contemplation: Thinking about changing but not ready to change
   - Preparation: Committed to and getting ready to change
   - Action: healthy use of technology
   - Maintenance: maintaining healthy use (Miller 1991)

Session Objectives:

Helping People to change Internet use

It involves changing their excessive use of Internet as well as enhancing their motivation to maintain them.

Why people do not change Internet use:

There are usually four forces which govern change:

Explore the forces keeping a person in his/her current behavior:

- What I like about my current behavior: (enjoyment associated with meeting new people)
- What I fear about the new behavior (online friend give fake information)

Explores forces encouraging change to a new behavior:

- What I dislike about my current behavior (sexual gesture/comments—online/offline)
- What I imagine the advantages of the new behavior would be (controlled use lead to save time/development of lifestyle and can avoid mishappening)

When the sum of the two forces discouraging change is greater than the sum of the two forces encouraging change, people are encouraged to maintain the status quo. Ignorance about consequences of excessive use or inability to avoid the pleasure associated with it are the major factors that discourage change.

When people change

When the sum of the two forces encouraging change is greater than the sum of the two forces discouraging change, a person is likely to start thinking seriously about changing.

The desire to change is a dynamic phenomenon. Various psychosocial factors influence the maintenance of desire for change.

The health professional's goal is to help the person to maintain the change and develop various coping behaviors.

Follow up sessions can be planned once to twice per week in the first 3 months, subsequently, it can be planned at once in 15 days.

17.5.3 Cognitive-Based Therapy

Objective: Assessment

Those who have asserted that Internet addiction is primarily maintained cognitively believe that cognitive behavioral therapy may be a possible solution (Davis 2001). Davis (2001) stated that this addiction is formed once the patients feel they have no social and family support, thereby developing the so-called maladaptive cognitions (which are the mental evaluations or screeners of interpretation) about themselves and the world. It includes two components: functional analysis and skill training.

Functional analysis includes triggers/reason for use (e.g., boredom) that lead to a subject's maladaptive behaviors and the immediate beneficial consequences (e.g., feeling good) that maintained the maladaptive behaviors as well as the structured assessment on Internet addiction test, whereas skill training includes development of coping style and dealing with various triggers.

17.5.4 Technique

Cognitive restructuring: The Internet users generally believe that the virtual world treats them (i.e., get more pleasure) well in comparison with real world. It manifest in form of all-or-nothing maladaptive cognition such as " I am respected more in the virtual world" "Nobody care for likes and dislikes" "I always have to restrain myself or obey my parent/brother in the real world whereas in virtual world I can do anything"; these types of belief can be challenged in a therapeutic settings by dysfunctional method of fulfilling the unfulfilled need using virtual field as well as by imparting the skill training to develop alternative pleasurable activities in the real world. It can be done by helping the client to shift from virtual to reality: By understanding one's virtual social link/world and the needs it fulfilled, it can provide insights and facilitate the process of enriching the real lives and reduce their indulgence in the virtual world.

Coping strategies: It has been seen that excessive Internet users use avoidant coping/less problem-solving styles (Huanhuan 2009). Client can be helped to develop coping strategy based on their strength and resources, and it will help them to expand their offline activities. The client has been counsel to work on developing alternative pleasurable activities, i.e., she was interested in pottery/ yoga to make herself relaxed. She joined pottery classes and showed interest to persist them and acknowledge the lesser need to go to social networking sites.

Follow up sessions can be planned once to twice per week in the first 3 months, subsequently, it can be planned at once in 15 days.

17.5.5 Other Approaches

Young approach toward Internet management:

Young (1999) suggests eight therapeutic techniques:

1. **Practice the opposite**: Discover clients' patterns of Internet use and disrupt these patterns by suggesting new schedules. For example, if the patient goes online as soon as he or she arrives home from work and remains online until it is time to go to bed, the clinician may suggest that he or she takes a break for dinner, watches the news, and only then goes back to the computer.
2. **External stoppers**: Clients can use real events or activities to prompt themselves to log off of the Internet. For example, the use of an alarm clock to function as a warning for the patient that it is time to turn off the computer and carry out some other offline activity, such as going to work or school.
3. **Setting goals**: Help clients to come up with specific, achievable goals with regard to the amount of time spent online. For example, if the patient remains online all day long on Saturdays and Sundays, a schedule with brief sessions of use followed by brief, although frequent, discontinuations could be designed.
4. **Abstinence from certain applications**: Encourage abstinence to only those applications that the client is unable to control. This means that patients should stop navigating particular Web sites or even certain applications (e.g., MSN, Facebook, online games) that are most attractive for them, discontinuing the use from time to time, shifting to alternative forms such as sending and receiving e-mails, news search, bibliographical sources for their school works.
5. **Reminder cards**: Use visible cues that remind the clients of the costs of their Internet addiction and the benefits of breaking the addiction. For example, a card containing the five major problems caused by Internet addiction, as well as the five major benefits from reducing the use (or ultimately refraining from using a given application) should be listed.
6. **Personal inventory**: Help the clients to recognize the benefits of breaking their habit by showing them all the activities that they used to engage in or cannot find the time for because of Internet addiction.
7. **Support groups**: These are useful because many Internet addicts are said to use the Internet to compensate for a lack of social support.
8. **Family therapy**: Family interventions are necessary to address relational problems that may have contributed to or resulted from Internet addiction.

Family-oriented therapies: Evidence suggest the efficacy of family-based treatment in decreasing the Internet use (Doug 2012). The multidimensional family therapy (MDFT) targets three domains: adolescent, the parents (other family members), and the interaction of adolescents and the parents.

Objectives: To enhance the understanding of negative consequences of excessive Internet use, coping skills, increasing prosocial peer behaviors, and enhancing parenting practices.

Sessions: Individual sessions with adolescent focus on facilitating the engaging in treatment and enhancing motivation for alternative behaviors in coping with high-risk situations. Individual sessions with parents focus on enhancing the healthy use of Internet; increasing the parenting practices observing the child Internet use and other behaviors, explaining the rationale for developing healthy use of technology, and setting rule in relation to Internet use.

The joint session can focus on parental commitment to the adolescent as well as developing a positive parent–child relationship. It is an essential prerequisite for effective parental monitoring of child Internet use.

Barrier to treatment: The main barriers manifest in the form educating the clients about the healthy use; inability to see the problematic usages of available technology and to seek help in the formal mental health facility.

These can be overcome by raising awareness about the excessive use of technology (Internet/social networking, etc.) through mass media/educational material or individual contact/referral for help to community mental service to help to overcome stigma, and even telephone counseling or email contact can be facilitated to retain the person in the treatment.

17.6 Conclusion

We live in such an era where there is a consistent engagement with technology—culminating into our gradual dependence on it. There are times when it is necessary to use technology in ways that are meaningful and productive, but this dependence often blurs the line between necessity and addiction. Internet is a medium that has so radically changed our lives, by creating newer possibilities in the dimensions of information and communication. Yet too much dependence on Internet also has created new social problems of people becoming socially withdrawn, avoiding working in collaborative teams, fearing face-to-face contact, and preferring only online communication. Also, deserving of exploration are the more subtle psychological changes that occur in the virtual world, such as online disinhibition and increased risk-taking. Thus, owing to these negative consequences, the concept of Internet addiction as a psychiatric disorder has taken shape, though it is still in an infancy stage. One of the primary reasons for this is the lack of any standardized diagnostic or assessment tools. Exploratory research studies are required to help us in having a better understanding about the etiological factors and prevalence rates, thereby providing a better platform to carry out proper treatment interventions.

References

Beard, K. W. (2005). Internet addiction: A review of current assessment techniques and potential assessment questions. *CyberPsychology and Behaviour, 8*, 7–14.

Beard, K. W., & Wolf, E. M. (2001). Modification in the proposed diagnostic criteria for Internet addiction. *Cyberpsychology and Behaviour, 4*, 377–383.

Bernardi, S., & Pallanti, S. (2009). Internet addiction: A descriptive clinical study focusing on comorbidities and dissociative symptoms. *Comprehensive Psychiatry, 50*, 510–516.

Block, J. J. M. D. (2008). Issues for DSM-V: Internet addiction. *Amercian Journal of Psychiatry, 165*(3), 306–307.

Brenner, V. (1997). Psychology of computer use: XLVII. Parameters of Internet use, abuse and addiction: The first 90 days of the Internet usage survey. *Psychological Reports, 80*, 879–882.

Caplan, S. E. (2002). Problematic Internet use and psychosocial well-being: Development of a theory-based cognitive-behavioural measurement instrument. *Computer in Human Behaviour, 18*, 553–575.

Davis, R. A. (2001). A cognitive behavioural model of pathological Internet use. *Computers in Human Behaviour, 17*, 187–195.

Davis, R. A., Flett, G. L., & Besser, A. (2002). Validation of a new scale for measuring problematic Internet use: Implications for pre-employment screening. *CyberPsychology and Behaviour, 5*, 331–345.

Griffiths, M. (1999). Internet addiction: Fact or fiction? *Psychologist, 12*, 246–251.

Han, D. H., Kim, S. M., Lee, Y. S., & Renshaw, P. F. (2012). The effect of family therapy on the changes in the severity of on-line game play and brain activity in adolescents with on-line game addiction. *Psychiatry Research Neuroimaging, 2002*(2), 126031.

Heather, N., Luce, A., Peck, D., Dunbar, B., & James, I. (1999). Development of a treatment version of the readiness to change questionnaire. *Addiction Research, 7*, 63–83.

Li, H., Wang, J., & Wang, L. (2009). A survey on the generalized problematic internet use in Chinese College students and its relations to stressful events and coping style. *International Journal of Mental Health and Addiction, 792*, 333–346.

Liu, T., & Potenza, M. N. (2007). Problematic Internet use: Clinical implications. *CNS Spectrums, 12*, 453–466.

Miller, W. R., & Rollnick, S. (1991). *Motivational interviewing: Preparing people for change*. New York: Guilford Press.

Morahan-Martin, J., & Schumacher, P. (2000). Incidence and correlates of pathological Internet use among college students. *Computer in Human Behaviour, 16*, 13–29.

Murali, V., & George, S. (2007). Lost online: An overview of Internet addiction. *Advances in Psychiatric Treatment, 13*, 24–30.

Shapira, N., Goldsmith, T., Keck, P, Jr, et al. (2000). Psychiatric features of problematic Internet use. *Journal of Affective Disorder, 57*, 267–272.

Wieland, D. M. (2005). Computer addiction: Implications for nursing psychotherapy practice. *Perspectives in Psychiatric Care, 41*, 153–161.

Yen, J. Y., Yen, C.F., Chen, C.S., Tang, T.C., Ko, C.H. (2009). The association between adult ADHD symptoms and internet addiction among college students: the gender difference. *Cyberpsychololgy and Behavior, 12*(2), 187–191.

Young, K. S. (1996). Internet addiction: The emergence of a new clinical disorder. *Cyberpsychology and Behaviour, 3*, 237–244.

Young, K. S. (1998). Internet addiction test (IAT). Available on: http://www.netaddiction.com/resources/Internet_addiction_test.htm. Accessed November 28, 2011.

Young, K. S. (1999). Internet addiction: Symptoms, evaluation and treatment. In L. VandeCreek & T. Jackson (Eds.), *Innovations in clinical practice: A source book* (pp. 19–31). Florida: Professional Resource Press.

Chapter 18
Obesity

Tanu Gupta, Vandana Jain and A.C. Ammini

18.1 Introduction

Most of our parents and grandparents used to perceive a fat child as a healthy child, but unlike the past, today obesity is considered as a major health-risk condition. The greater concern is that the risks of overweight during childhood will persist into adolescence and adulthood (Shah et al. 2008). In the past two decades, the prevalence of adolescent obesity has risen greatly worldwide and this excessive fatness has become a major health problem in both developed and developing countries including India (Ebbeling et al. 2002). There is a shift in nutrition and lifestyle in terms of increased popularity of fast foods, soft drinks, sedentary lifestyle, physical inactivity, increased television viewing and computer use are the common trends adopted by adolescents today. These can be seen as the causal or maintaining factors of childhood obesity (Kumari et al. 2011). Fifty to eighty percentage of obese adolescents grow up as obese adults and fall into risk group of diabetes, coronary heart disease, hypertension, asthma, sleep apnoea and many more obesity-related diseases (Styne 2001; Sinha et al. 2002; Belamarich et al. 2000; Chan et al. 2004). Once established, obesity acquires a decisive influence on the adolescent's mental health as well. Obese adolescents are more likely to suffer

T. Gupta (✉)
Department of Psychiatry, All India Institute of Medical Sciences, New Delhi, India
e-mail: tanubathla@gmail.com

V. Jain
Department of Paediatrics, All India Institute of Medical Sciences, New Delhi, India
e-mail: drvandanajain@gmail.com

A.C. Ammini
All India Institute of Medical Sciences, New Delhi, India
e-mail: aca433@yahoo.com

M. Mehta and R. Sagar (eds.), *A Practical Approach to Cognitive Behaviour Therapy for Adolescents*, DOI 10.1007/978-81-322-2241-5_18

from peer problems, high level of anxiety, depression, negative self-esteem and body dissatisfaction in comparison with their normal weight peers (Isnard et al. 2003; Goldfried et al. 2010).

18.1.1 Definition of Obesity

The WHO Consultation on Obesity (1998) provides a simple definition of obesity as "*a condition of abnormal or excessive fat accumulation in adipose tissue to the extent that health may be impaired*". Body mass index (BMI) is considered to be the most suitable adiposity index for adolescents as supported by the European Childhood Obesity Group, the National Centre for Health Statistics (NCHS) and WHO. BMI is defined as body weight in kilogram divided by height, in metres squared. Operationally, the criteria for overweight or obesity are levels of adiposity exceeding some pre-specified BMI cut-off. Across the world, different BMI classification systems have developed, which has given rise to various definitions arising from the use of different cut-off points for different reference populations.

18.2 Prevalence of Adolescent Obesity in India

Obesity is one of the most prevalent nutritional diseases of adolescents in many developed and developing countries (WHO 1998). The World Health Organization (2002) declared overweight as one of the top ten health risks in the world. India is adapting to globalization, western culture and lifestyle changes rapidly and following a trend of other countries that are steadily becoming obese. Adolescent obesity and overweight is emerging problem in India (as indicated by recent prevalence studies of obesity in India). Number of school-based studies conducted in the last decade reported that approximately 3–10 % of Indian adolescents are obese. Obesity was found to be more prevalent in boys and adolescent belonging to urban background (Mohan et al. 2004; Rao et al. 2006; Sharma et al. 2007; Jain et al. 2010; Kotian et al. 2010; Saraswathi et al. 2011)

18.3 Causes of Adolescent Obesity

Obesity develops as a result of various factors such as genetics, environment, psychosocial, eating habits and lifestyle. Generally, obesity occurs when a person's energy intake is more than the energy expenditure. Genetic factors and heritability plays an important role in the development of obesity in adolescents. Genetic factors interact with the obesogenic environment and put the child on higher risk of being obese. There are some medical conditions (such as Cushing's syndrome, hypothyroidism and Prader-Willi syndrome) which can cause obesity. The common causes of obesity in adolescents are poor eating habits, physical inactivity, overeating or binging, peer problems, family history of obesity, sedentary lifestyle adopted by parents and family, depression, emotional problems and stressful life events such as divorce of parents or death of beloved one.

18.4 Cognitive Behavioural Therapy

Cognitive behavioural therapy (CBT) is a psychological treatment based on the assumption that obesity is maintained by certain dysfunctional cognitions and beliefs. Thus, CBT uses behavioural techniques to change behaviours by changing antecedents and consequences and combines these with cognitive techniques designed to identify, challenge and restructure dysfunctional cognitions.

18.5 Background and Theoretical Basis of CBT

The behavioural approach to weight management originated in the 1960s from the application of learning theory to the problem of weight loss (Stuart 1967). Behaviourists started working on weight loss treatments based on the assumption that the behaviours that cause overweight were learned and could, therefore, be unlearned and replaced with more adaptive behaviours. Behavioural approach applies principles of classical and operant conditioning to the regulation of body weight.

Classical conditioning paradigm posits that eating behaviours are associated with different activities and become conditioned to occur together, e.g. when a child eats chips/junk food while watching the evening cartoon show. If these two behaviours are paired repeatedly, they develop strong association with one another that even turning on the TV alone triggers a craving for chips.

Operant conditioning approach emphasizes the importance of reinforcement and consequences to change the behaviour. An adolescent who uses food as a reward or to temporarily relieve stress will associate food with a more pleasurable state, which further increases the likelihood of the occurrence of that behaviour again and again.

Initially, behavioural approach views obesity as the result of maladaptive eating and exercise habits and thus emphasizes on the development of healthy eating and exercise behaviour. However, later on, behaviour therapist encounter with other important issues such as body dissatisfaction, low self-esteem, anxiety and stress that affect the outcome of behavioural intervention of obesity. Cognition affects emotions and behaviour thus becomes important to target for behaviour change. Then, the combination of cognitive therapy and behaviour therapy came into the existence. In the last decade, CBT has become an important part of obesity management.

18.6 Rationale of CBT for Adolescent Obesity

Till date, most of the intervention studies of adolescent obesity have recommended the use of comprehensive interventions that include behavioural therapy along with changes in diet and physical activity is the most successful approaches to improving long-term weight and health status (Jelalian et al. 1999). American Dietetic Association (2006) and the Expert Committee on the treatment of child and adolescent overweight and obesity (2007) also recommended cognitive behavioural intervention as an essential component of treatment. Considerable empirical support exists for programmes that incorporate some combination of techniques such as stimulus control, self-monitoring, goal setting, problem-solving, cognitive restructuring, parent skills training and relapse prevention in the treatment of adolescent obesity (Spear et al. 2007; Johnston et al. 2008; Stewart et al. 2008).

Recent literature also supports and recommends the use of CBT for adolescent obesity. Cochrane review of 54 randomized clinical trials on lifestyle interventions with the aim to ascertain the most effective intervention in the treatment of childhood obesity found that a behavioural lifestyle intervention with parental involvement is preferred over standard care or self-help (Oude Luttikhuis et al. 2009). Kirschenbaum and Kristen (2013) reviewed five recent expert recommendations on the treatment of adolescent obesity and found that all of the expert committees support the use of intensive dietary intervention, physical activity and cognitive behavioural counselling.

CBT has been found to be effective treatment of adolescent obesity as clearly evident in the literature. With the increasing prevalence and the recognition of the potential physical and psychosocial consequences of obesity, the need for evidence-based treatment has become an important issue for health care professionals in India. Adolescents become important target for early intervention and prevention because adolescence is a time when habits (eating and exercise) develops and it is easy to modify behaviour of adolescent in comparison with an adult. With this rationale, the present chapter has tried to target most of the obesity-related issues found in obese adolescents with the help of different evidence-based cognitive behavioural techniques.

18.7 Approaching Obese Adolescent for CBT

Specific age-related difficulties are associated with weight management in adolescents. Discussing weight could be very sensitive issue for them. The normal concerns of adolescence are independence from family and conformity with one's peer group and have positive self-esteem and satisfaction with body image. Adolescents are extremely dependent on peers for social support, identity and self-esteem. However, Overweight adolescents are more likely to be socially isolated than normal weight adolescents (Strauss and Pollack 2003). Similarly, Eisenberg et al. (2003) also reported that weight-based teasing was common by peers and family members, and these adolescent often suffered from low self-esteem, low body satisfaction and high depressive symptoms. These sensitive issues need to be handled with care while approaching obese adolescent for treatment. A non-threatening approach should be adopted by posing questions to the adolescents and encourage them to come with a best possible answer. It is important to ask right type of questions, e.g.

"*Who was the first to bring to your notice that you are gaining weight? When did that happened? What did you do when you noticed this? What happened then?*"

The above question reflects the therapist curiosity to know about the history of the problem, previous weight loss attempts and reason for relapse.

Another type of questions could be those that start with if, e.g.

Therapist: Do you want to lose weight?
Child: No
Therapist: if it were easy to lose weight then would you like to do something about it?

The second question framing would allow the child to think about it rather than simply refusing.

These small issues would help the therapist in rapport formation and allow the adolescent to open up and at the same time to maintain their need for independence and autonomy.

18.8 Assessment of an Obese Adolescent

There are some important factors to include in the comprehensive assessment of obese adolescents. It can be divided into two parts: first could be related to general history-taking approach and second could be related the behavioural and psychosocial factors associated with the obesity that needs to be targeted in the psychological intervention (Fig. 18.1; Table 18.1).

Based upon the assessment of these important aspects, therapist psycho-educate the family and adolescent about the important findings of the detailed interview and plan out the intervention.

Case Example of Assessment Findings in Obese Adolescent Girl

The mother of a 12-year-old girl came for consultation for her daughter's weight concerns and comments that the girl is concerned about her weight and is being teased about this at school and in the family. There is a family history of obesity in parents and grandparents. During the assessment it was found that the girl's main interests are sedentary activities like watching T.V., internet use and playing video games. Physical activity is limited, 'screen time' is 4–5 h a day and dietary habits put her at risk of weight gain (skipping breakfast, frequent snacking, consuming soft drinks, and high preference of junk food). The girl has not attained menarche and has a BMI above the 95th percentile on the US-CDC growth chart and normal lipid profile, liver function test, glucose and insulin levels. On psychosocial assessment, she was found to be anxious and depressed due to her increasing weight,

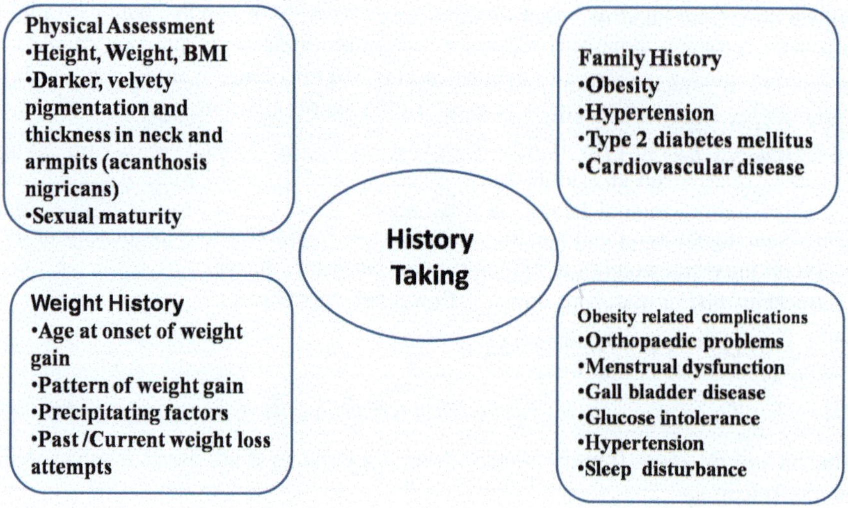

Fig. 18.1 History taking

Table 18.1 Behavioural and psychosocial assessment of obese adolescent

Behavioural assessment	Psychosocial assessment
Behavioural Analysis (ABC Charting) • Antecedent (what happened just before the behaviour) • Behaviour (detailed description of the behaviour) • Consequences (what happened after the behaviour) *Eating behaviour (Food logs)* • Foods and beverages consumed/per day • Pattern of food intake (meals, fast food, snacks) including interval between eating • Dieting, meal skipping, night time eating *Exercise behaviour (Physical activity/inactivity logs)* • Hours per day of sedentary activities (e.g. TV and video games, computer use, reading, listening to music, sleeping) • Exercise type, intensity, frequency and duration • Physically active daily routines (e.g. walking home from school, stairs climbing at home or school)	• Psychopathology (Child Behaviour Checklist by Thomas M Achenbach 1991) • Anxiety (Depression anxiety stress scale (DASS) by Lovibond and Lovibond 1995) • Stress (Stressful life event scale for Indian children by Malhotra 1993) • Body image (Body shape questionnaire by Cooper et al. 1986.) • Self-esteem (Rosenberg self-esteem scale by Rosenberg 1965) • Disordered eating pattern (Dutch eating behaviour questionnaire by Van Strein 1986, Children eating behaviour questionnaire by Wardle et al. 2001) • Isolation, Teasing, bullying, Social Support, Level of concern, motivation and stage of readiness for behavioural change (Semi-structured interview schedule)

body image concerns and previous failed attempts of weight loss. She lost her confidence and has low self-esteem. She indulged in emotional eating as well to overcome her stress. She has fewer friends as most of the people tease her about her weight. So she prefers to stay alone

Impression *Obese with high risk of further weight gain and psychosocial problems.*

18.9 Components and Structure of Cognitive Behavioural Therapy

There is enough evidence to support the effectiveness of comprehensive behavioural intervention programme that includes dietary modification and exercise routine as treatment of choice for the management of adolescent obesity. Nowadays, behavioural treatments are delivered as a package or module that includes multiple components such as psycho-education, goal setting, self-monitoring, stimulus control, diet modification, lifestyle intervention, cognitive restructuring, problem-solving, slowing the rate of eating and relapse prevention. Cognitive behavioural treatment done in group format along with individualized counselling is considered to be more efficient and less expensive to administer. Most outpatient-based behavioural interventions included 8–16 initial weekly group sessions lasting 45–90 min along with the follow-up sessions for a total duration of 4–12 months (Spear et al. 2007).

The current behavioural treatment module includes 12 weekly sessions lasting for 45–60 min followed by monthly booster sessions for a total duration of 4–12 months. It can be delivered in the group format as well as individual format as per the need of the target group. Table 18.2 presents an overview of the programme that includes the brief description of each sessions and techniques used.

Detailed description of the module is given below:

18.9.1 Session 1: Psycho-education and Self-Monitoring

Objective of the session

- To form a rapport with the adolescent
- Psycho-education of the adolescent and family
- To give brief orientation of the therapy process
- Teaching self-monitoring

Content of the session

Initial session is basically devoted to the rapport formation along with the psycho-education of obese adolescents and their parents. They are informed about the findings of the detailed assessment. A brief orientation to therapy process is also provided by specifying the number and frequency of the session. Therapist emphasizes the collaborative approach of CBT and encourages the active participation of adolescents and parents. Parents are also informed about their important role in the treatment process and how their involvement can affect the treatment outcome in a positive manner. They should be informed about the long-term aspect of treatment, weight loss and weight maintenance phase of the therapy. It is also important for

Table 18.2 Cognitive behaviour therapy module for childhood obesity (an overview)

Session no.	Session description	Techniques
Session 1–2	Psycho-education of the adolescent and family, goal setting, monitoring of food intake and physical activity/inactivity, weight	Psycho-education, goal setting, self-monitoring (food and activity logs)
Session 3	Reviewing the food and activity logs	Lifestyle intervention (targeting eating and exercise behaviour by including parent as an active agent for change)
Session 4	Homework reviewing, assessing problems and barriers	Stimulus control (environmental restructuring)
Session 5	Reviewing progress and discussing problems	Rewards, reinforcement, behavioural contract (encouragement and feedback)
Session 6	Review progress and discuss issues such as comorbid anxiety, depression and stress	Relaxation training (breathing exercises)
Session 7–8	Review progress and discuss problems and specific issues such as body dissatisfaction, low self-esteem and teasing	Cognitive restructuring
Session 9–10	Homework review and Feedback	Problem-solving and cognitive restructuring continued,
Session 11	Reviewing the change (eating and exercise behaviour), therapist also reviews the self-monitoring logs and gives positive feedback for change observed and encouragement for consistent efforts	Positive feedback, rewards, problem-solving
Session 12	Review progress, identification of high-risk situations, discuss weight maintenance and relapse prevention, review all the skills learned during the programme	Positive feedback, problem-solving, behavioural rehearsal, goal setting, self-monitoring for follow-up
4–12 months follow-up	Follow-up (reviewing the progress and barriers)	Booster sessions

the therapist to ensure that the adolescent and parents understand the rationale of different CBT techniques to target the specific behaviour change.

Psycho-education for obese adolescents and family does not mean that therapist is educating them about their weight and associated risks; however, therapist assumes that they know about their weight problems. With this assumption in mind, therapist can simply explain the BMI status of the child and ask them in a very non-judgemental manner "what do you think about it", and this approach allows the adolescent to open up about the problem and get more involved in the process of behaviour change. After listening to the adolescent's perspective, therapist educates the adolescent and parents about the need for healthy lifestyle changes and weight control.

The first session also incorporates the rationale and importance of self-monitoring. By using this technique, therapist asks the adolescent to record one's own eating and exercise behaviour. Adolescents are asked to keep a detailed record of their food intake, physical activity/inactivity and weight throughout the treatment. They are asked to maintain food logs that incorporate information regarding the type and amount of food eaten per day, calories taken in each food and frequency of specific foods and other eating-related factors such as eating situation, mood, food preferences and availability of food. Similarly, types and amounts of physical activity/inactivity are also recorded in physical activity logs. Activity logs records the structured physical activity (games, exercise routine), unstructured physical activity (walking, climbing stairs, etc.) and physical inactivity in terms sleep duration, number of hours spent on watching television and computer-related activities. They are instructed to record their behaviour daily and bring their self-monitoring logs to the sessions, providing an opportunity for feedback from therapist as well as self.

18.9.2 Session 2: Goal Setting

Objectives of the session

- Review the food and activity logs
- To set short-term and long-term goal of the therapy

Content of the session

After reviewing the food and activity logs, therapist encourage the adolescent and family to set specific, measurable, achievable, recordable and timed (SMART) goals. Adolescents are encouraged to set clearly defined behavioural goals for the target behaviour identified during assessment. Therapist helps the adolescents and parents to understand that the goal setting is a continuous process and will be continued throughout the treatment.

Goals can be divided into long-term (weight maintenance) and short-term goals. Short terms goals include relatively modest behaviour changes because long-term goals of weight management can take months or years to achieve. Therapist asks the child to set small and specific short-term goals with progressive changes in behaviour (e.g. adding 2 serving of fruit and vegetable in a day and reducing 1 serving of high calorie food/beverages, 15 min of physical activity per day and increase it up to 30 min in a week's time by adding 5 min each day, reduce television viewing from 4 to 3 h/day then 2 h/day). Setting and achieving these small goals will enhance the feelings of self efficacy in adolescent and increase their motivation for consistent efforts.

18.9.3 Session 3: Lifestyle Interventions

Objectives of the sessions

- To introduce lifestyle intervention.
- To involve parents as an agents of behaviour change.

Content of the session

The main objective of behaviour treatment of obesity is lifelong change of unhealthy behaviour. Therefore, behaviour therapist encourages the child to take low calorie food of his/her preference that they can continue to eat for rest of their life and ask them to engage in simple exercise in the form of walking that can be a part of their daily routine. Session 3 focuses upon the lifestyle intervention for the family as a whole. In lifestyle intervention, therapist targets the eating and exercise behaviour of adolescents. With the help of self-monitoring, therapist first identify eating behaviours that lead to weight gain in adolescent and then target them one by one in the process. Eating behaviours that are generally identified in obese adolescents are skipping breakfast/meal, frequent snacking, eating out, eating fast, preferences for junk food and binge eating in response to negative emotional state.

It is well known that eating habits of adolescents are largely a family affair especially in India. Thus, therapist involves parents as active agents to bring a change in their children's eating behaviour by establishing a healthy lifestyle for the family as a whole. Therapist educates parents about their role in behavioural change and asks them to use following tips to help adolescents in achieving their goals. Parents are asked to keep the handout of the following tips with them and paste it in their most frequent used room.

18.9.4 Session 4: Stimulus Control

Objective of the session

- To help the adolescent and parents in restructuring environment for promoting healthy eating and exercise behaviour

Content of the session

Session 4 focuses upon the environmental restructuring by using the technique of stimulus control. It involves controlling stimuli or cues that encourage or maintain the unhealthy behaviour (overeating, eating in absence of hunger and physical inactivity) and at the same time, providing cues that promote necessary lifestyle changes. Adolescents are asked to control stimuli by avoiding high-risk situations such as fast-food restaurants, buffets food, sweets shop and convenience stores. It is assumed that reducing exposure to such situations and problem foods is likely to reduce their consumption. Parents are also involved in the process by asking them to avoid buying and bringing into the home high sugary/high fat snacks, keep tempting items out of sight and serving small portions, as it may help to reduce overeating. Stimulus control is also used to increase physical activity of the adolescents by asking them to keep walking shoes and exercise clothes readily available. Stimulus control is basically based on the problems identified in self-monitoring logs. Therapist helps the adolescent to restructure the environment in such a way that leads to less chances of overeating, e.g. if an adolescent reports that he has a habit of eating a packet of chips/high fat snacks while sitting in front of TV in the evening, then by repeated pairing, this high fat snacks consumption has become associated with watching television. In this case, therapist suggests restricting eating behaviour only on the dining table.

18.9.5 Session 5: Reinforcing the Positive Behaviour

Objectives of the session

- To establish behavioural contract indicating specific rewards for specific behavioural change
- Motivate adolescent using rewards and reinforcement

Content of the session

It is well known that reinforcement/rewards work well while working with children and adolescents. It becomes easy to change children's behaviour by using reinforcement or rewards. For obese children, rewards received in terms of social acceptance, wearing smaller size clothes, decreased health risks, compliments from others can be very reinforcing in the early stages of weight loss, but the difficulty of maintaining weight loss suggests that additional positive reinforcement is needed. This module incorporates specific homework assignments with positive reinforcement contingent on successful behavioural change for motivating children. Parents are instructed not to use food as rewards for obese adolescents rather than involving them in pleasant activities such as an evening out, watching movie with friends, a weekend outing, or time spent on a favourite hobby or giving materialistic things such as new clothes and watch can be rewarding for them. Rewards can be decided by adolescent and parents together and should be related to something that encourages positive behaviour, e.g. sporting equipment such as cricket bat, badminton racket and football.

In this session, therapist also establish behavioural contract with the child, in which adolescent sign a written statement with therapist indicating specific reward for specific behaviour change. Contracts are used to help the adolescent in keeping their focus on the goal. Parents and adolescent are taught to keep the goal realistic and identify appropriate rewards. Parents are also taught the importance of providing rewards soon after they are earned. The signing of a "behavioural contract" enhances the child's commitment towards his goals within the predefined allotted time period.

18.9.6 Session 6: Addressing Comorbid Conditions

Objectives of the session

- Assessing and understanding the mental state of the adolescent.
- Targeting comorbid issues such as anxiety, stress and depression.

Content of the session

Session 6 focus upon the specific issues related to comorbid depression, stress or anxiety. Therapist reviews the homework and praise the child for his/her consistent efforts. At the same time, therapist tried to explore the mental state of the child by discussing the child's feelings in general and specific to the treatment process, e.g.

Therapist: *So how are you feeling now days?*
Child: *ok.*
Therapist: *tell me your experience about therapy*?
Child: *It's ok but I feel it's taking too long. It is not easy to keep records of everything and control myself everywhere. Sometimes I feel frustrating.*
Therapist empathize with the child by saying that "*I know weight loss is a long term, difficult and frustrating process*"
Child: "*Yes, you know, I am doing everything to lose weight but still have not lost much. What is the use of putting so much effort? Sometimes I am worried that nothing is going to change in me*"

The above statement clearly reflects the child's anxiety, stress and feelings of hopelessness. Therapist tries to help the child to be realistic about his/her expectation of weight loss. Therapist also teaches deep breathing relaxation exercises to the child and asks to practise them three times in a day and stay relaxed. Before closing the session, therapist asks the child to note down all the negative thoughts or feelings in their self-mooring logs and bring them to the next session.

18.9.7 Session 7: Restructuring Negative Cognitions

Objectives of the session

- To target negative cognitions
- Teaching adolescent to identify negative thoughts, challenge and correct them with the alternative thought

Content of the session

Session 7 focus upon the negative cognitions that generally undermine the weight control efforts. Adolescents are taught to identify their negative thoughts (through self-monitoring) and then challenge and correct them with more rational thoughts. These negative thoughts are known as cognitive errors and can take several forms, such as dichotomous thinking (e.g. "If I can't exercise for 30 min, I should not do it at all") and rationalization (e.g. "I've had a stressful day; I deserve my favourite ice cream"). With this technique, therapist helps adolescent to understand the relationship between their thoughts and behaviour. As part of cognitive restructuring, adolescent develops more positive self-statements to assist in behaviour change. Cognitive restructuring also targets the negative thoughts associated with previous failed attempts of weight loss and discrepancy between the expected and real weight loss. While entering into the treatment setting, most of the adolescents expect fast and a highest level of weight loss; however, when they encounter with the opposite then disappointment come in place. These disappointments affect the process and motivation of weight loss.

These disappointments also lead to excuses such as

"Everyone in my family is overweight, I am born with this so can't change" counter argument for this negative thought is "that makes weight loss harder for me; not impossible; I have faith that my efforts will get succeeded."

"It's taking too long to lose the weight" counter argument is "but more important is that I am losing it"

18.9.8 Session 8: Addressing Body Image Concerns and Low Self-esteem

Objectives of the session

- To discuss specific issues such as teasing, body image disturbances and low self-esteem.
- To improve self-esteem and body satisfaction.

Content of the session

In this session, therapist discusses the issues such as teasing faced by obese adolescents, body image disturbances leading to low self-esteem and try to enhance their self-esteem by using cognitive restructuring. In adolescents, self-esteem and self confidence is largely dependent on their own physical appearance and how other people perceive them. Most of the time obese adolescents are perceived as lazy, stupid and not good looking even by their friends and relative. Sometimes parents or siblings may also get involved in teasing overweight adolescents. These perceptions and comments strongly affect child's self-esteem. Therapist discusses all these issues with the adolescent and parents by involving them in a simple exercise. Therapist asks adolescent to write down their positive characteristics other than their physical appearance. Similarly parents are also asked to write down the positive aspects of their child's nature other than their appearance. After this exercise, parents are encouraged to focus on the positive traits of the child other than the physical appearance and praise their children for academic successes, good sense of humour, caring and responsible nature. Therapist also encouraged adolescent to accept their body and positive look of themselves and motivate them to engage in the process of weight management.

18.9.9 Session 9: Problem-Solving Skills Training

Objectives of the session

- Teaching effective problem-solving skills to adolescents and parents

Content of the session

Session 9 focus upon the discussion of the day to day problems encountered by the adolescents and parents. These problems make the process more difficult and frustrating for the adolescent and family. So problem-solving skill training becomes an important part of the module. Therapist asks adolescent about the problems that they have faced in the past week and problems that they anticipate in the coming weeks. Adolescents and parents are encouraged to devise solutions to their problems, asking them how they have solved similar problems in the past, or how they might advise a close friend to solve the same kind of problem.

This problem-solving skill training also involves the teaching effective problem-solving steps to adolescents as well as parents that they can practise to solve their day to day problems. These steps are given below:

1. Identify and define the problem
2. Identify several potential solutions
3. Evaluate each alternative
4. Choose a solution
5. Implement the solution
6. Evaluate results

Therapist demonstrates the use of all these steps by taking an example of a recent problem identified by the child and encourages the child to apply this effective problem-solving approach to future difficulties.

18.9.10 Session 10: Cognitive Restructuring and Problem-Solving

Objectives of the session

- Review progress and continue cognitive restructuring.

Content of the session

Therapist reviews child's attempts of effective problem-solving and suggests improvement if needed. Cognitive restructuring continued targeting negative cognitions and issues related to body dissatisfaction and self-esteem.

18.9.11 Session 11: Review Change

Objectives of the session

- To assess change in eating, exercise, weight and cognitions

Content of the session

Therapist reviews the self-monitoring logs (change in eating and exercise behaviour, cognitions, weight) and gives positive feedback for change observed and encouragement for consistent efforts. In this session, therapist also prepares the adolescent and parents for termination of the therapy and asks the child to anticipate and note down the future high-risk situations and discuss in the next session.

18.9.12 Session 12: Weight Maintenance and Relapse Prevention

Objectives of the session

- To discuss high-risk situation.
- Teaching adolescent how to handle such situations.

Content of the session

Session 12 emphasize on weight maintenance and relapse prevention before terminating the therapy. It is well known that weight maintenance is often a challenge for obese adolescents. Weight regain after completion of treatment is very common. To handle this situation, therapist teaches adolescents to anticipate problematic or high-risk situations such as birthday parties, family functions and holidays that might result in overeating and develop specific strategies for overcoming these lapses. Therapist asks the adolescent to imagine such situation and practise how to cope in such situations by using role play or behavioural rehearsal at the end of the treatment. Self control and self regulation skills along with problem-solving is used to find out the best solutions (e.g. to avoid the situation, distract yourself by doing something else, participate in the situation with less eating, have some healthy snacks at home then go out for party, participate with a plan to do some extra exercise afterwards, etc.) of the problems anticipated by adolescents. Adolescents are encouraged to have a plan in advance so that one overeating slip or lapse does not develop into a full-blown relapse. Parents are also suggested to encourage adolescents for doing daily self-monitoring of their eating and exercise behaviour and establish new goals and contracts.

18.9.13 Follow-up

Booster sessions are a very important component of the cognitive behavioural treatment of adolescent obesity in order to review the progress and barriers after the intensive phase of the treatment. Therapist plans booster session on a monthly basis for a total duration of 12 months and explains the rationale and importance of the same to parents and adolescents. Booster session usually includes the assessment of the weight status and problems faced in the last month along with the revision of the previously learned techniques.

18.10 Barriers to Treatment

There are number of barriers to treatment that make the initial process difficult and also hinder the weight maintenance. Here is the list along with the possible ways to overcome these barriers:

1. Adolescent's lower level of readiness/motivation to change (can be handled by motivating the child within the therapy process)
2. Parental attitude that fat child is a healthy child. (parental attitude can be changed by psycho-educating them about the risks associated with obesity)
3. Obesogenic environment (can be handled using environmental restructuring or stimulus control)
4. Lack of social support and encouragement from family and friends (social support can be enhanced by educating the significant others about their role in the treatment)
5. Previous failed attempts (can be handled by cognitive restructuring)

All of these barriers need to be dealt within the therapy process in the intensive phase of the weight loss and in the booster sessions of weight maintenance phase.

18.11 Conclusion

CBT as a treatment of choice for adolescent obesity has been well established in the literature. Although it is difficult to assess the effectiveness of specific CBT technique, overall it has been found that CBT produce positive behavioural changes in obese adolescents. Some of the CBT techniques have been evaluated and proven to have a positive effect in adolescent populations—such as self-monitoring (Kirschenbaum et al. 2005), stimulus control (Golan et al. 1998) and problem-solving (Graves et al. 1988). Behavioural programmes for childhood obesity integrate most of these CBT techniques as it can be seen in the above description that most of the techniques are useful throughout the process be it a self-monitoring, goal setting, cognitive restructuring or problem-solving. All of the techniques have their significance in bringing up behaviour change at different stages of therapy.

Appendix-I: Handout for Parents

1. **Be a good example or role model for the child**
   Your involvement is important for your child to learn healthy eating habits. Be a role model for your child by eating fruits, vegetables and other healthy food/snacks, so it becomes easier for the child to adopt such habits.
2. **Provide a variety of healthy snacks to your child at home**, e.g. fruit salad, sprouts, cheese and corn salad , so that craving for eating unhealthy snacks available in the market decreases. Try to change the long-term preferences of food in terms of avoiding junk food and develop a taste for fruits and vegetables
3. **Fix up regular family meal time and avoid frequent snacking in between**.
4. **Eat only when hungry**.
5. **Encourage your child to eat slowly and without distractions such as watching T.V or reading while eating**
   Obese adolescents have been observed to eat very rapidly so that large quantities of food are consumed in very brief periods. By slowing down the process of eating, the child is instructed to put a small amount of food in his mouth and to be more aware of each bite. This process also helps the child to derive more enjoyment from his food so that he can replace quantity with quality in his eating.
6. **Increase physical activity**
   Help the child in increasing his or her physical activity to at least one hour per day. Adolescents are encouraged to involve structured physical activity in terms of participating in sports or regular exercise (swimming, jogging, aerobics, etc.) More emphasis is given to increase lifestyle activity in terms of walking to school, cycling to market, use of stairs than lifts, etc., so that these habits becomes an important part of their daily routine and help them in long-term weight loss.
7. **Take a break**
   Encourage adolescent to "take a break" or a "timeout" from a situation where they are feeling angry or upset.
8. **Develop realistic goals and reward the child for each achievement**
   Developing specific and realistic goals that can be easily measured (e.g. walking/running for 40 min, five times per week). Give them rewards for achieving goals.
9. **Don't use food as reward.**
10. **Limit sedentary behaviour**
    Limiting television/computer/video game time gradually from 3 to 2 h/day, finally to 1 h/day (most of the time the strategy of reducing children's sedentary behaviour can be more effective than a strategy of promoting physical activity).

11. **Teach self-monitoring to the child**
    Give responsibility to monitor his/her eating behaviour and physical activity by maintaining logbooks/diaries. Verbally praise the child for taking responsibility.
12. **Enhance open communication with the child**
    Let the child be comfortable in sharing his/her feelings with you because many a times child would resort to food to overcome these negative emotions/feelings.

References

American Dietetic Association. (2006). Position of the American Dietetic Association: Individual, family, school, and community-based interventions for pediatric overweight. *Journal of American Dietetic Association, 106*(6), 925–945.

Achenbach, T. M. (1991). *Manual for the child behavior checklist/4-18 and 1991 profile*. Burlington, VT: University of Vermont, Department of Psychiatry.

Belamarich, P. F., Luder, E., Kattan, M., Mitchell, H., Islam, S., Lynn, H., et al. (2000). Do obese inner-city children with asthma have more symptoms than non-obese children with asthma? *Pediatrics, 106*(6), 1436–1441.

Chan, J., Edman, J. C., & Koltai, P. J. (2004). Obstructive sleep apnea in children. *American Family Physician, 69*, 1147–1154.

Ebbeling, C. B., Pawlak, D. B., & Ludwig, D. S. (2002). Childhood obesity: public-health crisis, common sense cure. *Lancet, 360*, 473–482.

Eisenberg, M. E., Neumark-Sztainer, D., & Story, M. (2003). Association of Weight-based teasing and emotional well-being among adolescents. *Archives of Pediatrics and Adolescent Medicine, 157*, 733–738.

Golan, M., Fainaru, M., & Weizman, A. (1998). Role of behaviour modification in the treatment of childhood obesity with the parents as the exclusive agents of change. *International Journal of Obesity and Related Metabolic Disorders, 22*, 1217–1224.

Goldfried, G. S., Moore, C., Henderson, K., Buchholz, A., Obeid, N., & Flament, M. F. (2010). Body dissatisfaction, dietary restraint, depression and weight status in adolescents. *Journal of School Health, 80*(4), 186–192.

Graves, T., Meyers, A. W., & Clark, L. (1988). An evaluation of parental problem solving training in the behavioral treatment of childhood obesity. *Journal of Consulting and Clinical Psychology, 56*, 246–250.

Isnard, P., Michel, G., Frelut, M., Vila, G., Falissard, B., Naja, W., et al. (2003). Binge eating and psychopathology in severely obese adolescents. *International Journal of Eating Disorder, 34*, 235–243.

Jain, S., Pant, B., Chopra, H., & Tiwari, R. (2010). Obesity among adolescents of affluent public school in Meerut. *Indian Journal of Public Health, 54*(3), 158–160.

Jelalian, E., & Saelens, B. E. (1999). Empirically supported treatments in pediatric psychology: pediatric obesity. *Journal of Pediatric Psychology, 24*, 223–248.

Johnston, C. A., & Dalton, W. T, I. I. I. (2008). Application of empirically supported treatments to clinical settings. In E. Jelalian & R. G. Steele (Eds.), *Handbook of childhood and adolescent obesity* (pp. 425–443). New York: Springer.

Kirschenbaum, D. S., Germann, J. N., & Rich, B. H. (2005). Treatment of morbid obesity in low-income adolescents: Effects of parental self-monitoring. *Obesity Research, 13*, 1527–1529.

Kirschenbaum, D. S., & Kristen, J. G. (2013). Five recent expert recommendations on the treatment of childhood and adolescent obesity: Toward an emerging consensus—A stepped care approach. *Childhood Obesity, 9*(5), 376–385.

Kotian, M. S., Kumar, S. G., & Kotian, S. S. (2010). Prevalence and determinants of overweight and obesity among adolescent school children of South Karnataka, India. *Indian Journal of Community Medicine, 35*(1), 176–178.

Kumari, D. J., & Krishna, S. H. K. (2011). Prevalence and risk factors for adolescents (13–17 years): Overweight and obesity. *Current Science, 100*(3), 373–377.

Lovibond, S. H., & Lovibond, P. F. (1995). *Manual for the depression anxiety stress scales* (2nd. ed.). Sydney: Psychology Foundation. ISBN 7334-1423-0.

Malhotra, S. (1993). Study of Life Stress in Children with Psychiatric Disorders in India.*Hong Kong Journal of Psychiatry, 3*, 28.

Mohan, B., Kumar, N., Aslam, N., Rangbulla, A., Kumbkarni, S., Sood, N. K., & Wander, G. S. (2004). Prevalence of sustained hypertension and obesity in urban and rural school going children in Ludhiana. *Indian Heart Journal, 56*, 310–314.

Oude Luttikhuis H., Baur, L., Jansen, H., Shrewsbury, V. A., O'Malley C., Stolk R. P., et al. (2009). Interventions for treating obesity in children. *Cochrane Database of Systematic Reviews*, 1, CD001872.

Rao, S., Kanade, A., & Kelkar, R. (2006). Blood pressure among overweight adolescents from urban school children in Pune, India. *European Journal of Clinical Nutrition, 61*, 633–641.

Rosenberg, M. (1965). *Society and the adolescent self-image*. Princeton, NJ: Princeton University Press.

Saraswathi, Y. S., Najafi, M., Gangadhar, M. R., & Malini, S. S. (2011). Prevalence of childhood obesity in school children from rural and urban areas in Mysore, Karnataka, India. *Journal of Life Science, 3*(1), 51–55.

Shah, C., Diwan, J., Rao, P., Bhabhor, M., Gokhle, P., & Mehta, H. (2008). Assessment of obesity in school children. *Calicut Medical Journal, 6*(3), e2.

Sharma, A., Sharma, K., & Mathur, K. P. (2007). Growth pattern and prevalence of obesity in affluent school children of Delhi. *Public Health Nutrition, 10*(5), 485–491.

Sinha, R., & Fisch, G. (2002). Prevalence of impaired glucose tolerance among children and adolescents with marked obesity. *New England Journal of Medicine, 346*(11), 802–810.

Spear, B. E., Barlow, S. E., Ervin, C., Ludwig D. S., Saelens B. E., Schetzina K. E., & Taveras E.M. (2007). Recommendations for treatment of child and adolescent overweight and obesity. *Pediatrics, 120*(4), S254–S288. doi:10.1542/peds.2007-2329F.

Stewart, L., Reilly, J. J., & Hughes, A. R. (2008). Evidence based behavioral treatment of obesity in children and adolescents. *Child Adolescent Psychiatric Clinics of North America, 18*, 189–198.

Strauss, R. S., & Pollack, H. A. (2003). Social marginalization of overweight children. *Archives of Pediatrics & Adolescent Medicine, 157*(8), 746–752, doi:10.1001/archpedi.157.8.746.

Stuart, R. B. (1967). Behavioral control of overeating. *Behaviour Research and Therapy, 5*, 357–365.

Styne, D. M. (2001). Childhood obesity and adolescents' obesity. *PCNA, 48*, 823–847.

Van Strein, T., Frijters, J. E., Bergers, G., & Defares, P. B. (1986). The Dutch Eating Behavior Questionnaire (DEBQ) for assessment of restrained, emotional, and external eating behavior. *International Journal of Eating Disorders*, *5*(2), 295–315.

Wardle, J., Guthrie, C. A., Sanderson, S., & Rapoport, L. (2001). Development of the Children's Eating Behaviour Questionnaire. *The Journal of Child Psychology and Psychiatry and Allied Disciplines*, *42*(07), 963–970. doi:10.1017/S0021963001007727.

WHO Consultation on Obesity. (1998). Special issues in the management of obesity in childhood and adolescence. In: *obesity preventing and managing the global epidemic Geneva* (pp. 231–247). Geneva: World Health Organization.

World Health Organisation. (2002). *The world health report: Reducing risks, promoting healthy life*. Geneva: World Health Organisation.

Chapter 19
Effectiveness of Cognitive Behavioural Therapy in Adolescents

Rajesh Sagar, Manju Mehta and Anamika Sahu

19.1 Introduction

Adolescence is the most crucial and challenging period of life where a child goes through significant transition from childhood to adulthood. Sometimes children and adolescents struggle to cope with these changes. As a consequence, they develop emotional disorders, such as anxiety, depression, and obsessions (Laufer 1997; Meltzer et al. 2003) and become functionally impaired (Friedman et al. 1996). Thus, the need of effective treatment for emotional problems of children and adolescents is urgent. It has been found that this population faces various limitations in metacognition and difficulty in labelling their feelings along with major deficits in social skills or interpersonal problem-solving. Therefore, cognitive behavioural therapy (CBT) has proven well its effectiveness form mental disorders in children and adolescents. In recent times, there has been an increasing trend among mental health professionals towards application of CBT in the treatment of emotional and behavioural disorders in children and adolescent population. In addition, there have been numerous studies from the west, which have tried to see efficacy and feasibility of CBT for adolescents with different disorders (depression, anxiety disorders, phobias, OCD, PTSD, obesity, substance use disorders, etc.). It is important to mention that there are very few studies in this

R. Sagar (✉) · M. Mehta (✉) · A. Sahu
Department of Psychiatry, All India Institute of Medical Sciences,
New Delhi 110029, India
e-mail: rsagar29@gmail.com

M. Mehta
e-mail: drmanju.mehta@gmail.com

A. Sahu
e-mail: cpanamika159@gmail.com

M. Mehta and R. Sagar (eds.), *A Practical Approach to Cognitive Behaviour Therapy for Adolescents*, DOI 10.1007/978-81-322-2241-5_19

field from India. Hence, most of the international studies have been discussed in this chapter. Along with this, the effectiveness of CBT of different disorders mentioned in this book is also reviewed in this chapter.

19.2 Specific Application and Efficacy Evaluation

In comparison with CBT for adults, there have been limited studies on CBT for children and adolescents. However, existing studies about CBT with children and adolescents have demonstrated its effectiveness in those experiencing the problems in Fig. 19.1.

19.2.1 Anger

Aggressive behaviours often co-occur with emotional, behavioural, academic, and social relationship problems (Özabacı 2011). Children and adolescents with aggression often exhibit increased rates of school dropout, depression, delinquent behaviour, substance abuse, and poor peer relationships. CBT is one of the most extensively researched form of psychotherapy for aggressive children and adolescents (Sukhodolsky et al. 2004; Blake and Hamrin 2007; Özabacı 2011).

Specifically, cognitive behavioural interventions do not involve a single therapeutic technique, but rather consist of multiple intervention components: (1) problem-solving and social skills education, (2) coping models, (3) role playing, (4) in vivo experiences and assignments, (5) affective education, (6) homework assignments, and (7) operant conditioning, most typically response cost (Kendall and Braswell 1993; Kendall 2006). In addition, therapeutic interventions include self-awareness training, relaxation techniques, cognitive therapy, and conflict management skill training (Deffenbacher 1999).

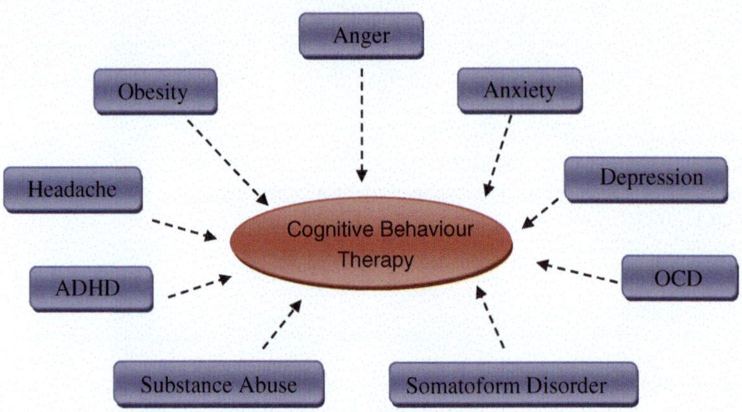

Fig. 19.1 Specific application of CBT in different disorders

A meta-analysis was done by Sukhodolsky et al. (2004) on the treatment outcome studies of CBT for anger-related problems in children and adolescents. In this study, they included 21 published and 19 unpublished reports. They found medium range of mean effect size (Cohen's $d = 0.67$) of CBT and it is consistent with the effects of psychotherapy with children in general. The CBT treatment for anger includes skills training, problem-solving, affective education, and multimodal interventions (differential effects $d = 0.79$, 0.67, 0.36, and 0.74, respectively). For reduction in aggressive behaviour and improvement in social skills, the skills training and multimodal treatments were more effective. However, for reduction in subjective anger experiences, problem-solving treatments were more effective. In addition, Blake and Hamrin (2007) found that cognitive behavioural and skills-based approaches are the most widely studied and empirically validated treatments for anger and aggression in youth.

Özabacı (2011) has reviewed the literature on the use of CBT for treating children and adolescents who demonstrate high levels of violence. Six studies were identified, and all of them indicated beneficial results of using CBT.

19.2.2 Anxiety Disorders

CBT has been shown to be highly effective in treating children and adolescent with anxiety disorders (Santacruz et al. 2002; James et al. 2005; Butler et al. 2006; Ishikawa et al. 2007). Many studies report that between 50 and 85 % of youth, who receive CBT, no longer met criteria for their primary anxiety diagnosis at the end of treatment (Kendall 1994; Barrett et al. 1996; Kendall et al. 1997) and its effectiveness maintained over time (Kendall and Southam-Gerow 1996; Barrett et al. 2001; Kendall et al. 2004; Craske et al. 2006; Garcia-Lopez et al. 2006; Saavedra et al. 2010).

CBT for children with separation anxiety disorder, generalized anxiety disorder, and social phobia is evidenced as effective as short-term treatment (Walkup et al. 2008). In addition, computer-based CBT has demonstrated positive outcomes in case studies of spider phobia (Nelissen et al. 1995) and selective mutism (Fung 2002), in randomized controlled trial of the treatment of spider phobia in children (Dewis et al. 2001) and in anxiety disorders (Calear et al. 2009; Cuijpers et al. 2009; Andrews et al. 2010; Spence et al. 2011).

In his study, Spence et al. (2006) also found positive outcomes for a CBT intervention, in which half of the sessions were presented over internet and half in the clinic. This study revealed that combined internet and clinic-based treatment produced significant reduction in anxiety symptoms as compared to non-intervention programme and there were only minimal differences between partial internet intervention and the entirely clinic-based intervention. March et al. (2009) reported that the participants in internet-based CBT group demonstrated small but significantly greater improvements in anxiety compared to the participants in the wait list. These improvements were enhanced to near about 75 % during the 6-month follow-up period.

Gearing et al. (2013) have studied the effects of booster sessions of CBT for children and adolescents with mood or anxiety disorders in case–control studies. They examined booster sessions using effect sizes (ES): pre–post and pre–follow-up (6 months). They found pre–post studies with booster sessions had a larger effect size ($r = 0.58$) than those without booster sessions ($r = 0.45$). Similarly, pre–follow-up studies with booster sessions showed a larger effect size ($r = 0.64$) than those without booster sessions ($r = 0.48$).

For post-traumatic stress disorder, American Academy of Child and Adolescent Psychiatry (AACAP) practise guidelines recommended TF-CBT as a first-line treatment for child trauma (Cohen et al. 2010). The published randomized controlled trials (RCTs) of TF-CBT have supported its effectiveness in reducing PTS symptoms and PTSD, emotional problems, shame, and trauma-related and general behaviour problems, in comparison with non-CBT interventions, e.g. supportive or client-centred therapies, waitlist control, and usual care (Cohen and Mannarino 1996, 1998, 2008; Cohen et al. 2004; Deblinger et al. 1996, 2001; King et al. 2000; Silverman et al. 2008).

The results of recent meta-analyses by Kowalik et al. (2011) and Cary and McMillan (2012) showed significant differences between TF-CBT and highly similar CBT treatments, compared with non-CBT therapies or treatment as usual, in reducing symptoms of PTSD, depression, and internalizing behaviours across 18 studies ($n = 24–229$). In addition, TF-CBT has also demonstrated efficacy for children experiencing other traumas, including community violence/terrorism (Hoagwood et al. 2006), childhood traumatic grief (Cohen et al. 2004, 2006), multiple traumas resulting in foster care placement (Weiner et al. 2009), and domestic or interpersonal violence (Cohen et al. 2011; Puccia et al. 2012).

Follow-up studies have also shown the positive treatment gains and evidence of sustained benefit at 6-months, 1-year, and 2-year post-treatment (Cohen and Mannarino 1997; Deblinger et al. 1999, 2006; Cohen et al. 2005).

19.2.3 Depression

There are a number of studies that show the effectiveness of CBT for adolescents with clinical depression (Lewinsohn et al. 1990; Kroll et al. 1996; Weisz et al. 1997; Harrington et al. 1998). Brent et al. (2002) did a meta-analytic review of 15 articles, on the efficacy of CBT with depressed adolescents. They found that CBT reliably outperforms the control conditions, such as wait list and placebo, with medium to large ES (1.27, Lewinsohn and Clarke 1999; 1.06, Reinecke et al. 1998). Butler et al. (2006) did a meta-analytic review on treatment outcomes of CBT for a wide range of psychiatric disorders. They found large ES of CBT for adolescent depression ($ES = 0.84$) and anxiety disorders ($ES = 0.74$) and moderate effect size ($M = 0.62$, $SD = 0.11$) for CBT of childhood somatic disorders. A study by Wood and Moore in 2006 included fifty-three children and adolescents with depressive disorders who were randomly allocated to brief CBT or to a control treatment, relaxation training. Results of this study showed a clear advantage of CBT over relaxation on measures of both depression and overall outcome. Klien et al. (2007) have also demonstrated the effectiveness of CBT in the treatment of adolescent depression ($ES = 0.53$). In addition, follow-up studies also reported that CBT for depression was strong, but still in the medium effect size range across meta-analyses (Santacruz et al. 2002).

Computerized CBT for adolescent depressive disorders via internet has the capacity to provide effective, acceptable, and practical health care for adolescents (Calear et al. 2009; Andrews et al. 2010).

19.2.4 Obsessive Compulsive Disorder

CBT is known to produce larger ES and greater rates of clinically significant improvement compared to medication in OCD (Abramowitz et al. 2005). CBT, in particular, exposure and response prevention (ERP), has been reviewed and studied in children and adolescents (March 1995) and is considered the first-line treatment approach for children and adolescents with OCD (Expert Consensus Guidelines; March et al. 1997).

Several published narrative reviews of the paediatric OCD treatment are available (e.g. Grados et al. 1999; Rapoport and Inoff-Germain 2000). These reviews are informative but they do not quantify the effects of treatment across studies. In contrast, meta-analyses (Abramowitz 1997) do quantitatively determine the magnitude of treatment effectiveness but are limited in respect to paediatric OCD.

First meta-analysis of the paediatric OCD treatment was done by Abramowitz in 1997. Results of this study indicate that SSRIs and ERP are effective in reducing paediatric OCD symptoms. Specifically, ERP was more effective and associated with larger ES on OCD measures and fewer residual symptoms than SSRIs, which were more effective than placebo (p s_0.01). Thus, this meta-analytic finding, in general, supports the clinical recommendations of the OCD expert consensus.

19.2.5 Somatoform Disorder

Though, a number of studies related to intervention (pharmacotherapy and psychotherapy) for somatoform disorders in adults have showed the efficacy of CBT across several types of somatoform disorders. However, there is a lack of evidence-based treatment of somatoform disorders in children and adolescents. In children and adolescents, persistent somatoform pain disorder (recurrent abdominal pain, joints pain, and other aches and pain) and undifferentiated somatoform disorder (multiple medical unexplained symptoms) are the most common type among all variants of somatoform disorder. CBT has been found to be effective in the treatment of functional paediatric recurrent abdominal pain. It includes activity scheduling, self-monitoring of symptoms, relaxation training, distraction, coping skills, problem-solving, and cognitive restructuring etc. (Sanders et al. 1989, 1994; Janicke and Finney 1999; Robins 2005; Warner et al. 2011; Van der Veek et al. 2013).

Warner et al. (2011) studied the feasibility and efficacy of CBT (treatment of anxiety and physical symptoms—TAPS) for children experiencing somatic complaints along with anxiety disorder and found TAPS to be acceptable and superior to the waiting list in the reduction of somatic and anxiety symptoms.

19.2.6 Headache

Non-pharmacological treatments for headache in children and adolescents are adopted from treatment of headache in adults (Nicholson 2010; Nicholson et al. 2011) and from treatment of other forms of pain experienced by children and adolescents. Among the existing treatments, CBT focuses on both, headache experienced by children and adolescents and other mental health problems associated with headache (e.g. anxiety, depression, substance abuse, etc.). Thus, CBT has been successfully used for the treatment of paediatric headaches (Palermo et al. 2009, 2010).

Eccleston et al. (2012) have reported in their meta-analysis that CBT including cognitive pain coping skills training and relaxation training (with or without biofeedback assistance) for the management of chronic and recurrent pain in children and adolescents has shown an approximately threefold greater likelihood of clinically significant improvement in headache as compare to control conditions.

Powers et al. (2013) conducted an RCT and found superior outcomes in headache and migraine-related pain and disability, when CBT was used in conjunction with a prophylactic medication (amitriptyline) as compared to use of headache education plus amitriptyline.

19.2.7 Attention Deficit and Hyperactivity Disorder (ADHD)

In the context of ADHD, two treatments and their combination have been empirically known to be effective for ADHD: stimulant treatment (methylphenidate, etc.), psychosocial treatment (behavioural or CBT), and the combination of both (Richters et al. 1995; Kutcher et al. 2004). The existing literature reports that CBT may be more efficacious for adults with ADHD (Safren et al. 2005) as compared to those with adolescents. However, few focal studies on CBT for adolescent ADHD have been conducted, and the results are variable.

Some studies have not found CBT as beneficial for children with ADHD (Abikoff and Gittelman 1985; Dush et al. 1989; Baer and Nietzel 1991;

Bloomquist et al. 1991; DuPaul and Eckert 1997). However, in a meta-analysis, Van der Oord et al. (2008) found some efficacy of CBT, though it was not superior enough as compared to medications in the treatment of adolescent ADHD.

Antshel et al. (2012) did a study to see the efficacy of manualized CBT for managing adolescent ADHD and concluded that an empirically validated adult ADHD CBT protocol can be beneficial for some adolescents with ADHD.

19.2.8 Substance Use Disorders (SUDs)

SUDs among adolescents have been a public health concern for decades. Adolescents with substance use disorders differ from adults in several ways. For instance, adolescents may be more susceptible to peer influences, be more vulnerable to adverse effects from substances and have smaller body size and lower tolerance levels and experience long-term cognitive and emotional damage from substance abuse (Brown et al. 2000; Tapert et al. 2004). Thus, they may have different treatment needs. The number of studies focusing specifically on the effectiveness of psychosocial interventions for adolescent substance abuse have grown over the last decade (Dennis et al. 2004; Waldron and Turner 2008; Williams and Chang 2000), with a significant rise in both the quantity and the quality of the treatment outcome studies.

The most prevalent treatment types are family therapy (Liddle and Dakof 1995; Stanton and Shadish 1997; Waldron 1997), motivational interviewing (MET) (Colby et al. 1998; Tevyaw and Monti 2004; Walker et al. 2006), and CBT (Kaminer and Burleson 1999; Waldron and Kaminer 2004).

In the context of adolescent substance use, CBT shows promise in treating adolescent substance use (Latimer et al. 2003). It includes functional analyses (identify stimulus cues–antecedents and consequences), self-regulation, coping skills (use various strategies to avoid situations that may trigger the desire to use), communication skills, and problem-solving.

A study was carried out on 32 adolescents (age range: 13–18 years) with dual diagnosis (AOD abuse and other psychiatric disorders, such as disruptive disorders (e.g. conduct disorder or attention deficit/hyperactivity disorder) or internalizing disorders (e.g. depression or an anxiety disorder). CBT or interactional group therapy was given for 12 week in an outpatient setting. The CBT sessions included didactic presentations, modelling, role playing, and homework exercises. CBT group showed significant reduction in severity of substance use (Kaminer et al. 1998).

In Kaminer et al. 2002, carried out a study again and compared CBT with psycho-educational therapy in treating adolescents with substance use disorders with dual diagnosis. The participants (n-88, aged-13–18) were randomly assigned to 8 weeks of either CBT or psycho-educational group therapy, for 75–90 min/week. Adolescents of CBT group exhibited better treatment retention and better outcomes at follow-up. However, both groups had similar relapse rates at the 9-month follow-up.

In addition, one study (Liddle et al. 2008) conducted to examine the efficacy of two adolescent drug abuse treatments: individual CBT and multidimensional family therapy (MDFT), with 12–17.5-year-old adolescents (n-224). In comparison with other randomized controlled trials testing CBT, both treatments showed approximately equivalent or larger reductions of cannabis consumption and slightly significant reduction in alcohol, both during treatment and at the 6-month follow-up (Waldron et al. 2001).

19.2.9 Obesity

In recent years, CBT has received an increasing amount of attention in the management of obesity. It is similar to the treatment of substance use disorders involving teaching children and families to monitor for triggers. Inspite of this, researches on efficacy of CBT to treat obesity in adolescent population have provided mixed results (Mellin et al. 1987; Duffy and Spence 1993; Braet and Van Winckel 2001; Warschburger 2001; Jelalian 2006). The review studies reported that outpatient CBT often produces positive effects (Stice et al. 2006). A meta-analysis has also documented decrease in per cent overweight at follow-up by 8.9 % for outpatient CBT programmes (Wilfley et al. 2007).

Brennan et al. (2006) have found 6 % reduction in body fat relative to the control group that sustained for 12 months after the delivery of 12-week CBT programme (CHOOSE HEALTH; L Brennan, Melbourne, Australia) in adolescents. Further, Tsiros et al. (2008) examined the effectiveness of shorter version of this same CBT programme (CHOOSE HEALTH) for improving body composition, diet, and physical activity in overweight and obese adolescents. He found improvement in body composition (BMI, weight, body fat, and abdominal fat) more in CBT group as compared to controls.

Immersion CBT has also produced promising results. Kelly and Kirschenbaum (2011) did the first comprehensive review of this research (involving 22 outcome studies). They concluded that compared to results of outpatient treatments, these immersion programmes produced an average of 197 % greater reductions in per cent overweight at post-treatment and 130 % greater reduction at follow-up. Further, follow-up evaluations showed decreased per cent overweight at follow-up by an average of 30 % for CBT immersion programmes versus 9 % for programmes without CBT.

Kirschenbaum and Kristen (2013) reviewed five recent expert recommendations on the treatment of childhood and adolescent obesity and found that all of the expert committees support and advised the use of intensive dietary intervention, physical activity, and cognitive behavioural counselling.

19.3 Efficacy of Different Approaches of CBT

Before looking at some of the subtle differences between various approaches of CBT in child and adolescent problems, it is necessary to get some view of the existing approaches of CBT. Followings are the various approaches of CBT:

- Individual CBT
- Group CBT
- Self-help
  - Computerized
  - ICBT
  - Manual
- Telephonic CBT

A traditional CBT is conducted in the form of face-to-face individual CBT in which sessions are held between the patient and the therapist. It consists of 6–18 weekly sessions of around an hour each. The therapist would write a session plan with the help of patient to ensure that everything that is important will be covered in a structured way. On the other hand, group CBT is extended form of individual CBT, in which sessions are held between a group of patients and a therapist.

Self-help CBT is given through computer, internet, or a manual. Computerized cognitive behavioural therapy (cCBT) is implemented through a computer, not a human, in which a computer programme is used to deliver some of basic explanations and planning of CBT. In other words, cCBT is a generic term for delivering CBT via an interactive computer interface delivered by a personal computer, internet, or interactive voice response system, instead of face-to-face with a human therapist.

In manualized approach, the patient receives a standardized treatment method with which he can help himself without major help from the therapist. It includes workbooks, and leaflets.

Another version of CBT, telephonic CBT, has recently been developed to overcome some of the practical barriers involved in conducting face-to-face psychotherapy, for example physical impairments interfering with attending regularly scheduled appointments, transportation problems, lack of available, and appropriate services in the patient's geographic area (Hollon et al. 2002). In telephonic CBT, therapist caters to the rising needs of the patients through telephonic conversation to target the depressogenic thoughts and behaviours.

Many studies have been conducted to see efficacy and feasibility of different approaches to assess efficiency of CBT (Face-to-face individual or group CBT, computerized CBT, telephonic CBT, reading self-help approach) in different disorders (depression, anxiety disorders, phobias, OCD, PTSD, obesity, substance use disorders, etc.). However, results of these studies are variable.

Computer-assisted/internet-based therapies have great potential to make psychological assessment and treatment more cost-effective than other approaches of assessment and treatment. These forms of therapies are also very feasible and efficacious with respect to anxiety and depressive disorders and can reduce the stigma of visiting a therapist.

March et al. (2009) found that children with anxiety disorders in internet-based CBT (NET) condition showed small but significantly greater reduction in anxiety symptoms and increases in functioning than waitlist (WL) participants. These improvements were enhanced during the 6-month follow-up period, and 75 % of NET children were free of their primary diagnosis. In addition, a meta-analysis of 23 randomized controlled studies (RCTs) performed by Cuijpers et al. (2009) in which they compared computerized psychotherapy (CP) with non-computerized psychotherapy (non-CP) in anxiety disorders (phobias (n = 10), panic disorder/agoraphobia (n = 9), PTSD (n = 3), and obsessive–compulsive disorder (n = 1). The author founds large effect size of CP compared with non-CP approach ($ES = 1.08$, 95 % confidence interval: 0.84–1.32) and no significant difference between CP and face-to-face psychotherapy (13 comparisons, $d = -0.06$). Further, a small difference between online therapy interventions and self-help accessed from static information was found in a study in the context of depression (Clarke et al. 2009).

Cornelius et al. (2011) also found long-term (2 years) efficacy of manual-based cognitive behavioural therapy/motivation enhancement therapy (CBT/MET) (in addition to the SSRI medication fluoxetine or placebo) compared to naturalistic care among comorbid MDD/AUD youth (15 and 20 years). They found that patients receiving CBT/MET demonstrated superior outcomes compared to those who had not received protocol CBT/MET therapy (41 vs. 17 %, chi-square = 5.3, $p = 0.021$).

Many studies comparing computerized CBT with traditional face-to-face CBT have found both modes to be equally beneficial with maintenance of gains after follow-up and good patient adherence (Andrews et al. 2010). However, CBT was found highly efficacious and feasible when minimal therapist support or therapist-guided sessions after or during the use of the web-based CBT or manual–guided or sequential self-care was incorporated (Spence et al. 2011). This is also true for other approaches of CBT. Hence, these approaches of CBT are suitable for only some individuals, having mild to moderate severity of symptoms.

19.4 Efficacy of CBT as Compared to Other Therapies

A number of studies have confirmed that CBT is superior to medication and other therapies (e.g. wait list, pill–placebo, relaxation therapy, supportive therapy, family therapy, interpersonal psychotherapy, psychoanalytic therapy, etc.).

When a line of comparison was drawn with medication, in some disorders (e.g. depression, anxiety, OCD, PTSD, etc.), CBT proved to be superior to serotonin reuptake inhibitors (clomipramine and fluvoxamine) due to reduced chance of side effects and greater cost-effectiveness (Phillips 2003; Haby et al. 2004; Guggisberg 2005; Wilson et al. 2005). In addition, in comparison with other forms of psychotherapy, CBT has proven to be more effective treatment, especially in internalizing disorders. For example,

- In depression and anxiety, CT/CBT is superior to wait list, relaxation therapy (Reinecke et al. 1998), supportive therapy (Brent et al. 1997; Reinecke et al.1998), family therapy (Brent et al. 1997), equivalent efficacy to pill–placebo (Treatment for Adolescents With Depression Study (TADS) Team, USA 2004), and interpersonal psychotherapy (Rosselló and Bernal 1999; Brent et al. 2002).
- In OCD, CBT has significantly better outcomes as compared to alternative approaches (no treatment, other psychosocial treatments, and medications) (Phillips 2003; Guggisberg 2005).
- In the context of PTSD, TF-CBT has greater effectiveness in comparison with non-CBT interventions e.g. supportive or client-centred therapies, waitlist control, and usual care (Cohen and Mannarino 1996, 1998, 2008; Cohen et al. 2004; Deblinger et al. 1996, 2001; King et al. 2000; Silverman et al. 2008).

Though, CBT has established effectiveness for the management of internalizing disorders. However, CBT has limited effectiveness than other form of therapy in some disorders. For example:

- In the field of ADHD, disruptive classroom behaviours and aggressive/antisocial behaviours, CBT has not been superior to pharmacological approaches (Löseland Beelmann 2003; Van der Oord et al. 2008).
- CBT was reported less effective than multidimensional family therapy in the treatment of substance use disorders.
- CBT has performed outstandingly when combined with medication and involvement of family (Walkup et al. 2008) (Table 19.1).

Table 19.1 The six content areas showing the efficacy of CBT in various disorders of child and adolescent population

Disorders	Therapy approaches	Efficacy
Anger	CBT	+
Anxiety	CT/CBT	++
Depression	CT/CBT	++
OCD	CBT/ERP	++
Somatoform disorders	CBT	+
Headache	CBT	+
Substance use disorders	CBT/MET	+
ADHD	CBT	+
Obesity	CBT/immersion CBT	+

Note ++ indicates stronger positive evidence, + indicates positive evidence

19.5 Training and Supervision in CBT

The question is who can deliver CBT? Is training essential before applying CBT? CBT primarily addresses dysfunctional emotions, maladaptive behaviours, and cognitive processes where therapists examine the thoughts, feelings, and behaviours related to situations, including reactions to the therapist, and relevant childhood experiences to understand the underlying core beliefs and conditional assumptions for each client. However, CBT has been tailored many folds to meet the symptom-based needs of each patients. As a result, different forms and approaches of CBT have been developed. Thus, understanding the concept and updating knowledge of therapy is prerequisite for a therapist, which requires an extensive training. Here, Pretorius (2006) also noted that supervised practice is an essential part of psychotherapy training because it cannot be learned through lectures or independent study only.

Pretorius (2006) concluded in his review that training and supervision in therapy always enhances the following skills of the trainees:

- Helping the therapist to adopt the philosophy of CBT (basic approach of changing clients' cognitions, emotions, and behaviour) facilitates the improvement or recovery
- Teaching the therapist specific skills or techniques (understand cognitions and emotions of patients, to develop case conceptualization, to consider treatment options and techniques, and to discuss goals as well as stumbling blocks towards them), improves the therapeutic competency
- Offers an opportunity to acknowledge, explore, challenge, and modify the cognitions and emotions of the therapist within the setting of therapy as well as during supervision
- Enable trainees in using their level of experience in different situations

However, often it has been found that many trainees rely completely on their theoretical orientation and personal experience in practising the therapy and fails to get appropriately trained under close supervision. Such patterns of learning rather impede the growth of trainees as therapists. As a result, same techniques are applied in multiple ways by different therapists, resulting in inappropriate and ineffective therapeutic outcome. Moreover, this also violates the basic ethics of therapy where only a trained clinician is supposed to practise the evidence-based therapies on patients. Overall, this pattern of learning fails to provide effective treatment to the patients. Hence, this is the need of the hour for the therapist to get appropriately trained and profess the therapy with utmost efficiency.

19.6 Conclusion

Although the evidence summarized above, highlights the treatment effectiveness of CBT for adolescents, these studies are limited by small sample sizes, small to moderate ES, and few follow-up assessments. Hence, there are important research questions which still need to be answered, such as replication and extension of more such studies to establish efficiency, issues concerning the applicability of methods in different settings, and with different populations, most importantly with members of different ethnic groups and with females as well as males.

The major conclusion that can be drawn from the existing literature is that CBT is effective treatment method for the management of internalizing and externalizing disorders of adolescents. CBT efficacy is rather enhanced many folds when it acts in combination with pharmacological treatment and involvement of family. Moreover, it is quite easily accessible and affordable to most of the patients. However, training and supervision is one of the prerequisites for teaching the therapy to ensure therapists' credibility and better therapeutic outcomes.

References

Abikoff, H., & Gittelman, R. (1985). Hyperactive children treated with stimulants: Is cognitive training a useful adjunct? *Archives of General Psychiatry, 42*(10), 953–961.

Abramowitz, J. S. (1997). Effectiveness of psychological and pharmacological treatments for obsessive-compulsive disorder: A quantitative review. *Journal of Consulting and Clinical Psychology, 65*(1), 44.

Abramowitz, J. S., Whiteside, S. P., & Deacon, B. J. (2005). The effectiveness of treatment for pediatric obsessive-compulsive disorder: A meta-analysis. *Behavior Therapy, 36*(1), 55–63.

Andrews, G., Cuijpers, P., Craske, M. G., McEvoy, P., & Titov, N. (2010). Computer therapy for the anxiety and depressive disorders is effective, acceptable and practical health care: A meta-analysis. *PLoS One, 5*(10), e13196.

Antshel, K. M., Faraone, S. V., & Gordon, M. (2012). Cognitive behavioral treatment outcomes in adolescent ADHD. *FOCUS: The Journal of Lifelong Learning in Psychiatry, 10*(3), 334-345.

Barrett, P. M., Dadds, M. R., & Rapee, R. M. (1996). Family treatment of childhood anxiety: A controlled trial. *Journal of Consulting and Clinical Psychology, 64*(2), 333–342.

Barrett, P. M., Duffy, A. L., Dadds, M. R., & Rapee, R. M. (2001). Cognitive–behavioral treatment of anxiety disorders in children: Long-term (6-year) follow-up. *Journal of Consulting and Clinical Psychology, 69*(1), 135–141.

Bear, R. A., & Nietzel, M. T. (1991). Cognitive and behavioral treatment of impulsivity in children: A meta-analytic review of the outcome literature. *Journal of Clinical Child and Adolescent Psychology, 20*(4), 400–412.

Blake, C. S., & Hamrin, V. (2007). Current approaches to the assessment and management of anger and aggression in youth: A review. *Journal of Child and Adolescent Psychiatric Nursing, 20*(4), 209–221.

Bloomquist, M. L., August, G. J., & Ostrander, R. (1991). Effects of a school-based cognitive-behavioral intervention for ADHD children. *Journal of Abnormal Child Psychology, 19*(5), 591–605.

Braet, C., & Van Winckel, M. (2001). Long-term follow-up of a cognitive behavioral treatment program for obese children. *Behavior Therapy, 31*(1), 55–74.

Brennan, L., Wilks, R., Walkley, J., Fraser, S., & Greenway, K. (2006). Efficacy of cognitive behavioral therapy in the treatment of overweight and obese adolescents. *Obesity Reviews, 7*, 87–89.

Brent, D. A., Holder, D., Kolko, D., Birmaher, B., Baugher, M., Roth, C., et al. (1997). A clinical psychotherapy trial for adolescent depression comparing cognitive, family, and supportive therapy. *Archives of General Psychiatry, 54*(9), 877–885.

Brent, D. A., Gaynor, S. T., & Weersing, V. R. (2002). Cognitive-behavioral approaches to the treatment of depression and anxiety. *Child and Adolescent Psychiatry: Modern Approaches*, 921–937.

Brown, S. A., Tapert, S. F., Granholm, E., & Delis, D. C. (2000). Neurocognitive functioning of adolescents: Effects of protracted alcohol use. *Alcoholism, Clinical and Experimental Research, 24*(2), 164–171.

Butler, A. C., Chapman, J. E., Forman, E. M., & Beck, A. T. (2006). The empirical status of cognitive-behavioral therapy: A review of meta-analyses. *Clinical Psychology Review, 26*(1), 17–31.

Calear, A. L., Christensen, H., Mackinnon, A., Griffiths, K. M., & O'Kearney, R. (2009). The youth mood project: A cluster randomized controlled trial of an online cognitive behavioral program with adolescents. *Journal of Consulting and Clinical Psychology, 77*(6), 1021–1032.

Cary, C. E., & McMillen, J. C. (2012). The data behind the dissemination: A systematic review of trauma-focused cognitive behavioral therapy for use with children and youth. *Children and Youth Services Review, 34*(4), 748–757.

Cohen, J. A., & Mannarino, A. P. (1996). A treatment outcome study for sexually abused preschool children: Initial findings. *Journal of the American Academy of Child and Adolescent Psychiatry, 35*(1), 42–50.

Cohen, J. A., & Mannarino, A. P. (1997). A treatment study for sexually abused preschool children: Outcome during a one-year follow-up. *Journal of the American Academy of Child and Adolescent Psychiatry, 36*(9), 1228–1235.

Cohen, J. A., & Mannarino, A. P. (1998). Interventions for sexually abused children: Initial treatment outcome findings. *Child Maltreatment, 3*(1), 17–26.

Cohen, J. A., Deblinger, E., Mannarino, A. P., & Steer, R. A. (2004a). A multisite, randomized controlled trial for children with sexual abuse–related PTSD symptoms. *Journal of the American Academy of Child and Adolescent Psychiatry, 43*(4), 393–402.

Cohen, J. A., Mannarino, A. P., & Knudsen, K. (2004b). Treating childhood traumatic grief: A pilot study. *Journal of the American Academy of Child and Adolescent Psychiatry, 43*(10), 1225–1233.

Cohen, J. A., Mannarino, A. P., & Knudsen, K. (2005). Treating sexually abused children: 1 year follow-up of a randomized controlled trial. *Child Abuse and Neglect, 29*(2), 135–145.

Cohen, J. A., Mannarino, A. P., & Staron, V. R. (2006). A pilot study of modified cognitive-behavioral therapy for childhood traumatic grief (CBT-CTG). *Journal of the American Academy of Child and Adolescent Psychiatry, 45*(12), 1465–1473.

Cohen, J. A., & Mannarino, A. P. (2008). Trauma-Focused Cognitive Behavioural Therapy for Children and Parents. *Child and Adolescent Mental Health, 13*(4), 158–162.

Cohen, J. A., Bukstein, O., Walter, H., Benson, R. S., Chrisman, A., Farchione, T. R., et al. (2010). Practice parameter for the assessment and treatment of children and adolescents with posttraumatic stress disorder. *Journal of the American Academy of Child and Adolescent Psychiatry, 49*(4), 414–430.

Cohen, J. A., Mannarino, A. P., & Iyengar, S. (2011). Community treatment of posttraumatic stress disorder for children exposed to intimate partner violence: A randomized controlled trial. *Archives of Pediatrics and Adolescent Medicine, 165*(1), 16–21.

Colby, S. M., Monti, P. M., Barnett, N. P., Rohsenow, D. J., Weissman, K., Spirito, A., et al. (1998). Brief motivational interviewing in a hospital setting for adolescent smoking: A preliminary study. *Journal of Consulting and Clinical Psychology, 66*(3), 574–578.

Cornelius, J. R., Douaihy, A., Bukstein, O. G., Daley, D. C., Wood, S. D., Kelly, T. M., & Salloum, I. M. (2011). Evaluation of cognitive behavioral therapy/motivational enhancement therapy (CBT/MET) in a treatment trial of comorbid MDD/AUD adolescents. *Addictive Behaviors, 36*(8), 843–848.

Craske, M. G., Roy-Byrne, P., Stein, M. B., Sullivan, G., Hazlett-Stevens, H., Bystritsky, A., & Sherbourne, C. (2006). CBT intensity and outcome for panic disorder in a primary care setting. *Behavior Therapy, 37*(2), 112–119.

Cuijpers, P., Marks, I. M., van Straten, A., Cavanagh, K., Gega, L., & Andersson, G. (2009). Computer-aided psychotherapy for anxiety disorders: A meta-analytic review. *Cognitive Behaviour Therapy, 38*(2), 66–82.

Deblinger, E., Lippmann, J., & Steer, R. (1996). Sexually abused children suffering posttraumatic stress symptoms: Initial treatment outcome findings. *Child Maltreatment, 1*(4), 310–321.

Deblinger, E., Steer, R. A., & Lippmann, J. (1999). Two-year follow-up study of cognitive behavioral therapy for sexually abused children suffering post-traumatic stress symptoms. *Child Abuse and Neglect, 23*(12), 1371–1378.

Deblinger, E., Mannarino, A. P., Cohen, J. A., & Steer, R. A. (2006). A follow-up study of a multisite, randomized, controlled trial for children with sexual abuse-related PTSD symptoms. *Journal of the American Academy of Child and Adolescent Psychiatry, 45*(12), 1474–1484.

Deblinger, E., Stauffer, L. B., & Steer, R. A. (2001). Comparative efficacies of supportive and cognitive behavioral group therapies for young children who have been sexually abused and their nonoffending mothers. *Child Maltreatment, 6*(4), 332–343.

Deffenbacher, J. L. (1999). Cognitive-behavioral conceptualization and treatment of anger.*Journal of Clinical Psychology.*

Dennis, M., Godley, S. H., Diamond, G., Tims, F. M., Babor, T., Donaldson, J., & Funk, R. (2004). The cannabis youth treatment (CYT) study: Main findings from two randomized trials. *Journal of Substance Abuse Treatment, 27*(3), 197–213.

Dewis, L. M., Kirkby, K. C., Martin, F., Daniels, B. A., Gilroy, L. J., & Menzies, R. G. (2001). Computer-aided vicarious exposure versus live graded exposure for spider phobia in children. *Journal of Behavior Therapy and Experimental Psychiatry, 32*(1), 17–27.

Duffy, G., & Spence, S. H. (1993). The effectiveness of cognitive self-management as an adjunct to a behavioural intervention for childhood obesity: A research note. *Journal of Child Psychology and Psychiatry, 34*(6), 1043–1050.

DuPaul, G. J., & Eckert, T. L. (1997). The effects of school-based interventions for attention deficit hyperactivity disorder: A meta-analysis. *School Psychology Review.*

Dush, D. M., Hirt, M. L., & Schroeder, H. E. (1989). Self-statement modification in the treatment of child behavior disorders: A meta-analysis. *Psychological Bulletin, 106*(1), 97.

Eccleston, C., Palermo, T. M., Williams, A. C. D. C., Lewandowski, A., Morley, S., Fisher, E., & Law, E. (2012). Psychological therapies for the management of chronic and recurrent pain in children and adolescents. *Cochrane Database System Review, 12.*

Friedman, R. M., Katz-Leavy, J. W., Manderscheid, R. W., & Sondheimer, D. L. (1996). Prevalence of serious emotional disturbance in children and adolescents. *Mental Health, United States, 996*, 71–89.

Fung, D. S., Manassis, K., Kenny, A., & Fiksenbaum, L. (2002). Web-based CBT for selective mutism. *Journal of the American Academy of Child and Adolescent Psychiatry, 41*(2), 112–113.

Garcia-Lopez, L. J., Olivares, J., Beidel, D., Albano, A. M., Turner, S., & Rosa, A. I. (2006). Efficacy of three treatment protocols for adolescents with social anxiety disorder: A 5-year follow-up assessment. *Journal of Anxiety Disorders, 20*(2), 175–191.

Gearing, R. E., Schwalbe, C. S., Lee, R., & Hoagwood, K. E. (2013). The effectiveness of booster sessions in CBT treatment for child and adolescent mood and anxiety disorders. *Depression and Anxiety, 30*(9), 800–808.

Grados, M., Scahill, L., & Riddle, M. A. (1999). Pharmacotherapy in children and adolescents with obsessive-compulsive disorder. *Child and Adolescent Psychiatric Clinics of North America.*

Guggisberg, K. W. (2005). *Methogological review and meta-analysis of treatments for child and adolescent obsessive-compulsive disorder* (Doctoral dissertation, Department of Educational Psychology, University of Utah).

Harrington, R., Wood, A., & Verduyn, C. (1998). Clinically depressed adolescents. *Cognitive-Behaviour Therapy for Children and Families*, 156–193.

Hoagwood, K. E., Radigan, M., Rodriguez, J., Levitt, J. M. D. F., Fernandez, D., & Foster, J. (2006). *Final report on the child and adolescent trauma treatment consortium (CATS) project for the substance abuse and mental health services administration.* Washington, DC: Department of Health and Human Services.

Hollon, S. D., Muñoz, R. F., Barlow, D. H., Beardslee, W. R., Bell, C. C., Bernal, G., et al. (2002). Psychosocial intervention development for the prevention and treatment of depression: Promoting innovation and increasing access. *Biological Psychiatry, 52*(6), 610–630.

Ishikawa, S. I., Okajima, I., Matsuoka, H., & Sakano, Y. (2007). Cognitive behavioural therapy for anxiety disorders in children and adolescents: A meta-analysis. *Child and Adolescent Mental Health, 12*(4), 164–172.

James, A. A. C. J., Soler, A., & Weatherall, R. (2005). Cognitive behavioural therapy for anxiety disorders in children and adolescents. *Cochrane Database of Systematic Reviews, 4.*

Janicke, D. M., & Finnev, J. W. (1999). Empirically supported treatments in pediatric psychology: Recurrent abdominal pain. *Journal of Pediatric Psychology, 24*(2), 115–127.

Jelalian, E., Mehlenbeck, R., Lloyd-Richardson, E. E., Birmaher, V., & Wing, R. R. (2006). 'Adventure therapy'combined with cognitive-behavioral treatment for overweight adolescents. *International Journal of Obesity, 30*(1), 31–39.

Kaminer, Y., Burleson, J. A., Blitz, C., Sussman, J., & Rounsaville, B. J. (1998). Psychotherapies for adolescent substance abusers: A pilot study. *The Journal of Nervous and Mental Disease, 186*(11), 684–690.

Kaminer, Y., & Burleson, J. A. (1999). Psychotherapies for Adolescent Substance Abusers: 15-Month Follow-up of a Pilot Study. *The American Journal on Addictions, 8*(2), 114–119.

Kaminer, Y., Burleson, J. A., & Goldberger, R. (2002). Cognitive-behavioral coping skills and psychoeducation therapies for adolescent substance abuse. *The Journal of Nervous and Mental Disease, 190*(11), 737–745.

Kelly, K. P., & Kirschenbaum, D. S. (2011). Immersion treatment of childhood and adolescent obesity: The first review of a promising intervention. *Obesity Reviews, 12*(1), 37–49.

Kendall, P. C., & Braswell, L. (1993). *Cognitive-behavioral therapy for impulsive children.* New York: Guilford Press.

Kendall, P. C. (1994). Treating anxiety disorders in children: Results of a randomized clinical trial. *Journal of Consulting and Clinical Psychology, 62*(1), 100–110.

Kendall, P. C., & Southam-Gerow, M. A. (1996). Long-term follow-up of a cognitive–behavioral therapy for anxiety-disordered youth. *Journal of Consulting and Clinical Psychology, 64*(4), 724–730.

Kendall, P. C., Flannery-Schroeder, E., Panichelli-Mindel, S. M., Southam-Gerow, M., Henin, A., & Warman, M. (1997). Therapy for youths with anxiety disorders: A second randomized clincal trial. *Journal of Consulting and Clinical Psychology, 65*(3), 366–380.

Kendall, P. C., Safford, S., Flannery-Schroeder, E., & Webb, A. (2004). Child anxiety treatment: Outcomes in adolescence and impact on substance use and depression at 7.4-year follow-up. *Journal of Consulting and Clinical Psychology, 72*(2), 276–287.

King, N. J., Tonge, B. J., Mullen, P., Myerson, N., Heyne, D., Rollings, S., et al. (2000). Treating sexually abused children with posttraumatic stress symptoms: A randomized clinical trial. *Journal of the American Academy of Child and Adolescent Psychiatry, 39*(11), 1347–1355.

Kirschenbaum, D. S., & Gierut, K. J. (2013). Five recent expert recommendations on thetreatment of childhood and adolescent obesity: toward an emerging consensus—Astepped care approach. *Childhood Obesity, 9*(5), 376–385.

Kirschenbaum, D. S., & Gierut, K. J. (2013). Five Recent Expert Recommendations on the Treatment of Childhood and Adolescent Obesity: Toward an Emerging Consensus—A Stepped Care Approach. *Childhood Obesity, 9*(5), 376–385.

Klein, J. B., Jacobs, R. H., & Reinecke, M. A. (2007). Cognitive-behavioral therapy for adolescent depression: A meta-analytic investigation of changes in effect-size estimates. *Journal of the American Academy of Child and Adolescent Psychiatry, 46*(11), 1403–1413.

Kowalik, J., Weller, J., Venter, J., & Drachman, D. (2011). Cognitive behavioral therapy for the treatment of pediatric posttraumatic stress disorder: A review and meta-analysis. *Journal of Behavior Therapy and Experimental Psychiatry, 42*(3), 405–413.

Kroll, L., Harrington, R. C., Gowers, S., Frazer, J., & Jayson, D. (1996). Continuation of cognitive-behavioural treatment in adolescent patients who have remitted from major depression. Feasibility and comparison with historical controls. *Journal of the American Academy of Child and Adolescent Psychiatry, 35*, 1156–1161.

Kutcher, S., Aman, M., Brooks, S. J., Buitelaar, J., van Daalen, E., Fegert, J., et al. (2004). International consensus statement on attention-deficit/hyperactivity disorder (ADHD) and disruptive behaviour disorders (DBDs): Clinical implications and treatment practice suggestions. *European Neuropsychopharmacology, 14*(1), 11–28.

Laufer, M. (1997). *Adolescent breakdown and beyond* (1st ed.). Karnac Books.

Latimer, W. W., Winters, K. C., D'Zurilla, T., & Nichols, M. (2003). Integrated family and cognitive-behavioral therapy for adolescent substance abusers: A stage I efficacy study. *Drug and Alcohol Dependence, 71*(3), 303–317.

Lewinsohn, P. M., & Clarke, G. N. (1999). Psychosocial treatments for adolescent depression.*Clinical psychology review, 19*(3), 329–342.

Lewinsohn, P. M., Clarke, G. N., Hops, H., & Andrews, J. (1990). Cognitive-behavioral treatment for depressed adolescents. *Behavior Therapy, 21*(4), 385–401.

Liddle, H. A., & Dakof, G. A. (1995). Family-based treatment for adolescent drug use: State of the science. *NIDA Research Monograph, 156*, 218–254.

Liddle, H. A., Dakof, G. A., Turner, R. M., Henderson, C. E., & Greenbaum, P. E. (2008). Treating adolescent drug abuse: A randomized trial comparing multidimensional family therapy and cognitive behavior therapy. *Addiction, 103*(10), 1660–1670.

Lösel, F., & Beelmann, A. (2003). Effects of child skills training in preventing antisocial behavior: A systematic review of randomized evaluations. *The Annals of the American Academy of Political and Social Science, 587*(1), 84–109.

March, J. S. (1995). Cognitive-behavioral psychotherapy for children and adolescents with OCD: A review and recommendations for treatment. *Journal of the American Academy of Child and Adolescent Psychiatry, 34*(1), 7–18.

March, J. S., Frances, A., Carpenter, D., & Kahn, D. A. (1997). The Expert Consensus Guideline Series: Treatment of obsessive-compulsive disorder. *Journal of Clinical Psychiatry, 58*, 4–6.

March, S., Spence, S. H., & Donovan, C. L. (2009). The efficacy of an internet-based cognitive-behavioral therapy intervention for child anxiety disorders. *Journal of Pediatric Psychology, 34*(5), 474–487.

Mellin, L. M., Slinkard, L. A., & Irwin, C. E, Jr. (1987). Adolescent obesity intervention: Validation of the SHAPEDOWN program. *Journal of the American Dietetic Association, 87*(3), 333–338.

Meltzer, H., Gatward, R., Goodman, R., & Ford, T. (2003). Mental health of children and adolescents in Great Britain. *International review of Psychiatry, 15*(1–2), 185–187.

Nelissen, I., Muris, P., & Merckelbach, H. (1995). Computerized exposure and in vivo exposure treatments of spider fear in children: Two case reports. *Journal of Behavior Therapy and Experimental Psychiatry, 26*(2), 153–156.

Nicholson, R. A. (2010). Chronic headache: The role of the psychologist. *Current Pain and Headache Reports, 14*(1), 47–54.

Nicholson, R. A., Buse, D. C., Andrasik, F., & Lipton, R. B. (2011). Nonpharmacologic treatments for migraine and tension-type headache: How to choose and when to use. *Current treatment options in neurology, 13*(1), 28–40.

Özabacı, N. (2011). Cognitive behavioural therapy for violent behaviour in children and adolescents: A meta-analysis. *Children and Youth Services Review, 33*(10), 1989–1993.

Phillips, A. S. (2003). *A meta-analysis of treatments for pediatric obsessive-compulsive disorder.* Manhattan, Kansas: Kansas State University.

Palermo, T. M., Eccleston, C., Lewandowski, A. S., Williams, A. C. D. C., & Morley, S. (2010). Randomized controlled trials of psychological therapies for management of chronic pain in children and adolescents: An updated meta-analytic review. *Pain, 148*(3), 387–397.

Palermo, T. M., Wilson, A. C., Peters, M., Lewandowski, A., & Somhegyi, H. (2009). Randomized controlled trial of an Internet-delivered family cognitive–behavioral therapy intervention for children and adolescents with chronic pain. *Pain, 146*(1), 205–213.

Powers, S. W., Kashikar-Zuck, S. M., Allen, J. R., LeCates, S. L., Slater, S. K., Zafar, M., et al. (2013). Cognitive behavioral therapy plus amitriptyline for chronic migraine in children and adolescents: A randomized clinical trial. *JAMA, 310*(24), 2622–2630.

Pretorius, W. M. (2006). Cognitive behavioural therapy supervision: Recommended practice. *Behavioural and Cognitive Psychotherapy, 34*(04), 413–420.

Puccia, E., Redding, T. M., Brown, R. S., Gwynne, P. A., Hirsh, A. B., Hoffmann Frances, R. J., et al. (2012). Using community outreach and evidenced-based treatment to address domestic violence issues. *Social Work in Mental Health, 10*(2), 104–126.

Rapoport, J. L., & Inoff-Germain, G. (2000). Practitioner Review: Treatment of Obsessive-Compulsive Disorder in Children and Adolescents. *Journal of Child Psychology and Psychiatry, 41*(4), 419–431.

Reinecke, M. A., Ryan, N. E., & DuBois, D. L. (1998). Cognitive-behavioral therapy of depression and depressive symptoms during adolescence: A review and meta-analysis. *Journal of the American Academy of Child and Adolescent Psychiatry, 37*(1), 26–34.

Richters, J. E., Arnold, L. E., Jensen, P. S., Abikoff, H., Conners, C. K., Greenhill, L. L., & Swanson, J. M. (1995). NIMH collaborative multisite multimodal treatment study of children with ADHD: I. Background and rationale. *Journal of the American Academy of Child and Adolescent Psychiatry, 34*(8), 987–1000.

Robins, P. M., Smith, S. M., Glutting, J. J., & Bishop, C. T. (2005). A randomized controlled trial of a cognitive-behavioral family intervention for pediatric recurrent abdominal pain. *Journal of Pediatric Psychology, 30*(5), 397–408.

Rossello, J., & Bernal, G. (1999). The efficacy of cognitive-behavioral and interpersonal treatments for depression in Puerto Rican adolescents. *Journal of Consulting and Clinical Psychology, 67*(5), 734–745.

Saavedra, L. M., Silverman, W. K., Morgan-Lopez, A. A., & Kurtines, W. M. (2010). Cognitive behavioral treatment for childhood anxiety disorders: Long-term effects on anxiety and secondary disorders in young adulthood. *Journal of Child Psychology and Psychiatry, 51*(8), 924–934.

Sanders, M. R., Rebgetz, M., Morrison, M., Bor, W., Gordon, A., Dadds, M., et al. (1989). Cognitive-behavioral treatment of recurrent nonspecific abdominal pain in children: An analysis of generalization, maintenance, and side effects. *Journal of Consulting and Clinical Psychology, 57*(2), 294.

Sanders, M. R., Shepherd, R. W., Cleghorn, G., & Woolford, H. (1994). The treatment of recurrent abdominal pain in children: A controlled comparison of cognitive-behavioral family intervention and standard pediatric care. *Journal of Consulting and Clinical Psychology, 62*(2), 306.

Santacruz, I., Orgilés, M., Rosa, A. I., Sánchez-Meca, J., Méndez, X., & Olivares, J. (2002). Generalized anxiety, separation anxiety and school phobia: The predominance of cognitive-behavioural therapy. *Behavioral Psychology*, *10*(3), 503–521.

Safren, S. A., Otto, M. W., Sprich, S., Winett, C. L., Wilens, T. E., & Biederman, J. (2005). Cognitive-behavioral therapy for ADHD in medication-treated adults with continued symptoms. *Behaviour Research and Therapy, 43*(7), 831–842.

Silverman, W. K., Ortiz, C. D., Viswesvaran, C., Burns, B. J., Kolko, D. J., Putnam, F. W., & Amaya-Jackson, L. (2008). Evidence-based psychosocial treatments for children and adolescents exposed to traumatic events. *Journal of Clinical Child and Adolescent Psychology, 37*(1), 156–183.

Spence, S. H., Holmes, J. M., March, S., & Lipp, O. V. (2006). The feasibility and outcome of clinic plus internet delivery of cognitive-behavior therapy for childhood anxiety. *Journal of Consulting and Clinical Psychology, 74*(3), 614.

Spence, S. H., Donovan, C. L., March, S., Gamble, A., Anderson, R. E., Prosser, S., & Kenardy, J. (2011). A randomized controlled trial of online versus clinic-based CBT for adolescent anxiety. *Journal of Consulting and Clinical Psychology, 79*(5), 629–642.

Stanton, M. D., & Shadish, W. R. (1997). Outcome, attrition, and family–couples treatment for drug abuse: A meta-analysis and review of the controlled, comparative studies. *Psychological Bulletin, 122*(2), 170–191.

Sukhodolsky, D. G., Kassinove, H., & Gorman, B. S. (2004). Cognitive-behavioral therapy for anger in children and adolescents: A meta-analysis. *Aggression and violent behavior, 9*(3), 247–269.

Tapert, S. F., Caldwell, L., & Burke, C. (2004). Alcohol and the adolescent brain: Human studies. *Alcohol Research and Health, 28*, 205–212.

Tevyaw, T. O. L., & Monti, P. M. (2004). Motivational enhancement and other brief interventions for adolescent substance abuse: Foundations, applications and evaluations. *Addiction, 99*(s2), 63–75.

Treatment for Adolescents with Depression Study (TADS) Team. (2004). Fluoxetine, cognitive-behavioral therapy, and their combination for adolescents with depression. *JAMA: The Journal of the American Medical Association, 292*(7), 807–820.

Tsiros, M. D., Sinn, N., Coates, A. M., Howe, P. R., & Buckley, J. D. (2008). Treatment of adolescent overweight and obesity. *European Journal of Pediatrics, 167*(1), 9–16.

Van der Oord, S., Prins, P. J., Oosterlaan, J., & Emmelkamp, P. M. (2008). Efficacy of methylphenidate, psychosocial treatments and their combination in school-aged children with ADHD: A meta-analysis. *Clinical Psychology Review, 28*(5), 783–800.

van der Veek, S. M., Derkx, B. H., Benninga, M. A., Boer, F., & de Haan, E. (2013). Cognitive behavior therapy for pediatric functional abdominal pain: A randomized controlled trial. *Pediatrics, 132*(5), e1163–e1172.

Waldron, H. B. (1997). Adolescent substance abuse and family therapy outcome. In *Advances in Clinical Child Psychology* (pp. 199–234). US: Springer.

Waldron, H. B., & Kaminer, Y. (2004). On the learning curve: the emerging evidence supporting cognitive–behavioral therapies for adolescent substance abuse. *Addiction, 99*(s2), 93–105.

Waldron, H. B., & Turner, C. W. (2008). Evidence-based psychosocial treatments for adolescent substance abuse. *Journal of Clinical Child and Adolescent Psychology, 37*(1), 238–261.

Walker, D. D., Roffman, R. A., Stephens, R. S., Wakana, K., & Berghuis, J. (2006). Motivational enhancement therapy for adolescent marijuana users: a preliminary randomized controlled trial. *Journal of Consulting and Clinical Psychology, 74*(3), 628–632.

Walkup, J. T., Albano, A. M., Piacentini, J., Birmaher, B., Compton, S. N., Sherrill, J. T., et al. (2008). Cognitive behavioral therapy, sertraline, or a combination in childhood anxiety. *New England Journal of Medicine, 359*(26), 2753–2766.

Warner, C. M., Colognori, D., Kim, R. E., Reigada, L. C., Klein, R. G., Browner-Elhanan, K. J., et al. (2011). Cognitive-behavioral treatment of persistent functional somatic complaints and pediatric anxiety: An initial controlled trial. *Depression and Anxiety, 28*(7), 551–559.

Warschburger, P., Fromme, C., Petermann, F., Wojtalla, N., & Oepen, J. (2001). Conceptualisation and evaluation of a cognitive-behavioural training programme for children and adolescents with obesity. *International Journal of Obesity and Related Metabolic Disorders, 25*.

Weiner, D. A., Schneider, A., & Lyons, J. S. (2009). Evidence-based treatments for trauma among culturally diverse foster care youth: Treatment retention and outcomes. *Children and Youth Services Review, 31*(11), 1199–1205.

Weisz, J. R., Thurber, C. A., Sweeney, L., Proffitt, V. D., & LeGagnoux, G. L. (1997). Brief treatment of mild-to-moderate child depression using primary and secondary control enhancement training. *Journal of Consulting and Clinical Psychology, 65*(4), 703–707.

Wilfley, D. E., Tibbs, T. L., Van Buren, D., Reach, K. P., Walker, M. S., & Epstein, L. H. (2007). Lifestyle interventions in the treatment of childhood overweight: A meta-analytic review of randomized controlled trials. *Health Psychology, 26*(5), 521–532.

Williams, R. J., & Chang, S. Y. (2000). A comprehensive and comparative review of adolescent substance abuse treatment outcome. *Clinical Psychology: Science and Practice, 7*(2), 138–166.

Wilson, D. B., Bouffard, L. A., & MacKenzie, D. L. (2005). A quantitative review of structured, group-oriented, cognitive-behavioral programs for offenders. *Criminal Justice and Behavior, 32*(2), 172–204.

Appendix

- Assessment
- Intervention Tools

Assessment Tools

(Ia) ABC Charting

The Antecedent, Behaviour and Consequence chart is a simple form for observation and reporting of maladaptive behaviours. The ABC chart can be maintained by parents, teachers or the adolescent. It helps to record information about contributing as well as maintaining factors of maladaptive behaviours. The ABC chart is a useful method that can guide the therapist about the intervention. Following is a template of an ABC chart (Table A.1):

M. Mehta and R. Sagar (eds.), *A Practical Approach to Cognitive Behaviour Therapy for Adolescents*, DOI 10.1007/978-81-322-2241-5

Table A.1 .

Date/Time	Situation	Antecedent (A)	Behaviour (B)	Consequence (C)
10:45 a.m.	Father was reading newspaper and M was watching a cricket match. Mother was in kitchen and sister was drawing in her book	Father asked for a glass of water and M said it is a very crucial point in the match; he refused to fetch water at that moment. Father shouted at M	M threw the remote control and kicked the cushion from the sofa	Father raised his hand and M started to argue with father. His mother interrupted and M pushed the mother away. After that M became shocked and silently left the room

Date/Time date/time when the behaviour occurred
Situation what was going on when the behaviour occurred? What was the adolescent doing? What were others doing at that time?
Antecedent what happened just before the behaviour that may have triggered the behaviour? What was the adolescent thinking or doing just before the behaviour occurred?
Behaviour description of the behaviour in detail. The actual behaviour and its duration is to be described
Consequence what happened following the behaviour, or as a result of the behaviour? Did it increase or decrease the behaviour? For example, how did others respond to the behaviour?

(Ib) Self-monitoring Form

See Table A.2.

Table A.2 .

Day/Time	Situation	Emotions	Thoughts	Behaviour
	What were you doing? Whom were you with? What exactly happened?	What was the emotion you experienced? How did you feel? Rate your feelings on a scale of 0–10, where 10 is the maximum intensity	What were you thinking just before? Rate how much you believe in these thoughts on a scale of 0–10, where 10 is the maximum strength of belief	What did you do? What happened after that?

Intervention Tools

(IIa) Activity Scheduling

The goal of an activity schedule is to increase the adolescent's engagement in mood elevating tasks. An activity schedule is usually preceded by self-monitoring where the adolescent may be asked to record his/her activity through the day. He/she rates each task on a scale of 0–10 on level of 'pleasure' (enjoyment, happiness, positive mood) and on mastery (sense of achievement, gained after completing a task). Following this, the therapist, in collaboration with adolescent and parents, develops a schedule of daily activities. The activities are chosen to maximize the feelings of happiness and increase a sense of mastery in the adolescents. This technique also helps to reduce procrastination or postponement, lack of motivation and inactivity arising out of poor decision-making or cognitive distortions. The activities however, may be graded in difficulty and broken into parts. The activity schedule may be revised periodically by the parents and adolescent, based on the need. The adolescent may be encouraged to rate his/her mood along with carrying out these activities. Following is an example of an activity schedule (Table A.3):

Activity schedule* for ______________________ (name of adolescent)
Monday/24.03.2014

Table A.3 .

Time	Activity	Rating
8:00–8:30 a.m.	Get up, use toilet, brush your teeth	P (Pleasure)
		M (Mastery)
8:30–9:00 a.m.	Have breakfast	
9:00–10:00 a.m.	Water the plants, take the pet for a walk	
10:00–11:00 a.m.	Take a bath, get ready for tuition	
11:00 a.m.–1:00 p.m.	Tuition class	
1:30–2:00 p.m.	Eat lunch	
2:00–2:30 p.m.	Watch friends on star world	
2:30–3:00 p.m.	Lie down on bed and relax	
3:00–4:00 p.m.	Tuitions/homework	
4:00–5:00 p.m.	Leisure activities	
5:00–6:30 p.m.	Going to the park and chat with friends	
6:30–7:00 p.m.	Have evening snacks and relax	
7:00–8:00 p.m.	Study mathematics	
8:00–8:15 p.m.	Take a break, eat a fruit/drink something cold	

(continued)

Table A.3 (continued)

Time	Activity	Rating
8:15–9:15 p.m.	Read a story book/magazine	
9:15–10:00 p.m.	Have dinner, talk with parents, help mother clean-up kitchen	
10:00 p.m.	Bedtime	

[a]This appendix is only to be used as an example; activities may vary depending on the need of the adolescent and in collaboration with the practitioner and parents

(IIb) Star Chart

Adolescents are attempting a change in their behaviour, for which they may need encouragement. Some adolescents suffering from depression, who have anhedonia, require reinforcement for trying out new behaviours and to persist with change. Rewarding positive behaviours indicates that you are attentive to the adolescent's progress. If given consistently, rewarding can go a along way in building desirable behaviours in the adolescents. It is also useful for self-reinforcement.

The star chart is most appropriate for use with children up to 12 years of age, however, it may be used with adolescents with some modifications. A more creatively designed chart can be used in a developmentally appropriate way. The chart can be pinned at a place where it is accessible and visible to the adolescents like cupboard, mirror, door, etc. The star chart technique is based on the principle of reinforcement.

There are creative ways of preparing a star chart. One such example is the use of snakes and ladders game. The ladders indicate sustained improvement and snake may indicate performance of a maladaptive behaviour. The star chart can be used along with the snakes and ladder where there may be built in reward for reaching significant levels like 25, 50, 75 and at 100 a big reward may be given. Smiley faces as stars for positive behaviour and sad face for maladaptive behaviours can also be used.

After the adaptive behaviour is firmly established, response cost may be employed to decrease the frequency of maladaptive behaviours by reducing the number of stars gained by adolescent for any maladaptive behaviour shown based on a pre-decided and mutually agreed upon ratio.

How to Use a Star Chart

- Choose one behaviour that you would like to change in the adolescent. Goals need to be identified and set as a collaborative activity between adolescent, parent and practitioner. An example could be: Setting the Table A.4
- On a chart such as the one drawn, give the adolescent a star for each day he/she performs the task. These credits can be given by parent or adolescents
- When he/she has earned a predetermined number of stars, he/she may be rewarded with a small token, that has been pre-decided by both parents and adolescents together. e.g. a favourite meal, an extra hour on the Internet, etc.

Table A.4 .

Activities	Monday	Tuesday	Wednesday	Thursday	Friday	Saturday	Sunday
Arranging cupboard	☺	☺	☺	☺		☺	
Filling water bottles	☺	☺	☺	☺	☺		
Studying	☺	☺	☺	☺	☺	☺	
Cutting vegetables for salad	☺	☺	☺			☺	
Total stars earned		**20**					

Illustration

Star Chart with smiley face for completed activity each day (Table A.5).

Star Chart with Response Cost smiley face for completed activity each day and tick mark for presence of maladaptive behaviour each day.

Table A.5 .

Activities	Monday	Tuesday	Wednesday	Thursday	Friday	Saturday	Sunday
Arranging cupboard	☺	☺	☺			☺	☺
Filling water bottles	☺	☺	☺	☺	☺	☺	☺
Studying	☺		☺	☺	☺	☺	☺
Cutting vegetables for salad	☺	☺	☺	☺		☺	☺
Hitting sister	√					√	
Total stars earned (No. of smileys–No. of tick marks)		**24 − 2 = 22**					

(IIc) Relaxation Techniques

During anxiety, our body is in a state of hyperarousal. Both mind and body need to relax so that the arousal may come down to an optimum level. Relaxation can be used in conditions like anxiety, headache, sleep difficultie, etc. To begin with, the adolescents need to understand the rationale for relaxation. Examples can be given to help gain an understanding of what is relaxation, why it is needed and how it works after this, the adolescent is demonstrated relaxation technique in session. He/she is asked to practise it once if it is diaphragmatic breathing; if, however, Jacobson Progressive Muscle Relaxation is taught, then a minimum of six supervised sessions need to be held in session before the adolescent is allowed to practise alone at home. There are various kinds of relaxation techniques; a few of them have been included here:

Diaphragmatic Breathing Exercise

Sit comfortably with your back straight. Let your limbs be loose. Stretch your legs out, relax your arms on the chair. Close your eyes and breathe in through your nose. Then, without holding your breath, exhale through your mouth. Make your breathing slow and effortless.

Continue to breathe in through your nose and exhale through your mouth. While, breathing focus on your breath, if however, you have any thoughts running through your mind, try not to stop them. Let the thought come and let them pass away. Return your focus to your breathing.

If you find it difficult breathing from your abdomen while sitting up, try lying on the floor and carry out this exercise.

Jacobson Progressive Relaxation Exercise

JPMR is a relaxation technique used for both adolescents and adult population. To administer this technique one needs supervised training. The instructions for this relaxation exercise are therefore not included as a part of this book.

Imagery/Visualizations

Imagery or visualization is a relaxation technique which involves imagining a scene and experience a sense of touch, taste, smell and sound. The rationale for the imagery is explained to the adolescent. It is best to assess the adolescent on the ability to imagine or visualize. This can be done by asking the adolescent in session to describe an object as vividly as possible in the session. He is asked to rate the ability to visualize it on a scale of 0–10. If the teen is not able to imagine the scene vividly, other therapist directed imagery techniques can be employed or a more structured relaxation exercise may be carried out like JPMR.

In identifying a stimulus for imagery, the adolescent is asked to recall any personal event, pleasant memory, a recent experience or any other scene of choice. The adolescent is asked to rate these in order of most to the least pleasant. The adolescent may be asked a few questions regarding the sounds heard, the color, the smell, etc. The adolescent is asked to relax by the use of diaphragmatic breathing or JPMR. Then the adolescent is asked to visualize the scene as vividly as possible at a slow pace, focusing on each detail, attending to sound, touch, smell and taste.

This is a technique in which the scenes may be created in the context of anxiety provoking situation like reading a book chapter aloud in a class of English. The scene is created and the adolescent is asked to visualize it. Homework assignments are given and adaptive coping statements may be taught to the adolescent to use sublingually while imaging a scene.

Mindfulness Meditation

Instructions for Body Scan Meditation

"In the next few minutes we will allow your attention to dwell completely within your body, without any other place to go, without any other thing to do. But simply to be present in this moment as it is… taking this time to settle yourself in a posture of some comfort- it might be lying down on the floor or mat or cushion. You can also do the body scan sitting up or even standing. Take a few minutes to settle in, if you are lying down, notice the points of contact between your body and the supporting surface, notice where the surface is supporting you, where it may not even be touching. Just begin to have a sense of the body as it is. Become aware of any activity in the mind, any sensations in the body, any lingering effects of the moments leading up to this one. Just take a note of them. No need to push anything away, thoughts of here and simply noticing that they are here and choosing to be aware of the body itself.

Become ready to allow the beam of attention to become narrow, to become a spot light, a very narrow beam that moves down your body, down your left leg, down to your left foot, into your left big toe… bringing attention to just this one small area of the body and taking note of what you find here… you are aware of sensations, the touch of clothing, warmth, coolness, numbness, tingling, lack of sensation… just noticing that. And to whatever degree you may notice other things, other sensations of the body, passing sounds in the environment, simply bringing your attention back to just this one point in the body, taking in what you are aware of… just here, just now. Not having to strain to become aware of anything in particular but taking a note of what is here. And now you are ready to move that beam of attention to the rest of the toes of your left foot, moving toe by toe… aware of whatever arises here, aware of tension, relaxation, lack of sensation… See if you can actually be playfully aware of the points between the toe, where one toe ends and the other begins, being curious about what you can find, without meaning to find anything in particular… simply being aware of these toes in this moment in this body.

And beginning to move your attention to encompass the rest of the left foot, the paw of the foot, the sole, the arch, the heel, the top, sides, even the bones and tissue that is inside the left foot. If you find yourself straining to feel something, or focussing diligently on any particular part, see if you can just soften your awareness… to allow whatever arises to arise… aware perhaps of the complexity of this part of your body to which you rarely paid much attention unless it has given you some difficulty and challenge.

Perhaps aware of the point of contact between your foot and the surface on which you are lying or sitting, noticing where the foot ends and where the mat begins.

In each time you notice your attention wandered to some passing sound or thought or feeling simply but firmly bring the attention back, in this case, to the left foot… not having to push away whatever you begin to become attached to but simply choosing to feature your left foot in the centre of your awareness, in the beam of that spotlight of attention…

Taking the time now to move that attention to the left ankle, leaving behind the toe, the paws and the foot, featuring the left ankle, another part of the body that you may not have attended to unless it gave you some pain or discomfort, difficulty… being curious about what you find here…

And as you are ready move the attention to the lower leg, the calf, the muscles and bone and tissue inside the left lower leg, just holding this part of the awareness just as it is. You may notice a sense of touch where this part of the body touches the surface upon which you are lying, you may notice tension or relaxation. You do not have to do anything about what you are noticing. Simply take a note of what you are experiencing as it is.

Allow your attention to move to the left knee. Take a note of whatever you discover here. It may be a slight twist or no sensation at all. See if you can encounter whatever you are observing with a sense of a playful curiosity and willingness to be present with it just as it is in that moment.

Whenever you find yourself attending to anything else, re-focus your attention.

Now move that beam of attention to your left thigh. Acknowledge your experience and simply observe your sensations. Simply notice where you feel what you feel, what is here and just now. Let go of any feeling of wanting it to be different from what it is. You may be aware of a variety of different sensations, one part may feel warmer than another, one may feel tenser than another. Simply take it into your awareness. Allow the experience to be what it is and let go of any feeling of changing or improving it.

Gather the attention and move it now to the right leg, all the way down to the right foot and to the right toe. Observe the toe just as it is, simply tune to the experience in this toe at the present moment… even if you feel no sensation at all. Now slowly move your attention to the rest of the toes one by one, simply noticing them, simply noticing the experience.

Now move your attention to the rest of the right foot- the paw, the heels, the arch, the sides, the top, taking in the right foot as a whole, including the muscles and bones inside. Allow the attention to move to the ankle. Notice the curve. Observe it just as it is.

Slowly move the attention to the lower leg, the calf, just hold it in awareness and notice what you are observing. If any emotion appears, then adopt the same awareness, the willingness to only observe things just as they are, acknowledge the presence of whatever comes.

Now move your attention to the right knee and simply notice what you are observing.

Now move your attention to the right thigh. Just explore. Become aware of the back of the thigh, the front, the outer and inner thigh. Simply be curious about what you find here. Simply observe. Let go of any tension, if you feel.

You may also have become aware of the effects of breathing on body. You may observe the subtle and gentle way in which parts of your body are moving forward and back.

If you find yourself thinking about other things, simply choose to come back here.

Now move your attention from the right thigh to the lower back. This is an area where many of us feel some discomfort. Whether you experience discomfort or tightness or relaxation or no particular sensation at all, just choose to attend here. Feel the movement of your breath. Notice whether this part of your body is in contact with the mat below, feeling the touch.

Now move your attention to your stomach. Observe the organs inside and the movements of the breath… the gentle moving out and in and its coinciding with the breath. If you feel the need to breathe in any particular way, let go of this feeling. Just be aware of your breath in this area.

Now move that spot light of attention to your chest and upper back. Become aware of the heart and lungs and the movement or sensation you feel associated with it. Simply be aware of the subtle changes happening in this area as you inhale and exhale. Observe the subtle effects of the heart beating and the blood moving from this area to the rest of the body. Do not strain yourself to be aware of any of these sensations. Just take a note of what you are aware of… your awareness of your upper body.

Now allow your attention to fall on your shoulders. Simply be aware of the experience and sensations coming from this part of the body. If you notice any tension, let go of it, and bring to your awareness your letting go of this tension. If your attention wanders, gently but firmly bring it back.

Now shift your attention down to your left arm, your left elbow and your left hand. Focus your attention slowly on each of the fingers, the palm and back of the hand, any points of contact between the hand and any surface upon which it rests. Allow your attention to move to the left wrist… a part of the body we rarely attend to, unless it gives us some difficulty… move your attention to your left forearm and notice what you find here, even if you find no sensation.

Move your attention to the left elbow and the left upper arm. Notice all muscles in this area, the inside, outside, the feel of the air if any, simply being aware of it.

Now move that beam of attention up the left shoulder and across to the right shoulder, down to the elbow and the right hand and fingers. Observe what you find in the right arm just now. Become aware of each finger, playfully, any sensation, the tips of each of your finger, the joint, the palm.

Now move your attention to the right wrist and forearm. You find that your attention wanders, bring it back to the right arm. If you notice any thoughts or sensations coming to your mind, simply allow them to be present in the background, behind the beam of your attention. Bring your attention to the right elbow and the right upper arm. Just notice what is here.

Move your attention to your neck. Simply observe what you find here. Bring to your awareness the flow of the breath in this area or the muscles or bones and tissues. Any tension, discomfort, or relaxation, whatever arises in this area, simply allowing it to arise and simply observing it.

Move your attention to your chin, jaws, teeth, lips, tongue. Just observe these areas. Become aware of the cheeks, the nose, the area around the eyes, the eyes, the forehead.

Notice the sensation of any facial expression that you may be holding. Simply notice it without having any urge to change it.

Move your attention to the sides of your head, your ears, the back of your head, the point of contact with the surface. Now bring your awareness to the top of your head.

Now as you are aware, allow that narrow beam of attention to widen and soften and spread back into a floodlight of attention that slowly spreads across the rest of the head, the neck, the shoulders, the arms, the body, the thighs, the lower legs and the feet. Become aware of this entire body, lying here, the whole body breathing. Take this opportunity to be present with yourself, with no other agenda, but simply to be present."

(IId) List of Positive Self-affirmation Statements

- I think I can do good work.
- I have very good friends.
- I have good control over my thoughts and feelings.
- I can find a solution for my problems.
- I have the capacity to successfully live through my adversities.
- I can take care of myself even when things are bad.

(IIe) Distraction

Distraction techniques can be helpful in the management of anxiety/pain symptoms. They are based on the premise that distraction involves defocusing attention from one stimuli to another. In case of anxiety, it involves redirecting attention to something other than what is thought to be anxiety provoking. Some common distraction techniques include:

- *Focus on object*
  The adolescent may be trained in a session to focus on an object of choice. The object chosen must be of the adolescent's preference and he/she is asked to describe it. Cue questions may be asked like, "What is its colour? How big is it? Where is it kept?" After sufficient practice in session, the adolescent may practice it at home to distract from negative thoughts.

- *Sensory awareness*
  The adolescent may be taught to focus on his/her surrounding. The focus may shift from outside to oneself. The cue questions may be, "What can you see in the surroundings? What can you hear? What else? Can you feel your clothes? Can you feel your hair?"

- *Mental exercises*
  These include some activities such as counting backwards, imagining a relaxing scene.
- *Pleasant memories*
  The adolescent may be directed to recall a pleasant memory and visualize it as vividly as possible. In the session, he/she may be asked to rate the vividness on a scale of 0–10 and may then be facilitated to imagine more clearly by the use of cue questions.
- *Absorbing activities*
  The adolescent may be asked to select activities that may be mentally occupying like:
  - Solving crossword, puzzles, sudoku
  - Reading a novel/book
  - Creating own scrap book
  - Surfing Internet
  - Doing something creative, such as drawing a picture or build a model
  - Playing music

(IIf) Postponement of Worry

When you notice that you are worried, say to yourself, "stop, this is only a thought, I am not going to engage in it right now, I'll leave it here and worry about it later". Next, allocate a particular time of the day, when you will allow yourself 15 min to worry. When that time comes, you can engage in your worry for as much as you want. However, you do not have to necessarily use this time period in worrying about what was bothering you during the day. If you still decide for using this period, please make a note for why you decided to use it.

(IIg) Problem Solving

The goal of problem solving is to train the adolescent in developing confidence in their own ability to help themselves meet challenges of daily lives. Before teaching the skill, the therapist emphasizes that problems are a part of everyday life and the adolescent needs to learn how to face them rather than avoiding them. Problem solving helps the adolescent become adept at generating alternatives in what may at first seem to be difficult situations. The adolescent can be taught the technique using examples from his/her daily life and then as a homework assignment. Later, they can be asked to pick another problem bothering them and look for a solution to it. Following are the stages of solving problems effectively:

Step 1—Defining the problem. The adolescent is encouraged to define and operationalize the problem so that it appears a 'workable' problem rather than something that is impossible to solve. Some ways to describe the problem are:

(1) Stating the situation as clearly and specifically in terms of what is happening, what was the other person saying or doing?

(2) Using an objective stance and avoiding blaming and stating the situation in a matter of fact way.

Step 2—Generating alternatives. Through use of brainstorming, all possible solutions, no matter how outlandish they may seem, are generated. The therapist needs to enable the adolescent to come with as many solutions as possible even if they do not seem viable. The therapist can model good brainstorming skills by generating both pragmatic and improbable alternatives, and encouraging the adolescent to follow.
Step 3—Evaluating alternatives. The adolescent is asked to evaluate each alternative for its viability as well as positive and negative consequences.
Step 4—Choosing the best solution and implementing it. After weighing all possible solutions, the adolescent puts into action the best possible solution.
Step 5—Re-evaluating. The last stage involves evaluating the merits of the chosen action. In case the solution does not seem to work, one has to go back to the pool of alternatives and look for another suitable solution again.

(IIh) Common Cognitive Distortions

See Table A.6.

Table A.6 .

Type	Description	Example
All or none thinking	Splitting things into black-and-white categories with no shades of grey in-between	"It's all going totally against me"
Jumping to conclusions	Guessing what people are thinking, with no facts to support our assumption	"She hates me, so much for her friendship"
Should statements	Rigid forms of thinking can lead to feelings of guilt and anger	"I must never forget the way he insulted me"

(continued)

Table A.6 (continued)

Type	Description	Example
Blaming	Holding ourselves or others responsible for something that happened that was out of our control	"I got angry because they messed up today"
Labelling	Very quickly giving ourselves or others a negative label	"He is irritating"
Overgeneralization	Seeing a single event as part of a regular pattern	"That's it, I'm always unlucky"
Magnification/ Catastrophization	Exaggerating the importance of a problem	"How terrible, I've got no clothes to wear for the evening party, this is the end!"
Emotional reasoning	Taking emotion as evidence for the truth	"I feel angry, that proves that my friend must have treated me badly"
Personalization	The adolescent tends to see himself/herself as the cause of some negative external event which he/she may not be actually responsible for	"My parents are unhappy because I am no good at academics"
Disqualifying the positives	Rejecting the positive qualities/experiences by insisting that they "don't count" for some reason or other	"I cleared the entrance exam as I was lucky"
Mental filter	To pick out a single negative detail and dwell on it exclusively discounting the actual situation	"The trip was all a waste as we could not spot a tiger at the tiger reserve"
Mind reading	Believing that one surely knows how someone else is feeling or what they are thinking without any evidence	"I know everybody is now thinking how poor my sense of dressing is"
Fortune telling	Believing that one can predict a future outcome, while ignoring other alternatives	"I know I will never succeed in life"

(IIi) Assertiveness Training

In stressful situations that involve others, using effective communication skills can decrease demands (e.g. you are able to politely, but firmly, tell someone who is asking for your time that you are unable to help, which results in less to do) or it can increase your resources (e.g. you can effectively ask for someone's help to do a task, which means it can get done faster). The goal of assertive communication is to honestly communicate your thoughts and needs in a respectful manner. Assertiveness skills include the following:

Using "I" statements

It is one of the most effective assertive communication strategies. Here you speak about things from your perspective. You are not blaming or accusing another person, you are simply stating things the way you see them. Using "I" statement can be effective in expressing your needs, especially when you wish for another person to change their behaviour. Here you can use the format "When (you)… , I feel…. What I need is…". For example, "When you constantly interrupt me, I feel like you have no interest in what I have to say. What I need is for you to listen to what I am saying without interrupting".

Be clear and direct

Use short and simple statements. Speak only about what is important and avoid going off the topic. Take a few seconds to think about what you are going to say and how you are going to say it before you actually speak. Avoid giving a mixed message.

Use assertive non-verbal communication

We communicate with words as well as through non-verbal elements such as body language. When nonverbal elements are inconsistent with our words, people tend to believe the non-verbal message more. For example, if you tell someone "That's a great idea" yet you roll your eyes, the other will probably think that you didn't really mean what you said. Assertive communication includes verbal and non-verbal messages that are consistent. Non-verbal assertive communications include the following:

- Maintain eye contact
- Smile, where appropriate
- Keep a relaxed, comfortable posture
- Speak in a clear, steady voice
- Use appropriate gestures

Practice/rehearse

Changing to an assertive communication style and being effective with it requires effort. Think through what you will say and even practice it out loud before you actually have a discussion with someone. This way, when the time comes you will likely be prepared to approach it in an assertive way.

Learn to say no

For some people, stress arises from a difficulty in saying "no" to the requests of others. As a result, extra tasks, projects or responsibilities pile up. Eventually stress can result as there isn't enough time in the day to do it all. Some points to consider when saying "no":

- You have the right to say "no": Your time is just as precious as anyone else's. You are not obliged to take on everything you are asked to do. Saying "no" is not selfish. It means that you are aware of your limits and that you want to honour the commitments you have already made.
- Focus on what is important: Before deciding to say "yes" to a request, think about how it fits with what is important to you. If it is important to you and you have the time to take it on, go ahead and say "yes".
- Be brief: It is acceptable to provide a reason for denying a request. However, don't go on-and-on about it. Provide a brief explanation—if you choose to do so.